PHYSICAL THERAPY MANAGEMENT
of Lower Extremity Amputations

Gertrude Mensch, M.C.P.A.
Director
Physiotherapy Services
Henderson General Hospital
Hamilton, Ontario, Canada

Patricia M. Ellis, Dip. P.&O.T., M.C.P.A., O.T.(C.)
Assistant Director
Physiotherapy Services
Henderson General Hospital
Hamilton, Ontario, Canada

AN ASPEN PUBLICATION®
Aspen Publishers, Inc.

1986

Gaithersburg, Maryland

Aspen Publishers, Inc.
200 Orchard Ridge Drive
Gaithersburg, Maryland 20878

Library of Congress Cataloging-in-Publication Data

Mensch, Gertrude.
   Physical therapy.

   Includes bibliographies and index.
   1. Amputation of leg. 2. Amputation of foot.
3. Physical therapy. 4. Amputees—Rehabilitation.
I. Ellis, Patricia M. II. Title. [DNLM: 1. Amputation—
rehabilitation. 2. Physical Therapy—methods.
WE 170 M548p]
RD560.M46   1986   617'.58062   86–10834
ISBN 0–87189–372–X

*This text has been awarded an honorable
mention in the physician's category in
the 1987 Medical Book Awards competion
sponsored by the American Medical
Writers Association.*

The authors and publishers have made every effort to ensure the
accuracy of the information herein, particularly with regard to drug
selection and dose. However, appropriate information sources
should be consulted, especially for new or unfamiliar drugs or
procedures. It is the responsibility of every practitioner to evaluate
the appropriateness of a particular opinion in the context of actual
clinical situations and with due consideration to new developments.
Authors, editors, and the publisher cannot be held responsible for
any typographical or other errors found in this book.

Printed in the United States of America
5

This book is dedicated to

Angus H. MacMillan M.D., F.R.C.S.(C.)
Orthopaedic Surgeon

who initiated and inspired the Amputation Rehabilitation Program at the
Hamilton Civic Hospitals, Hamilton, Ontario, Canada

Contents

Foreword
Preface
Acknowledgments

1 Introduction to Lower Extremity Amputations   1

Gait   1
Amputation Incidence, Causes, Associated Diseases and
    Conditions   21
Amputation Levels: Stump Characteristics and Treatment
    Considerations Related to Gait   31

**2 Preoperative and Postoperative Care and the
    Responsibilities of the Physical Therapist   45**

Part 1
The Amputation Rehabilitation Team   45
Preoperative Care   46
Postoperative Care   52
The Immediate Postoperative Phase   52

Part 2
Preparations for Prosthetic Fitting   97
Physical Therapy Assessment for Rehabilitation Potential   97
Patient Education   112
Hygiene   114
Stump Shrinkage and Shaping Techniques   119
Contractures   140

v

Stump Complications and Conservative Treatment
Indications   162
Stump Motions: Their Relationship to Gait Functions and Resultant
Treatment Considerations   191

3   Prosthetics and Prosthetic Gait   201
A Physical Therapy Overview of Prosthetics   201
Gait Training   246
Gait Deviations   282
Prosthetic Prescription and Checkout   283
Bilateral Amputations   326

4   Other Points of Interest   337
Recent Developments in Prosthetics   337
Sports   343

Conclusion   353

Index   355

Foreword

The large majority of amputations performed today result from limb ischemia. These individuals are for the most part elderly. Many have had previous surgical vascular reconstructive procedures. Approximately one-half have diabetes. These circumstances have changed traditional management to create increasing responsibility and an increasing challenge for physical therapists directing their rehabilitation. This changing patient profile does not in any way diminish the knowledge and skill requirements attendant to adults undergoing amputation for trauma, tumors, and other pathological states. The large and increasing number of those among us in the Western world experiencing amputation for peripheral vascular disease additionally compounds needed educational requirements. That is the purpose of this excellent and authoritative text.

The primary axiom of amputee rehabilitation is team care. Although a considerable number of health care disciplines may be involved with varying degrees of responsibility, the three absolute essential team members are the surgeon, the prosthetist, and the therapist. Their skills and contribution are indispensable. Whenever possible, each should be involved from the inception of treatment.

The surgeon's role in limb ablation carries with it the unattractive aura of a completely destructive technique. Surgical removal of a visible and vital part of the body is, at best, an unpleasant experience not only for the surgeon but often more so for the patient and family. Unfortunately, this "mind set" has lead to amputation surgery occupying a low estate in terms of surgical research and interest. Such an attitude is totally unjustified. Amputation surgery is, in fact, reconstructive. The surgeon is committed not only to remove the offending part of the limb but to create a residual limb that will interface with the environment with maximum effectiveness through the prosthesis.

With appropriate prosthetic support, the physical therapist and patient embark together on the road back to functional recovery. The sensitivity and skill of the therapist will elicit hope and cooperation. This rehabilitation experience may be at times halting and difficult, but it is entirely positive. Surveys indicate that when questioned as to who was primarily responsible for their recovery, more than three-fourths of amputees relate recovery to the physical therapist. Certainly the therapist plays a central and personally gratifying role in the recovery process.

It is also essential that the physical therapist assume a key role in setting individual goals for optimum levels of functional restoration. This process can often be initiated preoperatively by the amputee team. Realistic rehabilitation goals are important for all involved: in particular, the amputee. The physical challenge is that of pain-free, comfortable mobility. The psychological challenge is the adjustment of the amputee to his or her disability and to the social circumstances responsible for an acceptable and worthwhile quality of life. Mobility in the elderly amputee whose health is impaired by diabetes, emphysema, cardiovascular disease, malnutrition, and the many other chronic disease states that so often accompany limb ischemia may be restricted to ambulating short distances with aids or even the transfer from bed to wheelchair. Nonetheless, mobility is the goal. We strive to assist the patient to move about as comfortably as possible within the environment.

There is increasing emphasis on recreation for physically disabled persons and, in particular, for amputees. Young active adult and adolescent amputees are often able to engage in vigorous sports and perform remarkable feats of physical accomplishment. Marathon running, soccer, racket sports of all types, snow and water skiing, hunting, backpacking, rock climbing, and many other types of physical recreation are being performed skillfully by athletic lower limb amputees.

The spectrum of amputee function is broad and challenging. The physical therapist is directly involved in bringing out and developing mobility skills, whether it be for an elderly parishioner walking with a cane down the aisle at church or, at the other end of the spectrum, a teenage amputee windsurfing or hang gliding. These abilities are gratefully appreciated.

Gertrude Mensch and Patricia Ellis have combined to prepare a remarkable and much needed book. It deserves wide acceptance. The principles and techniques outlined within its pages will serve well those professionals responsible for amputee rehabilitation. This service and this hope then extend directly to the quality of life of the person involved. It is a privilege to write this foreword for this timely and excellent book.

> Hope is a strange invention
> A Patent of the Heart
> In unremitting action
> Yet never wearing out

Of this electric Adjunct
Not anything is known
But its unique momentum
Embellish all we own

Emily Dickinson

ERNEST M. BURGESS, M.D.

Preface

In amputation rehabilitation each team discipline plays a vital role in caring for the recent lower extremity amputees, helping them to adjust physically, psychologically, and socially to an altered life style.

Present literature provides ample information related to medical and prosthetic problems that these amputees may encounter. However, a total approach to physical therapy treatment methods and techniques is not readily available. Therefore, this book concentrates on the physical aspects of rehabilitation and addresses mainly the physical therapist, with emphasis on treatment responsibilities. The book provides guidance in realistic treatment planning and discusses clinical approaches and specific treatment techniques.

For several reasons, treatment planning is becoming more complex. Our society now enjoys a longer life expectancy, and vascular surgeons have developed skills that delay the need for amputation surgery. As a result, the patient who eventually undergoes amputation surgery is a considerably more debilitated person compared with the peripheral vascular amputee of just a few years ago. Complex medical histories require equally complex treatment considerations.

It should also be noted that treatment discussions in this text are applicable solely to the adult lower extremity amputee. The child amputee will not be discussed because treatment considerations for children differ greatly from adults. Factors such as child development, locomotor ability, human growth pattern, congenital limb deficiencies, child psychology, and parent counselling are major concerns in treating children. Specialty centers providing ongoing care through the growing years have rehabilitation teams who are skilled in these specific areas.

This text will aid the physical therapist in understanding the complexity of the treatment responsibilities required to provide the best care and guidance to all recent amputees and their families.

Our experience has been that therapists themselves are searching for guidance, and we hope this book will help to provide some answers for improved care for all adult lower extremity amputees.

Acknowledgments

As we grew into our roles as authors, we quickly realized that one can only succeed in writing a textbook with the help, continuous support, and advice of many friends and colleagues. To all, we wish to express our sincere gratitude. Some of our colleagues provided outstanding assistance, and we feel that they deserve special recognition.

First, we would like to express our appreciation to Dawn Fitzpatrick and Anne Gilmore, who coped, above and beyond the call of duty, with our endless typing demands, all of which had to be "completed yesterday"; to Rosalie Andersen and Elaine Lapsley, who became "in-house" proofreaders; and to Joan Stansell, who entered the entire manuscript on the word processor, remaining "unruffled" through all changes.

We especially wish to thank all our physical therapists at the Henderson General Hospital who provided ongoing encouragement and valuable critical appraisal of our material throughout the entire project and to our physical therapy students and interns who, through their questions, made us more acutely aware of the need for the clinical information that we have provided in the text.

One picture is worth more than 10,000 words. Most of those found in our book were expertly provided by Jerry Farrell (artist) and Irma Tosoian (medical photographer) of the Department of Audio-Visual Services, Hamilton Civic Hospitals. Our thanks to both of you.

We are also grateful for the approval, support and the incentive provided by our Hospital's Administration in the undertaking of this project. The hospital seal is displayed on this page as a token of our thanks.

And last, but most certainly not least, a big hug and loving thanks from both of us to our husbands, who so amiably endured our authors' "Mucken" and eccentricities over these 3 long years.

1

Introduction to Lower Extremity Amputations

Effective amputation rehabilitation requires, as a prerequisite, a sound knowledge of normal human gait. One must understand the intricate interactions of components involved in locomotion. These include:

- the forces that are required to walk
- the functions of opposing motions
- the swaying patterns to and from the line of progression
- the effects of balance (see Balance Control, p. 17)
- the energy requirements in gait (see Energy Expenditure, p. 18)

Gait appears simple as one leg steps in front of the other. However, these alternating motions are complex and, in their complexity, comprise many factors involving the body and its environment.

Normal gait has a precise cycle (see Human Gait Cycle, p. 4), and the pattern of this cycle permits clinicians to methodically observe, analyze, and document all sequences.

However, one must also understand what occurs in pathological gait patterns (e.g., amputation) so that postural adaptations and deviations in prosthetic gait can be analyzed and corrected.

The basics of ''normal gait'' will be reviewed since the teaching and correction of prosthetic gait is based on the understanding of normal locomotor principles. Prosthetic gait training without knowledge of how the body moves is impossible (Koerner 1967, 1980).

A person's posture, anatomical build, ability to control balance, muscle coordination, walking speed, and the ground conditions (e.g., gravel, ice, incline) are some of the many factors that control and influence normal locomotion (Mensch, 1979). Walking and posture are also affected by age and by how a

Factors Affecting Gait

1

person feels (healthy or ill, well rested or tired, happy or depressed), which indicates that gait patterns, under normal circumstances, change without underlying pathology. The combination of these factors make each gait pattern unique, so that each person expresses, more or less, an evident gait "personality" that makes it possible to recognize some people by their gait characteristics (Inman et al., 1981).

Forces

The forces initiating and acting upon gait need equal consideration for understanding gait dynamics (Hughes et al., 1979; Inman et al., 1981). These forces consist of muscle forces, gravitational forces, and combinations thereof.

Muscle forces initiating gait are both voluntary and automatically controlled. Muscle dynamics in gait are transformed into motions and, therefore, the results of these forces are readily visible.

The results of other forces involved during locomotion are not obviously seen, e.g., the weight-bearing forces (W). These are exerted by the body onto the ground and are the combination of gravity (G) and body motion [velocity (V)]. The size of these forces is determined by a person's body weight and by the gait velocity. Each force instantly creates a counterforce, and the resultant response to the weight-bearing forces are the ground reaction forces (R). The ground reaction forces occur in equal size and in direct opposition to the weight-bearing forces.

(See Fig. 1–1)

The ground reaction forces depend on the ground conditions and can be illustrated as follows. An elastic surface (trampoline) absorbs the major part of the weight-bearing impact and so delays the return force, whereas a hard surface (cement) returns most of the weight-bearing impact immediately back to the body.

Figure 1–1   Forces affecting gait.

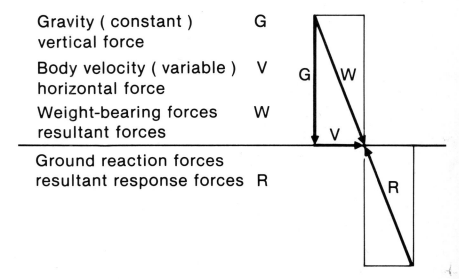

Gravity (constant)   G
vertical force

Body velocity (variable) V
horizontal force

Weight-bearing forces   W
resultant forces

Ground reaction forces
resultant response forces   R

In order to achieve harmonious movements during gait, all motions and forces have to be opposed by balancing or limiting counterforces. Examples:

- Hip flexion is reversed by hip extension.
- One leg supports the body weight while the other leg accelerates forward.
- The center of gravity sways from one support leg to the other.

All forces are dependent upon each other.

As a point of interest, a short comparison of quadrupedal and bipedal gait will emphasize the unique nature of human walking.

Gait Comparison

Most quadrupeds (e.g., dogs and cats) use all four limbs to support their body weight during locomotion because their spines are C curved. This postural position places the center of gravity in front of the hip joints. During quadrupedal gait the hind legs function as accelerators. This acceleration function is possible because the hip, knee, and ankle joints are anatomically flexed and, combined with muscular force, provide a strong forward thrust. The anatomical structure of the front legs is straight because they act as stabilizers.

Quadrupedal Gait

If quadrupeds attempt to walk temporarily in an erect fashion (e.g., some monkeys, trained circus dogs) excessive hind leg muscle power is required to maintain the upright position (Dagg, 1973). Biomechanically, the hind legs remain flexed during this forced bipedal gait, and the C curved spine cannot rise high enough to center the body weight over the balancing legs. Both the hind leg flexion position and the weight of the trunk keep the center of gravity in front of the hip joints, making this unnatural form of locomotion a most tiring experience (Mensch, 1979).

Bipedal gait is accomplished with comparative ease in healthy humans because the spine is S curved. The lordosis of the lumbar and cervical sections of the spine permit the trunk to be centered over the legs. In this vertical position, the center of gravity falls through the pelvis directly over the extremities. When standing, the line of gravity passes through the ear, the shoulder joint, the pelvis, and slightly anterior to the knee and ankle joints. This biomechanically efficient position requires little dynamic muscle effort to keep the body upright (Inman et al., 1981). However, if one body segment deviates from the support base, extra muscle work is necessary to maintain or recover the position.

Bipedal Gait

(See Fig. 1–2)

Gait requires:

- a base support
- correct functioning of the semicircular canals in the inner ear that hold the receptors for equilibrium and position sense
- muscular forces and counterforces to hold the body's center of gravity over the support base

Figure 1–2   The line of gravity.

Bipedal gait is accomplished by alternating steps that accelerate the body forward while the center of gravity is shifted from one support leg to another. All locomotor movements are so well tuned that the complexity of balance, coordination, forces, and counterforces during gait progression is hardly noticeable (Inman, 1966; Koerner, 1967; Inman et al., 1981).

The Human Gait Cycle

(See Fig. 1–3)

The gait cycle consists of a swing and stance phase. During the swing phase, which requires 40% of one gait cycle, the body is accelerated forward. During the stance phase, which takes up 60% of one gait cycle, the leg supports the body weight. The swing phase records acceleration, midswing and deceleration. The stance phase records heel contact, foot flat, midswing, heel off and toe off. A short period of double support occurs when the swinging leg reaches the ground and the supporting leg has not yet advanced into swing. The duration of double support shortens with an increase in walking speed until it is absent during running (Steinberg, 1966; Hughes et al., 1979; Inman et al., 1981; Murray et al., 1982).

One gait cycle is measured from heel contact to heel contact of the same leg. There is a right gait cycle and a left gait cycle. The rhythmic division (40% and 60%) is the result of *time* spent in each phase.

The *distance* covered during one gait cycle is also measured from heel contact to heel contact of the same leg. However, the distance is divided by two equal steps, a right one (50%) and a left one (50%). Therefore, two equal steps cover the distance of one gait cycle, and these two steps are referred to as one stride length.

To avoid an abrupt gait pattern as the leg positions change, the body sways in relation to the line of progression. It is held in balance by muscular forces that

The Undulating
Pathways

Figure 1–3 Schematic representation of the gait cycle.

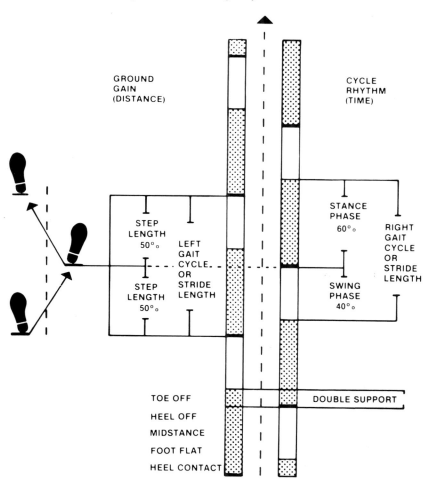

Figure 1–4   Diagrammatic illustration of the horizontal, vertical, and transverse planes.

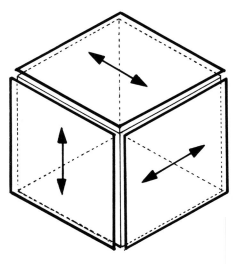

(See Fig. 1–4)

respond to changes in the position of the center of gravity, which is positioned approximately in front of the second sacral vertebra (Saunders, 1953; Murray et al., 1982). These postural swaying motions pass through different planes and provide a smooth transition between the angular motions involved in the gait cycle.

These swaying motions, called undulating pathways, are sinusoidal curves of about 2 in. amplitude (Saunders, 1953) that occur in different planes to the line of progression during ambulation. They are not easily observed but are a major factor in coordinated gait control. Their functions are:

- to make the gait smooth and rhythmic
- to balance the center of gravity over the support leg, thus holding the body in balance
- to equalize counterforces
- to reduce energy expenditure (Saunders, 1953; Inman et al., 1981).

To achieve these functions, each swaying motion has a balanced and coordinated countersway initiated by muscle forces that respond to movement, to position changes, and to the ground reaction force.

These pathways, or dimensional deviations from the line of progression, combine to create a rolling motion that may be compared with the rolling motion of a boat. For clarification, the undulating patterns of the individual pathways will be examined separately in the different planes.

Sagittal Plane (Sideview).   Viewed from the side, the pathway rises and

(See Fig. 1–5)

falls in relation to the line of progression. The peak is recorded at midstance, and

Figure 1–5   The sagittal pathway, computer tracing.

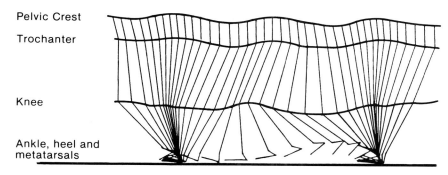

Source: Courtesy of Dr. H. DeBruin.

the lowest point is recorded when leg double support occurs. Wavelengths vary depending on step length, velocity, and leg length. The velocity slows slightly prior to reaching the highest point and accelerates again following midstance. These velocity changes can be compared with a roller coaster that slows to reach its peak and, just after the peak, gathers momentum and increases speed. The undulating pattern in the sagittal plane can be exaggerated by taking longer steps or by rising onto the toes during midstance.

Coronal Plane (Front or Horizontal View).   If the gait is viewed from the front or back, the pathway swings from side to side in relation to the line of progression. It also peaks at midstance and reaches its low point at leg double *(See Fig. 1–6)* support, only to rise again over the opposite stance leg. The side to side amplitude is shorter because the distance between the feet at midstance is less than the usual step length.

This pathway can be compared with the swing of a pendulum and can be exaggerated by walking with a wide base since this increases the distance the line has to travel away from the body midline.

Combination of Sagittal and Coronal Undulating Pathways.   When both of these undulating pathways meet, they transect at their lowest point and separate into a twisted figure eight pattern, looping toward their peak where they U turn to return to the point where they again meet. On observation, starting at midstance, the curve is at its lateral peak. By advancing the gait cycle to double support, the curve drops diagonally toward the body midline. This is the crossing point. When midstance occurs on the other side, the curve rises diagonally in the opposite direction to peak again over the support leg.

Reaching the peak requires energy as the body is "lifted" from its low position. The drop, beginning at midstance, adds momentum to the acceleration force within the cycle.

Figure 1–6   The coronal pathway.

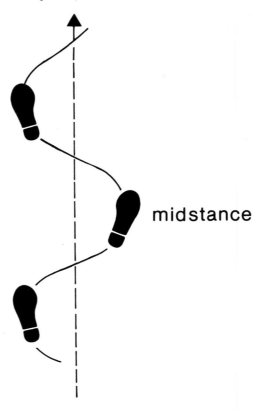

midstance

Transverse Plane.   The up and down, side to side swaying motions are interlinked with additional factors. These are rotational, tilting, and swaying motions that accommodate internal and external rotational forces and counterforces within the gait cycle. Rotational motions are recorded in the trunk, pelvis, arms, and legs. The spine counterbalances the opposing shoulder and pelvic rotations. Internal and external rotations of the femur, tibia, and foot are integrated into the leg acceleration and deceleration motions.

The Pelvis

The pelvis rotates clockwise and counterclockwise around its perpendicular axis. It changes direction with hip flexion and extension by following the leg from its forward and internally rotated position to its extended and externally rotated position (Prosthetic Devices, Research Project, 1947).

Simultaneously, the pelvis tilts diagonally and shifts laterally. The unsupported side drops toward midswing while the pelvis shifts sideways over the support leg. At this midstance phase the femur is positioned in slight adduction. This position is necessary to hold the body weight over the support leg without

(See Fig. 1–7)

Figure 1–7   Femoral adduction on stance.

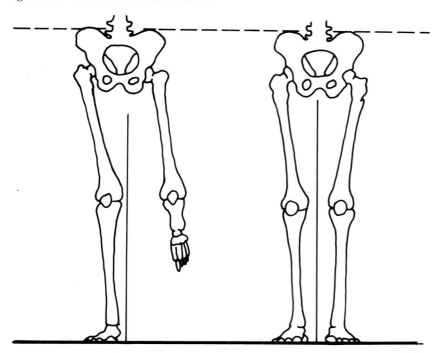

trunk bending. This femoral adduction on stance results in a slight leg abduction of the other leg during the swing phase. The abductor muscles on the support side control the pelvic position during stance. The counterbalancing motions keep the body in balance and contribute to energy efficiency (Inman et al., 1981).

The pelvic motions (rotating, tilting, and shifting), if viewed in isolation, result in an undulating pathway that is unique to the pelvis, peaking at midstance and progressing to its lowest point at double support.

(See Fig. 1–8)

The pelvis's horizontal axis to the line of progression is directly opposite the horizontal shoulder axis. This occurs to cushion the reverse motion of legs and arms.

Rotational Component of the Shoulder and the Pelvis

Lack of forward and backward movement in the shoulder girdle affects the pelvis and leg positions during the gait cycle, e.g., the support leg is held in more extension and external rotation, with limitation of shoulder girdle movement.

The body displacements that occur when all pathways are combined create a rolling motion and help to neutralize or cushion forces and counterforces that, without balance and muscular control, would appear sudden or abrupt. These normal displacements give the gait pattern a flowing appearance, so that the motion variations are hardly noticeable in normal gait.

Combination of Pathways

Figure 1–8   Pelvic movements—lateral displacement. (A) position at heel contact, (B) position at midstance, (C) positions combined.

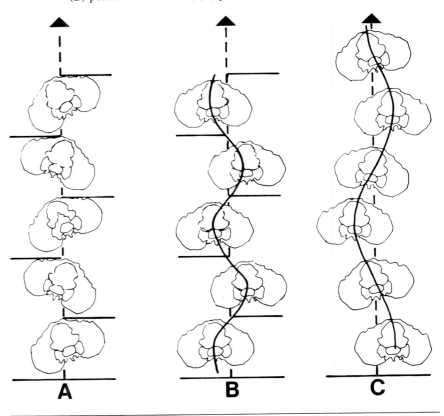

A   **B**   **C**

Factors Contributing to Joint Positions during Gait Phases

Flexion and extension movements can be observed best from the sagittal plane, whereas abduction, adduction, and rotational movements are best noted from the horizontal plane (Murray, 1967; Hughes et al., 1979; Inman et al., 1981).

Stance Phase

This is the support phase. The cycle begins when the swinging leg reaches ground contact (period of double support).

(See Fig. 1–9)

Heel Contact.   At heel contact, the ankle is held in joint midposition, the knee is almost extended, and the hip is flexed.

Forces.   The center of gravity has reached its lowest point (leg double support) and is centered between both lower extremities. The weight-bearing force in relation to heel contact passes in front of the hip joint and behind the knee and ankle joints. The ground reaction force affects plantar flexion, knee flexion, and hip flexion.

Figure 1–9 Heel contact.

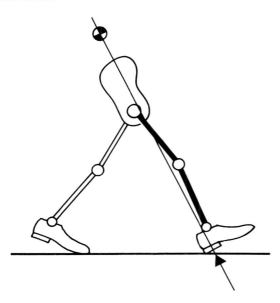

Electromyographic (EMG) Muscle Action. The dorsiflexors prevent the foot from advancing too quickly to complete ground contact. The knee extensors and the hamstrings stabilize the extended knee to reach the forward position. The gluteus maximus, assisted by the hamstrings, begins to contract in preparation for extending the hip, thus counteracting hip flexion. The hip abductors and adductors, combined with hip internal and external rotators, direct the foot placement on the ground in relation to the line of progression.

Foot flat. From heel contact the foot advances into foot flat. Knee flexion increases slightly, thus shortening the leg and making the transition to midstance less energy consuming. The hip is moderately flexed. *(See Fig. 1–10)*

Forces. As the trunk advances forward, the center of gravity begins to rise and shift toward the support side. The weight-bearing force passes in front of the hip joint, behind the knee, and slightly behind the ankle joint. The ground reaction force influences foot plantar flexion, knee flexion, and hip flexion.

EMG Muscle Action. The dorsiflexors reduce their activity because ground support has been reached. Quadriceps contraction increases and, together with the hamstring counterforce, holds the knee in slight flexion as the weight over the support leg increases. Gluteus maximus control is powerful at this point, drawing the leg into hip extension to help bring the center of gravity upward. The hip abductors contract moderately, to hold the pelvis level on the unsupported side.

Figure 1–10   Foot flat

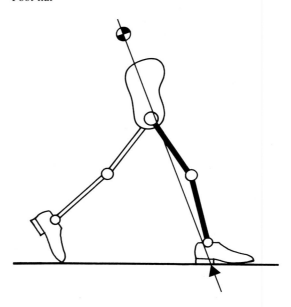

Figure 1–11   Midstance

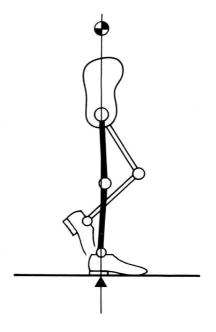

Midstance. At this point the foot reaches midstance. The ankle is slightly dorsiflexed; the knee once again is almost fully extended. The hip is in joint midrange.

(See Fig. 1–11)

Forces. The center of gravity has reached its highest and most lateral point and is centered directly over the support leg. The weight-bearing force passes through the hip joint, slightly behind the knee joint and just in front of the ankle joint. The ground reaction force gives momentum behind the knee joint but has no impact at the hip joint.

EMG Muscle Action. The dorsiflexors and plantar flexors now control the slightly dorsiflexed foot in an effort to maintain its position. Less effort is required from the quadriceps and gluteus maximus since the trunk is balanced directly over the stance leg. The raising of the center of gravity has been achieved. However, the abductor muscle groups on the support side are strongly active in holding the pelvis level. This action is assisted by the quadratus lumborum muscle on the unsupported side.

Heel-off. Body forward motion forces the heel off the ground. The ankle is dorsiflexed. This position is necessary to prepare the leg for the acceleration push. The knee appears extended but is actually very slightly flexed. The hip is extended.

(See Fig. 1–12)

Forces. The center of gravity begins to fall and passes in a medial direction toward the line of progression. The fall of the center of gravity gives

Figure 1–12 Heel-off.

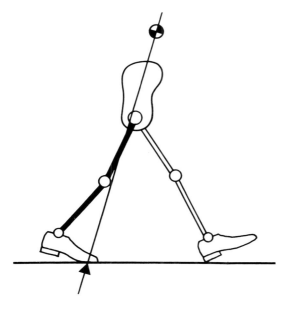

the body momentum in moving forward. The weight-bearing force, in relation to the heel-off position, passes just behind the hip, slightly in front of the knee, and way forward of the ankle joint. The ground reaction force has a dynamic effect on dorsiflexion, knee extension, and hip extension.

EMG Muscle Action.   The plantar flexors increase their action so that the foot can provide a powerful forward push in the upcoming plantar flexion position. The tensor fascia lata contracts to give stability at the end of stance phase and may assist the hip into flexion.

(See Fig. 1–13)

Toe-off.   Toe-off coincides with heel contact of the other leg, and the period of double support has once again been reached. The body weight is transferred to the forward leg. The ankle of the rear leg is in plantar flexion and the knee is in flexion (to shorten the leg and assist it into accelerating for the upcoming swing phase). The hip, still in extension, begins to flex.

Forces.   As the trunk moves forward, momentum is generated by the falling center of gravity. The weight-bearing line passes behind the hip, behind the knee, and in front of the ankle joint. The ground reaction force is minimized because the weight-bearing counterforce, in the toe-off position, is lessened.

EMG Muscle Action.   The plantar flexors reduce their activity and the dorsiflexors prepare to contract. The knee flexes because of the trunk forward motion. Hamstring action, to activate knee flexion, is minimal. The stance phase ends, and toe-off transfers the support leg into swing phase.

Figure 1–13   Toe-off.

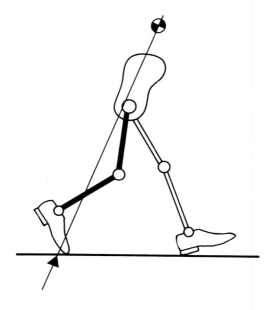

During swing phase the advancing leg is not in contact with the ground. The leg travels through space throughout the entire swing phase.

Acceleration. Following toe-off, the ankle changes from plantar flexion into dorsiflexion. The knee continues to flex as the hip passes from extension into flexion. All flexion positions shorten the leg to permit ground clearance during acceleration.

(See Fig. 1–14)

EMG Muscle Action. The dorsiflexors control the position change from plantar flexion after push-off into moderate dorsiflexion. Knee flexion is assisted by pendular motion as the iliopsoas muscle accelerates the leg forward, but is restricted by the quadriceps muscle action to bring the foot forward.

Midswing. Hip flexion increases further. Knee flexion reaches its maximum gait angulation and begins, thereafter, to change direction toward knee extension. The ankle remains in joint midposition.

(See Fig. 1–15)

EMG Muscle Action. The midswing phase depends on the acceleration momentum and, just as during the midstance period, major muscle action is not reported. Slight dorsiflexion is recorded. The knee motion is caused by pendular leg action.

Deceleration. The ankle remains in joint midposition, and the knee reaches full extension in preparation for heel contact to finish one complete cycle. The hip continues to flex.

(See Fig. 1–16)

EMG Muscle Action. At the end of the swing phase, the dorsiflexors prepare for heel contact. The hamstring muscles decelerate the forward swing

---

Figure 1–14 Acceleration.

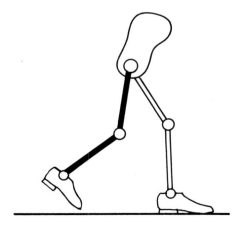

Figure 1–15   Midswing.

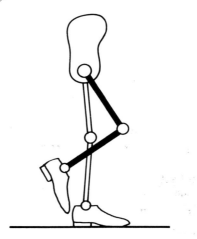

motion. The dorsiflexors, quadriceps, hamstrings, and adductors contract to prepare the leg for heel contact and foot placement.

Summary

The cycle is thus completed. It is worth noting that the strongest muscle activity takes place at the beginning and at the end of each swing and stance phase (Inman et al., 1981). At midstance, after intense muscle work, the muscles become comparatively less active in reaching the undulating peak. The swing phase acceleration is assisted by push-off and by active hip flexion and is reinforced by momentum. This forward motion is dampened by the hamstrings and, to some degree, the gluteus maximus prior to the next heel contact.

Figure 1–16   Deceleration.

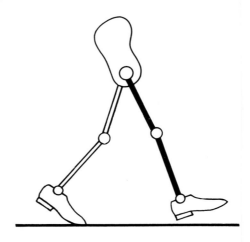

Although an effort has been made to explain leg movements in relation to the gait pattern, one must always remember that locomotion involves the total body. The trunk, arms, legs, and head all closely interact to produce a smooth, coordinated gait (Basmajian, 1979).

This overview of gait functions shows the interrelationship of movement, forces, and counterforces. In normal gait these factors are entirely balanced. However, if one link in this sequence is missing, the interruption of gait sequence causes rhythmic and postural disturbances, resulting in gait deviations.

This brief review of normal human locomotion provides a background for the critical observation and analysis of postural gait deviations as demonstrated by amputees.

Gait is considerably more complex, and clinicians who wish to further their knowledge in gait should investigate the intensive gait studies that have been carried out in leading gait laboratories (National Research Council Committee on Artificial Limbs, 1947; Inman, 1966; Murray, 1967; Inman et al., 1981) or view the videocassettes discussing "Observation of Human Gait" by Koerner, Health Sciences Audiovisual Education, University of Alberta (1984).

One of the basic criteria for amputee gait training is the ability to maintain balance. Maintaining balance requires the integration of reflex actions at higher levels in the brain and coordinated muscle reaction to brain signals. This occurs in the following sequence: **Balance Control**

- The body senses its positions (proprioception).
- The sensory (afferent) input is transmitted to the brain.
- The balance response is triggered automatically.
- Signals (efferent) are transmitted to the muscles to correct the postural imbalance.

Thus balance is maintained.

Balance is achieved by opposing muscle forces acting on the body over a support base. If the support base is wide, as in sitting, it is easier to maintain balance. If the support base is narrow, as in standing or walking, maintaining balance becomes more complex because it requires establishing a position of dynamic stability through synchronization of opposing movements. If the body weight shifts too far outside the support base, without adequate control, balance is lost and the person falls.

Following leg amputation, some of the distal proprioceptive sensors that aid in transmitting input to the brain to elicit balance control have been lost. Therefore, the neuromuscular system (i.e., proprioception, the inner ear vestibular mechanism, and the cerebellum) experiences a neurophysiological disturbance. This disturbance affects total body balance and initially deprives the amputee of the ability to walk without conscious thought. Body adaptation to this situation takes place within a short period of time. Therefore, the physical therapist must utilize this short time span, this period of learning how to walk following amputation surgery, to teach the amputee correct body and postural positions. This will enable the amputee to learn good postural control until balance once again becomes automatic.

During this learning period, the amputee will consciously try to sense posture and step positions (through touch, sight, and hearing) to compensate for the unilateral functional loss and to reestablish the former automatic gait pattern.

Clinical Example. The amputee can move the center of gravity directly over the sound foot by lateral trunk bending. If this incorrect postural adjustment, caused by the amputee's own balancing mechanism, becomes habit, it can lead to several undesirable gait deviations in the future. Instead, the physical therapist must teach the amputee to shift the pelvis laterally while keeping the trunk straight. This movement initially requires additional effort, but, eventually, it results in a smoother and more efficient gait pattern.

The importance of early physical therapy input cannot be over stressed. Teaching stump exercises and postural control immediately after amputation surgery helps the amputee to learn correct, precise muscle control. Efficient muscle control will facilitate prosthetic ambulation (see Basic Balance Exercises, p. 254).

If these activities are not taught, the amputee will learn through trial and error and the amputee's body balance mechanism will incorporate acquired postural gait deviations into the future gait pattern.

Gait deviations demand a higher energy output from the amputee because they require greater muscular counterforce to bring the body back into balance.

Balance, or the ability of opposing forces to adjust to each other during gait, must be diligently practiced to master prosthetic gait efficiently.

Energy Expenditure

Normally the human body is highly energy efficient. A healthy person, in reasonably good physical condition, uses a minimal amount of energy for ambulation. The amount of energy used can be determined by measuring the amount of oxygen consumed above the basic metabolic rate.

Normal energy expenditure varies with:

- the amount of physical activity
- the speed and intensity with which the movement is carried out
- the number of repetitions performed
- the time frame in which the task is completed
- the physical capabilities of the individual

Quiet activities such as sitting and standing require little energy expenditure, whereas activities such as walking, climbing stairs, and running necessitate an increase in energy spent (Inman et al., 1981).

Pathological factors such as musculoskeletal abnormalities or cardiovascular deficiencies affect the normal energy consumption required for all activities (Inman et al., 1981). Ambulation for the amputee necessitates a higher energy output because of the unilateral neuromuscular imbalance and the passive weight of the prosthesis.

Studies indicate that during walking the level of oxygen consumption increases for amputees (Kumar, 1982) if they walk the same distance under the same conditions at the same speed as nonamputees. Average figures quoted for amputees with vascular deficiencies compared with healthy nonamputees indicate an increase in oxygen consumption for:

- transtibial amputees from 9% to 20%
- transfemoral amputees from 45% to 70%
- bilateral transfemoral amputees up to 300% (Murray et al., 1982).

Therefore, one can generally state that the higher the level of leg amputation, the greater the energy expenditure necessary during ambulation (McColloch et al., 1971).

Studies conducted by Waters and his colleagues in 1976 and 1978 compared the energy consumption during normal walking speeds of healthy individuals and various levels of lower extremity amputees. One amputee group had an underlying pathology and the other group did not. These studies evaluated the oxygen consumed per minute as well as the oxygen consumed per meter walked in relation to stride length, cadence (number of steps), velocity (walking speed), pulse rate, and aerobic capacity (Waters et al., 1976, 1978). It is interesting to note that this comparison did not show an increase in energy consumption per *minute* walked for the amputees compared with the nonamputees, which indicates that the amputees' established oxygen consumption remained constant (English, 1981) during walking.

However, the results document that amputees walk with a shorter stride length and decrease the number of steps. Therefore, they walk a shorter *distance* per minute than nonamputees.

The heart rate of the amputee group increased only slightly because they lowered their walking speed. However, the oxygen used per distance walked recorded an increase compared with the nonamputee group. This shows that, by slowing down, amputees adjust to walking speeds that are compatible with their capacity for energy expenditure (English, 1981).

Clinical Consideration.   If the amputee is asked to walk at the same pace as recorded for nonamputees, energy requirements will increase tremendously. This implies that the amount of energy expended is directly related to the amount of physical effort required to perform the same task. If the physical task becomes increasingly difficult (e.g., through a higher level of amputation or through bilateral amputations) and if, in addition, the amputee has to adjust to an underlying pathology as well as to the loss of physical function, the additional energy requirements for walking become enormous. Some elderly bilateral amputees with vascular deficiencies will manage to walk limited distances on two prostheses under rehabilitation supervision. However, nearly all of them, after discharge from the rehabilitation center, will eventually revert to wheelchair mobility since the effort required for wheelchair mobility is negligible compared with the effort of donning and walking with two prostheses (Murray et al., 1982). The learned skills of using two prostheses are lost.

It is, therefore, imperative that long term goals, treatment programs, and gait-training activities be realistic, and that they consider the amputee's physical capabilities in terms of cardiovascular and respiratory tolerance, general strength, and amputation level.

References

Basmajian, J. "Human Locomotion." *Muscles Alive,* 4th ed. Baltimore, Md.: Williams & Wilkins, 1979, 253–263.

Dagg, A.I. "Gait in Animals." *Mammal Review 3,* no. 4 (1973): 135–154.

English, E. "The Energy Cost of Walking for the Lower Extremity Amputee." In J.P. Kostuik and R. Gillespie, eds. *Amputation Surgery and Rehabilitation: The Toronto Experience.* New York: Churchill-Livingstone, 1981, 311–314.

Hughes, J. and Jacobs, N. "Normal Human Locomotion." *Prosthetics and Orthotics International 3* (1979): 4–12.

Inman, V.T. "Special Article: Human Locomotion." *Canadian Medical Association Journal 94,* (May 1966): 1047–1054.

Inman, V.T., Ralston, H.J., and Todd, F. "Kinematics. Energy Expenditure. Kinetics Muscles." *Human walking.* Baltimore, Md.: Williams & Wilkins, 1981, 22–117.

Koerner, I.B. "The Gait of the Amputee." *Journal of the Canadian Physiotherapy Association* 19, no. 5 (December 1967): 321–329.

Koerner, I.B. *Normal Human Locomotion and the Gait of the Amputee.* Alberta: University of Alberta, 1980, 7.

Koerner, I.B. *Observation of Human Gait.* Videocassettes, Health Sciences Audiovisual Education, University of Alberta, 1984.

Kumar, V.N. "Normal Locomotion and Prosthetic Gait Deviation." In S.N. Banerjee, ed. *Rehabilitation Management of Amputees.* Baltimore, Md.: Williams & Wilkins, 1982, 237–254.

McCollough, N.G., Shea, J.D., Warren, W.D., and Sarmiento, A. "The Dysvascular Amputee: Surgery and Rehabilitation." *Current Problems in Surgery,* October, 1971, pp. 8–12.

Mensch, G. "Prosthetic Gait Observation: Comparison of Bipedal and Quadrupedal Locomotion." *Physiotherapy Canada.* 31, no. 5 (1979): 269–272.

Murray, D., and Fisher, F.R. "Normal Gait." *Handbook of Amputations and Prostheses.* Ottawa: University of Ottawa, 1982, 28–31.

Murray, M.P. "Gait as a Total Pattern of Movement." *American Journal of Physical Medicine.* 16, no. 1 (1967): 290–333.

National Research Council Committee on Artificial Limbs. *Prosthetic Devices Research Project: Study of Rotations during Locomotion, Using Pins. Subcontractor's Report on Fundamental Studies of Human Locomotion and Other Information Relating to Design of Artificial Limbs.* 1947, Section 1, 1–3.

Saunders, J.B.D.M., Inman, V.T., and Eberhart, H.D. "The Major Determinants in Normal and Pathological Gait." *The Journal of Bone and Joint Surgery,* 35-A, no. 3 (July 1953): 543–558.

Steinberg, F.V. "Gait Disorders in Old Age." *Geriatrics,* March, 1966, pp. 134–143.

Waters, R.L., Hislop, H.J., Perry, J., Antonelli, D., and the staff of the Pathokinesiology Laboratory, Rancho Los Amigos Hospital, Downey, California. "Energetics: Application to the Study and Management of Locomotion Disabilities." *Orthopedic Clinics of North America.* 9, no. 2 (April 1978): 351–456.

Waters, R.L., Perry, J., Antonelli, D.E., and Hislop, H.J. "Energy Cost of Walking of Amputees: The Influence of Level of Amputation." *The Journal of Bone and Joint Surgery.* 58-A, no. 1 (January 1976): 42-46.

Global statistics indicating the approximate number of individuals who have undergone limb or partial limb amputations are not available (Banerjee, 1982). Precise estimates are difficult to establish since the incidence of amputations varies in different cultures, geographical areas, and during times of war.

AMPUTATION INCIDENCE, CAUSES, ASSOCIATED DISEASES, AND CONDITIONS

Amputation Incidence

Estimated figures of amputation incidence have been published by Tooms (1980), who quotes that there are approximately 500,000 amputees in the United States. If one increases these figures by 10% to include Canada (since this country's population is one-tenth that of the United States), the total number of amputees on the North American continent may approach 550,000.

Figures for additional amputations performed each year are equally approximate. The committee on Prosthetic Research and Development of the National Academy of Sciences quoted 43,000 for 1971. An additional 10% would bring this total number of new amputations performed annually on the North American continent to a total of approximately 47,300.

Of these 47,300 amputations, 85% (Glattly, 1970; Tooms, 1980; Wagner, 1981), or 40,205, involve the lower extremities, whereas the remaining 15%, or 7,095 amputations, involve the upper extremities. Investigative data comparing the male and female ratio of amputation incidence indicate a male predominance (Hansson, 1964; Statistics Canada, 1975).

In comparing the ratio of transtibial to transfemoral amputation levels, the latter previously recorded a high rate of incidence. However, this ratio is now reversed (Burgess, 1969; Sarmiento, 1970) owing to the refinement of surgical techniques and the use of the rigid postoperative dressing in clinical practice (see Amputation Levels: Transtibial Amputations, p. 37).

The reasons leading to amputation vary considerably. It is therefore important to examine the different causative factors more closely, since they greatly influence rehabilitation treatment and the functional level that the amputee will be able to attain.

Lower extremity amputations occur, in order of highest incidence, as a result of (Murdoch, 1977; Tooms, 1980; Troup, 1982):

Amputation Causes

- vascular disease
- trauma
- malignant tumor
- infections
- limb discrepancies

An analysis of the causes of the estimated annually occurring 40,205 lower extremity amputations is significant: 80% (Kerstein, 1974; Tooms, 1980; Wagner, 1981), or 32,164, of all lower extremity amputations occur as a result of complications related to peripheral vascular disease, whereas the remaining 20%, or 8,041, are performed for the other reasons. The majority of these 32,164 amputees belong to the aging adult population, and many of them, between 50–70% (Wagner, 1981), have additional complications as a result of diabetes mellitus.

From these statistical estimates, the clinician can make the assumption that the majority of recent lower extremity amputees referred for rehabilitation will have a multitude of problems. The scope of assessment and treatment measures must, therefore, consider:

- functional loss
- medical complications
- socioeconomic factors
- psychological adjustment

The physical therapist must know and understand the extent of the disease process, the injury, and/or the condition that caused the amputation and the resultant physical effects that these may have on the amputee. This knowledge base will enable the therapist to synthesize the information obtained during the assessment (see Physical Therapy Assessment for Rehabilitation Potential, p. 97):

- to establish realistic treatment goals
- to implement an appropriate physical therapy program

Although the amputation itself is a major treatment concern, difficulties often arise during rehabilitation because of problems associated with the *cause* of the amputation as well as problems associated with the amputation itself.

In addition to the underlying cause and the physical impact of the amputation surgery, the amputee must also cope with emotional stresses associated with the amputation. This will further influence the course of recovery regardless of the reason for amputation (Friedmann, 1978).

All recent amputees require an individualized, coordinated amputation rehabilitation team approach (see The Amputation Rehabilitation Team, p. 45). Within that team, physical therapists have a key responsibility in ensuring that the maximum rehabilitation potential is achieved by each amputee.

Amputation Associated Diseases and Conditions

Although diagnosis(es) and medical treatment(s) are provided by the physician, the physical therapist must be able to interpret and monitor the clinical signs and symptoms that are manifested by the different amputation causes in order to adapt treatments to the amputee's current condition.

A major influence on amputation rehabilitation is the presence of peripheral vascular disease. Since vascular disease processes are complex, an attempt has been made to categorize and condense the information necessary to give the physical therapist an insight into these multifaceted conditions.

Vascular Disease

Vascular disease is a collective term for disorders affecting the vascular system: the blood vessels, the heart, the lymphatics, and the pulmonary and portal systems (Thomas, 1981). The etiology of these vascular deficiencies is not always clear. Vascular diseases occur in arteries and veins, and may affect large, medium, or small vessels. All vascular diseases ultimately impede blood flow and, therefore, compromise tissue nutrition, which, in extreme situations, will cause cell destruction (gangrene).

Arterial Degenerative Vessel Disease. Arteriosclerosis, or hardening of the arteries, is a term given to a group of diseases that involve thickening and/or loss of elasticity (calcification) of arterial walls (Robbins et al., 1984).

Atherosclerosis is the most common form of arteriosclerosis and is characterized by the laying down of atheromatous plaques on the inner walls of the arterioles. As the disease progresses, the plaques may block the lumen of the vessels, thereby impeding the rate of blood flow and weakening the affected arteries (Robbins et al., 1984).

Signs and symptoms may include:

- claudication pain
- skin blanching
- limb temperature changes
- trophic changes (poor nail growth, loss of sweat response)
- sensory loss
- ulceration

Ulceration progressing to gangrene in the lower extremities may necessitate amputation.

Atherosclerosis is a multisystem disease that may also cause (Robbins et al., 1984):

- decreased kidney function
- chronic obstructive pulmonary disease
- cerebral vascular disease
- ischemic heart disease

Venous Insufficiency. This condition results from weakening of the walls of the veins or failure of the valves. During valve failure, the blood backs up into the superficial veins, causing venous distention. Minor trauma can lead to skin ulceration (Doyle, 1983).

Signs and symptoms may include:

- edema
- pain
- varicose eczema
- fragile skin
- loss of hair
- ulceration

If ulcers become severely infected and/or do not heal, amputation may become necessary. However, amputation caused by venous insufficiency occurs less frequently than amputation caused by arterial vessel disease.[1]

Vasospastic Disorders. Buerger's disease is a chronic, inflammatory, vasospastic disease that causes vasoconstriction of the blood vessels. It affects the peripheral vessels (both arteries and veins) and starts in the small vessels of the hands and/or feet. It is believed that sheets of atheroma (emboli) dislodge proximally, causing distal irritation. This eventually leads to vessel inflammation, resulting in ischemic conditions.[2]

Signs and symptoms may include:

- parasthesia of the feet
- skin blanching
- muscle fatigue
- claudication pain in the instep
- ulceration or gangrene of the digits

Problems in the extremities are usually bilateral, and ulcers are commonly very painful and difficult to heal (Strandness, 1983). Often, bilateral amputation of the digits results. The clinician may also occasionally see higher levels of amputation related to this pathology.

Summary. If vascular disease is the cause of the amputation, the therapist must remember that, although surgery has alleviated the most severe problem, the disease process itself is still present. In some amputees, physical recovery may have limitations owing to other persisting conditions. For example, rehabilitation may require that the therapist also have some neurological expertise, if the amputee has suffered a cerebral vascular accident (CVA).

Although vascular surgeons are now able to improve the vascularity in the lower extremities by procedures such as sympathectomies or bypass surgery, amputation may still be indicated as the disease progresses. These amputees are often very ill, and stabilization of all medical problems is necessary before more intensive physical rehabilitation can proceed.

Conditions Accelerating or Affecting Vascular Disease

Additional factors that may accelerate or affect the severity or extent of existing vascular disease include:

- diabetes mellitus
- infection
- hypertension
- life-style
- aging

Diabetes

Diabetes is a chronic disorder of carbohydrate, fat, and protein metabolism (Robbins et al., 1984). Usually problems occur as the result of underutilization of glucose owing to either delayed or inappropriate insulin secretion or to resistance to insulin in the peripheral tissues, as opposed to problems caused by a deficiency of insulin (Robbins et al., 1984). The cells are unable to absorb glucose and, therefore, are deprived of nutrition and, subsequently, energy. Diabetes primarily affects the membranes of the small and medium diameter vessels. It may result in circulatory deficits that can lead to skin ulceration following any trauma. Damaged tissues supplied by the affected vessels heal poorly and are more prone to infection (Tooms, 1980). Diabetes can occur alone or in conjunction with atherosclerosis. If both are present the complications of one condition are superimposed upon the other.

Symptoms commonly include (Robbins et al., 1984):

- excessive urine production (polyuria)
- excessive thirst (polydipsia)
- increased food intake (polyphagia)
- weight loss
- itching
- tiredness

Test results will include:

- elevated blood sugar (hyperglycemia)
- sugar in the urine (glucosuria)

Long term effects of diabetes include (Robbins et al., 1984):

- atherosclerotic changes in the large vessels as well as in the small arterial walls
- renal failure
- retinopathy
- peripheral neuropathy
- sensory and motor involvement
- skin lesions

Diabetes, although incurable, can be well controlled by diet, insulin, and exercise.

Several excellent references are available that can provide the therapist with more in-depth information about atherosclerosis and diabetes (Krall, 1978; Robbins et al., 1984; Mannik et al., 1983).

Infections

Patients who have vascular disease and/or diabetes are prone to developing localized bacterial infections, especially at the site of existing skin lesions. The most common route of contamination of an open area is by direct or indirect contact. Pathogenic microorganisms (usually staphylococci) will enter the skin lesion and may cause a purulent condition and tissue destruction (Swartz, 1979). The infected ulcers may persist (see Stump Complications and Conservative Treatments Considerations–Delayed Healing, p. 163) owing to poor circulation. In diabetics healing may be further compromised because of the high glucose level present in the tissue fluids. If and when gangrene (tissue death) develops, amputation becomes imperative.

Osteomyelitis. This infection can develop in any bone and may be manifested in three ways: as a result of hematogenous spread of infection or trauma or secondary to a contagious infection. These types of osteomyelitis usually affect the long bones in younger patients. Osteomyelitis associated with vascular disease and/or diabetes primarily affects the toes and feet and is observed in middle-aged or older patients (Norden, 1979).

Signs and symptoms may include (Norden, 1979):

- fever
- pain
- swelling
- erythema
- ulceration

In osteomyelitis, prior to the advent of antibiotic drug therapy, amputation surgery was the only treatment possible. However, amputation surgery is now rarely necessary to control this infectious condition.

Hypertension

Blood pressure depends on the cardiac output, the peripheral resistance, and the blood volume. Several pathologies can affect the blood pressure level. In vascular disease, hypertension or increased blood pressure may be caused by vasoconstriction or occlusion of the vessels, which increases the peripheral resistance, thus increasing the blood pressure.

Symptoms may include:

- irritability
- reduced endurance
- headaches

Increased blood pressure places a constant stress on the vessel endothelium and may further weaken vessel walls already compromised by existing vascular disease.

Life-style Factors

Certain life-style factors are believed to have an adverse effect on already existing vascular pathology.

Cigarette Smoking.   Carbon monoxide and nicotine constrict the smaller vessels particularly, further affecting blood flow through the already weak or nonpatent vessels.[3] Abstinence from smoking is advisable for all patients who have vascular disease. However, it is especially recommended for patients with Buerger's disease.[4]

Nutrition.   Proper nutrition is essential for amputees:

- to provide energy
- to supply elements necessary for growth and tissue repair
- to prevent weight gain
- to control diabetes

A stable diet should contain water, proteins, fats, carbohydrates, fiber, vitamins, and minerals. Dietitians will review the amputee's food intake to ensure that the established requirements are met. In this way, the body's metabolic balance is controlled, and obesity, a result of an imbalance of food consumption and energy output, will be avoided.

Adhering to a balanced diet will ensure proper nutrition. The level of plasma cholesterol and other blood fats are partly determined by diet. Decreasing the amount of animal fat in the diet may curtail the development of atheromatous plaques, which are largely composed of cholesterol (Robbins et al., 1984).

During the normal aging process, changes occur in the mineral and protein structure of the major blood vessels. These changes result in a slow progressive loss of elasticity of the vessels and tend to limit the ability of the arterial system to increase blood flow to the organs and extremities (Adelman, 1982). As these changes occur, accumulation of lipids (blood fats) in the inner vessel wall increases (Adelman, 1982), leading to a potential obstruction of the arterial blood flow.

Aging

The physiological process of aging may also result in:

- decreased reflexes
- decreased joint mobility (Walker, 1981)
- sensory loss (auditory, visual)
- decreased skin sensation
- increased bone fragility
- increased incidence of chronic conditions (cardiovascular, respiratory)
- decreased efficiency of the central nervous system integrative functions (Johnson, 1978)

Amputation necessitated by trauma occurs because of irreparable tissue damage caused by:

Trauma

- nonunion of fractures following injury
- persistent infection resulting from contamination at the time of the injury or from complications developing later in the recovery period (osteomyelitis)
- exposure to temperature extremes

The general health status of these amputees is usually good. However, injuries occurring in addition to the amputation can present problems and may have treatment priority over specific stump treatments and preparations for prosthetic fittings.

An adolescent may require lower extremity amputation to remove a primary malignant bone tumor. Osteosarcoma is the most common form of this rare disease. It usually occurs near the epiphyseal line in long bones and nearly always involves the medullary cavity (Moss et al., 1973). Bone tumors may also occur in adult life in these and other areas and may also require leg amputation.

Primary Malignant Bone Tumor

Malignant growth presents a most complicated group of diseases necessitating a highly individualized treatment approach for each patient. A person may require radiation and/or chemotherapy prior to, or following, the amputation surgery. However, these methods are not always followed.[5]

In this group of amputees, the clinician will more commonly find higher levels of amputation because the removal of the entire tumor is a life-saving operation and has priority over preserving a joint for function.

If chemotherapy is indicated as a follow-up to the amputation, nausea can occur owing to the systemic effects of the drug. Chemotherapy may also temporarily affect the stump shape (Gillespie, 1981). Rehabilitation delays are not significant since these amputees recover quickly from these side effects.

Limb Discrepancies

Limb discrepancies include congenital deformities (absence of a limb or part of a limb) and other rare conditions such as paralysis or gross limb deformities.

Congenital Deformities

Congenital deformities occur as a result of suppression of growth during the different developmental stages in utero (Moore, 1982). Factors that can hinder or suppress growth during this time include genetic components and environmental components (Gillespie, 1981; Moore, 1982).

The extent of the body systems involved depends on the cause and time frame in which growth was interrupted. Limb amputation to improve function and for cosmesis may sometimes be indicated at a very young age or may be delayed until the maturation of growth.

A specialized team with expertise in dealing with child development, physical growth, parental anxieties, social implications, and adaptive prosthetic devices is required for these amputees (Atlas of Limb Prosthetics, 1981). Congenital deformities will not be dealt with in this book.

Other Conditions

The patient who has a limb that has been nonfunctional and troublesome because of paralysis, severe deformity (limb or joint), or pain may be anxious to discuss, and in some instances request, amputation to improve function and/or for cosmesis.

Summary

In highlighting the different causes of amputation, it is very difficult to categorize amputees into specific groups according to age. There are exceptions to the general concept that elderly amputees are all vascular amputees and that malignancy and trauma account for all adolescent or younger adult amputees. For example, a young juvenile diabetic amputee may have clinical signs of severe vessel changes that one might expect to find in a more elderly person. Similarly, a 65-year-old adult, who is otherwise very healthy, may have suffered an amputation because of trauma.

Clinically, one will also observe that the chronological and the biological age may differ greatly from one person to another.

There are several factors that affect the rate of aging, exclusive of underlying pathology. Some of these include social and cultural influences as well as the individual's attitude toward aging (McPherson, 1983).

Although aging cannot be controlled, it is a factor that must be considered during rehabilitation because, in the presence of vascular disease, the aging process may be accelerated when compared with the normal.

Although the effects of problems related to the cause of amputation should not be minimized for the younger age group, statistics indicate a marked increase in amputations for age 55 upward, with atherosclerosis, including diabetes, being the leading cause of amputation in Western societies (Banerjee, 1982).

In outlining some of the problems related to the causes of amputation, it becomes evident, and should be reinforced, that the physical therapist must consider the implications of *ALL* physical findings to effectively formulate a comprehensive, realistic treatment plan for each amputee patient. Since the life expectancy of the amputee with vascular disease and/or diabetes is considerably reduced, all treatment must aim to effectively expedite rehabilitation in the shortest possible time.[6]

References

Adelman, B.A. "Peripheral Vascular Disease." In J.W. Rowe and R.W. Besdine, eds. *Health and Disease in Old Age*. Boston, Mass.: Little, Brown, 1982, 224–231.

Aitken, G.T., Pellicore, R.J., Kruger, L.M., Lambert, N.C., Tooms, R.E., Hayes, R., Marquart, E., Laboriel, M.M., and Setoguchi, Y. *Atlas of Limb Prosthetics. Part Five: Surgical and Prosthetics Principles*. (American Academy of Orthopedic Surgeons.) St. Louis, Mo.: C.V. Mosby, 1981, 493–651.

Banerjee, S.N. "Limb Amputation—Incidence, Causes and Prevention." In S.N. Banerjee, ed. *Rehabilitation Management of Amputees*. Baltimore, Md.: Williams & Wilkins, 1982, 1–10.

Burgess, E.M., Romano, R.L., and Zettl, J.H. "Below-knee Amputation." *The Management of Lower Extremity Amputations*. Washington, D.C.: U.S. Government Printing Office, 1969, 13–39.

Doyle, J.E. "All Leg Ulcers Are Not Alike: Managing and Preventing Arterial and Venous Ulcers." *Nursing*, 13 (1983): no. 1, pp. 58–64.

Friedmann, L.W. "General Aspects of Amputee Psychology." *The Psychological Rehabilitation of the Amputee*. Springfield, Ill.: Chas. C. Thomas, 1978, 17–23.

Gillespie, R. "Congenital Limb Deformities and Amputation Surgery in Children." In J.P. Kostuik and R. Gillespie, eds. *Amputation Surgery and Rehabilitation: The Toronto Experience*. New York: Churchill Livingstone, 1981, 105–143.

Glattly, H.W. "A Preliminary Report on the Amputee Census." *Selected Articles from Artificial Limbs*. New York: R.E. Krieger, 1970, 319–324.

Hansson, J. "The Leg Amputee: A Clinical Follow-Up Study." *Acta Orthopaedica Scandinavica Supplement*, 1964, p. 69.

Johnson, L.A. "Gerontology." In H. Hopkins and H.D. Smith, eds. *Willard and Spackman's Occupational Therapy*, 5th ed. Philadelphia, Pa.: J.B. Lippincott, 1978, 450–452.

Kerstein, M.D., Zimmer, H., Dugdale, F.E., and Lerner, E. "Amputations of the Lower Extremity: A Study of 194 Cases." *Archives of Physical Medicine and Rehabilitation*. 55 (1974): 454–459.

L.P. Krall, ed. "Cardiovascular Complications." *Joslin Diabetes Manual*, 11th ed. Philadelphia, Pa.: Lea and Febiger, 1978, 178–179.

McPherson, B.D. "Types of Aging." *Aging as a Social Process*. Canada: Butterworth and Company, 1983, 6–11.

Mannik, M., and Gilliland, B.C. "Vasculitis." In R.G. Petersdorf, R.D. Adams, E. Braunwald, K.J. Isselbacher, J.B. Martin, and J.D. Wilson, eds. *Harrison's Principles of Internal Medicine*, 10th ed. New York: McGraw-Hill, 1983, 382–387.

Moore, K.L. "Limb Malformations." *The Developing Human*, 3rd ed. Philadelphia, Pa.: W.B. Saunders, 1982, 368–373.

Moss, W.T., Brand, N.W., and Battiford, H. "Osteosarcoma." *Radiation Oncology, Rationale, Technique, Results*, 4th ed. St. Louis, Mo.: C.V. Mosby, 1973, 544–549.

Murdoch, G. "Levels of Amputation and Limiting Factors." *Lower Limb Prosthetics*. New York: New York University, 1977, 43–46.

Norden, C.W. "Osteomyelitis." In G.L. Mandell, R.G. Douglas, and J.E. Bennett, eds. *Principles and Practice of Infectious Diseases*. New York: John Wiley and Sons, 1979, 946–956.

Robbins, S.L., Cottran, R.S., and Kuma, V. "Atherosclerosis." *Pathologic Basis of Disease*, 3rd ed. Philadelphia, Pa.: W.B. Saunders Company, 1984, 505–518.

Robbins, S.L., Cottran, R.S., and Kuma, V. "Diabetes Mellitus." *Pathologic Basis of Disease*, 3rd ed. Philadelphia, Pa.: W.B. Saunders Company, 1984, 973–986.

Sarmiento, A., May, B.J., Sinclair, W.R., McCollough, N.C., and Williams, E.M. "The Impact of Immediate Lower Extremity Amputation." *Clinical Orthopedic and Related Research*, 68 (1970), 22–31.

Statistics Canada. Surgical procedures and treatments. Ottawa, Canada: Ministry, Trade and Commerce. 1975.

Strandness, D.E. Vascular diseases of the extremities. In R.G. Petersdorf, R.D. Adams, E. Braunwald, K.J. Isselbacher, J.B. Martin, and J.D. Williams, eds. *Harrison's Principles of Internal Medicine*, 10th ed. New York: McGraw-Hill, 1983, 1491–1498.

Swartz, M.N. "Skin and Soft Tissue Infections." G.L. Mandell, R.G. Douglas, and G.E. Bennett, eds. *Principles and Practice of Infectious Diseases*. New York: John Wiley and Sons, 1979, 797–799.

Thomas, C.L. Taber's cyclopedic medical dictionary, 14th ed. Philadelphia, Pa.: F.A. Davis, 1981, 1541.

Tooms, R.E. "Incidence of Amputation." In A. Edmonson and A.H. Grenshaw, eds. *Campbell's Operative Orthopedics*, 6th ed. St. Louis, Mo.: C.V. Mosby, 1980, Vol. 1, 822.

Troup, I.M., and Wood, M.A. "Indications for Amputation." *Total Care of the Amputee*. London: Pitman Books, 1982, 24–33.

Wagner, W.F. "The Dysvascular Foot: A System of Diagnosis and Treatment." *Foot & Ankle*. 2, no. 2 (1981): 64–122.

Walker, J.M. "Development, Maturation and Aging of Human Joints: A Review." *Physiotherapy Canada*. 33, no. 3 (May/June 1981): 153–160.

Notes

1. Banerjee, S.N., Personal Communication, May 1985.
2. Frank, G.L., Personal Communication, May 1985.
3. Banerjee, S.N., "Introduction to Lower Extremity Amputations," Presented to Mohawk-McMaster Physical Therapy students. Hamilton, Ontario, April 1985.
4. Frank, G.L., Personal Communication, May 1985.
5. Muirhead, W., Personal Communication, May 1985.
6. Murdoch, G., "Amputation Levels," Advanced course in lower extremity prosthetics, East Meadow, New York, September 21–23, 1983.

Lower extremity amputations interfere with normal locomotion. They cause:

- a loss of physical function
- a change in weight distribution resulting from unilateral weight loss
- an interference in coordination and proprioception
- a disturbance of balance

To adapt to these changes the amputee, trying to maintain balance, compensates with postural adaptations. The extent of these postural adaptations depends upon the level of amputation and whether the amputation is unilateral or bilateral.

Each amputation level has its own specific characteristics (Murdoch, 1970). However, a few general comments concerning stump conditions and functions are indicated.

Although the loss of physical function increases proportionately with the height of the level of amputation, all stumps must act as levers to accelerate and control the prosthesis during gait.

The length of the stump (measured by bone length) influences:

- the amount of lever control
- the amount of available muscle tissue for muscular control
- the amount of stump surface available for

  1. weight-bearing distribution
  2. socket contact, which influences proprioceptive awareness and comfort

An amputation performed through a joint level (e.g., in ankle or knee disarticulations) results in an end-bearing stump. The long bone that flares out at the distal end remains intact (Baumgartner, 1979). The cancellous bone covered by articular cartilage provides a wide, smooth, weight-bearing surface. The bone functions in its natural state.

However, if the long bone has been severed (e.g., in transtibial or transfemoral amputations), total weight bearing through the stump end is not possible. The reasons for this are:

- The cut surface of cortical bone is sharp.
- The bone diameter is narrow.
- The anatomical cross section of long bones is tubular (Basmajian, 1975), reducing even further an already narrow weight-bearing surface.

To improve the stump weight-bearing properties, the distal bone end is surgically sculptured to smoothen the sharp edges, and muscle tissues are brought over the severed bone end to cushion and reduce the bone end sensitivity.

Socket construction and alignment further accommodate weight-bearing distribution. This distribution of weight bearing, imposed by surgical considera-

AMPUTATION LEVELS: STUMP CHARACTERISTICS AND TREATMENT CONSIDERATIONS RELATED TO GAIT

General Stump Comments

Weight Bearing

tions and prosthetic socket modifications, decreases the amount of weight bearing on the sensitive distal bone end.

When considering transfemoral amputations, the ischial tuberosity, which has some cancellous bone, is able to accommodate weight well because of its smooth surface and tendinous soft tissue coverage.

Amputation Levels

Each amputation level presents different problems in relation to the loss of physical function, treatment consideration, and gait adaptations.

Toe Amputations

Hallux or multiple toe amputations cause relatively minor functional problems. Equal leg length is preserved, and the weight-bearing surface of the foot remains intact so that balance is maintained. However, functional loss is experienced at toe-off as the toes help to accelerate the leg from stance into the swing phase.

(See Fig. 2–45)

Treatment Considerations. The physical therapist has to examine the surgical scar and, using caution, manually mobilize the tissues around it since they can become adherent. Mobile tissues reduce the chance of skin breakdown. A cotton filler, placed in the shoe, absorbs perspiration and provides contact. High-heeled shoes are not recommended because the elevated heel alters the weight-bearing distribution, transferring weight to the forefoot and decreasing the weight-bearing base. This adds stress to the amputation site.

Gait. Initially the patient compensates for the loss of acceleration by reducing the foot-rolling motion. Simultaneously, hip and knee flexion on the affected limb are slightly increased. A return to a normal gait pattern occurs quickly by wearing a comfortable supportive shoe. However, difficulties remain in tiptoeing, running, jumping, and squatting (Hunter, 1981).

Forefoot Amputations (Transverse)

Partial foot amputations (Bingham, 1970; Tooms, 1980) at the forefoot, midfoot, or hind foot levels, either through the metatarsal or at the midtarsal joint levels (Lisfranc and Chopart), result in forefoot lever loss. Midfoot and hind foot amputations are not frequently performed because they often result in foot deformities (Harris, 1981). However, midfoot amputation surgery, with appropriate shoe support, is a useful amputation level (Burgess, 1982) since the remaining foot portion provides equal leg length and is functional for weight bearing (over the heel portion). However, four necessary foot functions are missing, particularly in the shorter stump.

1. Balance loss. The forefoot contributes to body balance by its ability to invert and evert. Practice standing on one leg for a prolonged period of time and feel the functional control yourself. The shorter the remaining foot portion, the harder it is to balance.

2. Weight-bearing loss. The absence of the forefoot disrupts the foot-rolling motion, and so the transfer of body weight from the hind foot to the forefoot during gait is interrupted. Midstance is prolonged, and the knee remains extended

to compensate for the loss of forefoot weight-bearing function (Condie, 1970). Hip and knee flexion are increased following midstance, leading the leg into the swing phase.

3. Proprioceptive loss. The foot functions as a sensory organ (Burgess, 1982). The loss of foot surface and forefoot joints that contain proprioceptive sensors affects the feedback that the amputee receives from the ground, and thus proprioception is considerably decreased. The proprioceptive loss, as well as the forefoot weight-bearing loss, is comparatively high relative to the foot portion amputated.

4. Lever Loss. From heel-off to toe-off the forefoot acts as a support lever and, as such, contributes strongly in accelerating the stance leg into the swing phase by pushing forcefully against the ground.

Physical therapeutic treatments include the prevention of foot deformities. The remaining foot portion has a tendency to pull into equinus. This is caused by muscular imbalance and biomechanical changes.

Equinus Deformity

Tibialis anterior and tibialis posterior muscles are attached to the medial section of the midfoot and cause a strong inversion pull. This pull is no longer counteracted by the forefoot, which would normally control weight bearing and balance the body by inverting and everting.

The extensive biomechanical structural changes that take place in forefoot amputations contribute to the development of deformities. The collapse of the longitudinal arch shifts the remaining foot section downwards, thus changing the angular relationship between the tibia and the remaining bones of the foot (Harris, 1981; Foort, 1982). The remaining foot portion tilts into plantar flexion, and the directional pull of the gastrocnemius muscle forces the heel into equinus. The peroneii, which normally oppose the equinus position, are not strong enough to counteract the tibial and the gastrocnemius muscle actions.

(See Fig. 1–17)

Treatment Considerations. Stretching the medial border of the residual foot portion is essential to maintain mobility and to counteract contracture development. Scar mobilization is also advised since adherent tissues make the stump skin tight and tissue adhesions decrease skin tolerance to weight-bearing stresses.

(See Fig. 1–18)

A comfortable supporting shoe with a malleable sole allowing toe break action must be equipped with a filler. This filler provides standing and walking stability, aids in balance, and prevents the partial foot from sliding forward within the shoe. The distal contact of the stump with the filler also enhances proprioception.

Gait. Gait is possible without ambulation aids. The amputation level is functional and permits independent locomotion. The amputee adapts by terminating the stance phase on the amputated side immediately following heel off, picking the leg up before the cycle is completed. The swing phase, therefore, begins with intensified muscle action in the proximal joints, resulting in increased hip and knee flexion. This muscular action (not part of the normal gait cycle) restricts the

Figure 1–17 Change of angulation between the tibia and the stump following forefoot amputation.

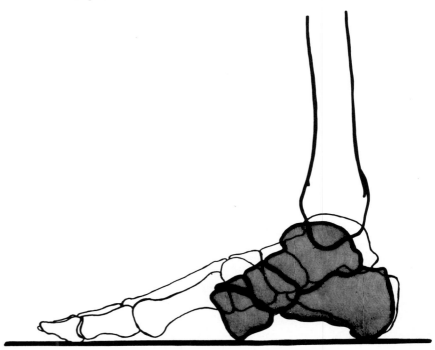

pendular movement of the shin during midswing and prolongs the stance phase on the sound side. It gives the gait a slightly arrhythmic appearance.

Partial Foot Amputations (Longitudinal)

Longitudinal foot amputation procedures are practiced[1] by surgeons who treat dysvascular feet. The physical therapist must assess the individual functional deficit of a longitudinal foot amputation prior to planning a rehabilitation program. As with transverse foot amputations, any longitudinal loss has an advantage: the preservation of equal leg length. However, the disadvantage in longitudinal procedures is the narrowing of the weight-bearing base, which diminishes foot balance control. Although lever length remains, the push-off strength and the elasticity of the remaining foot portions are reduced.

Ankle Disarticulations (Syme's Amputations)

In an ankle disarticulation (Syme's amputation) the foot is completely lost. The heel pad is brought forward and positioned under the distal end of the tibia. The heel cushion is sutured anteriorly, from side to side, providing the stump end with full end-bearing characteristics.

This amputation level is advantageous because the weight-bearing characteristics are enhanced by two factors: the preservation of the tibia provides a broad

Figure 1–18 Stretching the forefoot amputation stump.

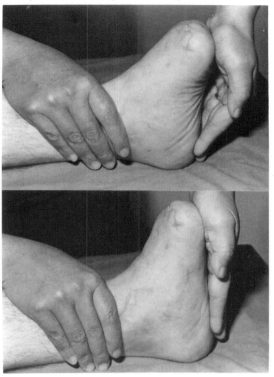

weight-bearing surface and the heel pad tissues that previously functioned in a weight-bearing capacity are utilized to cover the bone end. The stump shape is bulbous, and amputees often object to its appearance (Tooms, 1980; Burgess, 1982). Trimming of the malleoli in a second surgical procedure is possible (Wagner, 1981), thereby improving the distal stump appearance. The distal contours of the prosthesis are then less prominent. However, this reduces the lateral diameter of the bone, and with it some weight-bearing surface is sacrificed.[2]

Treatment Considerations. All foot motions such as inversion, eversion, dorsiflexion, and plantar flexion are missing, and the comparatively small heel cushion has to absorb and respond to weight-bearing shearing forces and floor reaction forces during all phases of prosthetic ground contact. Therefore, it is imperative that the heel pad and the bone end are firmly united and that the stump end is protected postsurgically by a walking cast. If unprotected and/or incorrectly aligned, weight-bearing shearing forces that are transmitted through the stump end can cause heel pad shifting.

Murdoch (1983) cautioned that stump protection is most important during the early postoperative phase because healing must occur where "thick skin" (tough heel skin) meets "thin skin" (tibial crest skin). This healing is vital in achieving a satisfactory outcome of this surgical procedure.

The stump is functional because of its weight-bearing ability. An amputee can get up at night to go to the washroom without donning a prosthesis. However, one should *strongly* advise amputees against this practice since heel pad shifting (without the external prosthetic socket support) results from incorrect weight bearing, and a mobile heel pad causes stump complications.

(See Fig. 1–19)

Dog ears may be observed on either side of the suture line when the cast is removed. They are not cut off during surgery because of abundant vascularity (Tooms, 1980). With correct bandaging, these dog ears will shrink (see Stump Bandaging, p. 134) and should not be a problem.

Gait.   A prosthesis compensates for the leg length discrepancy and the loss of all foot functions. Independent walking can be achieved provided the stump is painfree and correct prosthetic alignment is built into the prosthesis. Initially, the amputee demonstrates increased hip and knee flexion during gait. This occurs as a result of adaptation to the weight of the prosthesis and the lack of toe-off. However, in later stages the gait pattern becomes almost normal as the stump length and the contours of the socket design (extending to knee level) provide weight-bearing stability and excellent stump lever control. Patellar tendon-bearing (PTB) sockets can also be utilized for the Syme's stump to distribute some weight bearing through the patellar tendon.

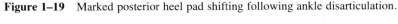

Figure 1–19   Marked posterior heel pad shifting following ankle disarticulation.

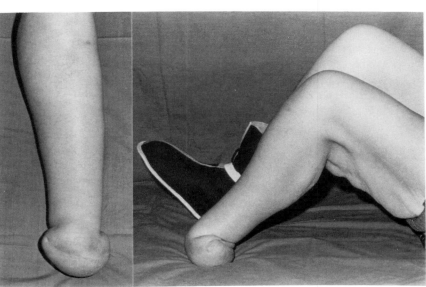

The gait appears somewhat stiff because the natural foot and ankle joints that have the ability to absorb the axial rotations of the tibia during gait are not present (Inman et al., 1981). This function, tibial external rotation on weight bearing, is now accommodated by the distal heel pad (Murray et al., 1981).

In transtibial amputations the amputee loses all the natural functions of the foot and ankle as well as the foot's weight-bearing characteristics. The stump is usually cylindrical and nonend bearing, but weight-bearing distribution to the patellar tendon and soft tissue areas makes this amputation level functional and useful.

Transtibial Amputations

The statistics of the early 1960s (Fernie, 1981) indicated that the majority of amputations performed for vascular problems were above the knee. It was felt that this level ensured healing. However, with the perfection of surgical techniques, muscle stabilization, and the reintroduction of the rigid postoperative dressing, the dysvascular amputee can heal at the transtibial level, enhancing a successful rehabilitation outcome because of the preservation of the knee joint (Burgess, 1969; Tooms, 1980). Consequently, the number of transtibial amputations has increased, whereas the number of transfemoral amputations has decreased.

The surgeon, utilizing plastic and reconstructive surgical techniques, sculptures the transtibial stump according to physiological principles by (Burgess et al., 1969, 1982; Tooms, 1980; Murray et al., 1981; Waddell, 1981):

- Conserving tibial length. This allows for lever control.
- Beveling the anterior tibial bone end and severing the fibula slightly shorter. This avoids protrusion of sharp bone edges into the soft tissues.
- Utilizing a longer posterior tissue flap and bringing these soft tissues over the bone end towards the front of the stump. This makes better use of the vascularity of the calf muscles, covering and cushioning the bone end as well as providing a cylindrical-shaped stump with an anteriorly placed surgical scar.
- Performing muscle stabilization (myoplasty). This means suturing the flexor and extensor muscles together to provide muscular counterattachment. This improves muscle contractability and avoids soft tissue retraction.

The stump is protected postsurgically by a cast that allows for a quiet wound healing environment and counteracts stump swelling, thereby permitting quicker healing.

Transtibial amputations performed prior to these refined surgical techniques presented with a conical-shaped stump, a distal surgical scar, and marked atrophy around the stump end. These stump shapes were the result of muscle retraction because muscle stabilization was not practiced. These stumps were often sensitive and painful on weight bearing. In many cases, proprioception was also appreciably diminished (Burgess, 1982).

When presented with a young and otherwise healthy patient, distal bone bridging between the tibia and fibula may be utilized when performing a transtibial amputation, whereby stump weight bearing is improved. It is not indicated, however, for amputees with vascular insufficiency because decreased vascularity may impede bone healing (Burgess, 1982).[3]

Treatment Considerations.   Transtibial stump tissues, although by nature not designed to carry body weight, have been surgically prepared to accommodate some weight bearing. Comfort and function in socket construction are based on the principle of compressing soft or pressure-tolerant tissues, while giving relief to hard or pressure-sensitive tissues (Murray et al., 1982). This is achieved by molding a total contact socket, allowing relief for the remaining tibial crest, fibular head, and distal fibula, as well as the hamstring and gastrocnemius tendons, and by compressing muscular areas and the patellar tendon. In this way, weight bearing is distributed over the total stump area.

Weight bearing is further controlled by aligning the socket in slight flexion on stance (see Alignment, p. 234). The amputee can feel patellar tendon weight bearing by contracting the quadriceps muscles. When this occurs, weight bearing is reduced at the stump end because of the flexion alignment of the socket and the muscular contraction against the patellar tendon bar. The flexion alignment of the socket also permits the amputee to walk and bear weight while the knee joint is in an anatomically correct position. Thus, a better gait pattern is possible.

The basic design of the patellar tendon bearing (PTB) socket can be adapted to specific functional needs, such as extending the lateral socket brim to a supra-condylar level (patellar tendon supracondylar [PTS] socket) to provide increased medial lateral knee stability. Also the type of suspension utilized depends on the stump shape and size. A PTB strap suspension and a PTS wedge suspension are least restrictive. A thigh corset relieves the stump of some weight bearing, while a sleeve suspension reduces stump piston action. (See Transtibial Prostheses, p. 218).

Gait.   The amputee's initial response to a transtibial amputation is to transfer weight to the sound leg when standing. This is caused by a shifting of the center of gravity over the support leg. As a result of this postural adaptation, the muscles of the remaining leg must work harder to maintain body balance.

During gait, prosthetic heel contact is absorbed by the prosthetic heel bumper. The slightly bent knee assists in cushioning the floor impact (Murray et al., 1982). As the prosthetic foot, by body forward motion, advances from the foot flat to midstance position, the amputee receives weight-bearing support by "kneeling" against the patellar tendon bar of the socket. Stump contractions of the remaining pretibial muscle group provide socket contact while the quadriceps and hamstring muscles control the degree of flexion. The center of gravity travels over the prosthesis as the gait cycle advances. Hamstring action decreases, and the remaining gastrocnemius muscles contract, maintaining stump contact with the socket and assisting the stump into knee flexion in preparation for the swing phase.

There is no active push off at the end of the stance phase, and the weight of the prosthesis is felt. Therefore, the amputee "hoists" the prosthesis, actively increasing the amount of hip flexion. This contributes to accelerating the prosthesis into swing phase.

Elderly amputees, many of whom experience a natural reduction in joint ranges, adapt to prosthetic gait by demonstrating a shorter step length and by sometimes eliminating prosthetic heel contact. The artificial foot is placed directly onto foot flat at the beginning of stance phase. Joint range limitations in aging also affect the rotational aspects of gait.

Generally, the transtibial amputee demonstrates a functional and satisfactory gait pattern. In young amputees, gait deviations are minimal; they are active and independent walkers. Elderly amputees may be independently mobile, often using only a single cane.

Amputees who have knee disarticulation amputations lose all foot, ankle, and knee movements. The stump has several distinct characteristics that permit gait with relative ease compared with transfemoral amputees, despite the similarity in functional loss (Harris, 1970; Kostuik, 1981; Murray et al., 1982; Mensch, 1983).

The stump is long, bulbous, and end bearing. The intact femur contributes to stump socket comfort. Muscular balance of all thigh muscles is preserved, permitting coordinated stump movements and good stump proprioception, resulting in an easier readjustment to balance and position sense (Baumgartner, 1979), as compared with transfemoral amputations.

The stump length and weight-bearing ability also provide axial rotational stability between the stump and socket, adding to prosthetic gait control. In addition, the stump permits secure socket suspension. This is achieved by contouring the socket above the femoral condyles. Additional pelvic suspension can be provided but is usually not necessary.

Treatment Considerations. It is important for the physical therapist to remember to work on hip extension because a hip flexion contracture (although not as common in the knee disarticulation stumps because muscle balance is maintained) at this amputation level interferes considerably with prosthetic gait. The prosthetist cannot build too much hip flexion into a knee disarticulation socket because it would bring the prosthetic knee too far forward, thereby making it more difficult for the amputee to maintain prosthetic stance stability (Mensch, 1983).

Gait faults are related to the actual stump length. The knee axis of the prosthesis falls below the anatomical position of the natural knee (Bell, 1970). This results, prosthetically, in an increased thigh length and shorter shank section, which interferes biomechanically with the gait cycle and gives the prosthesis a disproportionate appearance, which affects cosmesis. This can be partially corrected by the use of a four-bar linkage knee mechanism (see Prosthetic Knees, p. 207). However, many amputees still complain because floor contact during sitting is not always possible.

Knee Disarticulations

Coordination is decreased because two joints (knee and ankle), which function in opposite directions, are missing. This requires the stump to control the artificial knee joint by hip flexion and extension only. Prosthetic foot movements occur as a result of weight bearing and the forward propulsion of the trunk over the prosthesis. The loss of natural knee function presents more of a problem to the elderly, as compared with the younger age group. However, they must also practice perfecting prosthetic knee control.

Gait.   The prosthetic gait is functional and acceptable but unnatural because of the thigh/shank ratio. The beginning of the stance phase is prolonged, there is a pause at midstance, and then an increase in velocity is experienced following prosthetic knee flexion. This arrhythmic prosthetic stance phase increases the stance phase on the sound side.

The amputee also demonstrates a long prosthetic step. When trying to achieve prosthetic knee extension, the amputee has to increase the stump extension range compared with the hip extension needed to perform the same movement on the sound side. This increase in stump hip extension is due to the longer thigh lever and results in a stable prosthetic knee on midstance. As the gait cycle advances, the amputee often experiences difficulty in initiating prosthetic knee flexion, again due to the disproportionate thigh/shank ratio.

Despite these drawbacks, this amputation level is a good one for elderly people because of the end-bearing qualities of the stump (Kostuik, 1981). Weight bearing through the stump end helps the amputee to stand with comparative ease.

Elderly amputees often depend on one or two canes for prosthetic stance stability and to assist with balance.

Transfemoral
Amputations

The functional loss of foot, ankle, and knee movements is intensified in the transfemoral amputation stump. The length of the transfemoral stump determines the efficiency of stump leverage, proprioceptive adaptation, muscle coordination, and energy consumption.

The stump characteristics include a non-end-bearing stump and soft tissues that can be compressed to allow for total socket wall contact. Weight-bearing distribution is accommodated as the stump contracts against the walls of the socket. Weight bearing is also transferred through the ischial tuberosity by the provision of an ischial shelf that actually permits sitting in a standing position. These socket adaptations take into consideration that the cut femur is unable to bear total stump end weight.

Treatment Considerations.   The therapist must consider two major components in training the transfemoral amputee.

1. The counteraction of the development of a hip flexion contracture. The importance of this basic principle cannot be stressed often enough. A contracture reduces joint range, alters the step position, causes a long prosthetic step, causes difficulty in stabilizing the prosthetic knee, and eliminates the prosthetic push-off function because the stump cannot achieve its complete anatomical range. This limitation requires the hip flexors to draw the prosthesis into the swing phase

instead of propelling it by utilizing weight bearing and prosthetic push-off (see Contractures, p. 140).

2. The physical therapist must check, prior to gait training, that quadrilateral socket wall contact is ensured on all four sides since gait stability depends on stump socket wall contact (Radcliffe, 1970, 1981). If the socket is too loose, extra stump socks must be added to maintain an intimate socket fit.

A snug anterior-posterior socket diameter allows for acceleration and deceleration control, whereas a good medial-lateral socket fit allows for pelvic stability on stance. If the transfemoral socket is loose, gait training is not possible because the stump cannot brace itself against the lateral socket wall on stance. This causes instability as well as inaccurate socket feedback to the stump surfaces during the gait cycle.

Gait training becomes more involved as the amputee learns to balance over the prosthesis while controlling the artificial knee joint using stump hip flexion and extension. A common complaint is that the prosthesis feels too heavy, particularly from those transfemoral amputees with short stumps. The weight of the remaining leg is not felt despite the fact that it is heavier than the prosthesis. The feeling of excessive prosthetic weight can be reduced by well-controlled pelvic suspension with the use of a four-bar linkage knee mechanism (see Prosthetic Components, p. 207) and by choosing a shoe that is not too heavy.

Preparations for gait training include:

- stump exercises with emphasis on individual stump functions that enhance prosthetic control (see Stump Motions, p. 191)
- extensive balance exercises that provide the amputee with a feel for motion changes
- step practice that enables the amputee to learn how to activate the prosthesis

Gait. The gait in general appears stiff because the axial rotation of tibia and fibula in relation to the foot is missing and femoral axial rotation is reduced. The transfemoral amputee actually practices an unnatural gait pattern. In normal locomotion, the knee on weight bearing is held in slight initial flexion. However, to achieve stance stability, the amputee has to stand on the completely extended prosthetic knee. This means that hip extension must be held slightly longer on the prosthetic side compared with the sound side (Mensch et al., 1982).[4]

Most younger amputees, as well as those older amputees whose traumatic amputations were performed when they were young, are independent and safe walkers. However, each one of them adapts with moderate gait deviations. These are caused by:

- body adjustment to postural imbalance
- adaptation to the weight of the prosthesis
- reaction to the forces that affect gait (muscular, weight bearing, ground reaction forces) and result in increased energy consumption required to maintain body balance.

Elderly amputees, particularly amputees with vascular pathology, may have reduced joint ranges and considerably slower gait patterns. They should be permitted to walk with one or two canes at speeds comfortable to them, since the body is capable of adapting its locomotor system in its own energy efficient way (English, 1981) (see Energy Expenditure, p. 18).

Hip Disarticulations and Hemipelvectomies

These amputation levels present major problems since all functions of the foot, ankle, knee, and hip joints, together with all axial leg rotations and available weight-bearing surfaces, are absent. A hip disarticulation deprives the amputee of a stump with which to activate the prosthesis. The majority of these amputees are young, and the reason for amputation is, most commonly, malignancy.

Treatment Considerations.   Any edema in the tissues around the disarticulation has to be reduced to ensure an intimate socket fit to allow socket comfort and weight-bearing control through the prosthetic socket. The socket is suspended over the pelvic crest and is molded as a pelvic-bracing support. Prosthetic motion is initiated by prosthetic weight bearing, lumbar movement, and the functions of the sound leg. The exercise program prior to gait training includes activities for the sound leg, trunk movements, pelvic tilt exercises, and bilateral arm exercises. Scar mobilizations are beneficial in the prevention of adhesions.

Gait.   If the dynamic alignment of the prosthesis is correct, walking is stable and safe (McLaurin, 1970), although arrhythmic and slow. Pelvic tilting movements are required for activation of the prosthesis. This is extremely tiring. Often, hip disarticulation amputees ultimately elect to walk without a prosthesis because mobility on crutches is less cumbersome, speed of ambulation is faster, and less restriction is felt.

Summary

The various unilateral amputation levels present different functional problems to the amputee. The unique characteristics of each level indicate to the physical therapist specific training requirements.

One can basically state that a shorter stump length produces

- a reduced stump leverage
- a greater unilateral weight loss
- a more pronounced balance disturbance
- an increase in the weight of the prosthesis
- a greater evidence of gait deviations
- a more complicated prosthetic fit

These considerations intensify if bilateral amputation is necessary.

References

Basmajian, J.V. "Classification of Bone." *Grant's Method of Anatomy*, 9th ed. Baltimore, Md.: Williams & Wilkins, 1975, 4–6.
Baumgartner, R.F. "Knee Disarticulation versus Above-knee Amputation." *Prosthetics and Orthotics International*, 3 (1979): 15–19.

Bell, G. "Swing Phase Control for through-knee Prostheses." In G. Murdoch, *Prosthetic and Orthotic Practice*. London: Edward Arnold Publishers, 1970, 269–274.

Bingham, J. "The Surgery of Partial Foot Amputations." In G. Murdoch, *Prosthetic and Orthotic Practice*. London: Edward Arnold Publishers, 1970, 141–148.

Burgess, E.M., Romano, R.L., and Zettl, J.H. "Level Determination." *The Management of Lower Extremity Amputations.*" Washington, D.C.: U.S. Government Printing Office, 1969, 5–7.

Burgess, E.M. "Amputation Surgery and Postoperative Care." In S.N. Banerjee, ed. *Rehabilitation Management of Amputees*. Baltimore, Md.: Williams & Wilkins, 1982, 17–30.

Condie, D.N. "Biomechanics of the Partial-foot Amputations." In G. Murdoch, *Prosthetic and Orthotic Practice*. London: Edward Arnold Publishers, 1970, 149–160.

English, E. "Syme's Amputation." In J.P. Kostuik and R. Gillespie, eds. *Amputation Surgery and Rehabilitation: The Toronto Experience*. New York: Churchill Livingstone, 1981, 81–86.

Fernie, G.R. "The Epidemiology of Amputation." In J.P. Kostuik and R. Gillespie, eds. *Amputation Surgery and Rehabilitation: The Toronto Experience*. New York: Churchill Livingstone, 1981, 13–15.

Foort, J. "Prosthetic Fitting and Components—Lower Extremity Amputees." In S.N. Banerjee, ed. *Rehabilitation Management of Amputees*. Baltimore, Md.: Williams & Wilkins, 1982, 43–44.

Harris, E.E. "The through-knee Amputation Prosthesis." In G. Murdoch, ed. *Prosthetic and Orthotic Practice*. London: Edward Arnold Publishers, 1970, 253–267.

Harris, W.R. "Principles of Amputation Surgery." In J.P. Kostuik and R. Gillespie, eds. *Amputation Surgery and Rehabilitation: The Toronto Experience*. New York: Churchill Livingstone, 1981, 37–49.

Hunter, G.A. "Minor Foot Amputations." In J.P. Kostuik and R. Gillespie, eds. *Amputation Surgery and Rehabilitation: The Toronto Experience*. New York: Churchill Livingstone, 1981, 87–91.

Inman, V.T., Ralston, H.J., and Todd, F. "Introduction." *Human Walking*. Baltimore, Md.: Williams & Wilkins, 1981, 1–21.

Kostuik, J.P. "Amputations about the Knee." In J.P. Kostuik and R. Gillespie, eds. *Amputation Surgery and Rehabilitation: The Toronto Experience*. New York: Churchill Livingstone, 1981, 57–62.

McLaurin, C.A. "The Canadian Hip Disarticulation Prosthesis." In G. Murdoch, ed. *Prosthetic and Orthotic Practice*. London: Edward Arnold Publishers, 1970, 285–304.

Mensch, G. "Physiotherapy Following through-knee Amputation." *Prosthetics and Orthotics International*, 7, no. 2 (1983): 79–87.

Mensch, G., and Ellis, P. "Stump Mobility." In S.N. Banerjee (ed.), *Rehabilitation Management of Amputees*. Baltimore, Md.: Williams & Wilkins, 1982, 210–213.

Murdoch, G. "Indications, Levels and Limiting Factors in Amputation." *Prosthetic and Orthotic Practice*. London: Edward Arnold Publishers, 1970, 7–13.

Murray, D., and Fischer, F.R. "Below-knee Amputation." *Handbook of Amputations and Prostheses*. Ottawa: University of Ottawa, 1982, 50–59.

Radcliffe, C.W. "Biomechanics of above-knee Prosthesis." In G. Murdoch, ed. *Prosthetic and Orthotic Practice*. London: Edward Arnold Publishers, 1970, 191–198.

Radcliffe, C.W. "Prosthetic Knee Mechanisms for above-knee Amputees." In G. Murdoch, ed. *Prosthetic and Orthotic Practice*. London: Edward Arnold Publishers, 1970, 225–254.

Radcliffe, C.W. "Applications to Lower Limb Prosthetics." In V.T. Inman, H.J. Ralston, F. Todd, eds. *Human Walking*. Baltimore, Md.: Williams & Wilkins, 1981, 129–148.

Tooms, R.E. "Amputations." In A.S. Edmonson and A.G. Crenshaw, eds. *Campbell's Operative Orthopedics*. St. Louis, Mo.: C.V. Mosby, 1980, 821–861.

Waddell, J.P. "Below-knee Amputation." In J.P. Kostuik and R. Gillespie, eds. *Amputation Surgery and Rehabilitation: The Toronto Experience*. New York: Churchill Livingstone, 1981, 63–72.

Wagner, W.F. "The Dysvascular Foot: A System for Diagnosis and Treatment." *Foot & Ankle, 2*, no. 2 (1981): 64–122.

Notes

1. Wagner, W.F., ISPO's advanced course on B/K and T/K amputations and prosthetics, Køge, Denmark, May 10–13, 1982.
2. Murdoch, G. "Amputation Levels." Advanced course in lower extremity prosthetics, East Meadow, New York, September 21–23, 1983.
3. Ibid.
4. Mensch, G. "Prosthetic Gait Training." Advanced course in lower extremity prosthetics, East Meadow, New York, September 21–23, 1983.

2

Preoperative and Postoperative Care and The Responsibilities of the Physical Therapist

Part I

Rehabilitation is the combined and coordinated use of medical, social, educational and vocational measures for training or retraining the individual to the highest possible level of functional ability.

This statement was issued in 1969 by the World Health Organization (Expert Committee on Medical Rehabilitation).

Amputation rehabilitation teams are modelled, according to these principles, in an effort to provide the most efficient and effective care for the recent amputee. The coordinated efforts of this team of experts ensures that all bio-psychosocial issues are addressed during the rehabilitation program. It is important that the amputee constitute an integral part of this team, participating in decision making whenever possible. (Thompson et al., 1981; Gerhardt et al., 1982; Redford, 1982).

When considering the total concept of rehabilitation, one must realize that, ideally, team consultation should occur preoperatively. (Gerhardt et al., 1982; Varghese et al., 1982). The amount of input from each team member may vary during the different treatment stages. The core team, consisting of the physician, the nurse, the physical therapist, the prosthetist, and the social worker, will provide the initial care during the early pre- and postoperative rehabilitation stages (Gerhardt et al., 1982; Redford, 1982). As the amputee progresses to the pre-prosthetic, prosthetic fitting, and gait-training stages of rehabilitation, additional team members may include the occupational therapist, the psychologist, the dietician, and the vocational counselor. The expertise of these team members will enhance and complete the total treatment program.

THE AMPUTATION REHABILITATION TEAM

45

Education of the amputee is a total team responsibility. Learning to adapt to an irreversible disability, usually in the later stages in life, is often difficult for the amputee. Consistent and frequent input from all team members regarding such general topics as:

- the general medical care: diabetic protocol and general hygiene
- the care of the stump
- the care of the remaining leg
- the care of the prosthesis

will help amputees recognize the scope of their responsibilities in relation to their own rehabilitation. Education, regarding individual problems, is instituted as problems are identified following the team assessment or as they occur during the rehabilitation process.

An effective rehabilitation outcome requires coordination of the efforts of all team members. Each team member must earn the trust and confidence of the other team members by consistently demonstrating competence in their individual area of expertise, in relation to amputation rehabilitation (Mital et al., 1971). In this way, the team recognizes the individual expertise of its members and, consequently, each member will feel comfortable with any area of overlapping treatment responsibility.

References

Gerhardt, J.J., King, P.S., and Zettl, J.H. "The Team—Preoperative Planning." *Amputations, immediate and early prosthetic management*. Vienna: Hans Huber Publishers, 1982, 26–33.

Mital, M.A., and Pierce, D.S. "The Amputee Service Team and Its Role." *Amputees and Their Prostheses*. Boston, Ma.: Little, Brown, 1981, 41–57.

Redford, J.B. "Rehabilitation Team." In S.N. Banerjee, ed. *Rehabilitation Management of Amputees*. Baltimore, Md.: Williams & Wilkins, 1982, 150–163.

Thompson, R.G., and Kramer, S. "The Amputee Clinic Team." *Atlas of Limb Prosthetics*. St. Louis, Mo.: C.V. Mosby, 1981, 63–66.

Varghese, G., and Redford, J.B. "Preoperative Assessment and Management of Amputees." In S.N. Banerjee, ed. *Rehabilitation Management of Amputees*. Baltimore, Md.: Williams & Wilkins, 1982, 11–16.

PREOPERATIVE CARE

Physical therapy treatment should begin prior to the surgical event in order to provide the comprehensive care necessary to help the amputee achieve the highest level of biopsychosocial independence (Mital et al., 1971; Burgess, 1973, 1981; Banerjee, 1982; Gerhardt et al., 1982).

Amputation surgery has a major emotional impact on patients of any age. Full realization of the implications of the loss of physical function and uncertainty regarding the quality of the future lifestyle upsets and deeply concerns patients and their families (Fishman, 1961; Mital et al., 1971; Friedmann, 1978; Crowther, 1982; Bradway, 1984). The physical therapist's preoperative visit should be directed at easing some of this emotional stress so that the patient may better cope with the impending loss.

Geriatric patients with vascular pathology usually have long-standing histories that include several vascular procedures. Therefore, they have generally been debilitated for some time. These patients, as well as patients in whom neoplasm has been diagnosed, are usually scheduled for elective surgery. These situations permit the opportunity for an informative preoperative visit. However, a preoperative visit is not possible when severe trauma requires immediate leg amputation.

Explaining the sequence of rehabilitation to help alleviate fears and to permit the patient to have some feeling of control over future events is an integral part of total patient care.

The preoperative visit by the therapist serves two major purposes. The first is to share information so that the patient and the family have an opportunity to understand the rehabilitation process and discuss any concerns they may have. Emphasis is placed on the fact that amputation surgery should not be viewed negatively, as the end. With the recent improvements in surgical techniques, the stump is surgically prepared to maximize the previously lacking biomechanical functions of the affected limb. It is, therefore, the first step towards rehabilitation and the return to independence (Tooms, 1980; Burgess, 1981). With a prosthesis, the patient will again be able to walk, albeit in a modified way.

Elderly patients with a history of circulatory insufficiency and ischemic pain, including previous bypass surgery procedures, may express a feeling of relief (McCollough, 1971; Whylie, 1981), hoping that the amputation surgery will eliminate their pain.

The second purpose of the preoperative visit is to evaluate the patient's physical condition in preparation for postoperative activities and future ambulation (Burgess, 1973, 1981; Mensch et al., 1982; Varghese et al., 1982).

Information Visit

It is important to remember that the patient is already under stress and may also feel the effects of some administered medication. The therapist must, therefore, try to be understanding, informative, and supportive without further increasing the patient's anxiety.

The therapist's preoperative discussion should:

- reinforce the physician's diagnostic findings that make the amputation necessary
- explain the purpose of the postoperative stump dressing
- clarify the sequence of the rehabilitation process
- stress the importance of the patient's active participation in all treatment
- discourage unrealistic expectations without adversely affecting motivation
- discuss the functions of a prosthesis
- explain that a social worker is available to discuss the funding of the prosthesis, should this be a concern

The following information can also be given if indicated.

Phantom Sensation

This sensation, an awareness of feeling complete, is normal. It is useful and functional in learning to walk with a prosthesis. To avoid increasing the patient's anxiety level, the therapist should not dwell on phantom pain, but the patient should be made aware of the normal postoperative discomfort that is to be expected.

Increased Perspiration

This is common and occurs for several reasons:

1. Increased energy output. Walking requires effort, and doing the same work with only one leg is harder. Therefore, the body responds to the increased effort by perspiring more.
2. Loss of skin surface. Skin partially controls the body temperature. With the loss of skin surface through amputation, the remaining skin surface compensates in balancing the body temperature by perspiring more.
3. Effect of the amputation. The circulation must adapt to its new environment until the stump's collateral circulation has been formed.

The body adjusts to these changes, and the temperature balance following activities will gradually return to normal. This can take up to one year in high level amputations but rarely presents a problem in low level amputations.

The patient must also understand that the limb or partial limb loss is compensated for by the prosthesis and that this prosthesis, no matter how sophisticated, is only a substitute for the natural limb and walking with it has to be learned.

The therapist must convey all information in terms that the patient and the family can easily understand. Often these explanations must be repeated as many patients are not able to absorb and cope readily with all of this new information.

Typical Questions

From clinical experience, the most commonly asked questions prior to amputation surgery are:

How long will it be before I can walk?
Can I return to work and do the same job?
Will I be able to drive a car?
How much will a prosthesis cost?

All questions should be answered honestly and to the best of the therapist's ability (Friedmann, 1978). The answers will depend on the level of amputation and the patient's age, medical condition, and motivation.

Physical Assessment

A preoperative physical assessment indicates to a large degree the level of activity that can be expected after surgery. The extent of the assessment depends on the patient's preoperative condition. For example, if the patient is experiencing considerable pain, even gross evaluation in terms of muscle strength and range of motion may not be possible. The assessment requires investigation of the medical history and focuses on the patient's physical status (Burgess, 1973; Gerhardt et al., 1982; Mensch et al., 1982).

Respiratory Function

Chest expansion, deep breathing, and coughing ability are evaluated prior to surgery. Auscultation of the lung fields will determine the presence of any abnormal sounds. Existing respiratory problems such as chronic obstructive lung disease or previous respiratory complications following the administration of a general anesthetic are noted. A patient with optimal respiratory function is better able to cope with physical activities following amputation.

Muscle strength and range of motion of all joints are tested because, following amputation, the upper extremities take on the additional role of weight-bearing assistance during transfers and early ambulation. Any existing joint pathology or muscle weakness will decrease the patient's postsurgical mobility.

Upper Extremities

If possible, both extremities are examined. The pathological limb imposes test limitations. The focus is on the condition of the surviving limb.

Lower Extremities

Strength, Coordination, and Joint Range of Motion. Following surgery the remaining leg must assume the dominant role in all transfer and locomotor activities. Therefore, its strength, coordination, and range of motion must be investigated. This can be done even if the patient is unable to get out of bed. The therapist can test the leg with the patient supine. The hip and knee are flexed, the foot is cradled in the therapist's hand, and the patient is instructed to push. The directional resisted push is indicative of the patient's lower extremity coordination and total extension strength and indicates whether the extremity will support the patient when getting up after surgery. The nature and severity of preexisting contractures must also be investigated (see Contractures, p. 141).

Skin Condition and Sensation. The integrity of the skin surface is closely examined, and any existing skin lesions or abrasions are noted bilaterally. The surviving foot is examined, particularly for pressure areas that may have been caused by poorly fitting shoes.
Skin sensation is tested since peripheral sensation is often impaired, particularly in diabetic patients. The patient is advised to avoid bumping or bruising this leg since even superficial lesions can result in major complications. The awareness of the presence of diminished skin sensation will help to assist the patient in protecting and caring for the future stump and skin surface areas of the remaining leg.

Balance is the key to ambulation; if balance is not present, walking is impossible. Balance is tested in the sitting position, giving small amplitude directional stimuli. The therapist observes the patient's reaction to regaining and maintaining balance.

Trunk Balance

The assessment findings provide an indication of the patient's present physical capabilities and the level of postsurgical functional activities that can be expected.

Many elderly patients are debilitated from prolonged sitting or bed rest. This often results in muscle weakness, joint stiffness, and a decrease in general tolerance of activities (Holliday, 1981).

Exercises

Isometric muscle contractions are taught in preparation for future functional activities. Independent bed mobility and activities of daily living (ADL) within the patient's capability encourage the functional use of muscles and joints. Foot and ankle exercises assist in the prevention of deep vein thrombosis in the remaining leg. Deep breathing and coughing instructions are given to prevent postoperative chest complications.

Transfers

If possible, transfers should be practiced prior to surgery so that the patient is familiar with the sequence of transfer motions. This will increase the patient's confidence in the ability to perform transfers following surgery (see Transfer Procedures, p. 79).

Equipment

The preoperative preparation of equipment will facilitate postoperative activities.

Walker

A lightweight walker is adjusted to the patient's height and labelled with the patient's name and room number. Initially the walker is not kept at the bedside since walking with supervision is mandatory following surgery:

- to control balance
- to control weight bearing
- to prevent incorrect proprioceptive feedback to the stump
- to avoid falls

Shoes

A prosthetic foot can be adapted to any shoe that is given to the prosthetist. Therefore, the pair of shoes selected must be absolutely comfortable for the remaining foot. It is recommended that the shoes have a wide toe box to eliminate pressure on the foot and to allow for foot mobility. Flat block heels (not exceeding 2 in.) and nonslip soles are recommended. Heel height changes are not advised following the initial alignment of the gait device because then the prosthetic alignment is altered, causing either a knee flexion moment if the heel is higher or a knee extension moment if the heel is lower (see Incorrect Prosthetic Leg Length, p. 243). The transmission of forces from the ground to the stump is also changed by this height variation, causing incorrect pressures on the stump, pain, and postural compensation during gait activities.

The shoes are labelled with the patient's name, and the shoe for the side to be amputated is given to the prosthetist.

Amputee Visiting

A visit by another amputee prior to surgery is psychologically most beneficial provided the visitor is carefully selected. Choosing a visitor with a suitable personality is more important than matching age and level of amputation. Seeing an amputee who has successfully coped with the situation and sharing feelings with them will ease the patient's dread and will help the patient set more realistic goals. It must, however, be stressed to the patient that each person is an individual and that direct comparisons must never be made.

The physical therapist must provide the patient with strong emotional support by establishing a good rapport during the preoperative visit and by giving consideration to the amputee's psychological as well as physical needs.

In addition to the preoperative visit, Burgess (1973) advocates that the therapist be present during amputation surgery to observe:

- the amount of bleeding
- the condition of the muscle tissues and the skin
- the placement of the suture line
- the mobility of the joint proximal to the amputation level

This additional information will augment the physical findings and the preoperative assessment. These two sources of information will provide a baseline for the development and implementation of the postoperative treatment plan.

Summary

References

Banerjee, S.N. "Current Trends in Amputation and Prosthetics. In S.N. Banerjee, ed. *Rehabilitation Management of Amputees*. Baltimore, Md.: Williams & Wilkins, 1982, 429–447.

Bradway, J.K., Malone, J.M., Racy, J.L., Leal, J.M., and Poole, J. "Psychological Adaptation to Amputation—An Overview." *Orthotics and Prosthetics International, 38*, no. 3 (1984): 46–50.

Burgess, E.M., and Alexander, A.G. "The Expanding Role of the Physical Therapist on the Amputee Rehabilitation Team. *American Physiotherapy Journal, 53*, no. 2 (1973): 141–143.

Burgess, E.M. "General Principles of Amputation Surgery." *Atlas of limb prosthetics*. (American Academy of Orthopedic Surgeons.) St. Louis, Mo.: C.V. Mosby, 1981, 14–18.

Crowther, J.T. "New Perspectives on Nursing Lower Limb Amputees." *Journal of Advanced Nursing, 7* (1982): 453–460.

Fishman, S., Garrett, J.F., and Levine, E.S. "Psychological Practices in the Physically Disabled." *Amputations*. New York: Columbia University Press, 1961, 1–50.

Friedmann, L.W. "Patients Reaction to Amputation." *The Psychological Rehabilitation of the Amputee*. Springfield, Ill.: Chs. C. Thomas, 1978, 24–39.

Gerhardt, J.J., King, P.S., and Zettl, J.H. "The Team—Preoperative Planning. *Amputations, Immediate and Early Prosthetic Management*. Vienna: Hans Huber, 1982, 26–39.

Holliday, P.J. "Non-prosthetic Care." In J.P. Kostuik and R. Gillespie, eds. *Amputation Surgery and Rehabilitation: The Toronto Experience*. New York: Churchill Livingstone, 1981, 226–228.

Mensch, G. and Ellis, P. "Preoperative Procedures." In S.N. Banerjee, ed. *Rehabilitation Management of Amputees*. Baltimore, Md.: Williams & Wilkins, 1982, 166–168.

Mital, M.A. and Pierce, D.S. "Physical Therapy." *Amputees and their Prostheses*. Boston, Ma.: Little, Brown, 1971, 69–71.

McCollough, N.C., Shea, J.D., Warren, W.D., and Sarmiento, A. "Preoperative Period. The Dysvascular Amputee: Surgery and Rehabilitation." *Current Problems in Surgery*, October 1971, pp. 17–19.

Tooms, R.E. "Amputations." In A. Edmonson and A.H. Crenshaw, eds. *Campbell's Operative Orthopedics*, 6th ed. St. Louis, Mo.: C.V. Mosby, 1980, 821–872.

Varghese, G. and Redford, J.B. "Preoperative Assessment and Management of Amputees." In S.N. Banerjee, ed. *Rehabilitation Management of Amputees*. Baltimore, Md.: Williams & Wilkins, 1982, 11–16.

Whylie, B. "The Social and Psychological Problems of the Adult Amputee." In J.P. Kostuik and R. Gillespie, eds. *Amputation Surgery and Rehabilitation: The Toronto Experience*. New York: Churchill Livingstone, 1981, 387–393.

POSTOPERATIVE CARE

Following surgery, the amputee is actively involved in three stages of rehabilitation. These stages include:

- immediate postoperative treatment (lasting up to 14 days)
- preparations for prosthetic fitting (lasting from 2 to 6 weeks)
- prosthetic gait training phase (lasting from 2 to 6 months)

The suggested time frame allotted for treatment progression is realistic provided that the surgical wound heals by primary intention and that no other problems occur. The amount of physical therapy input varies in these phases of recovery and will depend on the amputee's physical ability, age, level of amputation and motivation.

The physical therapist's role in postoperative care is to plan and implement a treatment program based on the following considerations:

- the reasons leading to amputation
- the surgical procedure performed
- the dressing technique utilized
- the stump characteristics (related to the levels of amputation)
- the biomechanical implications of the loss of the whole or a part of the extremity
- the psychological and emotional effects of the amputation on the patient and their families
- the prosthetic requirements necessary to achieve a successful rehabilitation outcome

Physical progress and the development of self confidence during rehabilitation are greatly determined by the degree of empathy, guidance, support, and reassurance given by the physical therapist and other members of the rehabilitation team, combined with the effort, ability, and motivation demonstrated by the amputee.

THE IMMEDIATE POSTOPERATIVE PHASE

The initial treatment begins with chest care and circulatory exercises that start as soon as the amputee regains consciousness following surgery. A more specific physical therapy program dealing with the amputation itself begins the day after the operation.

Chest Care

A general anesthetic depresses the function of the respiratory center in the brain (Wylie, 1978). This may result in the accumulation of lung secretions because of depressed cilia action in the bronchi. This combination of events causes decreased air entry into the lungs and may affect the patient's ability to expel lung secretions. This, consequently, may result in complications, leading to (Bailey, 1981):

- atelectasis, caused by mucus plugs blocking air entry into segments of the lungs
- postoperative pneumonia if segmental atelectasis is not effectively treated

Therefore, it is necessary, as a preventive measure, to teach and encourage deep breathing exercises that will cause effective chest expansion, thus facilitating good air entry into all lung segments. The physical treatment should also encourage coughing in order to expel accumulated lung secretions. During early functional activities, deep breathing also counteracts the possibility of postural hypotension by providing extra oxygen to overcome the feeling of dizziness often associated with a sudden position change from lying to sitting (Mensch et al., 1982).

All future activities of the amputee will require an increase in cardiovascular respiratory efforts. Therefore, maintaining and, if possible, improving the amputee's respiratory status is essential after surgery.

Direct communication with the nursing staff will provide information about the amputee's postoperative condition. In order to get an objective overview prior to the actual physical therapy visit, additional data can be obtained from the patient's chart.

Postoperative Medical Status

Relevant facts to be investigated must include:

Vital signs. Blood pressure, pulse, and respiratory rate will signify if the amputee's condition has stabilized. However, problems with postural hypotension can still be expected when the amputee initially attempts to sit, transfer, stand, or walk with a walker.

Stump bleeding. A normal amount of bleeding may signify that sufficient vascularity is present in the stump and that normal healing is to be expected. Prolonged bleeding requires a delay in physical activities.

Biochemistry results. A temporary metabolic or electrolyte imbalance can occur postsurgically (Steinke et al., 1977; Hamburger, 1979), e.g., if the amputee's diabetes is out of control, a decrease in tolerance for activities will necessitate moderation in treatment progression (Becton-Dickinson Canada, Inc., 1981).

Pyrexia. The presence of a fever may cause symptoms such as general weakness, excessive perspiration and/or dizziness. Prolonged temperature elevation may indicate a possible systemic infection or a toxic stump condition resulting from a more localized type of infection.

Sleep pattern. Adequate sleep during the night provides important rest necessary to cope with physical activities during the day.

Pain. Stump pain may reduce the patient's tolerance for physical activity and will affect the accuracy with which movements are performed (see Clinical Evaluation of Pain, p. 65).

Medications. Narcotics dull pain. They may also adversely affect balance and reduce the ability to comprehend instructions as well as decrease the ability to judge stump sensation accurately. Therefore, activities must be curtailed. However, treatments can progress or resume when nonnarcotic analgesics have been administered. The physical therapist must always use discretion in judging the intensity of physical activity to be carried out at this time.

The goals of early treatment are:

- to heal the suture line
- to prevent complications (static pneumonia, contracture formation, delayed wound healing)
- to maintain and increase muscle strength
- to increase tolerance for activities
- to maintain and improve balance
- to retain and stimulate proprioception whenever possible
- to begin early controlled ambulation

Consequently, individual physical therapy treatment concentrates on

- stump dressing care
- positioning
- exercise program
- transfer procedures
- early ambulation

Stump Dressings

Postoperative stump dressings may be rigid, semirigid, soft, or pneumatic. The type of dressing applied depends on the surgical technique, the level of amputation, healing criteria, and the surgeon's preference when considering the functions and composition of each of these dressing techniques. The various textures of these postoperative dressings provide different stump healing environments (Redhead, 1973; Burgess, 1981). Physical therapists must provide follow-up care regardless of the type of dressing that has been applied. Therefore, it is essential to be familiar with the treatment protocol associated with each technique.

History of the Rigid Dressing

Immediate postsurgical fitting of an amputee with a temporary prosthesis was first practiced by Berlemont more than 25 years ago. It was accomplished with the application of a postoperative plaster of Paris rigid stump dressing and a pylon attachment for early partial weight bearing (Berlemont et al., 1969). Weiss then modified this technique and presented his clinical findings at the XIth International Prosthetic Course in Copenhagen in 1963. The physiological, psychological, and economical benefits were recognized, and an intensive research study was undertaken by the Veterans Administration in the United States. Burgess and his Seattle team investigated 280 lower extremity amputees between 1964 and 1969. This investigation resulted in further improvements and emphasized the importance of the interdependence of refined surgical procedures and early prosthetic fittings. Refined surgical procedures prepare the stump for its functional role, while early prosthetic fitting necessitates a precise casting technique to promote stump healing and to permit early ambulation (Burgess, 1969, 1981, 1982; Tooms, 1980;

Gerhardt et al., 1982.) This approach is now widely accepted and successfully practiced.

However, not all surgeons utilize this technique. Differences in surgical management, adaptations to the rigid cast dressing, and the use or nonuse of the detachable gait unit are some of the variations that the physical therapist will encounter in the clinical setting.

The rigid dressing is applied in the operating room immediately following surgery. The surgical wound is covered with sterile gauze, and a spandex stump sock is placed over the stump. Spray adhesive holds the stump sock in place. Pressure-sensitive areas are relieved by sterilized, precut felt pads. Finally, plaster of Paris is applied.

Rigid Dressing: Fundamental Concepts

As stump characteristics differ, (see Amputation Levels, p. 31) so do the rigid dressings (see Specific Rigid Dressings and their Ambulation Characteristics, p. 86). However, all rigid dressings have certain common principles.

The cast is molded according to socket principles (see General Information about Sockets and their Suspensions, p. 120). It must provide total contact and distal support. It must accommodate tissue sensitivity and conform to the stump contours by fitting snugly without restricting the circulation. Suspension must be used at all times to hold the socket in position (Burgess, 1969, 1981, 1982; Tooms, 1980; Gerhardt et al., 1982).

If applied according to these principles, the postoperative rigid dressing:

- provides a quiet wound healing environment
- prevents stump edema by maintaining even pressure to all soft tissues
- gives protection that is particularly important if stump neuropathy is a problem in diabetic patients (Helm et al., 1984)
- provides wound and distal soft tissue support, thus enhancing stump comfort and minimizing stump pain
- promotes stump circulation and aids in stimulating proprioception
- allows for early ambulation, which is psychologically and physiologically beneficial for the amputee

The disadvantage of the rigid dressing is that quick wound inspection is not possible because it necessitates cast removal. However, Burgess (1981) states that this disadvantage is, actually, an advantage because the wound is not disturbed during primary healing.

Gait-Training Attachment Unit. The postoperative plaster cast can be equipped with a prosthetic gait-training attachment unit to allow early weight bearing. However, the timing of the application of the attachment unit varies and depends on the reason for amputation (see Early Ambulation Activities, p. 84).

The prosthetic gait attachment unit consists of two parts. A base plate or disc is held in place at the distal end of the cast by malleable metal prongs incorporated into the plaster cast. This disc functions as a receptacle for the gait attachment unit, which consists of a pipe section and a SACH foot. For early weight bearing and

(See Fig. 2–1)

Figure 2–1   The prosthetic gait attachment unit.

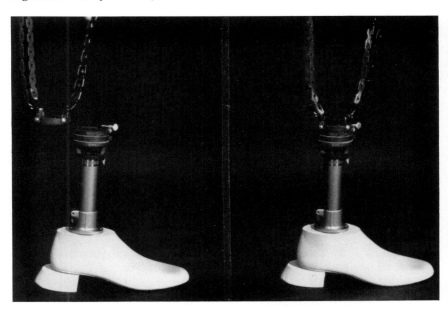

ambulation activities, the two segments are connected. During bed rest the gait unit is disconnected.

Cast Position and Suspension.   Maintaining cast position and controlling cast suspension are absolutely vital at all times since they are the key factors in effective stump tissue support. Cast slippage and/or cast rotation destroy the principles of the rigid dressing and damage the stump. Cast slippage permits distal stump edema to develop owing to a loss of distal tissue support. Cast slippage can also result in proximal circumferential pressure, which restricts circulation and thus delays healing and increases stump pain.

(See Fig. 2–2)

Cast rotation is equally detrimental since it malaligns the cast in relation to its anatomical contours and, therefore, imposes incorrect pressures on the stump tissues. This may lead to the development of pressure areas, skin irritation, and/or breakdown. It also causes discomfort.

Cast suspension is controlled partially by cast contouring and by straps incorporated into the cast during the cast application. These straps are fastened to a waist belt and must provide a straight suspension pull. A diagonal pull malaligns the cast and, in addition to pressure shifting, causes skin discomfort from friction.

Clinical Notes.

1. Both the cast position and suspension must be checked before and after every treatment.

Figure 2–2   The effects of cast slippage.

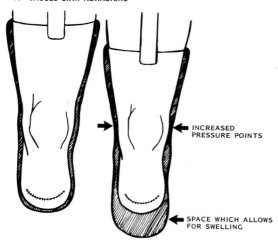

CAST SLIPPAGE
1. CAUSES LOSS OF TOTAL CONTACT
2. ALLOWS EDEMA TO DEVELOP DISTALLY
3. CAUSES SKIN ABRASIONS

INCREASED PRESSURE POINTS

SPACE WHICH ALLOWS FOR SWELLING

2. Should the cast lose its position or come off, it must NEVER be pushed back onto the stump. The skin friction caused by pushing upward may split the suture line. The resultant bulging of the proximal stump tissues is painful, and the cast position cannot be properly realigned. The cast must be removed immediately and a bandage must be applied in its place to prevent the swelling that will occur as soon as the cast is removed (Burgess, 1981; Gerhardt et al., 1982). A new cast application should take place as soon as possible.
3. If a double strap suspension is used, nurses and physiotherapists must ensure that the tension of the anterior and posterior strap is equal. Strap tension must be checked during bed care. For sitting, the posterior strap requires loosening. If the anterior strap is too tight, forced uncontrolled hip flexion results.
4. The suture line of an edematous stump heals slowly and the stump needs longer to mature, resulting in a delay in final prosthetic fitting.

Indications for Cast Changes.   A scheduled cast change for wound inspection usually takes place 10–14 days following surgery. However, it may be required earlier if complications arise. Cast changes are indicated:

- If the amputee complains of severe pain or excessive cast tightness.
- If the cast feels loose and slippage and/or rotation have occurred.
- If excessive piston action is observed (not all amputees are able to judge if the cast is loose).

- If the cast has been damaged.
- If the amputee complains of pressure areas. These may be caused by malalignment, a wrinkle in the stump sock, or a foreign body such as a piece of plaster of Paris between the sock and the cast.
- If the patient is febrile and/or cast odor is apparent. There may be an inflammatory process at the surgical site.

Summary. Exact cast management in this initial phase of amputation care is vital. Nurses and physical therapists alike must provide precise care since a stump that has been carefully surgically prepared can easily be damaged by indifferent or careless postoperative handling.

Semirigid Dressing

The semirigid Unna paste postsurgical dressing technique has been used primarily for transtibial amputations but may be utilized for other amputation levels as well. A gauze bandage, impregnated with Unna paste, is applied postsurgically and hardens to become a semirigid dressing (Ghiulamila, 1972; Kay, 1975). The dressing remains in place for approximately 10 days unless medical complications indicate the need for earlier removal.

The criteria for the use of the semirigid dressing are identical to those for the rigid dressing:

- to promote primary healing
- to provide wound protection and support
- to reduce postsurgical edema
- to permit early ambulation

The main difference between the dressings is in the nature and composition of the materials used to cover the stump. This results in some variations in the dressing and the gait unit (Ghiulamila, 1972).

Unna paste (commercially available as Dome™ paste) is a mixture of zinc oxide, gelatin, glycerine, and water (Hoover, 1975):

- Zinc oxide has a soothing and protective effect on the skin and possibly acts as an astringent.
- Gelatin is a mechanical protective agent, giving the paste a suitable consistency for application.
- Glycerine is a humectant and, as such, keeps substances moist. It also keeps water from evaporating too quickly. This regulates the rate of wound evaporation, preventing the wound from drying out prematurely.
- Water (warm) functions as a dilutant, softening the gelatin and permitting easy application.

Application: Transtibial Amputations. The suture line is protected by a Telfa™ pad. The first Unna bandage is applied in diagonal turns directly to the stump skin up to the midthigh level. More pressure is applied distally. Tension is

Figure 2–3   Unna paste bandage application (semirigid dressing).

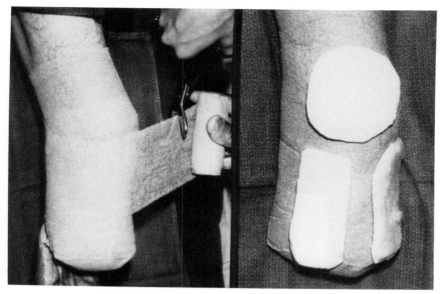

Source: Photograph courtesy of Dr. R.I. Ghiulamila.

reduced proximally. Felt pads are then positioned to protect the pressure-sensitive areas. These pads stay in place because the paste is sticky. A second Unna bandage is wrapped over the first one, again in diagonal turns to midthigh level. A Kling™ bandage covers the entire dressings.   *(See Fig. 2–3)*

Unna paste requires 24 hr to dry, and during this period stump positioning must be carefully monitored. Excessive knee flexion causes posterior bandage creasing and increases the possibility of developing a knee flexion contracture. The dressing is lightweight, and dressing changes for wound inspection are more easily accomplished than those necessitating cast removal (Ghiulamila, 1972; Menzies, 1978).

The ambulation device, constructed separately, is a polypropylene patellar tendon-bearing socket that is permanently connected to a gait attachment unit. For ambulation, the semirigid dressing is inserted into this pylon-type device. The   *(See Fig. 2–4)* socket remains in position on the dressing due to the fit and the adhesive character of the dressing; an auxiliary suspension system is added as well. Following ambulation the entire gait unit is removed. This temporary gait device is ready within 24 hr since it is a simple modular assembly.[1]

Initially, as with the rigid dressing, only minimal weight bearing is indicated to prevent trauma to the wound and to stimulate primary wound healing.

Summary.   The following areas of major difference can be identified in comparing the rigid and semirigid dressings:

Figure 2–4   The polypropylene gait attachment unit used in conjunction with a semirigid dressing.

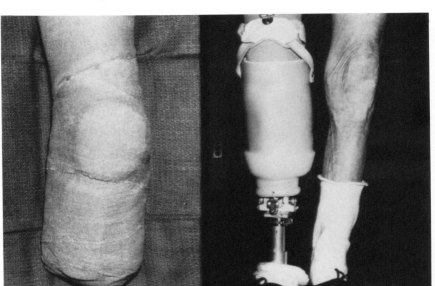

Source: Photograph courtesy of Dr. R.I. Ghiulamila.

- the texture of the materials used to fabricate the dressing
- the contact between the dressing and the stump skin
- the firmness of the dressing
- the method of application of the gait device

Each of these dressings has characteristics that will meet the individual amputee's requirements for stump healing postoperatively. However, the surgeon's preference dictates the technique selected.

Soft Dressings

Before the benefits of the rigid and the semirigid dressings were fully investigated, the stump was protected by a soft dressing using either an elastic bandage or a Kling™ bandage to cover the stump. Although somewhat outdated, the soft dressing techniques are still practiced in some areas today.

The surgical wound is covered by sterile gauze and a soft material, such as fluff gauze, and is then wrapped with a gauze bandage or with an elastic bandage using diagonal turns. The purpose of either bandage is to protect and support the stump and to apply distal pressure to counteract the development of postsurgical edema, thus promoting healing. Through the use of diagonal (never circular) bandage turns, with application of more pressure distally and progressively decreasing tension proximally, restriction of stump circulation is avoided.

Both dressings are lightweight and regularly removed for wound inspection. They are instantly reapplied by nursing staff.

However, this method of controlling primary stump wound healing has several major disadvantages.

1. The healing tissues are disturbed by frequent alteration of the healing environment, i.e., the support pattern alters when the bandage is removed and reapplied for wound inspection or after activities that may cause the bandage to loosen or to slip off.
2. The amount of tension in an elastic bandage cannot be accurately controlled since each person applying the bandage exerts different pressures that cannot be measured. Therefore, the method is unreliable (Redhead, 1973; Isherwood, 1975; Menzies, 1978; Burgess, 1981). Excessive bandage tension restricts capillary circulation, thus interfering with initial wound healing (Redhead, 1979). Insufficient bandage tension allows interstitial fluid to settle distally, producing stump swelling. This problem is intensified if the bandage is too tight proximally. The bandage then creates a "tourniquet" effect, and distal swelling occurs as the bandage "gives" to accommodate the increasing stump volume.
3. Neither bandage types provide the firmness necessary to immobilize the knee in the transtibial stump. Although they allow for active knee mobility, they also foster wound tissue mobility, and this may hinder suture line healing. There is also a greater tendency for joint contracture development (Burgess, 1981).
4. It has also been reported that stump pain is not as well controlled with the application of a soft dressing postsurgically as with the rigid and semirigid dressing techniques (Isherwood, 1975; Kane, 1980; Burgess, 1981). This may be attributed to the decreased amount of support provided by the bandage, the inconsistency of the bandage tension during application, or to a combination of these factors.

For these reasons, many physicians strongly oppose the use of a soft dressing as a primary stump healing environment (Redhead, 1973; Isherwood, 1975).

Clinical Note. It must be stressed at this time that there is a great difference between the use of an elastic bandage immediately postoperatively when it is part of the stump dressing and the utilization of a bandage during the preprosthetic phase. Postsurgically, the tissues are sensitive and wound healing may be precarious, particularly if vascular insufficiency was the reason for the amputation. Undisturbed wound healing is the prime concern, initially. In the later stages of rehabilitation, when the wound has healed, the tissues are much less sensitive, and bandaging is used for stump shrinkage, shaping, and maturation prior to prosthetic fitting (see Stump Bandaging, p. 120). The latter procedure is still commonly practiced in most rehabilitation centers.

Summary. Many practitioners advocate the application of the rigid dressing (Burgess, 1969, 1981, 1982; Tooms, 1980; Gerhardt et al., 1982) or the semirigid dressing (Ghiulamila, 1972; Menzies, 1978). Evidence from clinical studies indicates increased physiological benefits and improved rate of healing with these techniques as opposed to the use of the soft dressing (Mooney et al., 1971; Gerhardt et al., 1982).

Air Splints

Since practitioners constantly search to improve postoperative amputation care, attempts have been made to apply an air splint postsurgically mainly to trans-tibial amputation stumps. These splints have been used previously to successfully immobilize fractures. The procedure was developed to provide stump protection and to permit early ambulation when a prosthetic team was not available to apply and monitor the use of the rigid dressing technique.

(See Fig. 2–5)

The advocates of this technique (Little, 1970; Kerstein, 1974; Sher, 1974) attempted to simplify the rigid cast dressing procedure by inflating a clear plastic, double walled, long leg air splint over the stump immediately following surgery.

Figure 2–5   Air splint.

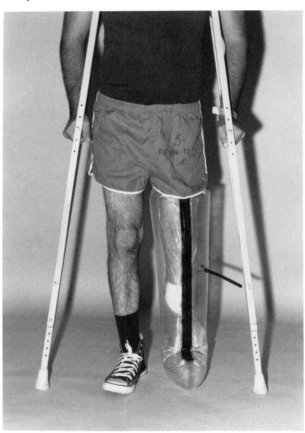

By applying controlled pressure (25 mm Hg), the splint is used for edema control, stump protection (by providing an ''air cushion'' effect), and as a temporary prosthesis to allow for early minimal partial weight bearing.

Following surgery the stump wound is protected with sterilized gauze and lambswool and covered with a stump sock. The sock and the felt relief pads (placed over the sock) are held in place with surgical adhesive spray. The air splint is applied so that it extends over the stump to the midthigh level and is aligned to obtain equal leg length; it is then inflated. The clear double-walled plastic splint provides uniformly controlled pressure to all encased tissues and is held in place by compression. The stump can be observed during both rest and activity, and the splint can be readily removed for stump wound care (Kerstein, 1974).

Disadvantages include air leakage and stump perspiration, since a plastic casing does not allow the stump tissues to breathe. Weight bearing is restricted and depends on the amount of air inflation. Too much weight exerted by the amputee causes the splint to buckle. (The inflated forefoot section bends in the toe-off position, and the shank has a tendency to give prior to midstance). Buckling also increases the danger of falling; therefore, weight-bearing progression is not possible (Little, 1970; Kerstein, 1974). Thus, in our clinical experience the value of the air splint in the immediate postoperative phase of treatment has proven to be questionable.

There are additional problems with the air splint. Knee mobility is restricted by the inflated airsplint, introducing postural deviations during early gait activities (see Balance Control, p. 17). The bulky splint also decreases the amputee's bed mobility and positions the hip joint in slight flexion in the supine position. This is of minimal concern in transtibial amputations but has definite negative implications for contracture development in transfemoral amputations. Sitting in a wheelchair with the inflated airsplint is clumsy and requires a cushion under the sound side to equalize sitting balance.

Controlled Environment Treatment (CET)

(See Fig. 2–6)

A special unit has been developed by the Biomechanical Research and Development Unit (BRADU), Roehampton, England in an attempt to provide a scientifically controlled stump wound-healing environment. The unit influences the stump-healing environment by controlling air pressure, temperature, sterility, and humidity (Kegel, 1976; Burgess, 1978; Troup, 1980; McCollough, 1981; Murdoch, 1983).

A transparent plastic air bag is placed directly over the stump postsurgically. Moderately heated, humidity controlled, filtered air is cycled from the CET via a hose into this air bag.

Alternate air pressure is applied to increase the stump circulation and to promote healing. The intensity of the air pressure can be regulated, and both the high and low pressure periods are timed. The high pressure phase (30–50 mmHg) counteracts the development of edema by encouraging lymphatic and venous return. The low pressure phase (10 mmHg) facilitates cutaneous blood flow to the distal stump. The surgical wound is kept sterile by air filtration, proper tem-

Figure 2–6   Controlled environment treatment (CET).

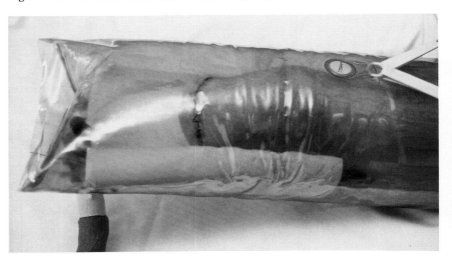

Source: Photograph courtesy of Dr. I. Troup.

perature control (approximately 5–6°C below body temperature), and a decreased humidity level to discourage bacterial growth and keep the wound relatively dry.

The bag has a flutter-type (Hovercraft™) proximal seal that is in contact with the skin at midthigh level. This seal eliminates the escape of air and, simultaneously, prevents proximal constriction (McCollough, 1981).

The plastic air bag permits immediate wound inspection since the stump and suture line are completely visible. Palpation of the stump through the bag is possible during the low pressure phase.

Physical therapy is started the day after surgery. At this time, emphasis is placed on routine chest care, isometric stump exercises, and active exercises for the remaining leg. Exercising is particularly important since the amputee, while connected to the unit, is less mobile. Standing and hopping with gait aids are possible, but the process is awkward. Two people are required: the therapist supervises the patient while another person moves the CET unit (Kegel, 1976). Active knee flexion in the bag is possible on a limited basis during the low pressure phase.

The amputee is usually connected to this unit for a 10-day period postsurgically. After initial wound healing has occurred, a rigid dressing is applied (Burgess, 1978). Weight bearing and bilateral gait activities can then begin.

Successful stump healing has been reported by several authors (Kegel, 1976; Burgess, 1978; Troup, 1980; McCollough, 1981; Murdoch, 1983).

Documented disadvantages of the CET method of postsurgical stump management include:

- the noise level of the CET unit during operation
- the hindrance of early weight-bearing progression
- the restriction of the amputee's mobility while connected to the CET unit.

The CET unit is a valuable adjunct to the techniques available for postoperative stump healing (Troup, 1980). However, the availability and expertise in the use of the CET unit is presently limited since only a few centers have clinically investigated the use of this treatment procedure.

Stump wound healing is the primary objective following amputation surgery. All stump dressing methods protect the surgical wound but provide environments that affect stump healing in different ways. The technique utilized depends on the surgeon's criteria for stump wound healing and also on the immediate availability of a prosthetic team.

Summary

Of all the methods available, the rigid dressing technique seems to be the most beneficial. The success of this technique is based on surgical preparation of the stump for function and the utilization of the three basic orthopedic principles for healing: immobilization, support, and early ambulation during the early postoperative phase (Burgess, 1981).

Regardless of the dressing technique utilized, physical therapists must know the protocol for the follow-up of all the various dressing procedures and must adhere strictly to detail when treating amputation stumps postsurgically.

Pain is a subjective experience that cannot be measured with accuracy (Jeans et al., 1979). It is also difficult to determine the precise nature of pain. However, the different kinds of pain encountered by amputees must be discussed since pain is a guide for treatment planning in clinical practice. It can affect the amputee's performance and influence treatment progression. Various pain experiences are often indicators of corresponding stump conditions. Pain in the remaining leg suggests how much walking the amputee is able to tolerate. The recognition of stump pain helps in determining whether or not an early postoperative cast removal is necessary.

Clinical Evaluation of Pain

For clinical use, the nature of the objective description of pain can be broadly classified into:

- pain of intrinsic origin
- pain caused by extrinsic factors
- phantom limb pain

Intrinsic pain, also referred to as internal pain, tissue pain, or physiological pain, is of an organic origin and is the result of an underlying pathology. It includes:

Pain of Intrinsic Origin

- bone pain
- vascular pain

- nerve pain
- wound pain

Bone Pain.   This pain is recognized as a deep ache and is often compared with a severe toothache. Bone pain may be present if a long weight-bearing bone has been severed because the periosteum that surrounds the bone (except for the articular surfaces) and is pain-sensitive, is responding to bone trauma. However, when a weight-bearing bone remains intact (e.g., knee disarticulation) bone pain is rarely a problem.

If the bone end that has been severed is sensitive to early partial weight-bearing, cast removal prior to the scheduled length of time may not be indicated immediately because the sensitivity of the periosteum will ease in time. The painful sensation will gradually diminish as healing takes place. Weight bearing should be deferred in order to avoid further irritation. However, if the intensity of the bone pain in the early postoperative phase persists and is present during rest, stump examination is indicated.

As ambulation activities progress, bone end sensitivity is more likely to be experienced when soft tissue coverage is minimal. Soft tissue coverage (as in a transtibial stump with a long posterior flap) should provide a weight-bearing "cushion" distally, thus helping to protect the sensitive bone end.

Vascular Pain.   Vascular pain may also be referred to as intermittent claudication or ischemic pain. It is described as a throbbing, pulsating, biting pain and is occasionally combined with a sensation of "icy" coldness. Amputees with a history of circulatory disease express a feeling of the limb being "caught in a vice." This pain results from muscle tissues being deprived of adequate blood supply when arterial spasm occurs or when plaque formation decreases the patency of the artery. Vascular pain can be severe and is felt predominantly in the remaining leg. It can also be present in the stump. If vascular pain occurs in the stump in amputees with advanced peripheral vascular disease, the amputee may be restless and may change the position of the stump frequently. Ambulation activities must be monitored carefully, allowing ample rest periods during treatment sessions (see Stump Symptoms Related to Amputation Associated Diseases, p. 185).

The presence of intermittent claudication is easily recognized by the onset of pain during ambulation and by an easing of the pain at rest. The intensity of pain will force the patient to rest. However, the symptoms will reduce or diminish with rest.

Cast removal in the early postoperative phase is not usually indicated because, if the cast is removed, swelling will occur and vascular pain will increase without cast support of the tissues. As an alternative to cast removal, rather than exercise, one can start with simple functional activities and increase these according to tolerance. Another factor to be considered is the resting position of the stump. This should not produce undue stretch stresses on the stump tissues. An uncomfortable, prolonged stretch (e.g., the hamstring muscles in a transtibial stump) will cause the amputee to tighten muscles in response to the stretch. This constant muscle tension can adversely affect stump vascularity and increase ischemic pain.

If muscle cramping is a postoperative problem, one can evaluate the amputee's tolerance for ambulation by practicing static muscle contractions. Treatment may then progress to active muscle work of the surrounding joints not inhibited by the cast (e.g., in a transtibial amputation the amputee exercises the major muscle groups of the hip). The amputee's ability to cope with this activity will indicate:

- the amount of activity the muscles will tolerate before requiring rest
- the amputee's readiness to progress to gait training and graduated weight bearing at this time

Nerve Pain.   Nerve pain is described as a sharp, shooting, flashing pain. Patients very often compare it with an electric shock. It should not be confused with phantom pain. It may be experienced as a radiating type of pain or it may be localized. Neuralgic pain occurs as a response to mechanisms such as compression of sensory nerves. Cast removal is not indicated.

Radiating, neuralgic pain is sometimes followed by muscle cramping or tetanus since this type of nerve pain causes the muscles to tense (Jeans et al., 1979). In patients with peripheral vascular disease, this muscle tension produces cramping or a tetanic type of contraction, thus superimposing vascular pain on the already present neuralgic pain. Radiating nerve pain may also be more central in origin (e.g., sciatic nerve irritation owing to exacerbation of a preexisting back problem).

Localized nerve pain can be diagnosed by palpation. A small area of acute pain may be triggered by localized pressure if a neuroma is present in that area. A neuroma, which does not develop immediately postsurgically, is recognizable during the active rehabilitation phase. It is a sensory fibrous growth with sensory fibers that develops at the end of the transsected nerve (Mital et al., 1971). If the neuroma is not deeply embedded in soft tissue, it can cause a considerable amount of pain on socket contact (see Stump Socket Interface and Weight-Bearing Problems, p. 180).

Wound Pain.   Surgical wound pain may be perceived as superficial or deep in nature. Superficial pain is not a cause for much concern. However, deep pain must be investigated immediately.

Superficial.   Superficial pain usually covers a localized area, and pain is experienced as a superficial skin burning or can be described as a skin friction or "soreness." Some amputees compare this discomfort with the feeling of "having hair pulled," others describe the sensation as skin "being pinched." Cast removal for this condition is not necessary.

Superficial wound pain may be aggravated when a fluid-soaked gauze dressing adheres to the open area, which then dries and becomes ''crusty.'' Each muscular contraction will then produce a slight pull on the dressing, thus increasing the sensation of superficial wound pain.

Deep (infection).   Deep wound pain, resulting from a serious soft tissue infection, is a constant, excruciating, burning pain that may be accompanied by a foul odor. Wound infection, if untreated, can produce necrosis and generalized toxicity (fever, disorientation). Pain in the stump can become so intense that cast removal is necessary to allow drainage of the wound, particularly if it is caused by local inflammatory edema pressing against the cast wall. The surgeon will decide on the subsequent treatment for infection control (see Delayed Healing, p. 163).

Pain of Extrinsic Origin

Extrinsically caused pain is produced by external influences such as pressure and leverage on the stump tissues. It is a pain resulting from an external mechanism.

Cast Pressure.   Cast pressure, if localized, is usually caused by either a wrinkle or by plaster of Paris crumbs in the stump sock. This irritant causes local pressure and can be compared with walking with a stone in one's shoe. It is an annoying pain sensation that usually results in a number of gait deviations.

Inadequate Socket Fit.   A socket that is too small or too tight produces stump choking and can lead to ischemic pain. A socket that is too large is malaligned either by slippage or by rotation, and causes incorrect pressures on the stump, because the position of the anatomical landmarks and the contours of the socket walls are misplaced (see Cast Positions and Suspension, p. 56).

Pressure areas are often visible on the skin when the cast, or the training unit, is removed. The causes of pain that are extrinsic in origin are more readily observed and can be more easily treated than pain that is caused by an underlying pathology.

Clinical Comments.   Postsurgically, when the stump is still protected by a nonremovable cast, a generalized continuous stump aching, if not diagnosed as ischemic pain, may indicate nonhealing or a breakdown of the suture line. (Delayed healing of the surgical site can occur if the amputation was performed at a marginal level, and/or if basic postoperative care principles were not met, e.g., loss of cast suspension, early uncontrolled weight bearing.) If this pain persists, the cast should be removed and the suture line evaluated. Following stump inspection and subsequent treatment, a nonremovable cast may be reapplied to give the stump an undisturbed wound healing environment. Gait training will be delayed.

Pain can also cause a problem when the amputee attempts to diminish stump pain by assuming the position of most comfort, which, unfortunately, tends to be flexion. If the stump pain persists for a long period and the amputee submits to the more comfortable, flexed position, a contracture can and will develop (see Contractures, p. 141, and Positioning, p. 70).

Prolonged pain will decrease the amputee's ability to cope (Jeans et al., 1979). It will reduce the tolerance level emotionally, as well as physically. It can also disturb the amputee's sleep pattern. If this occurs, the amputee's motivation and endurance for the rehabilitation program will be reduced, thus lengthening the rehabilitation time.

Phantom limb pain, affecting only some amputees, refers to pain in the part of the extremity that has been amputated and should not be confused with pain in the stump. Phantom limb pain can vary in nature and intensity. It is often described as a cramping or burning and is occasionally accompanied by the feeling or sensation that the amputated limb is in an awkward position (Melzack, 1971). Clinically, it has been observed that phantom pain does have a tendency to occur in patients who have experienced either prolonged or severe pain in their extremity prior to amputation surgery (Koerner, 1969; Melzack, 1971; Mital et al., 1971).

Phantom Limb Pain

It should be stressed that phantom limb pain does not always occur, but, if it is present, it is usually experienced by the amputee immediately following amputation surgery. As a rule, phantom limb pain will subside and become more of a phantom limb sensation (Melzack, 1971; Mital et al., 1971). This transition from phantom pain to phantom sensation, which may take place during the first few weeks following surgery, is gradual. Amputees often continue to describe their phantom limb feelings as pain when, in fact, it is no longer pain but a sensation that encourages an awareness of a complete body image. Phantom limb sensation or awareness is most useful in amputee gait training (Koerner, 1969) since it enhances proprioceptive feedback.

In extremely rare cases where severe phantom limb pain is permanently present, prosthetic rehabilitation is questionable since the phantom limb pain will be aggravated by muscular activity, forcing the amputee to avoid any attempt at gait training.

Summary. It must be understood that pain differentiation is seldom easy because the amputee's description of pain is often vague. Pain cannot be measured objectively. The pain threshold in individuals varies greatly, and emotional stresses can also affect the severity of existing pain.

The foregoing classification may be used as a guide in clinical evaluation of the various types of pain and will prove to be useful:

- in assessing the amputee's activity potential
- in judging if cast removal is indicated
- in determining the rate of treatment progression
- in reporting to physicians and to other amputation clinic team members

No attempt has been made here to provide the neurophysiological explanations of pain or an analysis of pain chemistry. However, diagnostic pain evaluation is clinically important since it will affect the treatment course that the physical therapist may take as a result of the amputee's pain.

It must be understood that since leg or stump pain are factors in amputation rehabilitation, normal gait patterns cannot be achieved because the amputee will try to avoid or decrease the severity of the pain and will compensate by demonstrating postural gait deviations.

Positioning

Controlled positioning prevents the development of contractures and reduces postural fatigue by providing adequate resting support. Positioning is ongoing, beginning immediately postsurgically and continuing throughout the entire rehabilitation program. It must be an integral part of the amputee's daily care. It is important to practice prophylactic techniques since contractures have a tendency to develop in the joint most proximal to the level of amputation shortly after surgery (Stryker, 1972). Positioning is primarily the responsibility of the nursing staff. Physical therapists act as consultants when individual requirements vary from conventional positioning procedures. Preparations for controlled positioning include the provision of a firm support base.

The Bed

A firm mattress is essential for all bed positions since a supportive base prevents the hips (by nature the heaviest part of the body) from sagging. A soft mattress will encourage hip flexion while lying supine (Stryker, 1972; Fuerst et al., 1974).

In early postoperative stages the amputee's position in bed must be changed frequently since, initially, the amputee will be unable to comfortably tolerate lying in one position for long periods.

Stump Positioning. Pillow support under the stump during rest periods is contraindicated for two reasons. It encourages joint flexion, which may lead to contracture development, and any prolonged stump elevation may cause a decrease in the peripheral circulation. This may compromise stump healing, particularly in the dysvascular amputee.

Clinical Note. The only indication for stump elevation is excessive postsurgical stump bleeding. This complication has treatment priority over positioning considerations.

The placement of a pillow between the stump and the remaining leg should also be avoided since this encourages stump hip abduction (Troup, 1982), which is of particular disadvantage to the transfemoral amputee.

Prone Lying. The prone position is beneficial and is recommended for up to half an hour several times a day for transfemoral amputees. It is comfortable and should be utilized for scheduled rest periods. The hip joints are, normally, relatively free of stress in this neutral joint midrange position.

In correct prone lying the head should face away from the amputated side, thus providing a gentle continuous stretch on the stump hip flexors. The head

Figure 2–7   The prone lying position: top, correct; bottom, incorrect.

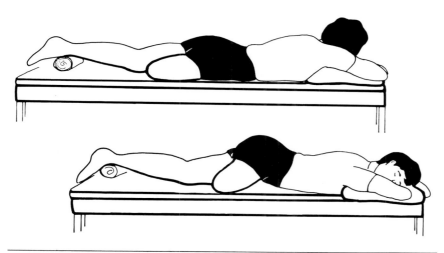

position stabilizes the hip stretch on the amputated side and eliminates, to some extent, the dual possibility of compensatory trunk side flexion and hip flexion. Trunk side flexion easily occurs if the head is facing toward the amputated side, allowing the transfemoral amputee to flex the affected hip, thereby defeating the purpose of prone lying.

(See Fig. 2–7)

A small pillow placed under the ankle of the remaining leg prevents the foot and toes from rubbing on the bed clothes.

Adaptations.   The physical therapist may be required to assist the nurses in adapting the prone-lying position to accommodate the amputee's individual needs.

Obese amputees require pediatric pillows placed under the shoulders to remove some of the pressure from the chest wall during prone lying. The same is true for female amputees with heavy breasts.

If respiratory or cardiac problems prevent the amputee from lying completely flat when prone, the entire head of the bed can be elevated on blocks, or the bed mechanism for the reverse shock position can be used. In this way, the bed is on an incline with the amputee's upper body elevated while the correct prone position is still maintained (Mensch et al., 1982).

Occasionally an amputee may have a medical or orthopedic condition that precludes prone lying. For example, patients who have spondylolisthesis cannot lie prone because the position causes pain and the irreversible joint condition will be further aggravated.

Clinical Note.   Transtibial amputees are not usually required to practice prone lying routinely since a knee flexion contracture, which is usually the presenting problem, is not counteracted by prone lying. If no contracture is present at the knee but there is tightness at the hip, prone lying can be beneficial to transtibial amputees. If there are contractures at both the hip and the knee, prone lying can be utilized to treat the hip contracture independently of the knee contracture.

Wheelchair Sitting Boards

As in lying, provision must also be made for a firm base of support when the amputee is sitting. The hammock effect of the standard wheelchair seat does not provide sufficient pelvic support. It encourages a pelvic drop in the transfemoral amputee because the amputee sits favoring the amputated side while at the same time adducting and internally rotating the stump. This sitting posture not only causes undue strain and muscle fatigue but also introduces spinal scoliotic com-

(See Fig. 2–8)

pensation as the amputee attempts to maintain an erect posture.

The placement of a wooden board in the wheelchair seat gives a firm sitting base while supporting the trunk and the stump and making sitting less tiring. It helps to prevent postural adaptations that, if maintained, could lead to gait deviations and/or contracture development.

Transfemoral amputees use a board that accommodates the wheelchair seat dimensions, whereas transtibial amputees use a board with either a right or left extension supporting the stump during sitting. This extension counteracts the development of a knee flexion contracture and also prevents dependent edema in the stump. Before getting out of the wheelchair, the amputee releases the spring-

Figure 2–8 Wheelchair sitting posture without (left) and with (right) support.

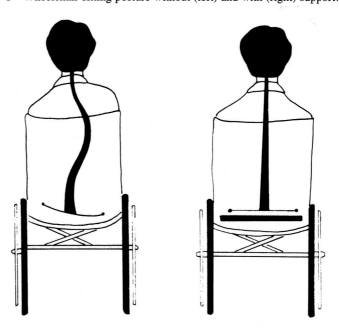

Figure 2–9   Transtibial sitting board with spring leaf extension mechanism.

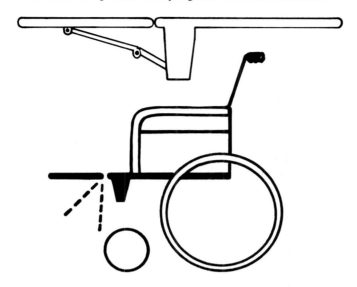

loaded dropleaf mechanism to lower the extension, thus providing an obstacle-free path for transfer and ambulation activities.

(See Fig. 2–9)

Another style of wheelchair sitting board is also available. The seat section is made up of two matching boards. Between these boards are two extensions that can be pulled out, like drawers, and pushed in when not in use. The length of the extension is limited by the anterior–posterior seat dimension. The advantage of this sitting board is that the same board can be used for most levels of amputation and for unilateral as well as bilateral amputees.

(See Fig. 2–10)

Effective positioning must be planned and scheduled (Fuerst et al., 1974). The recent amputee must be instructed as to why this postural control is necessary, and all team members must reinforce the importance of this routine.

Summary

In cases of delayed stump healing, positioning becomes even more important because these amputees are usually elderly and have additional medical and/or preexisting contracture problems. They are generally less active and spend longer periods in bed or in the wheelchair. The provision of a firm support base is vital for these patients.

Close liaison with the nursing staff is of utmost importance:

- to plan a consistent positioning schedule (e.g., times for prone lying) that can be integrated into the total treatment program
- to ensure the implementation of correct positioning during rest and activity periods
- to maintain ongoing patient supervision

Figure 2–10   Transtibial sitting board with pull out extension mechanism.

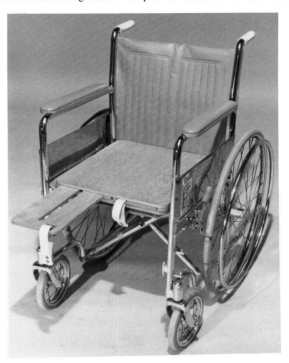

Unfortunately, correct positioning, which also provides comfort to the amputee, is often not consistently enforced (Getz et al., 1982). That "an ounce of prevention is worth a pound of cure" is clearly illustrated when clinicians must treat stump complications, some of which could have been avoided by immediately implementing these prophylactic measures (Mital et al., 1971).

Exercises   Muscle work increases circulation, improves muscle tone and strength, maintains joint range of motion, controls movement through coordination, and aids in maintaining balance skills. Muscles have the ability to work both isometrically (statically) and isotonically (kinetically). They can hold a position (isometric), lengthen during eccentric work, and shorten during concentric work (isotonic). Voluntary and automatic muscle work produce body movement (Gardiner, 1981).

The muscle work involved in gait is, for the most part, automatic. For example, one does not need to think about picking up one leg, swinging it forward, and placing it back on the ground. Following amputation surgery, this automatic pattern is disrupted. The amputee, trying to adjust posturally to the biomechanical change, initially moves willfully by thinking and consciously sensing body movement (see Balance Control, p. 17). An additional problem is weakening of the severed muscles.

The muscles required for ambulation must, therefore, be consciously exercised to regain their maximal level of strength. The physical therapist has the greatest influence over motion control during this learning phase. Precise input and correction of movements during this interim period, before gait activities are started, will help to reduce undesired compensatory movements before the automatic locomotor pattern reestablishes itself.

Muscle reeducation must be implemented as soon as possible to decrease the amount of muscle atrophy and to stimulate optimum functional output in the muscles affected by amputation. Exercise programs start with isometric muscle work and progress to isotonic muscle work, both eccentric and concentric. This order of progression will facilitate coordinated active movement.

Most muscles are actively involved in ambulation. However, selected muscle groups need special attention in preparing the amputee for future gait activities. These are:

- the trunk extensor muscles
- the abdominal muscles
- the hip and knee extensor muscles
- the hip and knee flexor muscles

The preparation of all extensor muscle groups is of prime importance in the reeducation of gait since they predominate in providing postural control and stabilization for the gait support phase.

The flexor muscle group, mainly responsible for initiating swing, also requires exercise practice, although not as extensively, however, as the extensor muscle group (Mensch, 1983) (see Stump Motions—Their Relationship to Gait Functions and Resultant Treatment Considerations, p. 191).

It is also important to note that, although amputation surgery results in a functional loss, the awareness of feeling complete remains intact. This phantom sensation is of great importance when preparing the amputee for locomotion (Koerner, 1969). The therapist incorporates this phenomenon into an exercise and gait training program by encouraging the amputee to perform bilateral movements.

Exercises begin with isometric muscle contractions the day after surgery. Ultimately, amputees will attempt to perform stump movements through what they sense and feel. Therefore, the physical therapist must provide sensory input to the stump by hand contact to focus on the isolated muscle group contractions. Ample time must be spent in reeducating and training the affected muscles in preparation for gait. The amputee is also taught to be responsible for repeating the exercise program every hour to stimulate active muscle work throughout the day.

Isometric Exercises

Quadriceps Contractions.   If the amputee has difficulty contracting and relaxing this muscle group, the following technique may help to elicit quadriceps muscle activity. The amputee is instructed to dorsiflex the ankle while simultaneously extending the knee of the remaining leg, since this movement enhances the quadriceps response. This is done to ensure that the movement is fully understood. The same movements, are then practiced simultaneously, with the amputated side. Bilateral contractions help the amputee to feel how the amputated side should be working.

A hand placed on the muscle, or above the cast, enables the therapist to feel the muscle contractions and at the same time provide sensory input to the stump. If the correct muscle action can be performed, progression is made to alternating contractions between the amputated and sound sides until the amputee can contract the quadriceps muscle groups on command.

Clinical Note. Following a Gritti–Stokes amputation (seldom seen clinically), quadriceps exercises should not be practiced. In this procedure, the patella is surgically positioned under the severed femur to reduce stump end sensitivity and also to provide stump end bearing. As bone has to heal to bone, quadriceps contractions the day after surgery would have a tendency to dislodge the patella from this position.

Gluteal Muscle Contractions. These muscles are of particular importance to knee disarticulation and transfemoral amputees. Practice begins by squeezing the buttocks together. The amputee can provide sensory input by placing the hands over the buttock area while attempting these contractions. The maximum contraction raises the pelvis slightly when the amputee is in a supine position.

Total Body Extension. Total body and trunk extension is practiced in the supine position. The amputee attempts to press the head and all extremities into the mattress. If this is forcefully done in combination with gluteal contractions, slight arching of the back occurs. Maintaining this position stimulates the correct trunk posture needed to control the shifting of the center of gravity during gait.

Clinical Note. Total body extension is often incorrectly performed since the amputee pushes the pelvis rather than the stump and the remaining leg into the bed.

Hip Abduction and Adduction. The physical therapist encourages isometric contractions of these muscle groups by giving sufficient resistance to the lateral and medial aspects of the thighs. Abduction and adduction against the therapist's resistance results in isometric work of these groups.

(See Fig. 2–11)   Once the contractions are correctly performed, the therapist's hand can be replaced by a towel. In this way, the amputee is able to work independently. Abduction is accomplished by wrapping a towel around both thighs, holding the ends of the towel firmly together to provide resistance. The patient must then attempt to practice an exact abduction movement without externally rotating the stump at the same time. Adduction is accomplished by placing a towel between the stump and remaining leg and trying to squeeze the towel. Again, the amputee must

Figure 2–11 Autoresisted hip abduction.

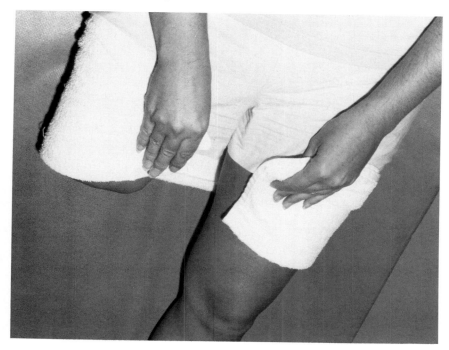

try to do a straight adduction movement so as not to introduce hip internal rotation by trying to squeeze the towel too tightly.

Abdominal Contractions.   The abdominal muscle groups are notoriously weak in the majority of amputees. Abdominal muscle strengthening requires attention, and contractions are practiced with the amputee in a supine position. The amputee bends the sound knee, resting the foot on the bed, and raises the head and shoulders. The stump remains on the bed. Progression of this exercise can be achieved by holding both hands behind the head and lifting the head and shoulders.

Young amputees with good abdominal strength may do half sit ups. This is not indicated for elderly amputees because their abdominal muscle weakness will cause undue strain on the back if this is attempted.

Summary.   Once isometric contractions for all major muscle groups are accurately performed, the patient progresses by holding the maximum contraction for 10 sec, followed by complete relaxation. The nurses reinforce the importance of exercising and make certain that the amputee carries out the exercise program at regular intervals. Isometric contractions maintain muscle tone and prepare the muscles for their functions.

Exercises for the
Remaining Leg

Active and resisted exercises for all muscles of the remaining leg are indicated immediately. They are necessary to prevent deep vein thrombosis and to prepare this leg for its dominant role. Standing on one leg posturally shifts the center of gravity over the supporting leg, requiring increased muscle work to control body balance and weight-bearing stability. Foot and ankle exercises as well as hip and knee exercises are, therefore, stressed.

The foot muscles must have strong inversion and eversion strength to accommodate the horizontal balance shifting and strong dorsiflexion and plantar flexion control to accommodate sagittal balance motions. The remaining foot provides a much narrower support base and must work harder to maintain balance. Simultaneously, the muscles controlling the knee must have enough strength and coordination to prevent the joint from buckling on weight bearing, while the hip abductor and extensor muscles must function with the weight shifted over the support side. Should the abductor muscles be weak, resulting in a positive Trendelenburg sign, the amount of work by the foot and ankle must further increase to maintain body balance.

The physical therapist can experience this increased work by standing on one leg and flexing the hip and knee of the other leg as much as possible. Initially, standing balance is easily controlled. However, when holding this position for a prolonged time, one suddenly realizes that additional muscular control of the foot is necessary to maintain balance.

The importance of maximal functioning of the remaining leg is often underestimated in this early stage of rehabilitation of the amputee.

Progression into
Motion

Isometric exercises progress to isotonic muscle action for both the stump and the remaining limb. Initially, stump proprioception is disturbed because the foot (a sensory organ) is gone and, therefore, the stump position sense is affected (Burgess, 1982). The weight of the amputated segment is missing, thus interfering with the performance of the stump motion. For example, if a large parcel is extremely light and one picks it up without knowing this, the muscle power exerted may be excessive and the motion, having little weight resistance, may be too fast.

Stump weakness resulting from surgical muscle severance makes control of the stump movement difficult. The physical therapist must, therefore, provide manual input to help the amputee control this movement. The input varies according to need and can be regulated to resist, assist, or provide a mere touch to direct the stump range of motion, while at the same time controlling the intensity and the speed of the movement. This allows the amputee to perceive through touch what the stump is able to do.

Active exercises vary and include muscle training in many different positions, e.g., side lying on the unaffected side allows the amputee to take the hip of the stump side past its neutral position into hip extension. Arm exercises condition the prime muscle groups in the upper extremities, the triceps, and wrist extensor muscles, providing and augmenting weight-bearing stability during bed mobility and early walking. Transfers and ambulation with gait aids provide the most functional muscle work.

The intensity of muscle conditioning and the level of activities are geared to the amputee's physical capabilities.

Muscles must be worked to maintain their efficiency for functional activities. A controlled exercise program is required for muscle reeducation and adaptation to the change in biomechanical function caused by amputation. Muscle strengthening is a vital prerequisite for ambulation activities.

Summary

The ability to safely transfer encourages independence in recent amputees. Transfer procedures (to the chair, the toilet, and, later, the car) must be taught and repeatedly practiced. They eventually progress from assisted and supervised to independent. Transfers require balance, coordination, and weight-bearing stability on the stance leg and through the upper extremities. Transfer procedures must be clearly explained and demonstrated before the actual transfer takes place. By doing so, the amputee is aware of the sequence of events and can more confidently attempt the transfer.

Transfer Procedures

Transfers from Bed to Chair.   The height of the bed should be such that the patient, in a bedside sitting position, can comfortably place the remaining foot on the floor.

1. The wheelchair is positioned next to the bed (on the nonamputated side), with the brakes secured and foot pedals up.
2. The amputee puts the shoe on the remaining foot while still lying on the bed. This protects the foot and is safer than having the amputee bend dangerously forward to put on the shoe in the bedside sitting position. Help is provided by the therapist if indicated.
3. The amputee rolls toward the remaining leg, pushing first the elbow and then the hand on the bed until the sitting position has been reached. If the amputee is unable to get into the sitting position independently, the physical therapist or the nurse can stabilize either the stump, or the remaining leg providing counter pressure with one hand while the amputee pulls on the other hand to achieve the sitting position. *(See Fig. 2–12)*
4. The remaining leg swings over the side of the bed for floor contact.
5. The position change from lying to sitting sometimes requires a pause for deep breathing, to overcome possible postural hypotension.
6. With both hands secured, one on the wheelchair armrest and one on the bed, the amputee leans forward to bring the trunk weight over the remaining leg. The amputee then pushes with the arms and the leg to reach a partial standing position, then pivots into position for sitting. Simultaneously, the therapist, by standing at an angle to the amputee, controls the transfer, guiding the chest or pelvis (through hand contact) and giving counterpressure through knee contact to prevent the knee from buckling and the foot from sliding forward (through foot contact). *(See Fig. 2–13)*

Figure 2–12   Assisting the amputee into the sitting position.

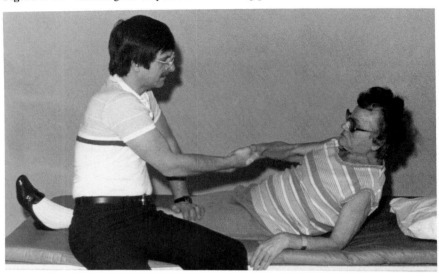

Figure 2–13   Transfer, from sitting to standing, showing knee stabilization by the therapist.

7. The amputee then places both hands on the wheelchair armrests and sits down slowly.

This transfer technique is practical for most amputation levels. One exception is the transtibial amputee, who has a nonremovable dressing and has progressed to ambulating with a gait attachment unit.

Transfers with Gait-training Unit in Place. When transferring the recent transtibial amputee from bed to chair, the base unit is secured to the cast prior to the transfer. The amputee still has bed support and can relax the stump so that the connection can be secured with ease. This is done because the rigid dressing extends to midthigh level, holding the knee in extension, and any active stump elevation would cause lever pressure over the anterior distal stump end.   *(See Fig. 2–14a)*

During the transfer, the therapist must hold the weight of the temporary prosthetic device and guide the unit over the side of the bed to the floor as the amputee moves from lying to sitting. In this way, lever pressure is avoided and stump comfort is ensured.   *(See Fig. 2–14b)*

Clinical Notes.

1. Amputees with higher levels of amputation who have been fitted with a rigid dressing always transfer without the gait unit in place, as described

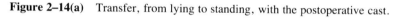

Figure 2–14(a)   Transfer, from lying to standing, with the postoperative cast.

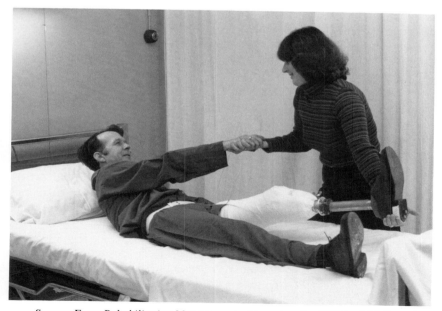

Source: From *Rehabilitation Management of Amputees* (p. 170) by S.N. Banerjee, 1982, Baltimore, Md.: The William & Wilkins Company. Copyright 1982 by The William & Wilkins Company. Reprinted by permission.

Figure 2–14(b)   Transfer, from lying to standing, with the postoperative cast.

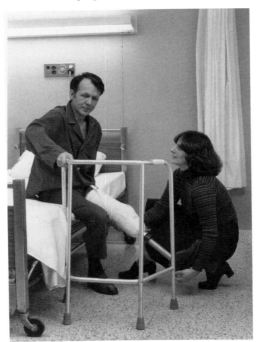

Source: From *Rehabilitation Management of Amputees* (p. 171) by S.N. Banerjee, 1982, Baltimore, Md.: The William & Wilkins Company. Copyright 1982 by The William & Wilkins Company. Reprinted by permission.

---

in the transfer sequence. It is easier and safer for these amputees to have the base section of the gait unit attached when they are securely seated.

2. Following ambulation, the gait attachment unit must be removed during bed rest and sitting periods. The weight and the length of the device hinders bed mobility and interferes with comfortable sitting. Also, if the amputee lifts the stump and its attachment, lever pressure is felt over the distal stump aspect and near the surgical wound. Hip external rotation with the temporary device connected results in stump skin friction by torque action because the weight of the unit accentuates the rotational movement.

Transfers with an Overhead Assist Device.   A trapeze or T-bar is not routinely installed since its use stimulates biceps muscle work rather than the more important triceps and wrist extensor muscle groups, whose functions are required for ambulation with gait aids.

However, in certain circumstances the use of one of these devices is indicated:

- To assist in transfers and independent bed mobility.
- To protect delicate sacral skin tissues from bed clothes friction when changing positions.
- To help in special cases with medical or orthopedic problems (obesity, weakness, fractures).
- To assist the bilateral amputee in attaining the sitting position since bilateral lower extremity weight loss drastically affects the body balance. This loss is most apparent when the amputee attempts to move from the supine to the sitting position.

The amputee using an overhead device is encouraged to use the "push–pull" method: one hand holds onto the overhead device while the other hand pushes on the bed. The pushing and pulling movements are alternated between both arms. *(See Fig. 2–15)*

Figure 2–15 Using the overhead bar.

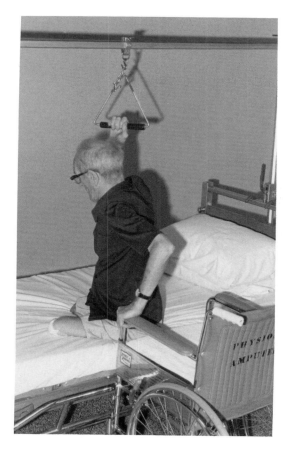

Summary

The outlined transfer techniques are guidelines. ADL transfers such as getting into a car, onto the toilet, or into the bath tub, for unilateral as well as bilateral amputees, require procedural changes and are taught at later stages of rehabilitation by the occupational therapist.

Clinicians will also notice that with increased independence some amputees develop their own methods of transferring. This is perfectly acceptable provided that the procedure is safe.

Early Ambulation Activities

Prolonged bed rest affects many of the body's physiological processes (Stryker, 1972; Caird et al., 1983) and increases the potential for complications. It may also have a detrimental psychological effect on many patients. Therefore, early mobilization and ambulation after surgery is very important since it will expedite the amputee's recovery and thus shorten the rehabilitation period.

Once the amputee has been established on a program of muscle-strengthening exercises and the remaining limb and upper extremities are strong enough to bear the body's weight, ambulation activities begin.

Weight-bearing Tolerance

Prior to the weight transmission through the stump, the therapist must evaluate the amputee's weight-bearing tolerance. This may be tested by giving gentle, upward manual pressure, which may be intermittent or constant, over the distal end of the cast. The amputee's comfort should be used as a partial guideline as to the amount of pressure applied. Most amputees express that the pressure "feels good." This is an indication that axial weight loading can be started.

The amputee can continue to practice increasing the weight-bearing tolerance independently, several times throughout the day, by carefully using a towel, in a sling-like fashion, either over the stump end or over the cast end.

(See Fig. 2–16)

Figure 2–16   Initial weight-bearing practice.

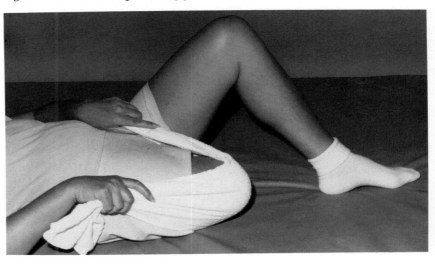

This technique also:

- aids in stump desensitization
- stimulates the stump weight-bearing sensation or proprioception
- reduces the stump throbbing sometimes experienced during the post-surgical stage or when the stump is held in the dependent position

Partial weight bearing through a rigid or semirigid dressing may begin shortly after surgery. The primary consideration in the timing of the application of the gait attachment unit is the ability of the stump to tolerate weight bearing without compromising wound healing.

Timing of Postoperative Weight Bearing

Immediate postoperative prosthetic fitting provides the means for gentle weight bearing 24–48 hr following the operation. Immediate application of the temporary gait attachment unit is indicated for young adults amputated because of cancer or traumatic injuries where stump healing should not be a problem. Therefore, gentle weight bearing should begin one or two days postsurgery. This weight-bearing stimulus will increase the circulation, promote stump healing through muscle activity, and encourage proprioceptive feedback from the floor to the stump.

Weight-bearing activities in these early postoperative stages are practiced by standing with the support of a walker, exerting only touch weight bearing through the amputated side. This is attempted for approximately 5 min twice daily. Any weight-bearing increase is not recommended until the first cast change indicates primary wound healing.

Immediate application of the gait attachment unit is also psychologically beneficial since the least amount of time elapses before the prosthetic device is integrated into the amputee's body image (Friedmann, 1978).

Early postoperative prosthetic fitting means that touch weight bearing through the gait attachment unit may be attempted 2–3 weeks postoperatively. This later progression to weight bearing is indicated if there are potential problems with stump healing (e.g., vascular deficiencies, arteriosclerosis, diabetes). These amputees will receive a gait attachment unit following the first cast change (10–14 days postoperatively) only if initial wound healing has progressed satisfactorily.

Weight-bearing activities are then practiced with equal caution, beginning with touch weight bearing through the amputated side. Weight-bearing progression, particularly for these amputees, is very individualistic, being closely linked to stump healing and to the tolerance of the remaining leg.

In preparation for ambulation, the physical therapist must assess

Preambulation Check-out

- the socket position
- the suspension system
- the alignment of the temporary prosthetic device

Any necessary adjustments are carried out by the prosthetist or by an experienced physical therapist, NEVER by a person who is unfamiliar with the principles of prosthetic alignment. This evaluation includes the observation and correction of the prosthetic components in relation to their position and to the stump functions.

The Base Unit.   Regardless of the type of receptacle used to attach the base unit to the cast, the connection must always be secure in order to provide a stable union between the socket and the base unit and to prevent the base unit from falling off. If the wing nut connection is not tight, axial rotational instability occurs, while an incomplete wedge connection results in an anteroposterior sliding motion.

The Suspension.   Adequate suspension contributes to an accurate alignment of the socket on the stump (see Stump Piston Action, p. 245). The suspension must always be snug:

- to provide an intimate stump-socket interface
- to minimize tissue piston action during gait
- to minimize stump-socket piston action during gait

Suspension control also contributes to making the prosthesis ''feel'' lighter to the amputee, thus improving stump lever control during gait.

(See Fig. 2–17)

The Prosthetic Leg Length.   Correct leg length is estimated by placing the hands over the amputee's iliac crests. The level of the hands will provide a rough guideline to the equality of leg length. Unequal leg length contributes to the development of several incorrect gait and postural habits (see Incorrect Prosthetic Leg Length, p. 243).

The Static Alignment.   To evaluate the static alignment of the temporary gait device, the amputee should stand in a walker with the trunk in an upright position, the feet flat and parallel to each other. Body weight is supported by the remaining leg and by the arms. When this position is viewed from the side, the weight-bearing line should fall through the hips, in front of the knee, in front of the ankle, and through the prosthetic forefoot. In evaluating alignment, the physical therapist must also check the position of the prosthetic foot in relation to the remaining foot. An excessive toe-in or toe-out position of the prosthetic foot must be corrected using the position of the remaining foot as a guide (see Prosthetic Alignment, p. 232).

Any problems identified during the preambulation check-out must be corrected prior to initial ambulation activities. The correction of these problems will minimize the potential for stump trauma and postural gait deviations.

Specific Rigid Dressings and their Ambulation Characteristics

Basic rigid dressing cast concepts apply to all stump levels and shapes. Each amputation level can be treated with a rigid dressing and can be equipped with a gait attachment unit to permit early weight bearing and ambulation. However, in order to function effectively, each level has distinct cast characteristics.

Figure 2–17 Checking prosthetic leg length.

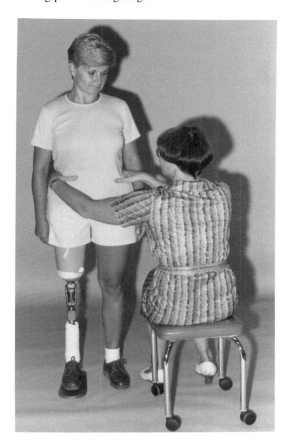

Ankle Disarticulation (Syme's Amputation). This rigid dressing extends to just below the knee, permitting free knee range of motion. With this method of application, the cast holds the distal heel pad in position. Relief is provided to the tibial crest by felt pads placed on either side, and counterpressure is accomplished by compression of the gastrocnemius muscle bulk. Suspension is achieved by contouring the cast above the malleoli. This contouring is generally a sufficient suspension for the cast since the distal stump is bulbous by nature. However, when the malleoli have been surgically trimmed for cosmetic reasons, or when contouring does not provide adequate suspension (as in cases of fleshy stumps), additional suspension is necessary. A fork strap must be used as auxiliary suspension and is *(See Fig. 2–18)* incorporated anteriorly and proximally into the cast. This strap is then connected to a waist belt.

Figure 2–18 Ankle disarticulation: rigid dressing with fork strap suspension.

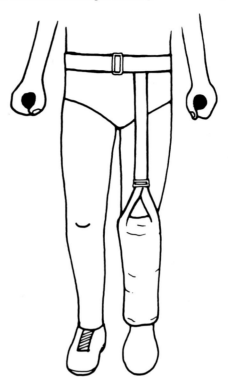

Weight bearing is accomplished by applying a rocker or a SACH foot to the cast. A rocker, equalizing leg length, does not provide forefoot lever function. The amputee responds with increased knee flexion at the beginning of the swing phase because toe-off action is missing. If a SACH foot is utilized, it must be aligned in slight dorsiflexion to facilitate a smooth foot-rolling motion.

Transtibial Amputations.   This cast extends to above midthigh level and is the only postoperative rigid dressing that immobilizes the joint proximal to the level of amputation, e.g., the knee. This ensures knee immobilization to provide undisturbed distal stump tissue support. If the cast was shorter, minimal knee mobility would be possible, and with attempted knee flexion, the posterior cast rim would press into the soft thigh tissues. Counterpressure would be felt over the knee as well as at the posterior distal stump end.

The cast is set in slight knee flexion (approximately 5°–8°) to avoid an excessive hamstring stretch, thus minimizing discomfort and allowing the amputee to completely relax the stump during rest periods (Gerhardt et al., 1982).

This slightly flexed position also places the knee in a more natural joint position for midstance during early ambulation activities.

A window is cut out over the patella to reduce pressure over this area and provide comfort. This window permits the therapist to visually and manually check quadriceps contractions during exercise and cast alignment. *(See Fig. 2–19)*

The cast is molded according to stump sensitivity (see Amputation Levels— Transtibial Amputations, p. 37) and is gently contoured above the femoral condyles. This contributes to cast suspension. An anteriorly placed suspension strap attached to a waist belt assists in holding the rigid dressing in place.

The gait attachment unit (see Gait Training Attachment Unit, p. 55) must be aligned slightly shorter than the remaining leg by approximately 5 mm. This reduces stump pressure during prosthetic heel-off. For the same reason, during gait training the amputee must only take small steps. Long steps require increased joint angulation and, since the knee is immobilized, postural compensations (e.g., hip hiking, abduction, trunk bending, etc.) have to make up for the lack of knee

---

Figure 2–19 Cast window over patella.

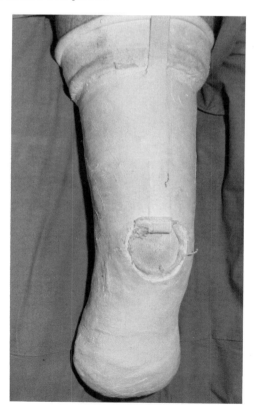

motion. Initial weight shifting in the correct postural position is easily accomplished.

Knee Disarticulation and Transfemoral Amputations.   These two amputation levels have similar postsurgical casting characteristics. The rigid dressing covers the entire stump. The proximal cast rim is molded with a casting device into a quadrilateral shape. The shape provides stump tissue comfort (see Transfemoral Prosthesis, p. 226) and reduces the possibility of cast rotation. It also accustoms the amputee's stump to its future socket shape.

In knee disarticulations, cast suspension is assisted by contouring the plaster of Paris above the femoral condyles. An additional strap suspension will control cast rotation as well as reduce skin friction and will prevent cast slippage, which may occur in fleshy stumps where the femoral condyles are not prominent enough to ensure adequate suspension by cast contouring alone.

In transfemoral amputations, the stump shape is conical and the cast rims extend anteriorly and laterally, similar to a quadrilateral socket (see Transfemoral Prosthesis, p. 226), while the posterior rim flares out to provide a shelf for the future weight-bearing surface, e.g., the ischial tuberosity. The adductor longus tendon is relieved. The duplication of the definitive socket shape is attempted by casting to provide a functional stump environment. Cast suspension must be maintained with three straps (anteriorly, laterally, and posteriorly).

Clinical Note.   Rigid dressings for these amputation levels are not routinely used in our clinical setting since transfemoral cast suspension is difficult for the nursing staff to control. It requires excellent team care since cast slippage and rotation occur relatively easily with the activities of daily living. For example, when the amputee raises the hips and abducts the stump for placement of the bedpan, the medial proximal stump tissues tend to ease out of the socket and cannot, or should not, be pushed back into the socket. However, other centers (the Seattle team) have successfully used the rigid dressing for this amputation level (Burgess et al., 1969).

A hip spica following transfemoral amputations, although providing a controlled quiet wound healing environment, is uncomfortable for the amputee. It causes difficulty in sitting and eliminates hip movements and is, therefore, not suitable for ambulation activities.

The gait attachment unit has an additional component, a knee joint. This knee unit should have a manual locking device for safety during initial standing and weight-bearing practice. As soon as possible, the knee unit should be used functionally to provide correct prosthetic feedback to the stump (see Basic Balance Control, p. 17).

(See Fig. 2–20)   In knee disarticulation amputations, the horizontal knee axis of the prosthetic device is located below the natural knee axis. This requires that the amputee become used to a gait sensation not previously experienced (see Amputation Levels: Knee Disarticulations, p. 39), whereas in transfemoral amputations the

Figure 2–20   The location of the horizontal knee axis in a knee disarticulation prosthetic device.

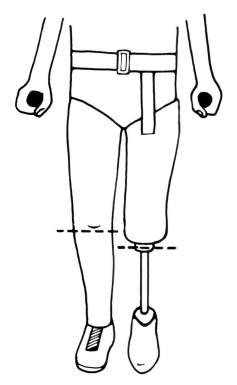

---

prosthetic knee axis is aligned to equalize the knee flexion and extension level during gait to that of the remaining leg.

Clinical Note.   As soon as standing balance and weight shifting has been accomplished, the prosthetic knee is activated to practice initiating hip and knee flexion in preparation for ambulation. It is advisable to begin this exercise in a step position by placing the temporary prosthetic device slightly behind the remaining leg. The amputee must learn to release the prosthetic knee and return it to the stable extension position (see Basic Balance Exercises, p. 254). This is best practiced between the parallel bars in front of a large mirror so that sensory and visual feedback can reinforce the movement. Again, small steps are indicated to assist the amputee in stabilizing the prosthetic knee joint.

A large prosthetic step forward followed by a step-to of the remaining leg will keep the center of gravity behind the prosthetic knee joint. Knee extension may then only be achieved by "bracing" (forceful heel contact and stump hip extension) and not by pelvic forward thrust. In this way, the skill of overstepping, necessary for a normal gait pattern, is not utilized.

Hip Disarticulations. The hip disarticulation postoperative rigid dressing has a bucket shape. It covers the entire pelvis and is secured over the pelvic crest on both sides, thus contributing to cast suspension. Iliac crest relief pads protect the bony protrusions. All cast rims must be smooth to avoid skin irritation when moving or ambulating.

Auxiliary suspension is provided by shoulder straps similar to commercial-type suspenders. These straps are incorporated into the posterior aspect of the cast and cross before they are placed over the shoulders. They are then buckled into the front straps. This provides a straight upward anterior and posterior pull on the socket.

(See Fig. 2–21) The receptacle for the gait unit is placed so that the medial side of the base plate is directly under the ischial tuberosity (Burgess, 1969). This is important since it determines the step width. The gait attachment unit consists merely of a pipe and a foot unit. Static use permits satisfactory weight bearing and practice for standing balance only and does not provide feedback for any joint motion. Burgess (1969) states that the simplicity of the design is accomplished at the expense of function. Dynamic use with an articulated temporary prosthesis would place too much stress on the plaster cast.

Progression from a rigid dressing to a temporary socket and gait practice with joint motions is indicated as soon as the surgical wound has healed.

Figure 2–21   The position of the base plate: hip disarticulation rigid dressing.

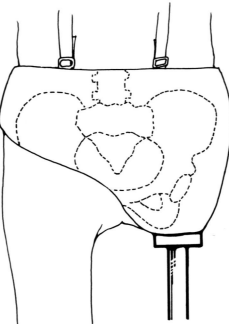

As standing tolerance improves, the amputee can progress to shifting weight from one leg to the other in a stationary position. The physical therapist guides the pelvis in lateral weight-shifting movements, with the amputee initially exerting only a minimal amount of weight bearing through the prosthetic device.

Weight Transference

Weight shifting is also practiced in an anteroposterior direction with both extremities alternately in a step position. Minimal step length is required, with the forefoot of the prosthetic foot positioned at the level of the heel of the remaining foot. This helps the amputee control the amount of weight shifting. Anteroposterior weight shifting with a long step and an immobilized knee necessitates increased weight bearing to correctly transfer the weight from one leg to the other. Caution must be taken since the weight bearing required initially may be too intense.

Weight-bearing Control

Initial weight-bearing attempts must be closely supervised. Too much weight transmission from the floor through the stump may cause stump trauma or may interfere with stump wound healing. The amount of weight bearing can be monitored in several ways.

Standing on two bathroom scales can help the amputee judge the amount of weight transmission through the gait device. The amputee can thus feel and see the amount of weight bearing needed to exert 5–10 pounds of force through the base unit to the stump. Weight shifting is then practiced without the scales. Although the procedure is logical, it does have certain limitations. The accuracy of controlled and graduated weight bearing is particularly difficult for the amputee to duplicate when only small amounts of weight initially are applied. The visual feedback provided by the scales is also limited to the standing position and must, therefore, be estimated when the amputee progresses to walking.

Another method that can be used to control weight bearing is the limb load monitor. An audio signal sounds when the desired amount of weight bearing has been reached, alerting the amputee to avoid a further increase in axial load to the stump. However, the limb load monitor is seldom used postoperatively to control weight bearing. It is more frequently utilized later in the rehabilitation program as a gait training tool when the amputee may tend to avoid weight transmission through the amputated side (see Limb Load Monitor, p. 268).

These two treatment adjuncts provide additional sensory input to help the amputee gauge more accurately the amount of weight being transmitted through the stump from the floor.

The therapist must also question the amputee as to whether weight distribution is felt equally over the entire stump surface. Incorrect weight distribution causes pressure pain and could interfere with normal stump functions (see Clinical Evaluation of Pain, p. 65).

The physical therapist can monitor weight-bearing progression by placing both hands between the patient's hands and the walker or parallel bars. As the

Weight-bearing Progression

amputee's ability to take weight through the temporary prosthesis increases, the amount of weight taken by the upper extremities should proportionately decrease.

Clinical Note. The amputee's judgment alone should not be used as a measure for weight-bearing progression. For example, a peripheral neuropathy will deprive the amputee of sensation and, because of this, the patient is unable to estimate the amount of weight the stump can tolerate.

The amount of weight transmitted through the stump remains difficult to judge. Weight-bearing control, particularly, will affect the amputee's balance, coordination, and proprioception. During these early weight-bearing activities, *meticulous* attention to controlled progression of weight bearing is necessary to protect the stump and to increase the amputee's confidence in the ability of the stump to bear weight and prevent postural deviations that can occur as a result of incorrect weight-bearing habits (see Gait Deviations, p. 282).

Postoperative Ambulation without a Gait Attachment Unit

If the postsurgical treatment course does not include initial stump weight bearing (e.g., soft dressing, wound healing complications), early ambulation can be accomplished with a walker. The amputee has to learn to swing the remaining leg forward smoothly, while both arms support the body weight on the walker. A fast, jarring, uncontrolled hop, although often demonstrated by amputees who have either balance problems or arm weakness, should be discouraged since the remaining leg will experience an impact with each step.

Disadvantages of the "jarring" experience include:

- increased throbbing of the stump
- increased incidence of claudication pain in the remaining limb
- decreased tolerance of the remaining leg

Occasionally, where stump circulation is marginal, stump healing may be delayed for some weeks or even months following amputation. Most of these amputees have to learn to ambulate with a walker and have to return home until stump healing occurs. Therefore, learning to use a smooth controlled step as soon as possible is an important part of early treatment for these amputees.

Summary

Rehabilitation up to this point takes place in a general hospital setting prior to the amputee's transfer to a rehabilitation center or unit. The role of the physical therapist in this initial phase is to provide precise care and patient education that will pave the way for all future activities.

The amputee has to experience many hitherto unknown life situations and, therefore, the quality of the physical therapy input at this stage will ultimately determine the success of the rehabilitation outcome.

References

Bailey, H., and Love, M. *Bailey and Love's Short Practice of Surgery,* 18th ed. by A.J.H. Rains and H.D. Ritchie, eds. London: Lewis, 1981, 749–751.

Becton-Dickinson Canada, Inc. "Better Diabetes Care." *Exercise and Its Benefits.* Mississauga, Ont. 1981, 8.

Berlemont, M., Weber, R., and Willot, J.P. "Ten Years of Experience with the Immediate Application of Prosthetic Devices to Amputees of the Lower Extremities on the Operating Room Table." *Prosthetics International, 3* (1969): 8–18.

Burgess, E.M., Romano, R.L., and Zettl, J.H. "General Principles. Below-knee Amputation Surgery." *The Management of Lower Extremity Amputations*. Washington, D.C.: U.S. Government Printing Office, 1969, 7, 17–19, 26–39.

Burgess, E.M. "Wound Healing After Amputation: Effect of Controlled Environment Treatment." *The Journal of Bone and Joint Surgery. 60A* (1978): 245–246.

Burgess, E.M. "Postoperative Management." *Atlas of Limb Prosthetics.* (American Academy of Orthopedic Surgeons.) St. Louis, Mo.: C.V. Mosby, 1981, 19–23.

Burgess, E.M. "Amputation Surgery and Postoperative Care." In S.N. Banerjee, ed. *Rehabilitation Management of Amputees*. Baltimore, Md.: Williams & Wilkins, 1982, 17–41.

Caird, F.I., Kennedy, R.D., and William, B.O. "The Bedfast State and Its Complications." *Practical Rehabilitation of the Elderly*. Marshfield, Ma.: Pitman, 1983, 85–91.

Friedmann, L.W. *The Psychological Rehabilitation of the Amputee*. Springfield, Ill.: Chas. C. Thomas, 1978, 49–50.

Fuerst, E.V., Wolff, L.V., and Weitzel, M.H. Posture and exercise. *Fundamentals of Nursing,* 5th ed. Philadelphia, Pa.: J.B. Lippincott, 1974, 319–362.

Gardiner, M.D. "Introduction to Movement." *The Principles of Exercise Therapy,* 4th ed. London: Bell and Hyman, 1981, 21–25.

Gerhardt, J.J., King, P.S., and Zettl, J.H. "The Rigid Dressing—Below-knee and Symes." *Amputations, Immediate and Early Prosthetic Management*. Vienna, Hans Huber, 1982, 59–84.

Gerhardt, J.J., King, P.S., and Zettl, J.H. "Advantages of Method." *Amputations, Immediate and Early Prosthetic Management."* Vienna: Hans Huber, 1982, 13–14.

Getz, P.A., and Blossom, B.M. "Preventing Contractures: The Little "Extras" that Help so Much." *R.N., 45,* no. 12 (December 1982): 45–48.

Ghiulamila, R.I. "Semi-rigid Dressing for Postoperative Fitting of the Below-knee Prosthesis." *Archives of Physical Medicine and Rehabilitation, 53* (1972): 186–190.

Hamburger, S. "Medical Management of the Surgical Patient with Diabetes Mellitus." *Journal American Medical Women's Association, 34,* no. 4 (April 1979): 155–167.

Helm, P.A., Walker, S.C., and Pullium, G. "Total Contact Casting in Diabetic Patients with Neuropathic Foot Ulceration." *Archives of Physical Medicine and Rehabilitation, 65* (November 1984): 691–693.

Hoover, J.E., ed. *Remington's Pharmaceutical Sciences,* 15th ed. Eaton, Pa.: Mack Publications, 1975, 714.

Isherwood, P.A., Robertson, J.C., and Rossi, A. "Pressure Measurements Beneath Below-knee Amputation Stump Bandages: Elastic Bandaging, the Puddifoot Dressing and a Pneumatic Bandaging Technique Compared." *British Journal of Surgery, 62* (1975): 982–986.

Jeans, M., Stratford, J.G., Melzack, R., and Monks, R.C. "Assessment of Pain." *Canadian Family Physician, 25* (1979): 159–162.

Kane, T.J., and Pollak, E.W. "The Rigid versus Soft Postoperative Dressing Controversy. A Controlled Study in Vascular Below-knee Amputees." *American Surgeon, 46,* (1980): 244–247.

Kay, H.W. "Wound Dressings—Soft, Rigid, or Semi-Rigid?" *Orthotics and Prosthetics, 29* (June 1975): 2, 59–68.

Kegel, B. "Controlled Environment Treatment (CET) for Patients with Below-knee Amputations." *Physical Therapy, 56* (1976): 1366–1371.

Kerstein, M.D. "A Rigid Dressing with a Pneumatic Prosthesis for Below-knee amputees." *American Surgeon, 40* (1974): 373–374.

Kerstein, M.D. "Utilization of an Air Splint After Below-knee Amputation." *American Journal of Physical Medicine, 53* (1974): 3, 119–126.

Koerner, I. "Clinical Experiences and Interpretation of the Phantom Limb Phenomenon in Amputee Training." *Journal of Canadian Physiotherapy Association,* 21 (April 1969): 90–100.

Little, J.M. "The Use of Air Splints as Immediate Prosthesis after Below-knee Amputation for Vascular Insufficiency." The Medical Journal of Australia, November 7, 1970, 870–872.

Melzack, J.G. "Phantom Limb Pain. Implications for Treatment of Pathological Pain." *Anesthesiology,* 35 (1971): 409–419.

Mensch, G., and Ellis, P. "Postoperative Activities." In S.N. Banerjee, ed. *Rehabilitation Management of Amputees.* Baltimore, Md.: Williams and Wilkins, 1982, 166–168.

Mensch, G. "Physiotherapy Following through-knee Amputation." *Prosthetics and Orthotics International, 7* (1983): 79–87.

Menzies, H., and Newnham, J. "Semi-rigid Dressings—The Best for Lower Extremity Amputees." *Physiotherapy Canada, 30* (1978): 225–228.

Mital, M.A., and Pierce, D.S. "Impact of Amputation on the Patient and Society." *Amputees and Their Prostheses.* Boston, Ma.: Little, Brown, 1971, 26–31.

Mooney, V., Harvey, J., McBridge, E., and Snelson, R. "Comparison of Postoperative Stump Management: Plaster vs. Soft Dressings." *The Journal of Bone and Joint Surgery, 53A,* no. 2 (1971): 241–249.

Murdoch, G. "The Postoperative Environment of the Amputated Stump." *Prosthetics and Orthotics International,* 1983, 75–78.

Murray, D.D., and Fisher, F.R. *Handbook of Amputations and Prosthesis.* Vancouver: University of British Columbia, 1979, 37–39.

McCollough, N.C. "Below-knee Amputation." *Atlas of Limb Prosthetics.* St. Louis, Mo.: C.V. Mosby, 1981, 341–368.

Redhead, R.G. "Discussion. Advanced course: Above-knee and through-knee amputations and prosthetics." Køege, Denmark: International Society for Prosthetics and Orthotics, May, 1979.

Redhead, R.G. "The problems of the postoperative 'stump/environment interface.'" *Congress Proceedings.* Vienna: International Congress for Prosthetics and Functional Rehabilitation, 1973, 65–73.

Sher, M.H. "The Air Splint." *Archives of Surgery,* 108 (May 1974): 746–747.

Steinke, J., and Soeldner, J.S. "Diabetes mellitus." In R.G. Petersdorf, G.W. Thorn, R.D. Adams, E. Braunwald, and K.J. Isselbacher, eds. *Harrison's Principles of Internal Medicine,* 8th ed. New York: McGraw-Hill, 1977, 581.

Stryker, R.P. "Reducing the Hazards of Bedrest." *Rehabilitative Aspects of Acute and Chronic Nursing Care.* Philadelphia, Pa.: W.B. Saunders, 1972, 24–28.

Tooms, R.E. "Amputations." In A. Edmonson and A.H. Crenshaw, eds. *Campbell's Operative Orthopedics,* 6th ed. St. Louis, Mo.: C.V. Mosby, 1980, 821–872.

Troup, I.M. "Controlled Environment Treatment (CET)." *Prosthetics and Orthotics International, 4,* no. 1 (1980): 15–28.

Troup, I.M., and Wood, M.A. The stump function and associated problems. *Total Care of the Lower Limb Amputee.* London, Pitman Books, Ltd., 1982, 76–79.

Wylie, W.D. "Affect of Anesthetic Agents on the Respiratory Centers." In H.C. Churchill-Davidson, ed. *A Practice of Anesthesia.* Philadelphia, Pa.: W.B. Saunders, 1978, 46.

Note

1. Ghiulamila, R.I. Personal correspondence, 1985.

Part II

The intensive rehabilitation phase of the amputee begins once the immediate postoperative phase has progressed satisfactorily. The extent of treatment protocol is based on the result of a detailed assessment performed by the rehabilitation core team.

PREPARATION FOR PROSTHETIC FITTING

Physical therapy objectives during this phase include

- the education of the amputee regarding all aspects of care
- the promotion of stump maturation
- the prevention and/or treatment of contractures
- the treatment of stump-healing problems
- the improvement of the amputee's general physical condition and tolerance

Initially, many amputees find this stage of rehabilitation extremely difficult because of the amount of physical and mental effort required to meet the demands of this escalated program. The support and encouragement provided by the team, the amputee's family, and friends is crucial during this stage.

Major input by the physical therapist is necessary in assessing amputees for rehabilitation potential. Therefore, a comprehensive assessment chart has been designed giving examples of pertinent data required along with their relevance to treatment planning.

PHYSICAL THERAPY ASSESSMENT FOR REHABILITATION POTENTIAL

The chart is meant to provide an organized approach to understanding the intricate interrelationship between problems and symptoms and their effect on treatment planning. It is also helpful for the physical therapist to obtain an overview of relevant problems in other areas (medical and social histories) as they pertain to physical therapy within the total scope of rehabilitation.

The guidelines will assist in precise, methodical data collection and will ensure that all areas of potential concern are evaluated. However, it must be stressed that the most detailed, objective assessment system cannot replace the sound clinical judgement necessary to correctly interpret the assessment findings that provide the basis for developing a realistic, appropriate treatment plan.

These guidelines are not meant to be used in a "cookbook" approach as the following example will illustrate.

The problem: stump edema
The treatment plan: bandaging

This simplistic conclusion would be workable in many instances. However, if stump swelling is associated with venous restriction (see When is the Bandage Removed?, p. 123), severe vascular pain could increase with the constant bandage compression. Therefore, bandaging would not be the treatment of choice. The treatment indicated in this situation would consist of frequent but short periods of exercise and ambulation, followed by adequate rest periods. The muscle-pumping action on the vessels produced by these activities would encourage a decrease in swelling. During nontreatment periods, a woolen stump sock should be worn instead of a bandage for warmth, protection, and comfort and stump dependency should be avoided. Knowledge of the underlying pathology and the evaluation of clinical signs and symptoms will help the therapist to judge the most appropriate treatment approach to counteract stump edema.

Assessment Chart

The assessment has been divided into categories to approach fact finding in a systematic way. The main categories are

1. The subjective data of medical history (Table 2–1, Part 1, p. 99) and social history (Table 2–1, Part II, p. 101)
2. The objective findings of physical examination (Table 2–1, Part III, p. 102)

Subjective Data:
Medical History

Subjective data collected from the patient and the hospital chart provides background information that will help determine the amputee's ability to fully participate in a structured physical therapy treatment program.

The following are examples of how information from the medical history can affect physical therapy treatment planning.

Trauma.   This could indicate that the amputee is young or middle aged with a history of good health. Stump healing may present complications caused by the initial injury (e.g., burns, fractures, or contusions). Taking into account other sustained injuries, the amputee should still be able to cope with a fairly strenuous physical program. In addition, treatment planning may include vocational considerations and, possibly, job retraining.

Treatment consists of extensive gait training and directs itself toward as close a return as possible to the preamputation level of fitness. Prosthetic considerations may also include the provision of special components designed to consider walking speed, certain sports activities, and vocational needs.

Malignancy.   These patients, usually in the younger age group, will often be excellent prosthetic users. They usually experience rapid healing and have problem-free stumps. Physical therapy may have to be deferred temporarily during chemotherapy sessions because of unpleasant side effects (e.g., nausea, fatigue, and weakness). Treatment planning and aims are somewhat similar to the traumatic amputee with regard to vocational and avocational interests.

Vascular Deficiencies and/or Diabetic Gangrene.   These reasons for amputation are more prevalent in the older age group, and one should keep in mind that the amputation surgery does not remove the underlying disease process. However, it may give relief from severe pain and may often end a long period of
(Text continues on p. 107)

TABLE 2–1 Physical Therapy Assessment of Rehabilitation Potential for Lower Extremity Amputations

Part I: Medical History

Major Investigative Headings	Examples of Pertinent Data Required	Relevance to Treatment Planning

Amputation Surgery	Date(s) of amputation surgery
	Level of amputation
	Type of postoperative dressing
	  rigid
	  semirigid
	  conventional
		time lapse from amputation surgery
		progression of healing
		stump weight-bearing possibilities
		weight-bearing status of the stump
		potential for stump lever control
		degree of loss of physical function

Amputation History	Reasons leading to amputation
	  trauma
	  disease
	  malignancy
	  other
	Symptoms prior to amputation surgery
	  pain
	    type
	    severity
	    onset
	  ulceration
	  loss of sensation
	Presurgical walking ability
	  endurance
	  average distance walked
	  walking aids used
	Surgical procedures relevant to amputation history
	  bypass grafting
	  sympathectomy
	  endarterectomy
	  skin grafting
	  other
		determines the expected tolerance level of the amputee for physical activity
		gives an indication of rehabilitation level which may be achieved
		indicates presurgical problems with mobility that may be compounded by the inherent difficulties associated with amputation

TABLE 2–1   continued

Part I: Medical History

Major Investigative Headings	Examples of Pertinent Data Required	Relevance to Treatment Planning

Present Medical Status	Diabetes
	  duration
	  control method (diet, insulin)
	  presently under control
	  neuropathy
	  other problems
	Cardiovascular and respiratory dysfunction
	  cardiac failure
	  cerebral vascular accident
	  chronic obstructive lung disease
	Arthritic joint changes
	  rheumatoid arthritis
	  osteoarthritis
	Chemotherapy
	  side effects
	Radiation therapy
	  side effects
	Injuries at other sites
	  fractures
	  burns
	  internal
	  other
		recognition of additional factors limiting amputee's ability to cope with rehabilitation activities
		recognition of potential problems with the higher energy consumption needed by the amputee during activity
		consideration of necessary treatment modalities
		implication of possible side effects of medications
		projection of needs for wheelchair independence

	Vital signs
	Medications
	  anti inflammatory
	  analgesics
		may affect the level of activities
		may reduce physical endurance
		may provide an indication of the amputee's expected tolerance in preparing for a structured rehabilitation program

	Life style
	  exercise
	  smoking
	  alcohol intake
	  dietary habits
		life long habits are difficult to change e.g., dietary control for obesity during rehabilitation is usually futile because on discharge the amputee will resume former eating habits and the socket will no longer fit.
		smoking is discouraged e.g., Buerger's disease, Renaud's disease

Part II: Social History

Major Investigative Headings	Examples of Pertinent Data Required	Relevance to Treatment Planning
Motivation	acceptance of the amputation initiation of the request for a prosthesis expectations of the prosthesis feelings regarding improvement in quality of life understanding the implications of a rehabilitation program	the patient's motivational level is extremely important as rehabilitation can be a lengthy process the amputee must take responsibility for following through with the program and ambulation even after discharge the decision to pursue prosthetic fitting is often dependent on the amputee's understanding of the rehabilitation process and all it entails the necessity of social work intervention
Communication	Ability to communicate functional dysphasia deafness Mental status well oriented depression senility	evaluation of ability to follow and retain treatment instructions modification of treatment techniques may be necessary indication of need for intervention by the psychologist and/or the speech pathologist
Vocational and Avocational Considerations	Professional skills Ability to resume previous work Work environment Hobbies active e.g., woodworking quiet e.g., stamp collecting Sports	consideration of vocational retraining programs consideration of adapting work environment to accommodate possible physical limitations adaptation to the prosthesis to planned physical activities adaptation of program to complement future vocational and avocational pursuits
Family	Spouse and children, their health status and ability to provide support Family coping mechanisms Reaction to amputation Circumstances precluding the amputee returning home	preexisting family coping mechanisms and adjustment to the amputation affect the patient's ability to benefit from the rehabilitation process support of family and friends affects the physical performance of the amputee
Home	Accessibility of home Layout of home bedroom bathroom stairs	determines whether the amputee can independently return home indicates liaison with occupational therapy to adapt home environment, to promote safety and function
Extended Care Facility	Previous patient accommodation e.g., custodial care Minimal level of functional ability needed to return to previous accommodation The amount of help which the amputee may need could change the eventual placement	occupational therapy assessment indicated social work intervention indicated criteria for admission to chronic care home must be specifically known

TABLE 2–1 continued

Part III: Physical Examination

Major Investigative Headings	Subheading	Examples of Pertinent Data Required	Relevance to Treatment Planning

Lower Extremity	Skin	Remaining leg
		  condition of toenails
		  trophic changes
		Stump
		  suture line
		  healing
		    abrasions
		    open areas
		    texture
		    dry
		    fragile
		  presence or absence of hair growth
		  healed scars from previous surgical procedures
		    bypass
		    skin graft
		    post trauma
		    scarring
			stump skin must toughen to take the stress of weight bearing and friction during ambulation
			stump condition influences stump weight-bearing
			skin breakdown—causative factors
			  infection
			  poor circulation
			  pressure
			  friction
			skin breakdown delays treatment progression
			pressure tolerant areas must be free of abrasions to allow socket fitting
			tissue mobility may be compromised by existing scars
			trophic changes indicate fragile skin, where breakdowns can easily occur
			absence of hair growth indicates impairment of superficial circulation

	Shape	peripheral edema
		  pitting
		  fluctuating
		foot deformities
		  depressed metatarsal heads
		  hallux
		  valgus
		conical
		cylindrical
		bulbous
		edematous
			reduction of edema promotes healing
			stump shape partially determines the comfort of the prosthetic fit
			matured stump permits an intimate socket fit
			undesirable shape (e.g. bulbous) leads to fitting problems, donning difficulties, and the formation of pressure areas
			fluctuating stump edema alters the shape and thus affects the socket fit
			foot deformities or problems in the remaining leg affect gait and must be accommodated for e.g. elastic stocking for swelling

	Measurements	girth length	girth measurements indicate if stump shrinkage should be implemented recording of reduction in edema indicates progression of shrinkage and efficiency of shrinkage method stabilization of stump measurements indicates stump maturation stump length is indicative of the amount of stump lever control

Category	Assessment	Rationale
Circulation	examination of peripheral pulses	poor circulation leads to skin problems and muscle fatigue
	coloration of skin	skin discoloration indicates trophic problems
	blanched	choking—venous restriction
	bluish	lymphatic involvement
	reddish	an "icy cold" stump may require gentle warming prior to activities
	pigmented	
	temperature of skin	
	perspiration	
Sensation	response to light touch and pressure	impairment of sensation to hot and cold will indicate caution in applying prior to exercising heat or cold modalities
	response to hot and cold	pressure sensation is vital for the amputee to be able to judge when weight-bearing stress becomes excessive
	response to pin prick	sensation acts as a guide in interpreting pressure, temperature, position, and motion and thus functions as a protective control mechanism to all tissues
	proprioception	poor skin sensation and proprioception require that strong visual and tactile input be incorporated into patient education regarding the observation and care of the stump and the remaining leg
	phantom awareness	phantom sensation is utilized to improve proprioception and body awareness during exercise and ambulation
		proprioception may be further impaired in the amputee with a CVA
Pain	bone pain	stump pain limits the amputee's tolerance and ability to participate fully in an active rehabilitation program
	vascular pain	pain increases stump sensitivity. Desensitizing techniques should be initiated as soon as possible
	nerve pain	pain is a causative factor in contracture development
	wound healing pain	claudication pain in the remaining leg limits the tolerance in ambulation activities
	phantom pain	neuropathy can range in symptoms from numbness to severe pain and can affect both the stump and the remaining leg
	intensity	phantom pain must be dealt with in terms of patient understanding of the phenomenon and physical treatment should be given in addition to prescribed analgesics
	duration	severe persistent phantom pain (rarely experienced) may affect the potential for prosthetic fitting
	frequency	
	description	
	intermittent claudication	
	preexisting nerve pain (e.g., sciatica)	
	neuropathy	

TABLE 2–1 continued

Part III: Physical Examination

Major Investigative Headings	Subheading	Examples of Pertinent Data Required		Relevance to Treatment Planning
		Stump	Remaining leg	
Lower Extremity (continued)	Motor function	Strength all joints tested tested muscle group function Tone hyper/hypotonus effects of the dominant synergic pattern (with cerebral vascular accident)		muscle actions propel and control the prosthesis muscle strength affects stump control and is an indicator of how much weight bearing is possible muscle strength aids body control and balance motor function partially determines walking speed muscle strength increases endurance stroke–stump side–motor deficit decreases ability to control prosthesis remaining leg–motor deficit causes inability to adequately weight bear to give stump a "rest" during gait cycle spasticity may increase with incorrect handling, positioning and the added weight of the prosthetic device
	Joint range of motion	all joints tested all ranges tested presence of contractures noted fixation severity characteristics duration		contracture prophylaxis is a major responsibility as a contracted joint affects postural body alignment increases energy consumption and causes gait deviations joint range limitations developing will probably respond well to conservative treatment chronic prevention of further increase in contracture adaptations in prosthetic alignment may be required postural compensation due to joint limitations may cause secondary complications postural gait deviations will be accentuated by the amputee in fixed preexisting limitations precise exercise and alignment considerations are necessary to avoid exacerbating existing arthritic hip and knee conditions if contractures are severe and fixed, prosthetic fitting may not be possible and either surgical contracture release or intensive occupational therapy input for wheelchair independence may be indicated

Upper Extremities	Motor Function	Strength
		  all joints tested
		  muscle group functions tested
		Tone
		  hyper/hypotonus
		  effect of dominant synergic pattern (with cerebral vascular accident)
			initially the upper extremities assume a dominant role in all mobility activities
			strong visual and tactile input are necessary to teach activities of daily living if there are motor changes in the hand

	Joint range of motion	all joints tested all ranges tested	joint range limitations affect use of ambulation aids and cause an increase in energy consumption
	Other significant findings	limitations due to chronic conditions rheumatoid arthritis deformities subluxation of hemiplegic shoulder wasting of intrinsic muscles of the hands sensory changes diabetic neuropathy pain	caution must be taken not to exacerbate joints that are affected by preexisting medical conditions arthritic changes may need adaption of walking aids stroke side effects: assistive walking device is carried on the sound side no matter which side the amputation is on standard progression from parallel bars to crutches is not possible external support to hemiplegic shoulder provides stability and decreases shoulder pain

Trunk	Motor function	all muscle group functions tested
		previous problems
		  surgical
		  conventional
			the trunk plays an integral role in balance
			strength and balance are necessary to maintain erect trunk posture
			range limitations in hip and knee are amplified in spinal posture

	Joint range of motion	limitations in spinal movements kyphosis scoliosis excessive lumbar lordosis	lumbar lordosis is increased if hip flexion contracture is present walking with an excess lumbar lordosis is energy consuming and affects the timing of prosthetic knee flexion controlled weight loss under the guidance of a dietician may be indicated for particularly obese patients

TABLE 2–1 continued

Part III: Physical Examination

Major Investigative Headings	Subheading	Examples of Pertinent Data Required	Relevance to Treatment Planning
Gross Motor Functions	Bed mobility	independent requires assistance	indicates amputee's level of independence

	Balance	sitting
		  attaining position
		  maintaining position
		standing
		  independent
		  requires assistance
		  aids used
			attaining sitting and standing positions helps to overcome prosthetic postural hypotension
			presence of claudication pain indicates level of ambulation the amputee can achieve
			if the remaining leg is affected by a stroke or other medical conditions, standing ability will indicate the amount of control the limb has on weight bearing

	Transfers	sit to stand bed to wheelchair	indicates body balance adaptation to the loss of the weight of the amputated limb
	Gait	postamputation level of ambulation amount of weight bearing aids used tolerance stairs—if applicable	

Subjective questioning will indicate the amputee's level of independence in activities of daily living

		bathing dressing toileting independent bandaging if applicable	demonstrates how the amputee is coping with problems imposed by amputation (resourcefulness) this gives some insight into the amputee's adaptability to other life situations after discharge demonstrates to some extent, motivation in learning to master skills demonstrates eye/hand coordination, hand skills and arm movements which are an integral part of donning and doffing the prosthesis. Occupational therapy intervention is needed if problems in these areas are observed

THOROUGH INVESTIGATION OF EXISTING CONDITIONS

plus

ANALYSIS OF IDENTIFIED PROBLEMS BASED ON SOUND CLINICAL KNOWLEDGE

plus

IMPLEMENTATION OF APPROPRIATE PHYSICAL THERAPEUTIC APPROACHES

equals

OPTIMAL TREATMENT OUTCOME

illness and inactivity. Treatment planning should consider a multitude of problems, which may include:

- delayed stump healing
- general debilitation or decrease of tolerance
- preexisting contracture problems
- poor balance and coordination
- aging factors

Treatment aims for the maximum level of independence that can be achieved safely by the individual. This can range from wheelchair independence to independent ambulation without walking aids.

It is obvious that the treatment focus depends largely on the reason for the amputation and also that treatment techniques may differ widely.

A comprehensive social history is an integral part of the complete assessment since psychosocial factors will have a bearing on treatment planning, progression, and outcome. The physical therapist needs to be aware of potential problems (financial, emotional, family, or job related, etc.) and discuss any of these, as expressed by the amputee, with the assigned social worker. The social worker will initiate any help required in the areas of concern.

Subjective Data:
Social History

Table 2–2 (p. 108) is comprehensive since this is the physical therapist's area of expertise. Although the chart is self-explanatory, the section dealing with stump examination will be discussed more fully in order to clarify the usefulness of the chart as an assessment tool. Assessment findings are listed, treatment considerations are suggested, and their rationale is supplied.

Objective Findings:
Physical Examination

The remaining leg. The remaining leg will become the dominant leg. It must function as the main support leg and, as such, has to exert greater effort. Increased muscle effort takes place around the foot and ankle to control the body's balance owing to the loss of the other leg. This causes particular problems for the geriatric amputee who may have complications such as:

Other Assessment
Considerations

- impaired sensation and poor proprioception due to peripheral neuropathy
- decreased muscle strength
- limitation of joint range
- foot lesions
- foot deformities

Any treatment strategy must ensure optimum function of the remaining leg (see Care of the Remaining Leg, p. 115).

The Upper Extremities. Initially, the upper extremities take on an important role in weight bearing during locomotion (e.g., crutch walking, transfers). Testing strength, range of motion, and functional capabilities of the upper

(Text continues on p. 110)

TABLE 2–2   Stump Assessment Findings

Assessment findings	Treatment considerations	Rationale
Delayed healing	whirlpool	to debride and cleanse the wound to increase circulation
	ultraviolet	to destroy bacteria, if present to increase circulation to promote growth of new skin to toughen skin
	suture line taping	to approximate wound edges to provide wound support
	bandaging	to reduce or prevent edema to give support and protection
	splinting	to provide a quiet wound healing environment to prevent contracture development to support positioning
	reapplication of the rigid dressing	to provide an undisturbed wound healing environment
	non weight bearing	to rest tissues which cannot yet tolerate weight-bearing stresses
Edema	bandaging	to aid shrinkage and shaping
	shrinker sock application	to aid shrinkage and shaping to maintain achieved shrinkage
	air splint	to aid shrinkage and shaping
	intermittent pressure pumping	to decrease lymphatic swelling
	pneumatic walking aid	to encourage lymphatic and venous return (Caution: See Pneumatic Walking Aid, p. 138)
	weight bearing with gait unit	to provide alternating contraction and relaxation of stump muscles against socket wall (this pumping action encourages reduction of edema)

TABLE 2–2 continued

Assessment findings	Treatment considerations	Rationale
Decreased strength	graded exercises	to increase strength in muscle groups where specific weakness is identified
	general exercises	to improve general condition tolerance
Decreased range of movement (ROM)	positioning	to maintain and passively increase existing ROM
	application of heat or cold modalities (Caution: Circulatory impairment limits the use of thermal applications. See Thermal Modalities, p. 186)	to decrease muscle tension to prepare for stretching to prepare for exercising
	manual techniques	to increase joint range
	exercises	to maintain and increase ROM
	ambulation with a gait unit	to encourage greater joint movement by the natural stretching produced during the gait cycle
	serial splinting	to maintain ROM achieved during treatment
Sensory impairment	vibration stroking percussion stump handling	to desensitize hypersensitive stump areas
	use of manual, visual, audio input	to increase proprioceptive awareness
	biofeedback	to establish or reinforce required muscle action for exercise and gait training
	education	to increase awareness of pressure-sensitive areas during self examination of the stump before and after treatment, e.g., checking for areas of excessive pressure on the stump after using the gait training unit to prevent stump trauma caused by excessive temperature changes

Table 2–2 continued

Assessment findings	Treatment considerations	Rationale
Stump pain	wound healing techniques (See Delayed Healing, p. 163)	to encourage wound healing
	positioning	to discourage contracture formation
	desensitizing techniques	to toughen stump
	application of thermal modalities	to decrease stump discomfort
	TENS	to decrease stump pain
	weight bearing	to encourage natural muscle function which will sometimes reduce stump pain

extremities is, therefore, an assessment consideration. Strength of the wrist extensors and grip are especially important because, even with adequate triceps strength, the amputee will not be able to use a conventional walker or crutches if grip or wrist stabilization cannot be maintained.

The Trunk. Trunk evaluation, so often overlooked, is a specific component in the physical assessment. One function of the trunk is to place the center of gravity over the support leg, thus keeping the body properly balanced. In normal gait this function occurs automatically. When the normal gait pattern is disrupted by amputation, gait symmetry is disturbed, affecting the counterforces required to balance the body (see Balance Control, p. 17). The amputee, exposed to the effects of gravity and trying to prevent falling, uses the trunk excessively to retain posture. Unnatural movements initially replace automatic locomotion until relearning permits adaptation to the gravitational forces and to the biomechanical changes. It is important that sufficient trunk strength and range of motion be present to permit facilitation of correct trunk movements at an early stage in the rehabilitation program because the deviant gait pattern will soon become automatic and these early gait adaptations very quickly become permanent habits.

Gross Motor Functions. The testing of bed mobility, sitting and standing balance, transfer skills, and postamputation ambulation levels are basic guides to establish the level of balance present (Gabell, 1982). If balance is poor or absent, prosthetic gait is not possible.

The amputee's present level of ambulation is tested. The ability to ambulate with a walker or crutches gives an indication of:

- the tolerance of the remaining leg
- the status of the cardiovascular respiratory system
- the independence of the amputee at this stage

In early stages, the amputee may experience postural hypotension caused by position change from lying to standing. All of these factors help to determine the amputee's general tolerance for rehabilitation.

Record Keeping.   All assessment findings are recorded. Precise and accurate record keeping is essential:

- to monitor patient progress
- to evaluate efficacy of treatment modalities (Day, 1981)
- to provide a data base for future reference in clinical research studies

When all data have been collected, a team conference becomes the forum for information exchange. Clinical findings, relevant observations, and existing problems are discussed, and a treatment course, with input from all team members, is outlined. A problem list is formulated. The diversity of problems that are identified reinforce the importance of ongoing information exchange throughout all stages of rehabilitation.

Team Conference

The amputee, THE most important member of the team, is then presented with an outline of the proposed rehabilitation program. The amputee, who is an active participant in the restoration of physical function, then has the opportunity to decide whether or not to accept this treatment course.

Once the decision has been made to pursue rehabilitation, the information from other team members pertaining to goal setting will help the physical therapist finalize a realistic individual physical therapy program for the amputee.

The aims of the physical therapy assessment are

Summary

- to evaluate the amputee's general health
- to determine the amputee's motivation in regard to rehabilitation
- to test physical capabilities
- to identify problem areas
- to project potential for prosthetic fitting

Once the assessment process has been completed, the physical therapist utilizes the accumulated data

- to set realistic short and long term goals
- to formulate a treatment program tailored to the needs of each amputee
- to implement the treatment program, accommodating changes in the amputee's status

Since rehabilitation is achieved, on the average, in 22 weeks (Kerstein, 1974), it is most important to utilize this time efficiently to achieve the planned treatment outcome.

Day, H.J.B. "The Assessment and Description of Amputee Activity." *Prosthetics and Orthotics International, 5,* no. 1 (1981): 23–28.

References

Gabell, A., and Simons, M.A. Balance coding. *Physiotherapy,* 68, no. 9 (September 1982): 286–288.

Kerstein, D., Zimmer, H., Dugdale, F.E., and Lerner, E. "Amputations of the Lower Extremity: A Study of 194 Cases." *Archives of Physical Medicine and Rehabilitation,* 55 (October 1974): 454–459.

PATIENT EDUCATION

Patient education is an integral part of the active rehabilitation program. By understanding:

- the physical limitations
- the emotional stresses
- the treatment procedures
- the preventive measures

related to the amputation, the patient is provided with a base for developing independence and self confidence, thus enhancing motivation. Patient motivation is of the utmost importance, since the amputee must increasingly participate in decision making and consequently become more involved in, and responsible for, the success of the rehabilitation outcome.

The aim of patient education is to help the amputee learn to shed the "sick" role (Imboden, 1972) by gradually accepting the fact that, although the amputation is permanent, functional independence is possible. The amputee may have to consider several factors during the process of learning to cope physically and emotionally with the impact of amputation. These factors include the knowledge that the future lifestyle and the role within the family may change and that new routines of activities of daily living must be implemented.

The physical therapist not only assesses and treats but also teaches, and thus assumes the role of educator to amputees and their families. During each treatment session, the therapist reinforces specific techniques such as bandaging, positions for contracture prevention, how to care for the stump and the remaining leg, and how to walk most efficiently and deals with all questions and concerns the amputee may express.

Teaching and/or education, geared to treatment progression, is provided through individual or group sessions. Groups permit social contact, reinforcement or synthesis of individual instructions and an environment in which to discuss and review more general issues. Groups also enable amputees to express their feelings openly. Amputees and their families are encouraged to voluntarily participate in these sessions. Various topics are presented by the different team members and may include:

- The pathophysiology of the disease process that caused the amputation.
- The care and maintenance of the prosthesis.
- The importance of proper nutrition. This is a valuable review for all amputees, particularly the diabetics. Avoidance of weight fluctuation is stressed as this will compromise the socket fit. Weight *gain* will also result in increased energy expenditure for all activities.

- The community resources available to amputees. This information may include sessions on:

  financial resources available
  local self-help groups
  adapted sports activities available
  specific regulations for driving
  wheelchair accessibility in the community, etc.

Group sessions not only give information but also provide an "experience sharing" environment for amputees and their families.

Under the guidance of a health care professional in individual and group sessions, amputees are encouraged to understand their unique psychological reactions to the amputation and how to cope with these feelings. Reactions to limb or partial limb loss vary in intensity in each individual. Some examples include:

- grief over the loss of the leg
- loss of self-esteem
- apprehension about interpersonal relationships
- worry regarding the future (Verwoerdt, 1972; Friedmann, 1978)
- denial of the existence of problems
- acceptance of the amputation as a life challenge that must be met

The primary focus of both the individual treatment and group sessions is to teach the amputee the *concrete* strategies that they will have to integrate into their future lifestyle. Although a review of pathophysiology given to the group may provide interesting information, the amputee may be more successful in relating to the significance of the presentation following discussion with the group and the health professional present. Setting goals, such as trying to give up smoking and/or altering eating habits, may be the outcome of these discussions.

Consistent contact by the same health care givers and consistent presentation of information are two factors that may help to facilitate the amputee's learning (Mazzuca, 1982). If the teaching is successful, an understanding of the "whys" of the different treatment procedures should, hopefully, increase the amputee's ability to comply with all physical therapy activities and instructions. The amputee must comprehend that the specific information provided will prevent problems only if they continue to practice what they have learned following hospital discharge.

Patient education enhances the rehabilitation program and attempts to improve   Summary

- The amputees' attitudes toward themselves. This will improve their self image and their ability to function successfully in the community.
- The existing lifestyle (e.g., smoking) that may have contributed to the primary cause for amputation (e.g., peripheral vascular disease).

- The amputee's ability and motivation to comply with postdischarge treatment follow-up. This may prevent problems with the stump and the remaining leg and may also help to ensure that the achieved level of independence is maintained.

The expected outcome of ongoing education is an amputee who is motivated, knowledgeable, and compliant with all treatment regimes. It provides the amputee with the tools necessary to independently implement the strategies that may help to encourage the maintenance of optimal health.

References

Imboden, J.B. "Psychosocial Determinants of Recovery." *Advances in Psychosomatic Medicine, 8* (1972): 142–155.

Friedmann, L.W. "Reactions to Amputation—Chronic." *The Psychological Rehabilitation of the Amputee.* Springfield, Ill.: Chas. C. Thomas, 1978, 26–60.

Mazzuca, S.A. "Does Patient Education in Chronic Disease Have Therapeutic Value." *Journal of Chronic Diseases, 35,* no. 7, (1982): 521–529.

Verwoerdt, A. "Psychopathological Responses to Stress of Physical Illness." *Advances in Psychosomatic Medicine, 8* (1972): 119–141.

HYGIENE

The importance of precise skin care related to the stump and the remaining leg cannot be overstressed. Skin care, a basic hygienic need for all amputees, is of even greater importance to patients who have peripheral vascular disease and/or diabetes. Healthy skin is a resilient organ and can cope with a fair amount of abuse before it breaks down (Levy, 1983). Dysvascular skin, however, is unable to tolerate continued stress and friction. Extra care must be taken to adhere to principles of good hygiene to ensure optimal functioning of the stump and the remaining leg through the prevention of skin problems. All procedures apply to all amputees, are based on common sense, and can be easily followed.

Care of the Stump

The stump, a motor and sensory end organ (Burgess, 1981, 1982), provides active prosthetic lever control and accommodates weight bearing during locomotion. It functions in a nonventilated enclosure (the socket), an environment that produces friction, skin tension, and perspiration, thus necessitating good stump hygiene.

Regular stump care must become part of each amputee's daily routine and must be continued after the stump has healed. Initial instructions are given by the nurse, while reinforcement is provided by the physical therapist during stump bandaging practice. Guidance during early rehabilitation gives the amputee ample opportunity to learn and to practice stump care under supervision. The simple but important daily routine includes:

- Washing the entire stump with mild soap and warm water. Evening bathing is recommended because the warm water, the dependent stump position, and the stimulus of washing can often result in skin "puffing." If skin puffing occurs in the morning, donning the prosthesis becomes more difficult.

- Cleansing and drying the bases of skin folds or indrawn scars gently with cotton swabs. This is indicated to prevent possible bacterial infections.
- Rinsing and carefully patting the skin dry. This will prevent skin roughness or flakiness due to air drying and will eliminate accumulation of moisture in skin folds.
- Using an emollient (optional). This helps to moisten dry and flaky skin. Weight-bearing areas (e.g., the patellar tendon in transtibial stumps), however, should not be lubricated as this will prevent the desired toughening.
- Examining the stump for lesions (bruises, abrasions, blisters, pressure areas). If skin sensation is poor, a hand mirror is useful for observing areas that are not easily visible (e.g., posterior stump). Any problems identified (see Stump Complications, p. 162) should not be treated without first notifying the physician. Something as simple as using adhesive tape to secure a dressing may cause damage to already fragile skin (Berkman et al., 1979). Gauze rolls (Kling™) or Micropore® tape are recommended.

The amputee is also advised to apply only *dry* socks or bandages to prevent chafing of the skin that may occur when it is in contact with damp materials, and only clean socks or bandages to prevent infection and friction from accumulation of salts due to perspiration.

Stump Coverings

The remaining leg becomes the dominant leg and assumes increased weight bearing, balance, and coordination responsibilities, especially during the early stages of rehabilitation when weight bearing through the stump is minimal or nonexistent. It is, therefore, necessary to avoid the development of potential problems in this limb. Possible signs and symptoms when examining the leg of a patient with peripheral vascular disease and/or diabetes include (deWolfe, 1973; Banerjee, 1979):

Care of the Remaining Leg

- blanched fragile skin
- ingrown and/or overgrown brittle toenails
- decreased skin sensation
- pitting edema
- coldness
- intermittent claudication
- unhealed or newly developed abrasions
- arterial or venous ulcers

(See Fig. 2–22)

(See Fig. 2–23)

The presence of surgical scars indicate previous vascular procedures performed in an attempt to improve distal circulation.

These conditions may delay or hinder gait activities, thus prolonging the total rehabilitation time for the amputee.

In the dysvascular, insensitive limb there are several areas more prone to develop problems. These are:

Common Problems, Sites, and Prevention

Figure 2–22   The diabetic foot: fragile skin and brittle toenails.

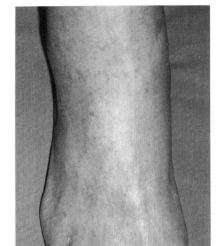

Figure 2–23   The diabetic foot: skin lesion.

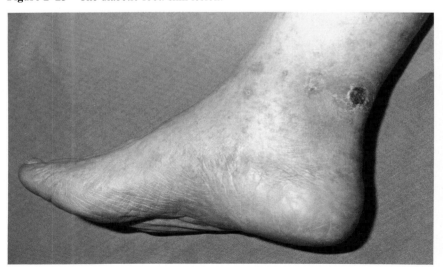

- the toes
- the heel
- the malleoli

The most common causes of trauma come from externally generated pressures or exposure to temperature extremes [e.g., ill-fitting shoe, rubbing of bed clothes, incorrect toenail cutting, or minor to severe burns that can occur during bathing (Brand, 1979)]. Resultant injuries heal poorly, and the open areas become prime targets for bacterial infection.

Preventive measures include:

- meticulous hygiene
- wearing a comfortable shoe
- using nonelasticized socks

Total leg care, like stump care, is part of the daily routine taught during rehabilitation and must be continued at home. It should include:

- Washing the leg in warm water, using mild soap. This removes skin secretions and reduces the possibility of infection.
- Patting the foot and leg dry, with special attention to the skin between the toes. Rubbing may injure the skin.
- Using an emollient to keep the skin moist and malleable. This may prevent "cracking" of the skin, especially around the heel (Wagner, 1981).
- Inspecting the foot and leg for any reddened areas, cuts or bruises, so that any lesions can be dealt with immediately.

The water temperature must always be checked with the part of the body that has normal sensation (e.g., hand, elbow) to avoid scalding the foot (Shipley, 1979).

When more specific care such as cutting the toenails is required, the amputee must exercise extra caution. Toenails must be cut straight across to prevent ingrowing (Berkman et al., 1979). Sometimes nail cutting and/or the relief of the removal of corns and callouses must be performed by a chiropodist.

Shoes.   During the day, a well fitting shoe (see Preoperative Care, p. 50) should always be worn for:

- protection
- comfort
- stability
- support

Custom made orthotic inserts are sometimes required to relieve pressure on the metatarsal heads and/or provide arch support.

If lesions on the foot prevent the amputee from wearing a shoe, then a slipper, enclosing toes and heel, or a plastazote boot is worn for protection.

Transfers, sitting in wheelchairs, or standing or walking while barefoot are absolutely not permitted.

Socks. The purchase of woollen or cotton socks is advised since they absorb perspiration. Nonbinding cuffs are recommended to avoid further circulatory restrictions. The sock must always be free of wrinkles since wrinkles can cause discomfort and pressure points when the shoe is in place. Ideally, socks should be laundered following each wearing in order to rid them of the crusty build up that occurs as a result of perspiration.

Heel and Malleoli. Prior to amputation surgery, the dysvascular amputee may have spent prolonged periods of time on bed rest. Preventive care initiated at this time to protect the heel and malleoli from localized pressure must continue. The amputee must also learn to inspect these areas and to change position frequently. A small rolled towel placed under the ankle will prevent pressure on the heel in the supine position. In the presence of fragile skin, the use of a lambswool-lined boot with a Velcro closure is helpful to dissipate pressure on these areas.

Clinical Comment. The amputee must also learn to avoid bumping and/or bruising the foot and the leg. Awareness of the potential causes of injury and the strategies to prevent problems is one of the primary aims of education and treatment. The amputee is instructed to use as much sensory input (visual, tactile) as possible to compensate for any lack of sensation. For example, teaching safe transfer techniques (see Transfer Procedures, p. 79) will prevent falls or abrasions to the leg that could occur if the brakes are not secured or if the foot pedals are not raised prior to the transfer. Female amputees are advised to use an electric razor to shave their legs.

Edema. Some amputees experience dependent edema in the remaining leg. If severe, range of motion is limited and increased skin tension also occurs in the edematous area. The use of an external support (e.g., bandage, Tubigrip™, antiembolism stocking) and exercise wearing the elastic support may encourage a decrease in edema and prevent additional swelling. It is recommended that the external support be applied first thing in the morning before getting out of bed since edema increases as the day goes on. During nonactive periods, the edematous leg should be elevated on the wheelchair leg rest or a foot stool.

Claudication Pain. If claudication pain is a problem, the amputee is taught to walk only to the limit of comfort. When ischemic pain begins, the amputee must sit and rest the leg *completely*. Walking, often for short distances, followed by adequate rest periods will gradually increase walking tolerance (deWolfe, 1973).

Increasing standing tolerance in the presence of ischemic pain is contraindicated; therefore, standing tolerance during ADL activities must be carefully monitored. An energy conservation program developed for the amputee by the occupational therapist will reduce unnecessary standing.

Prolonged cross-legged sitting, will tend to restrict the circulation and can also lead to ischemic pain.

Stump and leg self-care procedures are taught and reinforced throughout the rehabilitation period. Automatic integration of these routines into the amputee's adapted life-style usually only occurs after frequent and consistent repetition since patients often have difficulty in comprehending and retaining information and instructions given to them in the early stages of rehabilitation.

Summary

On discharge, the amputee should be independent in the performance of lower extremity skin care routines. However, simple written instructions can be provided to help ensure continued follow-up at home.

If an amputee has poor vision and/or eye-hand coordination and is unable to care for the stump and the remaining leg independently, a family member can be instructed in the procedures, or a referral to a community resource such as the visiting nurse can be arranged. Although it may be obvious from the amputation, the patient should always inform people who are providing skin or wound care that there is a vascular problem (Wagner, 1981).

Skin care is important because skin problems on the stump and/or the remaining leg hinder ambulation.

References

Banerjee, S.N. "Assessment and Management of the Ischaemic Foot." *Canadian Family Physician 25* (1979): 84–86.

Berkman, S. "Diabetes." *Care of the Feet*. Chicago, Ill.: Budlong Press, 1979, 57–59.

Brand, P.W. "Management of the Insensitive Limb." *Physical Therapy 59*, no. 1 (1979): 8–12.

Burgess, E.M. "General Principles of Amputation Surgery." *Atlas of Limb Prosthetics*. (American Academy of Orthopedic Surgeons.) St. Louis, Mo.: C.V. Mosby, 1981, 14–18.

Burgess, A.M. "Amputation Surgery and Postoperative Care. In S.N. Banerjee, ed. *Rehabilitation Management of Amputees*. Baltimore, Md.: Williams & Wilkins, 1982, 17–41.

deWolfe, V. "Arteriosclerosis Obliterans: Clinical Diagnosis and Treatment." *Geriatrics*, September, 1973, 93–101.

Levy, S.W. "Stump hygiene." *Skin Problems of the Amputee*. St. Louis, Mo.: Warren H. Green, 1983, 255–265.

Shipley, D.E. "Clinical Evaluation and Care of the Insensitive Foot." *Physical Therapy*, 59, no. 1 (1979): 13–17.

Wagner, F.W. "The Dysvascular Foot: A System for Diagnosis and Treatment." *Foot & Ankle, 2*, no. 2 (1981): 64–122.

STUMP SHRINKAGE AND SHAPING TECHNIQUES

Stump edema is common following amputation surgery since stump tissues swell in response to the operative procedure. Severe swelling affects the rate of stump healing (Menzies, 1978; Manella, 1981; Brady, 1982), thus delaying prosthetic fitting. The amount of edema varies in individuals, but, one can generally say that higher amputation levels and amputation stumps with bone severance tend to be more edematous postsurgically than lower amputation levels and joint disarticulation stumps.

Reduction of stump edema is a treatment priority since it helps the stump to heal and to stabilize; optimum lever control through an intimate prosthetic socket fit will only be achieved when the stump is fully matured. Stump stabilization occurs when stump shrinkage is complete and there is no further edema. Stump maturation has been reached when the stump is fully functional, free of edema, and able to accommodate all weight-bearing stresses.

Several techniques can be practiced to shrink, shape, support, and stabilize the stump. These include the use of:

- stump-bandaging techniques
- shrinker sock applications
- intermittent compression pumping
- pneumatic walking aid
- gait-training unit

These techniques are selectively utilized, either individually or in combination with each other.

Stump Bandaging

Bandaging is an acquired skill. If applied correctly, it is an effective and economical stump shrinkage and shaping tool. The bandaging must be done accurately, supervised continuously, and taught to the amputee (Holliday, 1981; Mensch et al., 1982). Bandaging techniques are not standard for all amputated stumps. Each application is adapted to the individual stump condition and length. Different bandaging techniques can be utilized provided each individual aim and goal is met.

Objectives

The purpose of bandaging is:

- to reduce edema
- to shape the stump
- to help counteract stump contractures
- to support the surgical wound
- to provide some stump protection and comfort
- to reduce adductor roll tissues (in transfemoral stumps)
- to diminish dog ear formation in stumps with redundant tissues

Stump shrinkage and shaping occurs when distal stump compression is maintained. This is achieved by carefully grading the bandage tension control from firmer tension distally to lesser bandage tension proximally (Mensch et al., 1982). Grading in this way encourages venous return and lymphatic drainage. Initially, stump edema decreases rapidly, but as treatment progresses the rate of decrease will be more gradual.

Positive aspects of stump bandaging are:

- Bandage material conforms to stump contours and sizes, making bandaging an adaptable and practical stump shrinkage and shaping method.
- Stump support and protection are provided.
- Stump observation is accessible.
- Stump hygiene can be regularly practiced.
- Bandages are readily available.

Negative aspects of stump bandaging are:

- Stump tissue damage can occur with excessive compression or with too tight a bandage.
- Bandage application is often difficult for older patients to accomplish.
- Bandage slippage resulting in loss of distal pressure can make this method of edema control ineffective.
- Increased staff time is required, initially, for frequent rebandaging during the day.
- Bandage tension control can only be estimated and may vary accordingly.
- Bandaging of the stump does not provide complete protection against accidental bumping or bruising.

It is necessary to be selective in the type of bandage used because different bandage textures fulfill different functions. A bandage that does not have diagonal stretch is not suitable for stump compression bandaging, since it cannot mold to the contours of the stump. Bandages are available in different widths; the choice of length and width will depend on the length and girth of the stump.

Lightweight Bandage. This net-like, multidirectional stretch bandage with indicator lines allows for good ventilation. The elasticity of the bandage is such that it provides gentle compression to the stump tissues.

The advantage of this bandage is that it is of adequate length to support the stump tissues to the desired level. It may be used over stump dressings and, because of the soft texture of the bandage, overlapping layers will not cause excessive compression.

Disadvantages of this type of bandage are that it loses its elasticity after washing and, if the finished end is cut, the bandage frays.

Standard Elastic Bandage. This heavier bandage has a stronger elastic fiber providing both lengthwise and diagonal stretch to permit more compression control. The advantage of this type of bandage is that it is suitable for active patients with healed stumps. The disadvantage may be that two, and sometimes three, bandage lengths must be sewn together to ensure that the stump can be covered to the correct level and that tension is not lost during bandage application, unless of course, longer bandages are available. Ventilation is marginal with this type of bandage.

Bandage Tension.   It should be noted that it is extremely difficult to achieve the same tension each time the bandage is applied, especially when a number of people are responsible for the application. Factors that contribute to bandage compression include:

- the elasticity of the bandage
- the amount of pull exerted when the bandage is applied (this will vary from person to person)
- the number of bandage layers utilized

The final result should always feel comfortable and provide support by equalizing the internal and external pressures on the stump. (Comparison: in order to cough effectively following abdominal surgery, a patient will support the suture line with both hands, which will give protective counter pressure.)

Tolerance to bandage tension and pressure varies in amputees. The clinical guide to a correct bandage application is the subjective expression of comfort and support by the amputee.

General Bandaging Comments

Successful stump bandaging requires a lot of practice and precision in the method of application by the physical therapist. A few key points must be remembered.

1. Bandage application starts immediately after the postoperative cast has been removed because of the quick development of edema when external support is gone (Burgess, 1969; Horne, 1982). However, if a postoperative soft dressing is applied initially, compression bandaging starts following primary healing of the surgical suture line.
2. The bandage should always be firm and supportive but never tight. It is worn day and night, except for short periods during wound care, and stump hygiene. It should not be worn when a prosthetic device is worn.
3. Bandage compression can act as an early desensitizing technique, preparing the stump for socket contact.
4. Compression markings (pale) seen on swollen stumps when the bandage is removed indicate that fluid reduction is being controlled successfully by bandaging. These markings, which will quickly disappear, must not be confused with irritated or angry looking skin areas. Irritated, dusky looking skin can be the result of too much bandage tension (choking).
5. Amputation stumps with bone severance are generally more edematous than joint disarticulation stumps. This occurs because with bone severance during amputation, muscles are also separated, causing a more extensive disruption of tissues, whereas during disarticulation, bone and muscles remain intact.

(See Fig. 2–24)

Figure 2–24   Compression markings on an edematous stump following bandage removal.

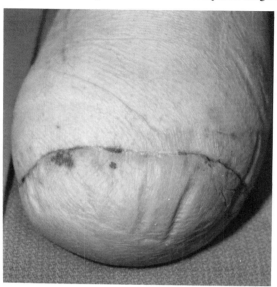

6. Dysvascular amputees will generally show more persistent stump edema than amputees without any underlying pathology.
7. The geriatric patient needs more time to learn correct bandaging. Health care workers must assist and supervise the patient until the correct tension and the position of the bandage are learned. Transtibial amputees usually master the skill of bandaging with comparative ease. Transfemoral amputees do not manage quite as well because it is often cumbersome for the elderly to cope with the anchoring pelvic turn of this bandage procedure.
8. The technique for bandage application should be uniform within each institution. If all staff use the same technique, it will be less confusing to the patient, but staff should ALWAYS adapt the standard techniques to any unusual stump conditions.

All stump bandages must be regularly removed (approximately every 4 hr) to allow for:

When is the Bandage Removed?

- surgical wound care
- general stump inspection
- stump hygiene
- unrestricted stump movement
- early detection of potential problems

Immediate rebandaging is necessary to ensure prevention of edema through ongoing distal stump compression.

However, certain pathological stump conditions require the discontinuation of bandaging. Bandaging is not indicated:

- When the stump pain is ischemic in nature and is combined with the sensation of excessive cold, as felt by the therapist or expressed verbally by the patient (Mensch, 1983).
- When the stump skin has a reddish blue discoloration, indicating venous restriction.
- When the stump skin is hypersensitive to bandage pressure and the skin compression marks show localized discoloration, blistering, or break-down, particularly over the bony areas.
- When numbness or tingling are experienced as the result of bandage tension.

How Long is Bandaging Necessary?

There is no firm answer to the question of how long bandaging is necessary. Circumstances, and the stage of rehabilitation, often determine the answer. During the stump maturation phase the bandage is worn continuously.

Once the amputee eventually uses the prosthesis regularly throughout the day, and stump measurements have been reduced with no fluctuation, then one may assume that the stump has stabilized. At this time the amputee can attempt to leave the bandage off.

When weaning from bandaging, the amputee should try to sleep one night without the bandage (Zimnicki, 1977). If swelling occurs during the night, making prosthetic donning difficult in the morning, then the stump has not matured sufficiently, and bandaging must be continued once again.

However, if the amputee only wears the prosthesis for short periods, once or twice daily, bandaging must continue in order to maintain the shape of the stump. These stump volume fluctuations will delay maturation and make the donning of the prosthesis difficult, if not, at times, impossible.

Basic Stump Bandaging Instructions

The bandaging techniques for the different levels of amputation have several common basic rules.

1. The physical therapist should stand to the right of the patient to bandage the stump regardless of whether the amputation is on the left or right extremity. Otherwise, one works against one's own wrist. Left-handed people reverse the position. When the therapist is teaching the amputee how to bandage, it is important NOT to use a mirror image when explaining and demonstrating the bandage turns. This way, the amputee can observe the procedure directly and correctly for later independent applications.
2. An emollient is used on the stump skin, but not over the weight-bearing areas, to help prevent the bandage from slipping off.
3. The bandage turns should be in a diagonal or a figure-eight pattern to facilitate the application of the bandage over the stump contours. The bandage should NEVER be applied in tight, circular turns since this restricts circulation and

causes a tourniquet effect that will result in tissue strangulation, adversely affecting stump edema and wound healing.

4. The suture line is supported by a directional bandage pull that approximates the wound edges (from posterior to anterior).

5. Wrinkles should be avoided because excessive compression caused by bandage wrinkles can be experienced as pressure points that may lead to skin irritation and/or breakdown.

6. The bandage should be fastened using a safety pin or masking tape. To avoid pricking the stump the therapist places the index finger under the bandage while the safety pin is inserted through the bandage layers. Metal clips should not be used since they can cause abrasions on the stump or the remaining leg and may introduce a route for infection. Metal clips can also come off, causing loss of bandage tension.

7. The bandage, once applied, can be held in place using elasticized net or tubing. This will also reinforce the distal firmness.

Although the initial teaching of stump bandaging is the responsibility of the physical therapist, correct bandage application is a team responsibility. Therefore, each team member, including the amputee, is equally responsible for ensuring that the bandage is correctly applied at all times.

Ideally, each amputee should learn to bandage. This can be accomplished in the majority of cases. Patients who have higher levels of amputation, combined with medical problems, or have reduced hand dexterity or eye–hand coordination will encounter some difficulty in applying the bandage correctly. These patients will need continuous help and encouragement to learn the correct bandaging technique. If this proves impossible, an alternative method of shrinkage and shaping may have to be investigated.

If the amputee has difficulty in applying the bandage and goes home on the weekends during the rehabilitation phase, it is advisable to have a family member or friend learn to apply the bandage. In this way, stump support, protection, and compression control can be maintained at all times.

Owing to the increased sweating that occurs following amputation surgery, the bandage will absorb perspiration and, as a result, will develop a salty crust. Therefore, the bandage, like a sock on the foot, should be worn for only one day and then washed so that it remains clean and comfortable at all times. A mild, nonirritating soap should be used to wash the bandage. It is important to rinse the bandage well. To dry, the bandage is rolled in a towel to eliminate excess moisture, then laid out flat. Other drying measures such as electric dryers or hanging may destroy the elastic fiber content. The amputee and, if appropriate, family members must be instructed in the care and hygiene of bandages. It should be emphasized that when elasticity is gone, the bandage is useless and should be replaced.

Bandage Hygiene

Specific Bandaging Techniques Related to Different Stump Levels

Specific bandaging techniques are necessary because the stump characteristics and the needs in preparation for prosthetic fitting vary for each amputation level.

Forefoot Stump Bandaging

(See Fig. 2–25)

Aims:

- shrinking and shaping of the remaining portion of the foot
- counteracting an inversion contracture

The bandage is started diagonally over the dorsum of the foot, directing the initial turn medially. Using figure-eight turns, the bandage is anchored over the remaining portion of the foot, including the heel. Bandage turns coming from the sole of the partial foot towards the stump end will pull the lateral border into the neutral position, counteracting the inversion tendency, and thus assisting the positioning of the remaining part of the foot into a stable stance position. The bandage direction from the bottom upward also approximates the suture line

---

Figure 2–25   Forefoot stump bandaging.

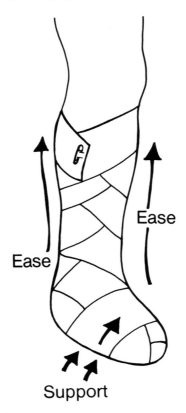

instead of applying a wrongly directed skin tension. To encourage shrinking of the remaining foot portion, the bandage should extend approximately 8–10 cm above the ankle joint.

Clinical Comment.   Do not force a bandaged forefoot into a shoe. Instead, a custom made shell of a more pliable material (e.g., Plastazote®) should be provided for protection. Swelling at this amputation level is generally not too pronounced. However, if any edema is present it will be slow to respond to treatment.

Aims:

- shrinking and shaping of the stump
- positioning of the heel pad centrally

Ankle Disarticulation (Syme's Amputation) Stump Bandaging

(See Fig. 2–26)

Due to its bony structure and heel pad, the stump is bulbous; therefore, most of the shrinkage occurs above the reshaped malleoli. To provide graded and equal compression control over the total stump, the bandage extends to just below knee level. The bandage turn sequence is important because the main aim at this

Figure 2–26   Ankle disarticulation (Syme's Amputation) stump bandaging.

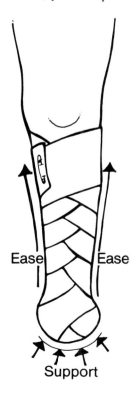

amputation level, in addition to shrinkage and shaping, is to brace the heel pad and prevent it from shifting (see Amputation Levels—Ankle Disarticulations, p. 34). The tendency to shift can be counteracted by bandaging. The bandage is started diagonally over the medial distal stump end and continued in a figure eight sequence. This allows for tension control and assists positioning the heel pad tissues in a neutral position. The bandage is continued proximally to below knee level, gradually decreasing the tension to provide support for the calf muscles.

Clinical Comment. Weight bearing in early stages is not permitted on the bandaged ankle disarticulation stump since the bandage does not provide enough support to prevent the heel pad from shifting on weight bearing.

Transtibial Stump
Bandaging

(See Fig. 2–27)

Aims:

- shrinking and shaping of the stump
- prevention of a knee flexion contracture

There are two methods practiced. In one application the entire knee joint is covered by the bandage, the other leaves the popliteal area uncovered.

Knee Joint Covered. The more common transtibial bandaging approach starts over the distal stump end in a figure eight pattern and extends in continued diagonal turns to midthigh level. The knee joint is covered completely so that the bandage provides graded total stump compression. This technique requires frequent bandage removal during the day to allow for an active range of motion of the knee.

Figure 2–27 Two methods of transtibial stump bandaging.

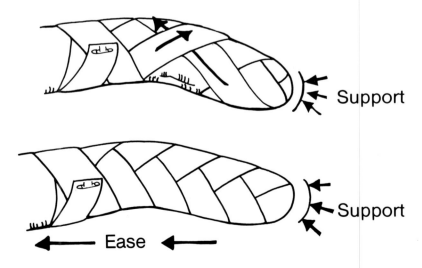

Caution. Too much bandage tension over the popliteal fossa can cause circulatory restriction, particularly if the knee is bandaged and held in a flexed and dependent position. For this reason, the stump should always be supported in the sitting position.

Knee Joint Uncovered. A less common method covers the stump below the knee joint level and then leads the bandage in front of the knee and above it. In this way, the directional bandage pull will aid knee extension. The popliteal space is kept uncovered to allow for unrestrained joint range motion. This technique is indicated for the younger, more active amputee where there is only a moderate amount of stump edema present. In the more edematous stump, when swelling will also tend to settle in the popliteal fossa, this method is not indicated.

Aim:

- shrinking and shaping of the stump
- prevention of hip joint contractures

Knee Disarticulation
Stump Bandaging

(See Fig. 2–28)

Figure 2–28   Knee disarticulation stump bandaging.

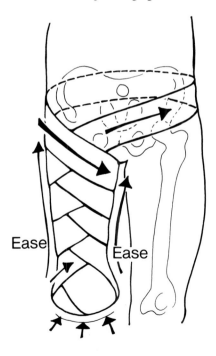

The stump is bulbous because of its bony structure. Therefore, the main concern is to reduce the edema above the femoral condyles because the condyles are utilized to suspend the prosthesis.

Two bandaging techniques may be practiced. The decision of which method to use should be based on the presence, or absence, of an adductor roll (see Adaptations to Bandaging Techniques, p. 132), a hip contracture, or an extremely fleshy stump. Bandaging starts anteriorly over the stump end. The bandage is directed diagonally towards the medial aspect of the stump. This initial directional turn is necessary because it will later help to draw the stump toward body midline, thus counteracting stump abduction. Bandaging is continued in a figure-eight fashion, repeating the stump end turns and decreasing the tension proximally. The bandage is then extended anteriorly across the pelvis and brought around the pelvis, posteriorly. The completed pelvic turn is directed from the stump side in front of the stump medially and placed high into the groin area, covering the adductor region. The pelvic turn is repeated and the bandage secured with a safety pin.

If a hip contracture, an adductor roll, or an extremely fleshy stump do not pose a problem, the same method is used, eliminating the pelvic turns.

Clinical Comment.   The occurrence of contractures in a knee disarticulation stump is rare because muscle tissues have not been severed by surgery. Also, an adductor roll may not be as common as in transfemoral stumps because the knee disarticulation stump, following surgery, retains its muscular balance (Baumgartner, 1979).

Transfemoral Stump
Bandaging

Aim:

- shrinking and shaping of the stump
- prevention of an abduction–external rotation contracture
- prevention and/or shrinking of an adductor roll (see Stump Complications and Conservative Treatment Indications—Stump Shapes, p. 175)

(See Fig. 2–29)

The bandage is started anteriorly and diagonally over the distal portion of the stump. The first bandage turn is directed medially. This is of major importance since this initial medial turn will, later, determine the direction of the bandage pull at pelvic level. The pull toward body midline counteracts stump abduction and external rotation. (If the reversed bandage direction is used, the stump would be placed into abduction–external rotation, thus encouraging poor hip joint positioning.) The bandage is continued by contouring over the stump end in a figure eight fashion, approximating the suture line. The tension is reduced as the bandage is applied proximally. The figure eight sequence is continued over the total stump length and brought around the pelvis. At this point, the stump is held in extension to avoid a flexion pull by the bandage, which would encourage the development of a flexion contracture. The pelvic turn begins, anteriorly, with the bandage resting on the pelvic crest and returns around the body to the stump side.

Figure 2–29   Transfemoral stump bandaging.

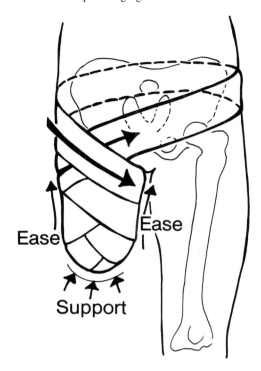

An adductor roll can be controlled by placing the bandage from the pelvic level anteriorly, high into the groin area (Alexander, 1978). This diagonal approach holds the bandage in position and prevents the proximal edge from rolling into a tight band which, in turn, would cut into the soft tissues and create an adductor roll rather than reduce it. The pelvic turn is repeated to reinforce the bandage suspension, and the bandage is fastened with a pin.

Clinical Comment.   In very short transfemoral stumps, bandaging can be started over the pelvic crest. This may be necessary to anchor the bandage securely so that greater distal pressure can be applied to the short stump. Again, it is important to place the bandage direction in such a way that the stump is assisted toward the adducted position to counteract abduction and external rotation.

Aim:

- shrinking and shaping of the residual tissues
- providing support to the surgical incision

The selection of a wider bandage allows for better stump support.

Hip Disarticulation Bandaging

(See Fig. 2–30)

Figure 2–30   Hip disarticulation stump bandaging.

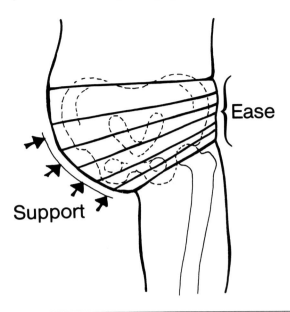

The bandage is secured around the pelvic crest and is then led from posterior to anterior in layers over the stump portion, giving distal and lateral support. Taping of the completed bandage will hold it more securely in place. A soft pad, placed over the surgical site, allows for comfort during sitting until the skin is toughened. Complete shrinkage of the disarticulated section is important to provide an intimate and comfortable socket fit.

Adaptations to the
Bandaging Techniques

Certain stump conditions require procedural adjustments to be effective in shrinking and shaping the stump.

(See Fig. 2–31)

Adductor Roll.   Shaping becomes difficult if the adductor roll is large in size and flabby in tissue structure. The contouring bandage disappears into the folds of the fatty tissue and does not provide the equal compression support necessary to achieve edema reduction and stump shaping. To counteract this, an adductor roll shell can be custom fitted to the individual size of the amputee's stump and can be incorporated into the bandage to provide equal shaping compression (Mensch et al., 1982).

(See Fig. 2–32)

The pattern made from Plastazote® is oval and when molded does not extend anteriorly as far as the anterior wall of a quadrilateral socket. The upper rim is shaped away from the stump to provide sitting comfort. A groove for the adductor longus tendon is incorporated into the splint, and the upper edge of the medial wall (similar to the medial wall of the quadrilateral socket) is placed

Figure 2–31 Adductor roll.

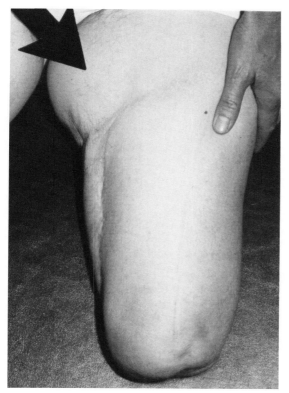

Figure 2–32 Adductor roll splint pattern.

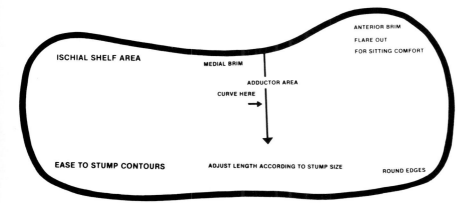

RIGHT
(REVERSE FOR LEFT)

ANTERIOR BRIM

FLARE OUT

FOR SITTING COMFORT

ISCHIAL SHELF AREA

MEDIAL BRIM

ADDUCTOR AREA

CURVE HERE

EASE TO STUMP CONTOURS

ADJUST LENGTH ACCORDING TO STUMP SIZE

ROUND EDGES

slightly lower than the top rim of the anterior wall. The medial rim is sloped gently away from the stump to prevent the shell from impinging on the pubic ramus. Only anterior and medial wall support is necessary to contain the adductor roll and provide equal pressure. The length of the shell from top to bottom depends on the stump length. If the shell extends below the stump end, it will hold the bandage away from the stump tissues, thus reducing the effectiveness of the bandage in shrinking the distal tissues.

Shell fabrication and adjustment can be easily accomplished. The shell is a useful tool in controlling an excessive adductor roll while shrinking and shaping the stump.

Bulbous Soft Tissues.   (see Stump Complications and Conservative Treatment Indications—Stump Shapes, p. 175). Some transtibial and transfemoral stumps are bulbous distally, which can cause difficulty when donning the prosthetic socket. The bulbousness can be reduced by bandage tension, giving firm diagonal, upward support distally. This directional control encourages reduction of fluid and enhances the desired stump shaping.

Dog Ear Control.   When redundant tissues shrink, dog ear formation can, at times, be observed. With increased shrinkage, tissue lipping can occur either at the medial or lateral end of the suture line, or both. It is important to apply equal pressure directly over the center of the section, which tends to shrink into a dog ear (see Stump Complications and Conservative Treatment Indications—Stump Shapes, p. 175).

(See Fig. 2–33)

If it proves difficult to control the dog ear section, one can use surgical or micropore tape and pull the skin into position so that the bandage can be molded

---

Figure 2–33   Counteracting a dog ear formation.

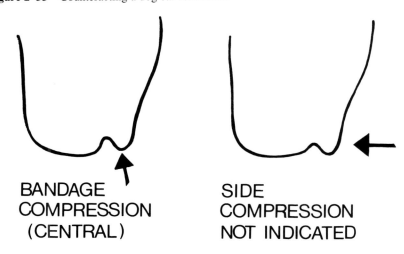

BANDAGE
COMPRESSION
(CENTRAL)

SIDE
COMPRESSION
NOT INDICATED

over this particular area and provide the correct, centrally directed upward, compression. With correct compression control, most dog ears shrink away.

Diversified Opinions to Stump Bandaging, or "To Bandage or Not to Bandage"

Some practitioners[1] (Manella, 1981) are not in favor of using bandaging as a treatment modality, particularly in stumps where superficial skin circulation is impaired and never as an immediate postoperative dressing. These practitioners report delayed healing caused by bandage choking (too much bandage tension) and further stump insults such as skin bandage burns.[2] This is of particular concern in the vascular patients and only reinforces the importance of being precise and selective in all treatment procedures used to reduce stump edema.

However, it can be argued that other rehabilitative treatment methods applied to aid stump shrinkage cause stress of a far greater intensity than bandaging. For example, when weight bearing during gait training, maximal compression is exerted on the stump tissues during prosthetic stance when the stump muscles contract against the socket wall to hold the artificial leg in position. The amount of compression on stump tissues in this situation cannot be controlled or measured. The pressures exerted can be further affected by body weight and balance ability.

Summary

Although there are negative reports regarding the efficacy of bandaging, it is, if applied with careful consideration of possible outcomes, a most useful and simple tool that gives support, shape and reduction of edema in recent amputation stumps. Stump bandaging, which we as authors recommend, is extensively and successfully practiced at our center. It requires staff competence that is maintained by frequent reviews of bandaging techniques. Comments from amputees indicate that stump comfort is achieved by bandage support.

Shrinker Sock Applications

Shrinker socks are elasticized stump socks that, if correctly fitted, function like support hose. The purpose of these socks is to aid stump shrinkage and shaping while simultaneously giving support and comfort. This is achieved, as with bandaging, by providing firm distal stump support, with socket tension decreasing proximally. Shrinker socks are marketed in different materials (e.g., Lycra®, Spandex®), sizes and shapes. Therefore, one should stock several sizes to accommmodate the clinical needs of all amputation stumps.

An elastic bandage adapts to all stump sizes, shapes, and contours. A shrinker sock does not and must therefore be fitted to approximate the stump contours as closely as possible. If the correct size is not available, clinicians must sometimes alter a shrinker sock accordingly.

(See Fig 2–34)

Selecting and Fitting Shrinker Socks

The concepts involved in the selection and fitting of the shrinker sock must be understood. If the proximal girth of the shrinker sock is not large enough, the sock material will place an increased amount of tension on the stump tissues. This can cause stump "choking." Choking is the result of proximal circulatory restriction resulting in stump damage distally (e.g., edema, claudication pain, wound healing problems). If the sock circumference is too large distally, the required support is not provided, and the stump stock is ineffective. If sock contact appears adequate but the lengthwise stretch of the sock has too much give, distal pressure is lost while lateral contact remains. This reduces the comfort provided by the sock. This problem can be resolved by sewing the distal sock portion to provide the required contact.

The shrinker sock make, size, and any necessary adaptations should be recorded on the chart to simplify replacements.

Suspension

The usefulness of shrinker socks as a shrinkage and shaping tool is dependent on effective suspension control. Some socks are suspended by an auxiliary system composed of suspenders attached to a belt. This method is somewhat cumbersome. The other method is one that incorporates the suspension into the stump sock design by extending the sock section laterally over the pelvic area. A belt is attached to the proximal border of this extension, resulting in a more even, comfortable suspension pull. By utilizing this method of sock suspension:

- The sock has a better chance of staying in place.
- The proximal sock cuff is prevented from rolling down (avoiding a tourniquet effect).
- The adductor roll remains covered.

Figure 2–34   Shrinker socks: left, standard sock, adapted to stump size, with auxiliary suspension; right, suspension incorporated.

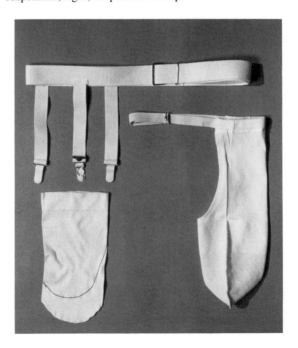

Most amputees can pull the shrinker sock on independently and secure the suspension belt, which usually has a buckle or velcro closure.

A shrinker sock, fitted correctly, is easily and quickly applied. The stump is readily accessible for wound care and is protected by the sock. It not only aids in stump shrinkage and shaping but, if properly fitted, maintains the stump shape and provides comfort for the amputee.

Advantages

Hand dysfunction, particularly a decrease in strength, will make it difficult for the amputee to pull on the sock and fasten the suspension independently. Size selection is not always easy. Shrinker socks for particularly unusual stump shapes are not commercially available, and existing socks may not be suitable to be adapted to fit the stump correctly. If a stump is bulbous, a shrinker sock should not be used since tissue compression for this stump shape cannot be correctly controlled with a commercially available shrinker sock.

Disadvantages

Even if the amputee will not be a prosthetic wearer, the use of a shrinker sock can be beneficial. It will give support and control stump swelling. A swollen stump feels ''heavy'' and is less mobile, whereas a maintained stump shape, even if the stump is nonfunctional for ambulation activities, gives comfort to the elderly patient who is aiming to achieve wheelchair independence or who requires chronic care.

Clinical Comments

To avoid placing too much tension on sensitive stump tissues, a shrinker sock should not be worn along with a stump bandage.

Stump shrinker socks, like bandages, must be regularly washed with mild soap, rinsed well, and laid out to dry to avoid breaking the elastic fibers.

Shrinker socks, because of the limitations posed by sizing, have restricted use and, as with any other shrinkage and shaping technique, must be carefully evaluated before being dispensed to the amputee.

Summary

Intermittent compression pumping, using a Jobst pump unit, is a treatment modality that aids in the reduction of lymphathic swelling. This treatment approach, although not routinely used to reduce stump edema, can occasionally be of benefit to some amputees who have excessively swollen stumps. It is only indicated if the surgical wound is completely healed and if the stump skin is free of abrasions and/or infection.

Intermittent Compression Pumping

Compression pumping, together with slight stump elevation, is administered with the amputee in a supine position. The treatment is lengthy and, therefore, requires the amputee to be inactive for several hours during the day.

In the initial stages, lymphatic swelling usually reduces quickly using this treatment technique.

Advantages

This treatment modality is a selective one for several reasons. The pneumatic stump sleeve is marketed in one size only. This results, primarily, in

Disadvantages

uniform lateral compression but does not necessarily provide equal distal stump pressure. The inflated sleeve is also bulky, and this tends to encourage flexion at the hip level. However, this treatment can be justified if initial shrinkage results are favorable.

Clinical Comments.   Some centers carry this treatment approach one step further by utilizing the inflated pneumatic stump sleeve, disconnected from the pump, for specific activity periods. The method is only suitable for young active amputees who demonstrate good standing balance. It allows the amputee to be mobile so that they can hop on one leg and participate in modified rehabilitation sports activities. The stump muscle action against the constant pressure provided by the pneumatic sleeve also encourages stump shrinkage during activities.

For very obvious reasons, wearing a constant pressure sleeve is contraindicated in the elderly in the presence of vascular problems. Many of these amputees have problems that make standing on one leg impossible. Ischemic reactions such as intermittent claudication can occur that may affect balance. Postural compensation owing to poor balance when standing on one leg and wearing the compression sleeve causes scoliotic adaptations that encourage postural deviations. Another consideration is that stump dependency does not encourage lymphatic or venous return.

Sitting with the disconnected inflated stump sleeve in place requires a pillow under the sound side to compensate for the pelvic imbalance that occurs because the air-filled compression sleeve is bulky.

Summary

Intermittent pressure pumping is an adjunct to other methods of shrinking and shaping. Immediately after the treatment is completed, reduction in swelling must be maintained by applying a stump bandage or another method of edema control.

Pneumatic Walking Aid

A pneumatic walking aid, developed in Roehampton, consists of a small inner stump support air bag, an outer pneumatic stump sleeve, and a pylon metal frame with a rocker bottom. The device is assembled by placing the inner support bag over the stump end and then donning the outer pneumatic sleeve. The frame is positioned over both stump covers. The assembled device is then inflated with a foot pump to 40 mmHg, first partially expanding the support bag and then the entire sleeve (Troup, 1982; Redhead, 1983). The frame provides stability and remains in position over the inflated outer sleeve, allowing the amputee to weight bear.

Advantages

The pneumatic walking aid is used as an early gait-training aid for stump shrinkage and shaping and to provide relief for the remaining leg during ambulation activities. Stance is stable because the air support provides total contact with stump comfort (Dickinson, 1982). Air compression can be adjusted. This feature, together with stump muscle action, facilitates venous and lymphatic return. Donning is uncomplicated but requires assistance. The unit can be reused later for other amputees.

Disadvantages

Walking with this gait device requires a stiff-legged, peg-like gait. Knee motion is not possible because the support frame is rigid. The pneumatic walking aid thus introduces incorrect proprioceptive feedback to the stump. During early gait activities, this may be detrimental because the amputees will adapt their prosthetic gait to what they feel and perceive initially. Incorrect sensory feedback facilitates gait deviations that later become permanent habits (see Balance Control, p. 17). This is of particular importance when training transfemoral amputees because a stiff-legged gait prohibits proprioceptive awareness of the hip extension function and thus deprives the amputee of the feeling of stance stability. Similarly, it deprives the amputee of experiencing the initiation of prosthetic knee flexion (Mensch, 1983). A stiff-legged gait introduces such gait deviations as hip hiking for ground clearance. The amputee may also abduct the prosthetic device, practice unequal step length, or vault with the remaining leg (see Transfemoral Gait Deviations, p. 292). Furthermore, this abnormal gait pattern requires a higher energy output by the amputee during walking (see Energy Expenditure, p. 18).

Summary

The physical therapist must carefully assess the advantages of stump shrinkage and shaping qualities of the pneumatic walking aid. The benefits must outweigh the disadvantages of introduction of early postural gait compensation. If one can predict that the amputee will eventually be able to walk independently with a free-swinging prosthetic knee, then a stiff-legged device should not be used, particularly not during early gait training. Other shrinkage and shaping methods are available.

However, if the amputee is unable to learn to control the artificial knee in extension, or achieve stance stability, then a device such as the pneumatic walking aid can be utilized. In this situation the device helps the more debilitated amputee to obtain stump maturation and at the same time allows limited walking independence.

Gait-training Unit

A gait-training unit has many functions (see Gait Training—Gait Training Unit, p. 246), one of which is to promote stump shrinkage and shaping. Walking regularly with this temporary device is one of the most effective ways to reduce stump edema.

Walking stimulates natural stump muscle activity. The gait cycle incorporates alternating contraction and relaxation of muscles. This natural physiological and functional activity aids in decreasing swelling. Contracting stump muscles against a snugly fitting socket wall, combined with stump weight bearing, encourages further stump shrinkage.

Shrinkage obtained during these walking sessions must be maintained by applying extra stump socks to preserve intimate socket contact and by immediately applying a bandage or a correctly fitting shrinker sock when the training unit is taken off.

Summary

The clinician selects the most suitable shrinkage and shaping methods by carefully considering the advantages and disadvantages of each technique and their implications to the individual amputee's stump condition.

References

Alexander, A. *Amputees Guide, Above-the-knee.* Issaquah, Wa.: Medic Publications Company, 1978.

Baumgartner, R.F. "Knee Disarticulation versus Above-knee Amputation." *Prosthetics and Orthotics International*, 3 (1979):15–19.

Brady, W.M. "Post-operative Management of Lower Extremity Amputees using Tubular Elastic Compression Bandaging." *Orthotics and Prosthetics, 6*, no. 2 (1982): 8–10.

Burgess, E.M., Romano, R.L., and Zettl, J.H. "Postoperative Management—General Principles." *The Management of Lower Extremity Amputations.* Washington, D.C.: U.S. Government Printing Office, 1969, 97–98.

Dickstein, R., Pillar, T., and Mannheim, M. "The Pneumatic Post-amputation Mobility Aid in Geriatric Rehabilitation." *Scandinavian Journal of Rehabilitation Medicine, 14*, (1982): 149–150.

Holliday, P.J. "Non-prosthetic Care." In J.P. Kostuik and R. Gillespie, eds. *Amputation Surgery and Rehabilitation: The Toronto Experience.* New York: Churchill Livingstone, 1981, 238–242.

Horne, G., and Abramowicz, J. "The Management of Healing Problems in the Dysvascular Amputee. *Prosthetics and Orthotics International, 6*, no. 1 (1982): 38–40.

Manella, K.J. "Comparing the Effectiveness of Elastic Bandages and Shrinker Socks for Lower Extremity Amputees. *Journal of the American Physical Therapy Association, 61*, (1981): 334–337.

Mensch, G., and Ellis, P. "Bandaging." In S.N. Banerjee, ed. *Rehabilitation Management of Amputees.* Baltimore, Md.: Williams & Wilkins, 1982, 190–194.

Mensch, G. "Physiotherapy Following through-knee Amputations." *Prosthetics and Orthotics International, 7*, no. 2 (1983): 79–87.

Menzies, H., and Newnham, J. "Semi-rigid Dressings: The Best for Lower Extremity Amputees." *Physiotherapy Canada, 30* (1978): 225–228.

Redhead, R.G. "Post-amputation Pneumatic Walking Aid." *British Journal of Surgery.* 65, (1978): 611–612.

Redhead, R.G. "The early Rehabilitation of Lower Limb Amputees Using a Pneumatic Walking Aid. *Prosthetics and Orthotics International, 7*, no. 2 (1983): 88–90.

Troup, M.I., and Wood, M.A. "Physiotherapy." *Total Care of the Lower Limb Amputee.* London: Pitman Books, 1982, 104–109.

Zimnicki, quoted by Holliday P.J. "Non-prosthetic Care." In J.P. Kostuik and R. Gillespie, eds. *Amputation Surgery and Rehabilitation: The Toronto Experience.* New York, Churchill Livingstone, 1981, 234.

Notes

1. Redhead, R.G. Discussion, ISPO's Advanced Course on B/K and T/K Amputations and Prosthetics, Køge, Denmark, May 10–13, 1982.
2. Ibid.

CONTRACTURES

In a contracted joint, the resultant reduction in range of motion affects the dynamic body alignment. Changes in the angular relationship between the contracted limb segments result in:

- minimized stump leverage
- postural adaptations

- increased energy expenditure to accomplish gait because the residual limb cannot move through its entire natural range

It is, therefore, a sound rehabilitation principle to practice contracture prophylaxis (Mital et al., 1971; Holliday, 1981).

If, however, a stump contracture has developed, treatment to counteract the range loss is of utmost importance. The objectives are:

- to make the gait as energy efficient as possible
- to avoid gait deviations
- to prevent secondary problems
- to encourage a more automatic and natural gait

To treat contractures successfully, one must recognize their characteristics, the factors that cause the diminished joint range, the tissues that are involved, and their response to conservative treatment measures.

A classification system has been developed to clarify the complexity of contracture characteristics. The analysis is based on

(See Table 2–3)

- tissue manifestations
- related causative factors
- single or multiple joint involvement
- severity of joint fixation

This essential information is followed by a listing of conservative physical therapeutic treatment approaches (see Specific Physical Therapeutic Treatment Measures, p. 147) that can be utilized to prevent the development of contractures and to counteract existing stump contractures.

Anatomically, stump contractures tend to settle postoperatively, in the joint next to the level of amputation. Joint range loss may also be present prior to amputation surgery. Contractures can be orthopedic or neurological in nature and may involve:

Contracture Characteristics and Possible Causes

- muscle tissues
- joints: capsular, ligamentous, and/or bony structures
- skin

These structures can contract alone or in conjunction with surrounding tissues.

Contributing causes to contracture formation can be determined during physical examination, and clinical findings will indicate the appropriate treatment plan.

In muscle contractures, the joint range is limited by soft tissue tightness either in the muscle bulk or the tendinous insertions. The shortening or tightness can affect one or several joints. On manual testing, the tissues respond to stretch with a springy or elastic feel at the end of the joint range (Kaltenborn, 1976). Stretch techniques to counteract the shortening are generally successful.

Muscle Contractures

TABLE 2–3 A Classification of Stump Contractures in Lower Extremity Amputations

Tissue Manifestations		Some Examples of Related Causative Factors	Contracture Characteristics	
			Extent of Joint Involvement	Fixed or Nonfixed
Muscle Contractures	Preexisting Muscle Tightness	Long standing low back pain with iliopsoas muscle tightness can cause reduced hip extension range in transfemoral amputees	Multiple joint involvement Principle joint range loss in hip, however spinal joints also involved	Nonfixed—responds to stretch
		Long standing effect of changes in muscle tone due to neurological disorder	Multiple joint involvement e.g., could result in hip and knee flexion contracture in the transtibial amputee	Nonfixed phasic muscle stretch may increase muscle tone tonic or maintained muscle stretch reduces muscle tone
	Postoperative Soft Tissue Retraction	Further tissue retraction than anticipated at the time of amputation surgery	Involvement of joint next to the level of amputation	Nonfixed—responds well to stretch
		Tissue retraction due to spasticity in the amputated limb; not as apparent while under general anaesthetic	Multiple joint involvement due to the effect of the synergic patterns on the total limb	Nonfixed—quick stretch may act as stimulant, only in the direction of the dominant synergy
Joint Contractures	Preexisting and Postoperative Joint Contractures	Rheumatoid arthritis	Multiple joint involvement	Nonfixed—early stages Fixed—later stages
		Osteoarthritis	Often single weight-bearing joint is affected	Nonfixed—in early stages improvement in joint range possible Fixed—in chronic condition, therefore passive stretch contraindicated
		Complicated fractures	Depends on severity and extent of trauma	Nonfixed or fixed
		Prolonged effects of flexor or extensor synergies on stump joints affected by a cerebrovascular accident	Multiple joint involvement	Can be fixed depending on the duration of the effect of the synergy
Skin Contractures	Surgical Scar Contractures	Adhesion of scar to underlying tissues restricting tissue mobility	Joint restriction rare	Nonfixed
	Hypertrophic Scarring	Tendency to develop after burns Fibrous tissue growth restricts tissue mobility to the extent that joint range can be affected	Joint involvement depends on the extent of burn trauma	Can be fixed following scarring Early post trauma contracture prevention is important

Fixed refers to contracture ranges that come to a bony or solid stop on testing.
Nonfixed refers to contracture ranges that demonstrate a "springy" or elastic end feel on testing.

Preexisting Muscle Tightness (Orthopedic). Preexisting muscle tightness may be apparent in patients who have a long-standing history of low back pain. One of the causative factors is a tight iliopsoas muscle that restricts hip range of motion.

The amputee experiences difficulty achieving hip extension. This is particularly significant for the transfemoral amputee. Range compensation affects the lumbar area, so that during ambulation a hip flexion contracture forces the amputee to either lumbar lordose (to accommodate for the muscle shortness) or to walk with trunk flexion to achieve the desired hip extension range for stabilizing the prosthetic knee joint.

If the transtibial amputee, prior to amputation surgery, had tight hip flexor muscles as well as tight hamstring muscles, the problem is intensified, creating *(See Fig. 2–35)* (owing to excess flexion in both joints) an apparent leg shortening. This will result in lateral trunk bending toward the amputated side during ambulation.

If a contracture combination involving lumbar lordosis and hip and knee flexion is evident, it probably cannot be corrected. The gait becomes tiring because the trunk demonstrates excessive anteroposterior swaying during gait. The body leans forward throughout the prosthetic stance phase and then arches in the lumbar spine to assist the prosthesis into the swing phase. This is, at times, accompanied by an increase in arm swing to assist leg acceleration and deceleration.

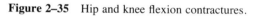

Figure 2–35 Hip and knee flexion contractures.

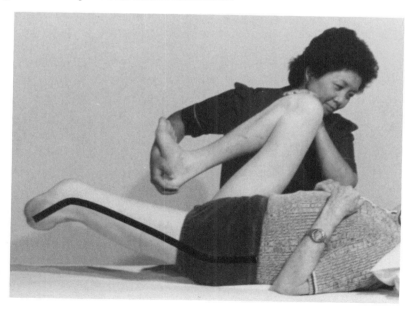

The patient who has a history of back problems and has previously been asymptomatic may experience an exacerbation of back problems owing to postural compensation during gait.

The contracture primarily affects muscle tissue and is nonfixed in nature. It responds well to controlled stretch techniques if only the hip is involved, but in multiple joint involvement, contracture treatment is often not successful because of excessive compensation in the joints around the one being stretched.

Preexisting Muscle Tightness (Neurological).   Spasticity on the side of the amputation is indicative of an increase in stump muscle tone owing to an increase in the excitability of the muscle spindle. Spasticity also decreases the functional movements of the stump. Added stress such as resisted movement or weight bearing can (depending on the stage of stroke recovery) cause the stump to draw into the dominant synergy (pattern of movement) (Brunnstrom, 1970). Because of this synergic pattern, all remaining joints in the stump are involved in the movement.

Initially, contractures resulting from spasticity are nonfixed, but as with orthopedic muscle tightness, the affected joints can become fixed if untreated.

Postoperative Soft Tissue Retractions (Orthopedic).   Different tissues respond to resection in distinctive ways. Skin and muscle, if severed, will retract, whereas bone retains its cut length.

These characteristics are considered during amputation surgery. Muscle tissues are prepared longer than the bone to provide enough length so that the soft tissues can be approximated over the distal bone end (Burgess, 1969; Tooms, 1980) without causing the sutures and tissues to be overstretched. The correct tissue tension and myoplasty provide the severed muscles with more controlled contractability and better proprioception, resulting in better function (Burgess, 1969; Tooms, 1980).

If, however, tissues retract further than anticipated following surgery, reduction in the joint range owing to soft tissue tightening can occur.

A postoperative soft tissue retraction contracture is nonfixed and responds well to conservative treatment provided excessive edema, which could limit movement, is not present. Passive stretching is contraindicated in cases where excessive edema is present.

Postoperative Soft Tissue Retraction (Neurological).   During amputation surgery the effects of the anesthetic cause nonspastic muscles to relax completely. Tension also subsides considerably in spastic muscles.

In amputation surgery on the stroke side, adequate stump tissue tension is estimated when suturing the severed opposing muscles to each other. However, it may happen that further tissue retraction is caused by increased spasticity postsurgically, drawing the residual limb into the dominant synergic pattern. Whether the dominant synergy is flexion or extension, there would be a resultant joint range restriction causing dysfunction in the gait pattern.

The postsurgical muscle retraction can indirectly act as a muscle spindle stimulus, thus increasing the tone or spasticity, even further limiting joint range motion; as a result of this, the degree of the contracture increases.

This increase in spasticity is part of a cycle of events whereby any movement of the body and/or residual limb puts tension on the muscle because the spastic muscle has lost the central nervous system inhibiting influence (Brunnstrom, 1970). The unopposed stimulus of moving the stump can cause the muscles of the stump to pull even more into the synergic pattern. This further motion again puts tension on the muscle, and the cycle is repeated. Thus a pathological pattern is set up around the remaining joints of the amputated limb, often resulting in muscle tissue shortening and contracture.

Contracture formation affects all remaining joints in the stump. They are nonfixed. Any sudden, intense stimulus should be avoided since it increases the synergic pattern and thus decreases functional movement.

Joint contractures are primarily bony in nature and involve the joint itself. The joint surfaces generate range limitations and adhesions or tightness in the joint capsule or ligaments, further solidifying joint range motions. On manual testing, the joint range will come to a firm sudden stop.

Joint Contractures

Joint contractures are usually fixed and are associated with either joint disease or trauma (e.g., fractured hip) and are, therefore, sometimes present in geriatric patients prior to amputation surgery.

Any forceful, passive effort to release fixed contractures may set up joint irritation or inflammation, thus further restricting the already limited joint range. Active muscle work is indicated for the muscles functioning around the contracted joint. The patient's own muscle power will not allow the joint to be forced beyond its restricted range capabilities.

Rheumatoid Arthritis. This disease can affect many joints, causing deformities as well as contractures. In early stages, the forming contracture is nonfixed. Fixation develops in later stages. A recent amputee who has rheumatoid arthritis needs detailed, holistic treatment considerations. A primary consideration is maintaining joint function for stump leverage. The prescription of a lightweight prosthesis is indicated since the weight of the prosthesis and weight bearing on the stump provide additional stress to pathological joints.

Osteoarthritis. Range limitations caused by osteoarthritis affect mainly weight-bearing joints. Surgical procedures such as osteotomies and hip or knee replacements are performed to provide pain relief to joints with degenerative changes. A secondary result of surgery is some permanent reduction in the range of motion of the affected joint. Passive stretch techniques are ineffective and contraindicated.

Often only one joint is affected, and contracture limitation, whether on the side of the amputation or present in the remaining extremity, will hinder gait performance.

Trauma.   Acute joint involvement following trauma depends on the nature of the accident that necessitated amputation surgery. Any fracture healing or surgical fixation for stabilization has treatment priority over mobilization techniques. Positioning and preventive rehabilitation measures are indicated.

In later stages, x-ray findings will help to indicate the potential for full joint function prior to initiating mobilization. Passive stretch in total joint fixation is contraindicated since resultant tissue tears would cause further intra- and extraarticular damage.

Prolonged Effects of Flexion and Extension Synergy.   Longstanding effects of marked spasticity involving the extremities affected by a stroke can restrict joint motion to such an extent that capsular tightness results and a fixed contracture develops. This will occur if a gentle, passive, maintained stretch has not been practiced regularly to maintain joint range as a preventive measure. An additional causative factor is that marked spasticity and the loss of normal volitional muscle control in the stroke-affected limb force joint inactivity.

Contractures affect proprioception, locomotion, and coordinated active as well as reflex movements.

Skin Contractures

Skin contractures can manifest themselves in the epidermis during wound healing. Scars have a tendency to adhere to the underlying fascia and muscle tissues. If scarring is superficial, more tissue elasticity is present. If deeper scarring takes place, skin mobility is reduced because adhesions, composed of fibrous tissue, have less elasticity and adhere to adjacent structures.

Surgical Scar Contractures.   Most surgical stump scars heal without complications. During healing, connective tissue replaces the severed skin. Scars are initially red, then bluish-purple, and in the end stage look whitish owing to the lack of pigmentation.

A contracted scar does not affect joint motion; therefore, the contracture is classified as nonfixed. Moderately tight scar tissues can be mobilized with conservative treatment methods.

Treatment is indicated since mobile stump soft tissues are more functional because of their ability to interface with the socket contours. There is also less tension on the scar, and skin breakdown is less likely to occur.

Hypertrophic Scarring.   Amputation surgery following severe burn trauma may result in stump problems that are caused by hypertrophic scarring. Problems arise when the scarring is not isolated to the surgical suture line but covers additional stump areas as well. Hypertrophic scars are raised and have increased vascularity (Larson et al., 1974).

Hypertrophic scarring can take up to one year to develop. Generally, in the initial posttrauma phase no scar contractures are present. Scarring becomes most active between 3 to 6 months following the burn (Larson et al., 1971, 1974). During this period, extreme caution in passive stretching is advised because any passive stretch may cause microtears at the scar base (which cannot be seen) and result in the development of more fibroblasts, which makes the scar less elastic and more intensely contracted.

Initially, scars are nonfixed. However, in later stages, hypertrophic scars can act like tight bands and restrict (depending on their position) joint range of motion, thus reducing stump function.

Precise identification of the nature of stump contractures is essential so that appropriate treatment methods can be applied.

Summary

During physical therapy treatment sessions, several approaches can be used to improve the nonfixed contracture and to maximize the efficiency of muscles acting around the fixed contracture. These include:

Specific Physical Therapeutic Treatment Measures

- prophylaxis (see Postoperative Care—Positioning, p. 70)
- pain relief
- manual stretch techniques
- active exercises
- ambulation
- splinting

A chart consisting of treatment considerations, techniques, and related clinical comments has been compiled to provide a clear outline of the various treatments.

(See Table 2–4)

The therapist must be aware of the baseline norms of range of movement in the joints prior to performing the assessment. A reliable reference for joint range and standardized measurement techniques can be found in *Joint Motion: Method of Measuring and Recording* (American Academy of Orthopedic Surgeons, 1965).

Measurement of Contractures

The therapist can use a goniometer or a tape measure (Mensch et al., 1982) to record ranges; the important point to remember is that fixed landmarks are essential to consistently measure progression in joint range improvement.

Clinical Comments. In the geriatric amputee, it is often more realistic to compare the stump joint ranges to those of the remaining leg, considering that limitations may be due to degenerative joint changes related to aging, other joint pathology, e.g., rheumatoid arthritis, or a decrease in the preamputation activity level. This may indicate that joint range decreases are generalized rather than specific to the joints of the amputation stump.

In planning long term goals, achieving for full range of movement in the affected joints is not always possible. Treatment emphasis should then be on attaining a functional range of movement so that future gait activities will require the least amount of energy expenditure possible.

Stump pain and, if present, phantom pain are contributing factors to contracture development (see Clinical Evaluation of Pain, p. 65).

Pain Relief

TABLE 2–4 Physical Therapeutic Treatment Approaches to Counteract Stump Contractures

Treatment Considerations	Techniques	Clinical Comments
Prophylaxis (See Postoperative Care—Positioning, p. 70)	Bed positioning firm mattress prone lying for transfemoral amputees Wheelchair positioning wheelchair board	Contractures develop because the amputee assumes a position of comfort which is usually flexion A firm mattress and sitting boards provide postural support counteracting contracture development Poor postural habits and lack of proper positioning may contribute to development of contractures Close liaison with nursing staff is vitally important to provide continuity in implementing contracture preventive measures
Pain Relief	Selected forms of moderate heat; ice; TENS; whirlpool; desensitizing methods; hold-relax techniques	Stump and/or phantom pain are contributing factors in contracture development Pain relief reduces muscle tension so that the stump can better tolerate stretch and exercises
Manual Stretch Techniques	Passive joint stretching Active joint stretching Contract—relax techniques	Stretching requires fixation above and below the joint being stretched and positioning of the body to prevent compensatory movements which would diminish the effect of the stretch. Should ONLY be done in the painfree range Stretching is only indicated in the nonfixed joint where tissue elasticity is able to accommodate stretch tension Stretching adversely affects fixed contractures causing joint irritation and can further decrease range of motion Scar mobilizations are practiced with two fingers (on either side of the scar). The fingers move simultaneously in a clockwise direction to avoid a separation pull on the scar An emollient may be used, on non weight-bearing areas to decrease uncomfortable skin friction
	Frictions	Frictions in hypertrophic scarring are used with EXTREME CAUTION over muscle tissue only (not over joint structures) Manual frictions may cause shearing which can easily lead to blistering and breakdown of tissue fibers An emollient is recommended as burned skin does not have normal oil and sweat glands
Active Exercises and Ambulation	Individual muscle reeducation programs active resisted Gait reeducation postural correction progression of weight bearing progression of gait aids Sensory feedback visual manual auditory EMG biofeedback	Active muscle contractions with emphasis on increasing strength and joint range of movement are effective in overcoming contractures Constant postural correction is necessary to prevent further contracture development and secondary compensatory problems Fixed contractures can be accommodated in the alignment of the prosthesis Walking with equal step length through the different phases of the gait cycle is most effective in stretching contractures in a natural way
Splinting	Bivalved cast Serial casting (plaster of Paris) Posterior backslab	Maintains joint range during the night Recommended only for single joint contractures. In stumps with two joint involvement, immobilizing one joint will cause the other joint to respond adversely to the added stretch on the muscle caused by the splint Occasionally used The backslab is held in position with an elastic bandage which still allows the knee to flex moderately because of bandage elasticity. This is not as effective in controlling joint positioning

To ease pain, the amputee assumes the position of greatest comfort, which too often is a flexion position. In this way the least amount of stress is exerted on the painful tissues. This is also true for the burn patient. Larson (1974) states that the position of comfort is the position of the contracture.

Pain relief reduces muscle tension and, therefore, is a prime treatment consideration. The painfree, contracted residual limb can better tolerate stretching and exercises.

Some pain can be relieved by utilizing different forms of moderate heat, ice, desensitizing techniques, and by applying transcutaneous electrical nerve stimulation (TENS) (see Desensitizing Techniques, p. 185).

Ultrasound may also be indicated to raise the temperature of the joint capsule, thus increasing extensibility; therefore, there may be a better chance of decreasing the contracture by stretching (Mital et al., 1971). However, temperature altering modalities must be selected with great caution in the dysvascular stump since the tissues are often unable to cope with sudden temperature changes.

These modalities are all soothing, provide an analgesic effect, increase circulation, and promote healing. Severe pain is treated with prescribed medication.

Manual Stretch Techniques

Stump joint stretching, which is often applied to achieve a full joint range of motion, can be practiced in different ways. It is somewhat forceful in that manual pressure is applied; however, it is an effective treatment approach. It must always be carried out within a painfree range to avoid tearing of tissues and further flexion that could result from a painful stretch stimulus (Kottke, 1966; Mensch et al., 1982).

Muscles may be prepared for stretch by giving moderate heat to provide comfort and increase circulation and by correctly positioning the patient for the stretching technique. The therapist stabilizes the patient so that only the contracted joint is stretched.

Passive Stretching. Passive stretch must be applied to a relaxed residual limb. The stretch is most effective if performed with moderate tension over a prolonged period as opposed to an intense stretch of short duration (Kottke, 1966). The controlled, gentle stretch is increased to the extent that the patient can tolerate. It is maintained and then released to allow for relaxation. The whole hand provides equal comfortable pressure. Pressure exerted by digging the fingers into the tissues is painful and is to be avoided because the muscles will contract against the painful stimulus; thus rendering the stretch ineffective.

(See Fig. 2–36)

Active Assisted Stretching. The amputee actively moves the joint to be stretched through the existing joint range. On reaching the restricted end range position, the amputee is encouraged to try to continue this motion further actively to increase the existing range. The therapist assists the active motion by simultaneously stretching in the same direction.

(See Fig. 2–37)

Figure 2–36   Passive stretching.

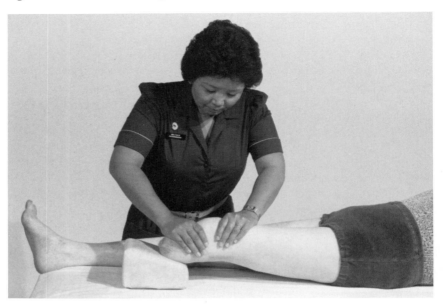

Figure 2–37   Active assisted stretching.

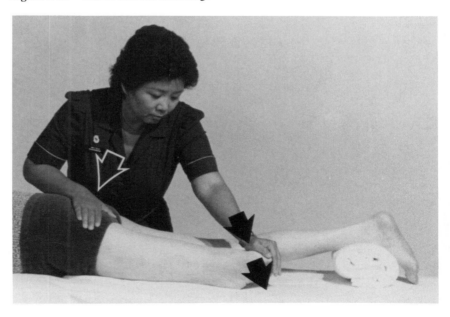

Hold–Relax Technique.   The hold–relax technique will facilitate greater relaxation of the antagonists. Strong contraction is followed by complete relaxation. This produces a decrease in tension in the antagonists; therefore, they are better prepared to allow the agonists to increase the desired range of motion (Gardiner, 1981).

(See Fig. 2–38)

Example: Knee Flexion Contracture.   The joint is actively positioned at the extreme of its extension capability. The therapist applies manual resistance to obtain a strong isometric contraction of the antagonists (hamstrings). Following this strong hamstring contraction, time must be allowed for complete hamstring relaxation. The amputee then attempts to actively extend the knee to its maximum. An increase in extension range is expected because of the decrease in tension in the hamstrings, the antagonists.

Clinical Note (Orthopedic).   Stretching of preexisting muscle shortness can be somewhat more vigorous, while postsurgical muscle tightness or tissue retraction has to be stretched more gently, due to the healing of the surgical suture. Also, postsurgical stump edema may be present and may restrict joint movement as well. Edematous joint stiffness, does not respond to stretch.

Contractures caused by ligamentous or capsular tightening may be effectively treated by using mobilization techniques as outlined by Maitland (1970) in *Peripheral Manipulation*. The problem that becomes most evident when working with the amputation stump is the lack of distal control owing to the missing part.

Figure 2–38   Hold–relax technique.

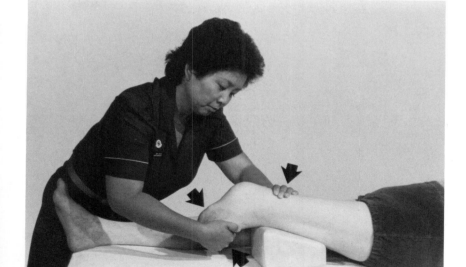

Careful evaluation of the feasibility of using these techniques must be made to ensure that total control of the movements can be maintained at all times during treatment.

Clinical Note (Neurological). A quick or phasic stretch would, by its stimulus, increase the muscle tone and, with it, the intensity of the spasticity. Thus, by repeating the quick stretch stimulus, contracture development is encouraged.

A tonic or gently maintained stretch will facilitate a reduction in pathological tone. Only permanently reduced spasticity will counteract muscle joint contractures of this nature. The aim in early postoperative CVA stump treatments is to maintain joint mobility.

The effective tonic stretching for amputees with long term stump spasticity may be facilitated by several types of muscle relaxant drugs, which inhibit pathological tone in muscles, e.g., dantrolene sodium. This medication is a skeletal muscle relaxant that diminishes spasticity by acting on the motor end plate of spastic muscles and not by acting as a central neuromuscular blocking agent. Thus, total loss of muscle function does not occur (Canadian Pharmaceutical Association, 1982).

Summary. Graduated stretch must be combined with positioning and active muscle contractions within the patient's tolerance to stimulate stump activity.

Stretch Positions

It is important that both amputee and therapist are positioned correctly to stabilize the joints proximal to the one being stretched. This is necessary to eliminate compensatory motion by other body segments that could reduce the stretch effect.

The relaxation phase is equally important. Complete muscle relaxation between stretching can be supplemented by gently massaging proximally and distally to the joint being stretched.

Hip Stretching. Two positions can be utilized to achieve effective stretching of the hip flexor muscles.

Side Lying. The transfemoral amputee lies on the sound side and bends the remaining leg at hip and knee level. This provides a wider, more secure base for stability in the side-lying position. The therapist can also kneel directly behind the amputee at hip level, lean forward, and fix with one hand the remaining leg by holding the flexed knee in position. The flexed position of the remaining leg and the hip support provided by the therapist's posterior kneeling position will eliminate spinal movement. The other hand is placed on the anterior distal aspect of the stump and directs the stretch into hip extension.

(See Fig. 2–39)

(See Fig. 2–40)

Postural fixation ensures an isolated hip joint stretch and prevents lumbar movement that would diminish the stretch effect. The stretch direction controlled

Figure 2–39 Hip stretching in side lying.

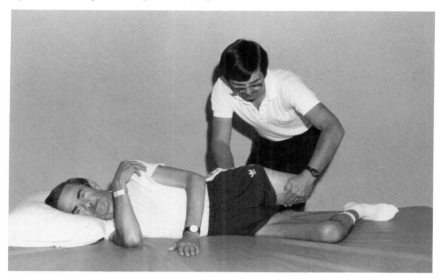

Figure 2–40. Hip stretching in side lying: a more forceful approach.

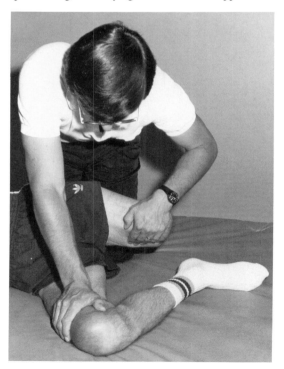

by the therapist can accommodate combinations of movement, including extension–internal rotation or extension–external rotation.

The side-lying position permits the therapist to exert an intensive controlled stretch on the hip flexor muscles and also allows for resisting hip extension to increase muscle strength for the extensor muscle group.

Prone Lying. This position places both hips in a neutral position. The foot of the remaining leg overhangs the treatment table to prevent excessive lumbar lordosis. The therapist places one hand over the buttocks, stabilizing the pelvis. The other hand cradles the stump end on its anterior medial or anterior lateral aspect to give directional guidance to the desired joint range movement.

(See Fig. 2–41)

Knee Stretching. Effective knee joint stretching can be practiced with the amputee in the sitting, supine, or prone position. The therapist selects the desired position.

Sitting and Supine. If the patella is adherent to the underlying structures and the range of motion in the knee joint is affected, patellar mobility is tested. Passive patellar mobilization is performed in preparation for stretching the knee (Maitland, 1970; Mensch et al., 1982).

(See Fig. 2–42)

The therapist can also use opposing hand positions for the actual joint stretch by giving an anterior, downward pressure on the femur with one hand while exerting an upward pressure on the posterior–distal end of the transtibial stump with the other hand to accomplish knee extension. The hand positions are reversed if the aim of the passive stump stretching is to achieve knee flexion (rare).

(See Fig. 2–43)

Figure 2–41   Hip stretching in prone lying.

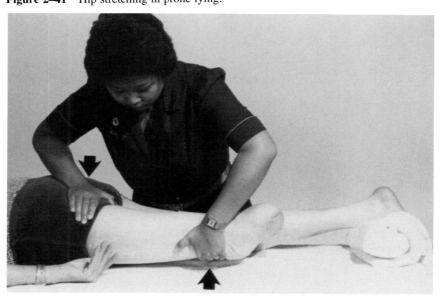

Figure 2–42   Patellar mobilizations.

Figure 2–43   One method of knee stretching in supine position.

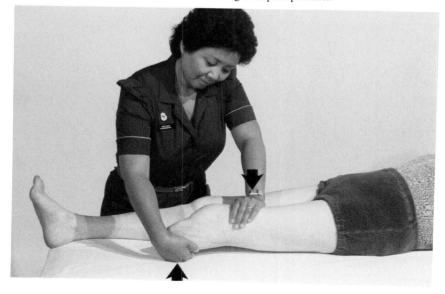

Prone.   The prone position is utilized when a combination of hip and knee flexion contractures is present. By prone lying, the hips are placed in a neutral position. The pelvis is stabilized when the therapist leans over the patient and exerts forearm pressure on the hip joints. The other hand then directs a steady downward pressure over the posterior distal aspect of the transtibial stump. Consistent pressure is needed over the pelvis to prevent hip flexion since the hamstrings are stretched at the knee level. A bony knee should have a towel as extra padding. Without the padding the amputee will feel an uncomfortable counterpressure above the patella during stretch, which would cause opposition to the stretch because of pain.

(See Fig. 2–44)

Clinical Note (Neurological).   The therapist has to be selective in applying stretch techniques to the amputee with the stroke on the amputated side. The same positions can be utilized as for the strictly orthopedic amputee. However, the therapist must carefully evaluate the patient's balance in sitting. Lack of sitting balance may prevent the patient from maintaining this position during the application of stretch techniques, and in prone lying care must be taken to ensure that the affected shoulder is not overstretched by incorrect positioning of the arm.

Frictions to Mobilize Scar Adhesions

Manual frictions, to break down adhesions, are practiced with both index or middle fingers. The fingers are placed in position on either side of the scar, and over a small area deep pressure is applied parallel to the adherent scar tissue. Simultaneous circular motions, with both fingers moving in the same direction,

Figure 2–44   Knee stretching in prone position.

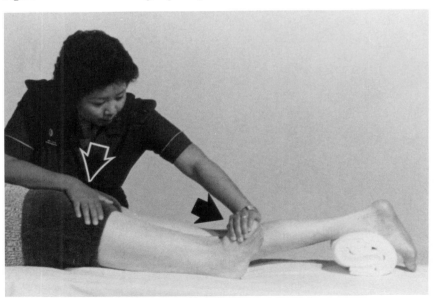

are applied. In this way, the scar is mobilized by deep frictional motions and is, at *(See Fig. 2–45)* the same time, protected from a separation pull that would occur if frictions were carried out with the fingers moving in opposite directions.

The use of an emollient is advisable; it lubricates the stump skin and makes the procedure more comfortable for the amputee. It also increases the tactile sensation helping the therapist to judge the intensity with which the frictions can be applied.

Surgical Scars. Most stump scars heal so that soft tissue mobility is maintained. However, sometimes during healing, scar adhesions develop, restricting soft tissue mobility around the scar areas. These adhesions can be treated with ultrasound and whirlpool. Both ultrasound and whirlpool increase the circulation, whereas ultrasound also increases the collagen stretch properties of the muscle fasciae (Mital et al., 1971; Murray et al., 1982). These modalities are utilized prior to applying frictions.

Hypertrophic Scarring. Conservative treatment of burn scars needs special attention. The treatment approach concentrates mainly on contracture prevention. Initially, postsurgical joint contractures are not present since mainly skin is involved. Therefore, maintaining joint range has priority. Other procedures such as skin grafting defer active exercises temporarily. Splinting should be avoided if at all possible unless range of motion cannot be actively achieved. However, if a splint is needed to maintain joint range during rest periods, it should be frequently removed to permit active motion (Larson et al., 1974).

Frictions applied WITH EXTREME CAUTION are a selective treatment modality and should ONLY be attempted over muscle tissue, NEVER over joint structures. Manual frictions cause shearing that can easily lead to blistering and

Figure 2–45   Mobilizing scar tissue.

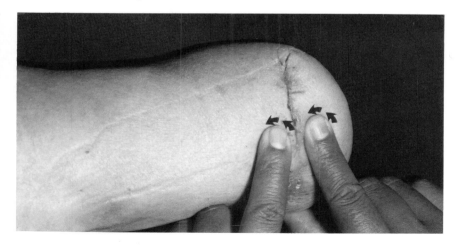

breakdown of fibers of the scarred dermis (Larson et al., 1974). The use of emollients is indicated because burned skin does not have normal oil and sweat glands. The emollient will also aid in reducing itchiness that is common on dry skin areas.

Joint contractures that may later develop may not necessarily be related to skin burns or hypertrophic scarring but may develop because of extensive soft tissue destruction, which causes tissue fibrosis (La Borde et al., 1978).

Prophylaxis provided by good positioning, utilization of splints if indicated, skeletal traction, and pressure dressings is the best method of treatment (Larson et al., 1979). Following treatment, a custom made Jobst sock is worn over the stump. The constant gentle pressure (approximately 25 mmHg) reduces and controls the severity of hypertrophic scar formation (Larson et al., 1974).

Clinical Note.   Emollients with a petroleum jelly base destroy the fibers of the Jobst sock. Cocoa butter is probably the best choice.

Summary

Stretching is indicated in the nonfixed joint contracture where tissue elasticity can accommodate stretch tension. Fixed contractures are permanent and do not respond to stretch. However, muscles that act within the existing joint range can be strengthened. To avoid adverse muscle reactions, several short periods of stretching per day within pain limits with moderate stretch are more beneficial than one long intensive stretching session (Kottke et al., 1966). All stretch treatment techniques aim to increase joint range of motion so that muscle forces can then act on the joint to eventually overcome stump contractures.

All passive stretching should be followed immediately by active exercises, and it should be stressed that the amputee should practice actively and intensively to maintain the joint end range achieved during the stretch. This should be done periodically throughout the day.

Active Exercises

Stump exercises, isometric, active, and resisted, are most important since they strengthen the stump muscles, improve stump leverage, increase joint ranges, and thus decrease the degree of contracture and prevent further contracture development. Therefore, they improve gait. The stump exercise program depends on the tolerance and capabilities of the amputee. The activity level of the amputee has to be carefully monitored since overfatigue may have adverse effects on the joint being treated.

Ambulation

"Walking a contracture out" is a frequently used term. Supervised ambulation with a prosthetic training unit is the most effective way of reducing joint contractures in amputation stumps.[1] The main advantage of walking in contracture treatment is that it provides a functional, alternating stretch and relaxation on the contracted joint as the prosthetic side goes through the different phases of the gait cycle.

A transtibial amputee with a knee flexion contracture experiences the greatest stretch on the knee joint from prosthetic heel contact to foot flat. Following this phase, the knee first flexes slightly (reducing the stretch) but extends again in midrange within the gait cycle. The second stretch has a lesser effect than the first.

A transfemoral amputee experiences the greatest stretch on the hip joint from prosthetic heel-off to toe-off.

Close liaison with the prosthetist is necessary to provide optimum alignment that will give sufficient stability while allowing maximum stretch on the contracted joint(s).

Clinical Note. Therapists should be aware that joint stabilization, as used in stretching techniques in static positions to prevent compensatory body movements, is not present during gait. The interaction of muscle groups acting on the trunk and pelvis as well as on the contracted joint becomes evident, and the patient will demonstrate postural deviations resulting from joint range limitations.

Various sensory feedback techniques (auditory, visual, tactile) are utilized in gait reeducation to facilitate joint stretching. Two examples have been selected.

Sensory Stimulation Techniques

EMG Biofeedback. EMG biofeedback is a practical tool in aiding muscle reeducation. It can be used to demonstrate to the amputee, by means of an audiosignal, if the contracted muscle is working to its maximum, if more muscle work is required, and if complete muscle relaxation is being achieved.

(See Fig. 2–46)

Figure 2–46 Muscle reeducation using EMG biofeedback.

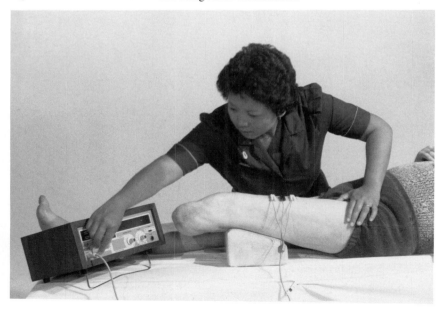

(See Fig. 2–47)

Tactile Stimulation. During gait practice, manual resistance applied in an anteroposterior direction on the pelvis teaches the amputee the pelvic thrust. This motion is important since the hip forward motion during gait controls pelvic balance and aids in transferring the center of gravity from one support leg to the other. This pelvic thrust is extremely difficult for an amputee who has a hip flexion contracture. If the pelvic thrust is not practiced, the hip "lags" behind, keeping the joint in flexion. This promotes the stooped trunk position and places the center of gravity in front of the hips, overstretching the hip extensors and requiring the quadriceps muscle to support the body for a prolonged period of time.

Manual resistance behind the head will encourage an erect posture that then counterbalances the often stooped trunk position that the amputee with the hip flexion contracture usually demonstrates (see Conventional Sensory Feedback Techniques, p. 266). The upright position balances the body dynamics and thus counteracts the flexion contracture.

Manual resistance applied at the same time behind the head and in front of the hips provides a directional tactile stimulus for postural correction.

Figure 2–47   Postural correction using tactile stimulation.

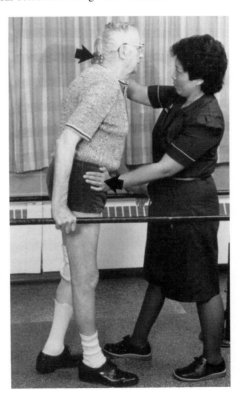

The purpose of splinting is   Splinting

- to maintain joint range
- to counteract contractures
- to give support
- to permit an undisturbed wound healing environment

The application of splints in contracture treatment is sometimes helpful, but it is not practiced routinely.

Transfemoral amputees with contractures are not splinted. Transtibial amputees with a knee flexion contracture may be considered for splint application provided the contracture affects *only* the knee joint. If the hip joint is involved as well, immobilization of the knee joint will only cause further hip flexion (hamstring action) because the distance the contracted muscle can accommodate is already taken up by the corrected knee position.

Splints should preferably be used only at night, and active exercises should be encouraged during the day to prevent joint stiffening.

Indications.   If a transtibial amputee sleeps in a fetal position, the range of motion achieved during the day is lost at night. A back slab is usually satisfactory. The back slab is constructed so that the amputee's *bandaged* stump is placed on the splint. In this way, stump edema remains under control even if the amputee removes the splint through the night.

Serial Casting.   This refers to the succession of cast fabrications that will adapt to the degree of contracture improvement achieved. The casts are bivalved for frequent removal and provide resting comfort during the night. This technique is time consuming but is better accepted by the amputee because the plaster of Paris shells provide more comfort than the bandaged back slabs.

Summary.   Whichever splinting method is used, it is important that the support extends at least two-thirds of the way up the thigh. Short splints dig into the tissue, cause irritation, and permit knee mobility in the splint.

An attempt has been made to classify contractures and to suggest physical   Conclusion
therapeutic treatment methods that can be beneficial in contracture prophylaxis and in treating existing contractures in lower extremity amputations.

Every effort should be made to initially treat contractures with conservative methods. However, if decreased joint ranges interfere with rehabilitation or if they cause pain during ambulation, or if the range loss is excessive, then surgical intervention is indicated to correct the deficit.

American Academy of Orthopedic Surgeons. *Joint Motion: Method of Measuring and*   References
   Recording. Chicago, Illinois, 1965, 46–66.
Brunnstrom, S. "Synergies. Recovery Stages and Evaluation Procedures." *Movement Therapy in Hemiplegia.* New York: Harper and Row, 1970, 3, 34–37.

Burgess, E.M., Romano, R.L., and Zettl, J.H. Below-knee Amputation Surgery. Above-knee Amputation Surgery. *The Management of Lower-extremity Amputations.* Washington, D.C.: U.S. Government Printing Office, 1969, 16–19, 45–46.

Canadian Pharmaceutical Association. *Compendium of Pharmaceuticals and Specialties.* Ottawa, 1982, 142.

Gardiner, M.D. "Rhythmic Stabilization." *The Principles of Exercise Therapy.* London: Bell and Hyman, 1981, 88–90.

Holliday, P.J. "Non-prosthetic Care." In J.P. Kostuik and R. Gillespie, eds. *Amputation Surgery and Rehabilitation: The Toronto Experience.* New York: Churchill Livingstone, 1981, 250.

Kaltenborn, F.M. "Types of Bone Motion. *Manual Therapy for the Extremity Joints.* Oslo: Olat Norlis Bokhandel, 1976, 8–9.

Kottke, F.J., Pauley, D.L., and Ptak, R.A. "The Rationale for Prolonged Stretching for Correction of Shortening of Connective Tissue. *Archives of Physical Medicine and Rehabilitation, 47* (June 1966): 245–253.

LaBorde, T.C., and Meier, R.H. III. "Amputations Resulting from Electrical Injury: A Review of 22 Cases. *Archives of Physical Medicine and Rehabilitation. 59* (March 1978): 134–137.

Larson, D.L., Abston, S., Evans, E.B., Dobrkovsky, M., and Linares, H.A. "Techniques for Decreasing Scar Formation and Contractures in the Burned Patient." *The Journal of Trauma, 11* no. 10 (1971): 807–821.

Larson, D.L., Abston, S., Willis, B., Linares, H., Dobrkovsky, M., Evans, E.B., and Lewis, S.R. "Contractures and Scar Formation in the Burn Patient." *Clinics in Plastic Surgery, 1,* no. 4 (October 1974): 653–666.

Larson, L., Huang, T., Linares, H., Dobrkovsky, M., Baur, P., and Parks, D. "Prevention and Treatment of Scar Contracture." In C.P. Artz, J.A. Moncrief, and B.A. Pruitt, eds. *Burns, a Team Approach.* Philadelphia, Pa.: W.B. Saunders, 1979, 466–491.

Maitland, G.D. "Lower Limb." *Peripheral Manipulation,* 2nd ed. London: Butterworth, 1970, 5, 50, 203–274.

Mensch, G., and Ellis, P. "Contractures." In S.N. Banerjee, ed. *Rehabilitation Management of Amputees.* Baltimore: Williams & Wilkins, 1982, 213–216.

Mital, M.A., and Pierce, D.S. "Contractures." *Amputees and their Prosthesis.* Boston: Little, Brown 1971, 175–176.

Murray, D., and Fischer, F.R. "Phantom Limb Sensation." *Handbook of Amputations and Prostheses.* Ottawa: University of Ottawa, 1982, 39–40.

Tooms, R.E. "Amputations." In A. Edmonson and A.H. Crenshaw, eds. *Campbell's Operative Orthopedics.* St. Louis, Mo.: C.V. Mosby, 1980, 845–846.

Notes   1. MacMillan, A.H. Personal communication, 1978.

STUMP COMPLICATIONS AND CONSERVATIVE TREATMENT INDICATIONS

Most stump complications occur during the period of stump maturation and are related to the progression of healing, the amputee's general health status, and environmental factors. Other stump problems may develop later and can be caused by intensive prosthetic use. It is the problem stump that needs extra care and treatment consideration. Stump complications, regardless of their severity, affect the amputee both physically and psychologically. They restrict and/or delay ambulation and, consequently, lengthen the rehabilitation time.

Most of the commonly identified stump complications will respond well to selective application of conservative physical therapy treatment measures.

For clarity, stump problems can be broadly divided into three groups

- problems related to delayed surgical wound healing
- problems pertaining to stump shape and joint range
- problems caused at the stump–socket interface and by weight bearing.

Factors Contributing to Stump Complications

(See Table 2–5)

A distinct separation of these groups is impossible because several components (physiological, pathological, biomechanical, and external), all interrelated, constitute causative factors. Available vascularity is a major determining component in stump healing. Stump pain, localized or generalized and varying in nature and severity, also accompanies most of these conditions and affects treatment progression.

Treatment decisions are based on the clinical assessment of the nature and factors contributing to the stump complication. Close liaison with other team members (physicians, nurses, prosthetists) is necessary to ensure optimum care.

Delayed healing is a broad term used to describe a range of superficial to deep skin and tissue lesions that can be either clean or infected. Underlying causes of delayed or nonhealing of the stump are:

Delayed Healing

- vascular insufficiency
- external forces exerted on the stump (correctly or incorrectly applied from early weight bearing or localized socket pressure)
- loss of or reduced skin sensation

Conservative physical therapeutic treatment techniques used to treat stump wounds aim toward increasing circulation and thereby promoting healing. These include:

- ultraviolet irradiation
- whirlpool bath
- wound taping
- stump immobilization

These treatments should be coordinated with the prescribed wound care techniques followed by the nurses.

Ultraviolet (UV) rays have a physiological effect on the skin. Depending on the dosage, they increase circulation, cause erythema, and kill bacterial growth. Wavelengths between 315 and 280 nm (UVB, erythemal effect) and less than 280 nm (UVC, germicidal effect) are the most beneficial for stimulating wound healing (Diffey, 1982).

Ultraviolet Irradiation

Stumps that have clean but slow-healing wounds will benefit from a daily suberythemal dose to the entire stump. This low dosage of general irradiation:

Clean Wounds

- increases the superficial circulation
- stimulates growth of granulation tissues

TABLE 2–5 Possible Clinical Manifestations of the Problematic Stump

Delayed Surgical Wound Healing		Factors Affecting Biomechanics		Prosthetic Problems	
Simple	**Complex**	**Stump Shape**	**Joint Range**	**Stump-Socket Interface**	**Weight Bearing**
open stitches (clean)	open suture line superficial deep infected sinus drainage ulceration necrosis	edema bulbous soft tissues redundant tissues skin folds adductor roll adhesions skin grafts	extensive scarring contractures preexisting joint pathologies spasticity	pressure areas abrasions blisters contact dermatitis verrucose hyperplasia sebaceous cysts	bone end sensitivity painful neuroma

Stronger generalized dosages are contraindicated, particularly for the dysvascular stump. Overexposure of slow-healing areas with marginal blood supply can cause destruction of tissues rather than stimulation of granulation tissue growth.

Infections and Ulcers. Infected, open wounds are irradiated locally with *(See Fig. 2–48)* calculated erythemal dosages:

- to destroy bacteria
- to provide a clean wound base for granulation tissue growth

The irradiation dosages (up to an E4) are given to the central area of the wound with the surrounding tissues masked (Scott, 1983) to prevent damage to the granulating wound edges by the high erythemal level.

Sinuses. Wound sinuses and cavities respond well to ultraviolet irradiation (Scott, 1983) because wound healing can be stimulated (UVC) at the level of the deeper structures.

Figure 2–48 Infected open wound.

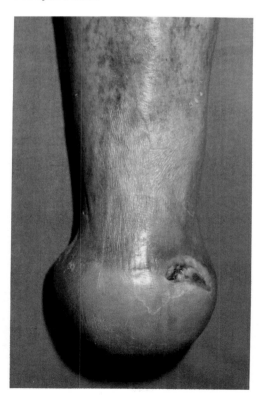

The Kromayer lamp is used for irradiating sinuses because the variety of shapes and sizes of quartz applicators permits effective sinus penetration (Diffey 1982). This technique is indicated only if the applicator can reach the base of the sinus so that healing occurs from the base outward while the sinus remains open to permit drainage.

(see Fig. 2–49)

Clinical Comments

- Irradiation dosages must be carefully calculated and recorded.
- Any topical medications or solutions (see Liaison with Nurse, p. 170) that have been applied to the stump wound must be removed prior to the ultraviolet exposure to allow for maximum penetration of the ultraviolet rays.
- Ultraviolet rays do not penetrate through Op-site® dressings (see Wound Dressings, p. 172).
- Eye protection must be used by patients and staff during treatment.

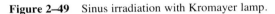

Figure 2–49   Sinus irradiation with Kromayer lamp.

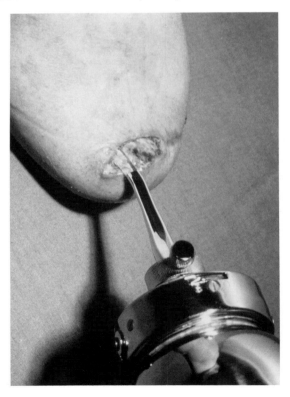

Whirlpool bath immersion is used:

- to stimulate stump circulation
- to help desensitize the tender stump
- to provide gentle rinsing debridement of the wound
- to disinfect the wound
- to contribute to a general feeling of well being

Clinical Comments. 1. Water temperature control is vitally important since the peripheral limb segments are cooler because of decreased vascularity. If the water temperature is too hot, stump circulation in amputations caused by vascular insufficiency may not be sufficient to dissipate the heat and may cause circulatory embarrassment or a burn, delaying rather than aiding the healing process[1] (Holliday, 1981). Clinically, the optimum water temperature for immersion of amputation stumps should not exceed body temperature. In extremely cold stumps, the temperature should be even slightly below body temperature.

2. The long low tub whirlpool bath is selected because the patient can be comfortably seated during treatment. Within certain limits the patient can exercise the stump and the remaining leg during immersion. In this position, the stump is not held in a dependent position.

The high-seated whirlpool bath, sometimes used for treatment of extremities, should not be used for several reasons:

- The amputation stump cannot be fully immersed.
- The stump is held in a dependent position, thus contributing to edema formation.
- The whirlpool seats are not comfortable and, therefore, the amputee is not relaxed during treatment.

3. For open wounds, Savlon® solution 1:100 is added to the water. The water turbulence produced by the air jet aids in debridement of the wound and Savlon, which has germicidal and disinfectant qualities, aids in wound cleansing and helps to prevent cross infection.

4. Extreme care must be taken to avoid cross infection when using whirlpool baths for other patients. An antiseptic cleanser dispensed through a spray hose (e.g., Microspray®) must be used to thoroughly clean the tub, the air jet, and the drain areas before and after treatment. Frequent swabs taken by the infection control officer will ensure the efficiency of the method of disinfection.

5. The stump is immediately wrapped in a sterile towel after whirlpool treatment.

6. During all wound care treatments, the physical therapist must practice sterile or other special techniques applicable for each wound.

This technique of wound support is indicated for suture line splits and small open wounds. It ensures that the amputee can proceed to ambulation activities without further traumatizing the stump tissues. The taping approximates the suture line and stabilizes the surrounding stump tissues.

Steri-Strips™ are used for taping. They must be of sufficient length to maintain their position. The use of regular adhesive tape which contains zinc oxide is strongly discouraged because it causes superficial abrasions on fragile skin when it is removed.

Suture Line Taping.   Equally spaced Steri-Strips™ are applied in parallel. These are stabilized distal to the scar line with a proximal tension pull applied over the wound to approximate the wound edges. Cross taping the Steri-Strips both anteriorly and posteriorly holds the suture line tape in place.

(See Fig. 2–50)

Wound Support.   A small round open wound can be reinforced by criss-crossing the tape. This permits all tissues to move simultaneously and avoids further tissue separation and shearing on weight bearing. It can be compared to bracing wounds.[2]

(See Fig. 2–51)

By utilizing these techniques, controlled weight-bearing activities can continue without further damage to the healing area from possible increased separation of the wound on weight bearing.

Stump Immobilization

In early postoperative stages, when it becomes evident that healing will not occur by primary intention, the rigid dressing is reapplied. However, some physicians choose to attempt healing by eliminating the rigid dressing and prescribing conservative therapy treatment methods in combination with the application of topical medication. If this course of action is not successful and stump healing remains particularly precarious, the rigid plaster dressing can be

Figure 2–50   Suture line taping.

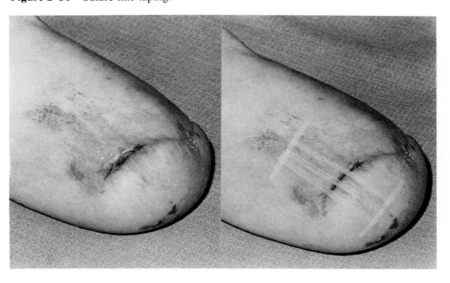

Figure 2–51 Wound support provided by criss-cross taping.

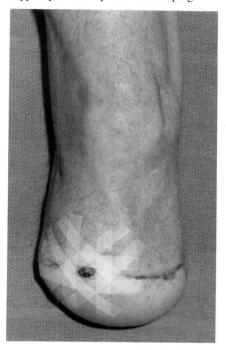

reapplied (see Cast Position and Suspension, p. 56). This non-weight-bearing resting cast:

- promotes healing by protecting the wound from external trauma
- controls edema
- prevents tissue mobility

The amputee is now able to continue with an exercise program, maintaining and increasing muscle strength and range of motion in the other extremities. Static exercises for the stump encourage muscle pumping action against the cast wall. This will promote healing by increasing the stump circulation and will also counteract the formation of edema.

Windowed Cast. Occasionally, a window is incorporated into the cast over the wound[2] (Mensch et al., 1982). This provides easy access to the wound for specialized care by both the nurse and the physical therapist.

Clinical Comments. Dressings under the window have to be of the same thickness after each treatment. The cast window closure must be both correctly aligned and replaced with equal pressure to prevent window edema or excessive compression over the already sensitive wound area.

(See Fig. 2–52)

(See Fig. 2–53)

Figure 2–52   Windowed cast open for wound care.

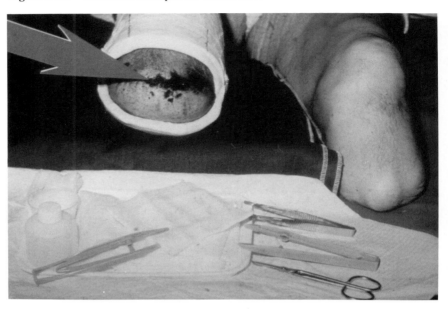

Adequate suspension control is imperative for the cast to maintain correct position. This prevents further trauma to the stump from friction and/or distal edema caused by cast rotation and/or slippage.

Liaison With the Nurse

Close liaison with the nursing staff is indicated throughout all phases of amputation rehabilitation. This is especially important when planning treatment for the problem stump. A coordinated program prevents unnecessary exposure of the stump wound. For instance, ultraviolet irradiation, or whirlpool bath treatments should coincide with the nursing schedule for wound care. Preferably, the nurse should come to the physical therapy department to provide immediate wound care following treatment. However, if this is not feasible, the patient should be returned to the ward with a sterile towel protecting the wound. There, further prescribed wound care can be immediately completed.

Nursing care may include selective physician-prescribed topical medications to further stimulate wound healing and/or oral antibiotics to combat any infection that may be present.

Examples of Prescribed Topical Medications

Some common topical medications that may be used are

1. *Hygeol*™ (dilute sodium hypochlorite solution 1%).
   Class: antiseptic, disinfectant.
   Use: wet compress or soaks.
   Recommended concentration: 1:20.

Figure 2–53   Closure after wound care.

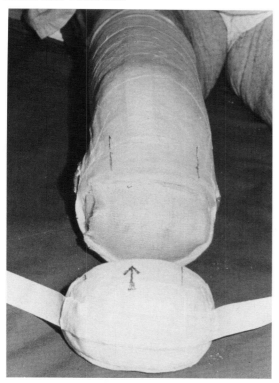

Other concentrations are requested, i.e., 1:12 or 1:16, although these have no
   real advantage over the common concentration of 1:20.
2. *Savlon®* (chlorhexidine gluconate-cetrimide).
   Concentrate contains (chlorhexidine gluconate 1.5% w/v and cetrimide 15%
   w/v.
   Class: germicide, detergent.
   Uses according to various concentrations:

Concentration	Use
1:100 (aqueous)	Disinfection of skin
1:30 (aqueous)	Cleaning contaminated abrasions

3. *Proviodine*™, *Betadine* (povidone-iodine).
   Class: antiseptic (iodophor).
   Supplied as 10% solution, 7.5% detergent scrub.
   Others: ointment, spray.
   Use: preop skin preparation, also postop wound disinfection, use as swab or
      scrub.
   Caution: known sensitivity to iodine, do not use with Hygeol.

4. *Hydrogen Peroxide*.
   Usual concentration 3%.
   Use: wound disinfection.
   Applied as wet compress or soaks.
5. *Cicatrin*™.
   Class: antibiotic, tissue healant.
   Supplied as a powder or cream.
   Use: minor wounds or burns.
   Note: inactivated by Hygeol™.
6. *Elase*™ (fibrinolysin-desoxyribonuclease).
   Elase™: Chloromycetin.
   Travase (sutilains ointment).
   Class: enzymatic debriding agent.
   Use: liquefaction and dissolution of purulent tissue exudates.
   Supplied as ointments (Elase™ also available in powder form) that must be
       stored in refrigerator.
   Dosage: apply topically one or more times/day.
   Enzymatic activity diminished and probably exhausted after 24 hr.
   Avoid using concurrently with Hygeol™.
7. *Debrisan*™ (Dextranomer).
   Class: wound cleansing agent.
   Use: cleansing or draining exudative wounds.
   Useful for serous rather than purulent wounds.
   Supplied as tiny spherical porous beads that will absorb liquid (1 gm of
       Debrisan™ will absorb 4 times its weight in fluid).
   Wounds treated with Debrisan should be thoroughly rinsed with saline between
       applications.

The therapist must know the prescription protocol to correctly integrate physical therapeutic treatment. For example, if Cicatrin™, Elase™, or Debrisan™ are used on the wound, they must be removed completely to ensure the desired depth of ultraviolet penetration.

Wound Dressings

The stump wound can be protected by:

Dry sterile gauze. This cover is used as protection over superficial wounds. The gauze, at times, is beneficial in mechanically debriding infected tissues. The moist slough will adhere to the gauze and thus be lifted away with each dressing change.

Telfa™ film. Telfa™ does not stick to the wound and is used to protect the newly forming granulation tissues during wound care.

Wet compresses. Compresses soaked with medicated solutions can be applied during dressing changes. The particularly "dirty" wound is packed for approximately 20 min with the solution-soaked gauze for more effective cleansing of the area. The compress is then removed, and a dressing is applied for wound protection. The wet compress is not usually left in place for longer periods because some medications (e.g., Hygeol™) can have adverse effects on the surrounding healthy skin.

Op-site® dressings. Op-site® acts as a substitute synthetic skin and is not removed as frequently as conventional dressings. The lesion heals by containing the serous exudate under the Op-site® film. It protects the lesion from external contamination and prevents crust formation by keeping the surface of the lesion moist and pliable (Op-site® product information pamphlet). Op-site® acts much like the skin over a blister, allowing healing from within.

(See Fig. 2–54)

Most physical therapeutic wound healing modalities, in liaison with meticulous nursing care, are effective. If more severe wound healing problems occur, such as:

Summary

- severe infection
- necrosis (cell death)
- gangrene (cell death caused by ischemia in conjunction with bacterial infection)
- bone protrusion (absence of soft skin over the bone end)

(See Fig. 2–55)

(See Fig. 2–56)

then surgical intervention becomes a consideration in achieving secondary stump closure and healing. However, during the interim stage, physical therapy wound healing techniques can attempt to help keep the stump wound tissues clean in preparation for further tissue or stump revision.

Figure 2–54   Op-site® dressing.

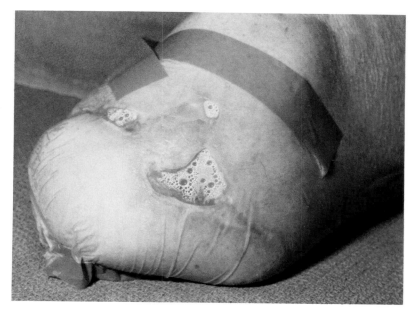

Figure 2–55   Severe infection.

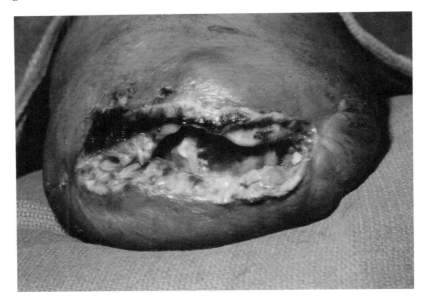

Figure 2–56   Bone protrusion.

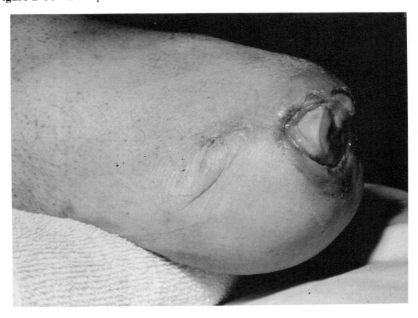

Unusual stump shapes and joint range restrictions interfere with an intimate socket fit, affect prosthetic alignment, and often complicate gait control. They may also cause stump discomfort. The majority of these complications respond well to physical therapeutic management.

Stump shape alterations are apparent in the soft tissues and affect the socket fit.

Edema. The most common postsurgical problem is stump edema. Edema increases stump volume, decreases circulation, and consequently slows wound healing. In severe conditions, the joint range of motion can also be affected. If not controlled, swelling can lead to secondary problems such as skin breakdown, pitting edema, ''hardening'' of edema, and reduced skin sensation (Levy, 1983). In later stages, uncontrolled distal stump end edema can eventually develop into verrucose hyperplasia (see Stump Socket Interface and Weight-bearing problems, p. 182). Edema control (see Stump Shrinkage and Shaping Techniques, p. 119) eliminates a great variety of stump problems.

Bulbous soft tissues. If the distal stump in transtibial and transfemoral amputations is bulbous, stump entry into the socket is difficult since the distal circumference of the stump is larger than the circumference of the midsection of the socket. This necessitates forcing the wider tissues through a narrow canal and may result in tissue damage and increased stump sensitivity, thus reducing stump weight-bearing capabilities. Bulbousness can be the result of insufficient myofascial flap contouring (Burgess et al., 1969) or distal edema caused by inadequate soft tissue support (Kumar, 1982). Following shrinkage, previously bulbous soft tissues may result in redundant tissues.

Redundant tissues. These excessive distal soft tissues are mobile and nonfunctional. Since stump lever control is determined by bone length only, these tissues do not contribute to actual functional stump length. Distal tissue mobility makes it difficult to don the prosthesis since tissue shifting may result in pinching. The correct way to don the prosthesis when distal redundant tissues are present is to hold the stump sock firmly under tension. This has a bracing effect on the tissues and gives control and support while positioning the stump correctly in the socket.

(See Fig. 2–57)

Excessive passive tissue motion within the socket during gait reduces position sense and decreases prosthetic control.

Skin folds. Skin folds are often referred to as ''dog ears'' and are situated on either side of the surgical scar. These are skin flaps that, if large and non-edematous, have a tendency to fold back onto themselves when donning the prosthesis and conversely slip down when doffing the prosthesis. They are prone to tissue tearing that, in turn, may lead to infection or other complications. Hygiene is important since perspiration collects under these flaps. The skin folds

(See Fig. 2–58)

Figure 2–57   Redundant tissue.

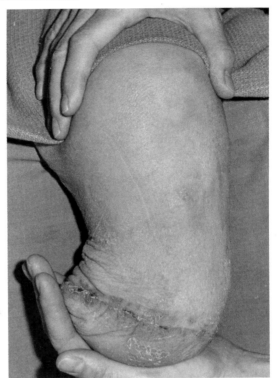

are a nuisance, but most can be effectively controlled by taping and bandaging (see Adaptations to the Bandaging Techniques, p. 132).

Skin grafts.   Although Harris (1981) states that skin grafts should be avoided on lower extremity stumps, they are sometimes necessary to retain stump length, especially in burn or degloving injuries. Grafts are very sensitive and do not readily tolerate stump socket pressures. Problems can arise with graft rejection and infection around the graft site if weight-bearing activities are started too early.

Physical therapy treatment considerations aim toward maintenance of mobility of the grafted tissues and prevention of skin contractures (see Skin Contractures, p. 146). Grafts usually "take" in 7 days. If graft infection or rejection occurs, then physical therapy modalities will not be of benefit and, if the site is extensive, regrafting is necessary. Small blisters can be kept clean and treated topically.

Adductor Roll.   This problem is typical in transfemoral stumps and is most commonly observed in elderly females. Excess adipose tissue may be present in

Figure 2–58   Skin (dog ear potential).

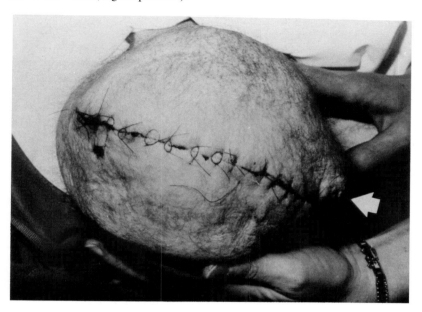

the adductor area and probably did not cause any difficulties prior to amputation. However, during prosthetic fitting this tissue bulges, interfering with stump placement into the socket. This creates a tissue barrier between the medial socket brim and the pubic ramus. The amputee sits too high in the prosthesis because the tissue bulge prevents complete stump penetration into the socket, thus making the prosthesis seem too long.

Most adductor rolls can be easily controlled by using stockinette to pull this soft tissue into the socket when donning the prosthesis. However, an adductor roll does not always remain problem-free since the excess skin tends to perspire and, thus, cause discomfort. An adductor roll responds well to bandaging techniques (see Adaptations to the Stump Bandaging Techniques, p. 132). In very rare situations, surgical removal of this tissue is indicated.

Whether the loss of joint range is caused by soft tissue shortening or joint range restriction, gait deviations result and, therefore, postural and biomechanical problems occur.

Joint Range Problems

Extensive Scarring and Adhesions.   A stump with extensive burn scars may demonstrate soft tissue and skin damage, resulting in permanent stump shape indentation.

(See Fig. 2–59)

Figure 2–59   Extensive burn scarring.

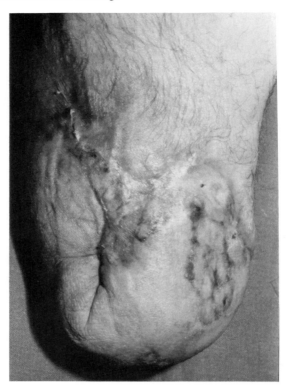

This:

- reduces soft tissue mobility
- affects stump muscle contractability
- affects the stump area available for weight-bearing distribution

Intimate socket wall contact is difficult to maintain. At times, severe scarring accompanied by scar adhesions can result in joint range loss. Stump treatments need specific considerations (see Contractures—Hypertrophic Scarring, p. 146).

(See Fig. 2–60)

Contractures.   Severe contractures interfere with gait (see Specific Physical Therapy Treatment Measures, p. 147). They affect step length and prosthetic alignment and consequently cause an increase in energy expenditure. If contractures are long-standing in that tissue shortening has occurred but improvement in joint range may still be anticipated, muscle tendon releases may be considered if intensive conservative physical therapeutic treatment has not been successful. The feasibility of eventual prosthetic fitting, and causative factors leading to contrac-

Figure 2–60   Joint contracture.

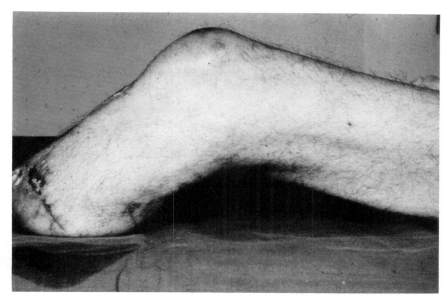

Source: From *WCPT World Congress Proceedings,* 1970, World Confederation for Physical Therapy. Reprinted by permission.

ture development, must be fully investigated to determine whether further surgery will improve joint function and, therefore, facilitate prosthetic ambulation.

Joint Pathologies.   Pathological joint conditions (e.g., rheumatoid or osteoarthritis) limit the joint range and can result in joint pain. Assessment of the joint condition will indicate treatment needs. Treatments may include:

- pain relieving methods (see Thermal Modalities, p. 186)
- graduated exercises
- prosthetic modifications

Example 1.   An unstable knee joint in a transtibial amputee may need socket rim alterations for medial-lateral stability on stance or may need side hinges and a thigh corset to prevent further stress on the knee joint during ambulation.

Example 2.   A fixed joint contracture will necessitate changes in prosthetic alignment that will affect the efficiency of the gait pattern.

Spasticity.   Changes in muscle tone can affect joint range of motion and controlled stump movement in varying degrees of severity (see Muscle Contractures, p. 141).

Summary

The amputee with an unusual stump shape or marked joint range limitation will continue to experience problems with the stump and with ambulation activities, despite the fact that the stump, in most cases, is well healed.

Stump–Socket Interface and Weight-bearing Problems

Stump–socket interface and weight-bearing problems are produced by mechanical actions that occur as the result of external forces acting on the stump tissues. They are caused by:

- piston action
- socket friction
- weight-bearing forces
- localized pressure points
  (wrinkle in a stump sock)

(See Fig. 2–61)

Pressure Areas and Abrasions.   Weight bearing, if not strictly supervised, can cause pressure irritation and/or abrasions over areas that are unable to tolerate friction or stress. These areas of breakdown often develop if the amputee does not

Figure 2–61 Tibial abrasions.

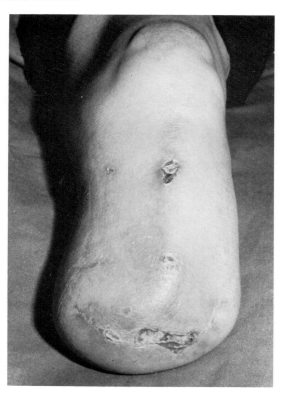

have sufficient skin sensation (e.g., diabetic neuropathy) to judge the amount of weight bearing occurring through the socket to the stump. Incorrect alignment of the socket walls in relation to the anatomical stump contours also causes problems since pressure-sensitive areas are compromised.

Blisters. Blisters develop as a result of friction and pressure. Fluid develops under the point of irritation. They can form in edema-prone, redundant tissues at the distal stump, over the patellar tendon, and at the point where the proximal socket brim contacts the skin. This applies to both transtibial and transfemoral stumps.

(See Fig. 2–62)

Abrasions and blisters must be protected in order to avoid escalating these complications into

- skin infections
- ulcer development
- gangrene

Amputees with minor stump lesions can continue limited ambulation provided the area is protected. Minor lesions either heal on their own or can be treated with topical medications. Dressing thickness must be kept to a minimum in order to avoid a further increase in pressure on the already irritated areas. Socket

Figure 2–62 Blisters.

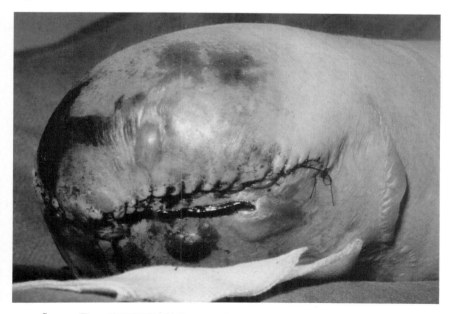

Source: From *WCPT World Congress Proceedings,* 1970, World Confederation for Physical Therapy. Reprinted by permission.

adjustments, such as the relief of pressure-sensitive areas or the redistribution of socket contact are indicated. The suspension must be checked frequently to avoid excessive piston action that contributes to skin friction.

It is advisable to restrict weight-bearing progression by keeping the amputee in the parallel bars so that the amputee can bear most of the weight through the upper extremities and on the remaining leg. However, the patient may continue with controlled partial weight bearing, transferring, and balance activities to stimulate stump proprioception, which will aid in future gait activities.

Weight-bearing activities for patients with severe stump-healing problems must be deferred until sufficient healing takes place. The risk of further trauma to the stump, which might occur as a result of sudden uncontrolled weight bearing, outweighs the benefits that can be achieved by the continuation of ambulation.

Venous Restriction. This problem (rare) is primarily caused by circulatory restriction at the posterior proximal stump level. It is typically observed in the transfemoral amputee who has vascular impairment. The long saphenous vein is partially compressed because of weight bearing on the ischial shelf, and the condition is further aggravated by the absence of distal stump socket contact.

Venous restriction is recognized:

- by distal stump discoloration (the distal stump end appears blue, then blanches and reddens proximally)
- by cool stump temperatures
- by distal stump pain
- by pressure discomfort over the ischial tuberosity on weight bearing

Socket alterations are indicated and, on rare occasions, the quadrilateral socket design has to be altered to a more triangular shape, to change the posterior socket counter pressure (similar to the European transfemoral socket design). Removal of the stump bandage may also have to be considered.

Contact dermatitis. This localized dermatitis develops as a result of skin reacting to one or several agents:

- the inner coating of the socket wall (resins, polyester, acrylics, leather)
- the stump socket materials (wools, man made fibers)
- detergents used for sock hygiene

Clinically, this skin reaction is confined to the stump, the skin may be itchy, and a skin rash is seen. The condition is further aggravated by perspiration and poor socket ventilation (Levy, 1980). Only the determination and elimination of the source of the irritant can alleviate this condition.

Verrucose hyperplasia. Verrucose hyperplasia develops gradually and is visible at the distal end of the very mature amputation stump. The skin thickens, develops a "putty" discoloration, and has a "mushroom-like" appearance. The skin loses tissue elasticity and is prone to cracks in the crevice sections. Skin

(See Fig. 2–63)

Figure 2–63   Verrucose hyperplasia.

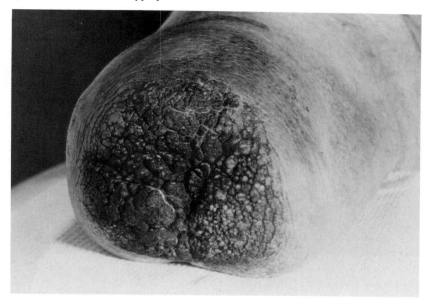

Source: Photograph courtesy of Dr. S. William Levy.

sensation becomes dull. This condition develops if longstanding distal stump edema is present (Levy, 1983). Levy (1983) observed that treatments by topical ointment and oral medications were not successful but that, in most cases, the stump did not have distal socket contact. By providing distal contact, accompanied by some weight bearing, the condition improved considerably (Kumar, 1982; Levy, 1983).

Sebaceous cysts, epidermoid cysts.   Cysts develop only on the stumps of active prosthetic users. These are not a postoperative problem. Transfemoral amputees are prone to cyst formation at the anterior and posterior socket brim, whereas transtibial amputees will develop cysts more frequently in the popliteal area and, to a lesser extent, in the patellar tendon area (Levy, 1983). These are areas where socket counter pressure is most pronounced.

Cysts develop as the result of socket pressure, skin friction, perspiration and dermal cells blocking the hair follicle opening. Occasionally the surrounding tissues become inflamed.

The treatment of cysts includes:

- surgical management by incision and drainage (Levy, 1983)
- antibiotic therapy
- ultraviolet irradiation to promote healing

Stringent hygiene is stressed. Weight bearing may be temporarily deferred until the inflammation has settled to avoid further irritation of the area.

Bone End Sensitivity. Distal bone pain on weight bearing may be the result of periosteal hypersensitivity. This discomfort occurs as a complication during early weight-bearing practice and is more pronounced if the bone end has minimal soft tissue coverage. Eventually, as the stump heals this sensitivity is reduced. Initially, these amputees will automatically avoid full weight bearing and will be strongly dependent upon the support of walking aids. Weight-bearing progression should not be considered during this time.

Bone Spurs. Sharp, bony growth may result in a weight-bearing problem at a later stage. This condition occurs if some shreds of periosteum have remained in the soft tissues following amputation surgery or if the stump has a rough bone end (Clark et al., 1980). If these spurs are embedded in soft tissues, they pose no problem. However, if these forms of exostoses are near the skin surface at the distal stump end, they can cause considerable weight-bearing discomfort. If superficial, one can feel the bone end spurs by gently rotating the tissues over the stump end. The resistance or grinding that is felt is similar to the crepitus felt in an arthritic joint. Revision or filing of the bone end may be necessary to allow pain-free ambulation.

Neuroma. Neuromas (see Clinical Evaluation of Pain, p. 65) do not pose a problem if they are deeply imbedded in muscle tissue. If a neuroma is unprotected by surrounding soft tissues, localized pain is triggered by palpation or pressure, and the amputee experiences ''pin-point'' pain. Pain may also radiate up the course of the nerve. An attempt to treat a painful neuroma with conservative methods is indicated before invasive treatment measures (injections, nerve blocks, or resection of the neuroma) are to be considered (Harris, 1981).

Conservative treatment methods include the application of transcutaneous electrical nerve stimulation (see Transcutaneous Electrical Nerve Stimulation, p. 187) and ultrasound.

Ultrasound

Ultrasound, a form of high frequency modality, produces a micromassage effect as a result of sound waves reflecting and refracting off the different tissue interfaces, producing heat. The heat is generated by the frequency and the intensity applied and also depends upon the tissue density. Ultrasound has a place in treating neuromas. If a painful neuroma is adherent to the superficial surrounding muscle tissues, muscle contractions will constantly irritate this sensitive area. Ultrasound may soften the adherent tissues and thus reduce the irritation on the neuroma. Treatment success is limited because of the low intensities necessary to prevent overheating of the deeper stump tissues. Ultrasound is contraindicated if stump skin sensation is reduced or absent.

Clinical Note. If the neuroma is too sensitive to tolerate contact pressure from the ultrasound heat, indirect application through water is the technique of choice.

As the amputee progresses in weight bearing and ambulation activities, it is imperative that the physical therapist maintains close liaison with the prosthetist at all times. This becomes even more important with the problem stump. Within the prosthetic socket, modifications are possible by relieving pressure-sensitive areas and/or by building up pressure-tolerant areas. Further prosthetic fitting changes are accomplished by alignment adjustments after initial attempts at standing and weight bearing have been made. These early corrective measures will prevent potential stump and skin problems, ensuring stump comfort and contributing to a controlled prosthetic gait. However, if a lesion develops on a stump weight-bearing area, it may not be possible to relieve the socket because this would compromise the fit and alter weight-bearing pressures in other stump areas. Ambulation may have to be deferred until this lesion has cleared.

Liaison with the Prosthetist

Symptoms caused by amputation associated diseases complicate existing stump problems and need equal treatment consideration.

These nonvisible, subjective symptoms are in contrast to overtly visible stump conditions and are experienced by the amputee. Examples of these problems include:

Stump Symptoms Related to Amputation Associated Diseases

- the hypersensitive stump
- the painful stump
    the cold stump
    intermittent claudication
- the insensitive stump

These symptomatic conditions are affected by the available stump vascularity and by the severity of pain experienced by the individual amputee.

The total stump area is excessively sensitive to external pressure (touch, stump bandage pressure, socket contact, and movement). This excessive sensitivity is a result of either vascular deficiency or the generalized bruising effect caused by handling of the stump tissues during surgery. The cause may also be of unknown etiology.

The Hypersensitive Stump

General stump hypersensitivity can be treated with:

- desensitizing techniques
- thermal modalities
- transcutaneous electrical nerve stimulation

Stump tissues, most particularly the skin, are not accustomed to weight-bearing pressures. They are initially sensitive and have to be toughened. Conventional techniques such as handling the stump, rubbing with a towel, tapping, percussions, and vibrations act as gentle counterirritants that can decrease stump sensitivity.

Desensitizing Techniques

Moist Salt and Sand Rubs. Moist salt and sand rubs, which have been suggested by some clinicians, will help to toughen and desensitize stump skin. However, these modalities have a very limited use. These techniques can be selectively applied over weight-bearing areas but should not be applied over areas of skin breakdown or irritation. Moist salt rubs are not recommended for the patient with vascular disease (Holliday, 1981) because of skin fragility.

Contrast Baths. The literature suggests the application of contrast baths. However, the temperature range between very cold water and very warm water is indeed extreme. Our recommendation is to avoid the procedure since the sudden temperature changes may cause vascular embarrassment, even to the recent healthy stump, because the collateral stump circulation has not yet developed sufficiently to cope with the range from cold to hot and vice versa. Recommended alternatives include mild and gradual application of warmth, which provides a gentle increase of circulation and easing of pain.

Vibrators. The vibrator functions as a pleasant and gentle counterirritant by providing electrically produced massage. For stump desensitization, the small hand-held unit is best.

The unit produces short, pulsating, rhythmic vibrations of different intensities. The amputee controls the vibration intensity, the contact pressure, and the extent of the stump surface to be treated. The head of the vibrator is moved gently around and gradually placed over the areas of greatest sensitivity.

Vibrator models used for chest therapy are contraindicated for stump desensitizations since their vibrations are too powerful.

Alternatives to Bandaging for Sensitive Stumps. The application of a stump bandage exerts pressure on the stump and this will, to some extent, encourage desensitization. However, the tension of the conventional stump bandage may be too great for some sensitive stumps (fragile skin). Skin irritation and breakdown may occur. To counteract this, stockinette coverage may be all that the skin can initially tolerate. When the stump skin eventually toughens, Tubigrip™, a mildly elasticized stockinette, can be used as a stump sock. When treatment progression is indicated, an alternative to Tubigrip™ is a lightweight net bandage (Elset™). This can be applied, providing gentle compression and distal support, until the stump skin can tolerate the customary bandaging procedure (see Stump Shrinkage and Shaping Techniques, p. 119).

Localized skin sensitivity to pressure over the tibial crest can be alleviated by using thin strips of soft felt or Spenco-dermal™ pads (an artificial fat substance). These are applied on either side of the tibia prior to stump bandaging. The felt strips are stabilized with hypoallergenic tape. The Spenco-dermal™ pad, once positioned, does not require additional stabilization. This technique incorporates the counterpressure areas that are built into the prosthetic socket to relieve prominent and at times, sensitive areas while the bandage is in place.

Thermal Modalities   Thermal modalities are used to provide mild warmth to counteract general stump pain. They increase circulation, decrease muscle spasm and provide comfort.

Infrared Irradiation. The supported stump is covered with a towel to protect the sensitive area and to absorb any possible perspiration. The standard distance from the lamp to the stump is doubled to provide a gentle heating effect. A 20–30 minute application increases stump comfort, enhances mobility, and reduces stump sensitivity.

Whirlpool Bath. With controlled temperatures the whirlpool bath is a pleasant way of desensitizing the stump. (see Delayed Healing, p. 163)

Ice Packs. These are rarely used on stumps and never considered for the dysvascular amputee. The stump is cool to begin with because of circulatory deficiency, and further cryotherapy increases the pain because the cold cannot be dissipated quickly enough by the available circulation. The application of ice does not have a numbing effect but produces initial vasoconstriction that results in ischemic pain.

Transcutaneous Electrical Nerve Stimulation

TENS treatment modality can be beneficial in reducing or controlling general stump pain, provided the pain is not caused by an infectious or febrile condition.

The analgesic effect of TENS is based on the principle of neuromodulation and the following assumptions:

- nerve impulses can be generated by electrical currents
- large and small fibers can be preferentially stimulated
- large fibers have a lower threshold and a faster conduction velocity than small fibers

Many hypotheses have been suggested to explain why TENS works. One of these is that the stimulation of the large fibers by high frequency TENS sets up a ''gating'' mechanism that inhibits afferent pain messages (Herman, 1977; Melzack, 1983). Evidence also suggests that low frequency high intensity TENS results in the release of endorphins and subsequent pain relief (Sjølund et al., 1979).

TENS is a symptomatic treatment and can serve as an alternative to, or at least to reduce, analgesic intake. However, it must be pointed out that not all amputees treated with TENS experience permanent pain relief. This may be due to the fact that different types of pain respond in different ways to stimulation and that the origin of pain is often difficult to diagnose (bone pain, vascular pain, neurogenic pain, wound pain). Therefore, the appropriate selection for TENS as a treatment modality is not yet specific enough. However, it has been demonstrated that pain due to peripheral nociceptive input responds best to this treatment modality[4] (Meyerson, 1983).

Electrodes can be placed locally or along the course of the appropriate nerve. It has been found to be most beneficial to place the anode over the nerve root and the cathode over the trigger point in treating painful neuroma.[5] Alternative electrode placements can be chosen when treating general stump pain. Selection depends largely on the subjective reports from the amputee regarding the improvement of pain. Objectively, a decrease in pain will result in improved gait and exercise performance.

The Painful Stump

Pain adversely affects the amputee's ability to walk. The prosthetic stance phase is shortened, and a variety of other gait deviations become evident. The origin of pain has to be determined (see Clinical Evaluation of Pain, p. 65) before treatment can be initiated.

The Cold Stump. An excessively cold or hypothermic stump (like cold feet) causes pain and general discomfort. Coldness and pain are felt (as in a hypersensitive stump) over the total stump surface, including the area above the joint closest to the level of amputation. Circulatory impairment, particularly the superficial circulation, affects the tissue temperature regulation. Clinically, cold stump symptoms include:

- blanched skin
- decreased skin sensation
- stump numbness
- decreased mobility of the proximal joint
- stump pain

Blanched skin and decreased skin sensation are usually indications of decreased superficial circulation that will eventually cause a feeling of stump numbness. Stump numbness can change to severe ischemic pain, making the wearing of the stump bandage and/or the prosthesis intolerable. Decrease in temperature also results in a feeling of stiffness that can inhibit joint mobility.

Any form of treatment that provides comfort, gentle warmth, and gentle active exercises without weight bearing and incorporates adequate rest periods is indicated.

Intermittent Claudication. An insufficient blood supply to the muscles causes muscle "cramping" that results in severe ischemic pain. Often observed in the calf muscle group, it stops the elderly person with occlusive arterial disease from walking. Only complete relaxation of the affected limb will reduce muscle cramping and permit increased blood flow, thus relieving the symptoms.

Intermittent claudication is often a symptom in the remaining leg. However, it may also occur in the stump. Treatment considerations include:

- Teaching energy conservation techniques.
- Resting frequently.
- Discouraging prolonged standing. Standing requires constant muscle work, while walking allows for rhythmic contraction and relaxation of the appropriate muscle groups.

If the disease process has advanced to the level at which ischemic pain occurs with ambulation activities, treatment aims must concentrate on a controlled gradual increase of functional walking tolerance, since moderate progressive activity is more beneficial than inactivity (deWolfe, 1983).

Neuropathies (diabetic, ischemic, alcoholic, or of unknown etiology) can vary in symptomatology from being severely painful to being completely insensitive (Wagner, 1981). Severely reduced sensation (hypoesthesia) and the absence of stump sensation (anesthesia) are both serious conditions because the amputee is unable to judge

The Insensitive Stump

- the amount of weight bearing
- the presence of localized socket pressure
- the amount of skin friction (pistoning)
- the correct prosthetic socket contact

In addition to these extrinsic factors, proprioception is diminished, and the danger of stump skin damage is high.

Patient education is vital because, too often, the amputee will be unaware of the high potential for stump injury and commonly states that "it doesn't hurt." The amputee with an insensitive stump has to learn:

- to keep the stump sock wrinkle-free
- to don the prosthesis by observing the socket landmarks to avoid prosthetic malalignment
- to always examine the stump after doffing the prosthesis
- to practice stringent stump hygiene

The amputee must also learn that when a pressure sore develops, the sensory impairment will affect the ability to feel this usually painful stimulus. The therapist must stress use of the visual senses to compensate for the absence of the "warning system" (feeling).

If stump skin sensation is reduced, skin sensation in the remaining leg is also affected (danger of injury).

Pain control is often difficult to achieve because pain is a very subjective entity and can originate from several causes. Several treatment methods can be utilized to alleviate pain. Depending on the nature of the pain and the success of the treatment, the effect can be long or short term.

Summary

It is important to remember that efficient prosthetic ambulation is not possible in the presence of stump pain.

All recent stumps have the potential for developing complications. Therefore, the prevention of stump complications has to be practiced, and ongoing patient education regarding all aspects of stump care is an integral part of the overall treatment plan.

Conclusion

The team approach ensures optimum results in the treatment of the problematic stump because, in a coordinated manner, each team member is able to contribute specialized skills to the treatment.

Indifferent care can have devastating effects on the recent amputation stump.

References

Burgess, E.M., Romano, R.L., and Zettl, J.H. "Below-knee Amputation Surgery." *The Management of Lower-extremity Amputations*. Washington, D.C.: U.S. Government Printing Office, 1969, 16–39, 45–48.

Clark, G.S., Naso, F., and Ditunno, J.F. Jr. "Marked Bone Spur Formation in a Burn Amputee Patient." *Archives of Physical Medicine and Rehabilitation, 61* (April 1980): 189–192.

deWolfe, V.G. "Arteriosclerosis Obliterans: Clinical Diagnosis and Treatment." *Geriatrics*, September, 1973, 93–101.

Diffey, B.L. "Ultraviolet Spectrum. Kromeyer Lamp." *Ultraviolet Radiation in Medicine*, Bristol, Eng.: Adam Hilger, 1982, 1–2, 32–33.

Harris, W.R. "Common Stump Problems." In J.P. Kostuik and R. Gillespie, eds. *Amputation Surgery and Rehabilitation: The Toronto Experience*. New York: Churchill Livingstone, 1981, 191–194.

Herman, E. "The Use of Transcutaneous Nerve Stimulation in Management of Chronic Pain." *Physiotherapy Canada, 29* (1977): 65.

Holliday, P.J. "Conditioning of the Amputation Limb." In J.P. Kostuik and R. Gillespie, eds. *Amputation Surgery and Rehabilitation: The Toronto Experience*. New York: Churchill Livingstone, 1981, 237–243.

Holliday, P.J. "Non-prosthetic Care." In J.P. Kostuik and R. Gillespie, eds. *Amputation Surgery and Rehabilitation: The Toronto Experience*. New York: Churchill Livingstone, 1981, 243–245.

Kumar, V.N. "Stump Complications and Management." In S.N. Banerjee, ed. *Rehabilitation Management of Amputees*. Baltimore, Md.: Williams & Wilkins, 1982, 385–388.

Levy, S.W. "Skin Problems of the Leg Amputee." *Prosthetics and Orthotics International*, 4, no. 1 (1980): 37–44.

Levy, S.W. "Verrucose Hyperplasia." *Skin Problems of the Amputee*. St. Louis, Mo.: Warren H. Green, 1983, 153–155, 280.

Melzack, R., and Wall, P.D. "Sensory Control of Pain (Electrical Stimulation of Nerves, Spinal Cord and Brain)." *The Challenge of Pain*. New York: Basic Books, 1983, 310–313.

Mensch, G., and Ellis, P. "Windowed Rigid Dressing. Physical Therapeutic Management for Lower Extremity Amputees in Rehabilitation." In S.N. Banerjee, ed. *Rehabilitation Management of Amputees*. Baltimore, Md.: Williams & Wilkins, 1982, 176–179.

Op-site® *Product Information*. Smith & Nephew Ltd., 2100 52nd Avenue, Lachine, Quebec, Canada, H8T 2Y5.

Meyerson, B.A. "Electrostimulation Procedures: Effects, Presumed Rationale and Possible Mechanisms." In J.J. Bonica, A. Iggo, and U. Lindblom, eds. *Advances in Pain Research and Therapy*, New York: Raven Press, 1983, vol. 5, 495–534.

Scott, B.D. "Uses of Ultraviolet Therapy." in K.G. Stillwell, ed. *Therapeutic Electricity and Ultraviolet Radiation*, 3rd ed. Baltimore, Md.: Williams & Wilkins, 1983, 245–252.

Sjølund, B.H., and Eriksson, M.B.S. "Endorphins and Analgesia Produced by Peripheral Conditioning Stimulation." In J.J. Bonica, A. Iggo, and U. Lindblom, eds. *Advances in Pain Research and Therapy*, New York: Raven Press, 1979, vol. 3, 587–592.

Wagner, W.F. "The Dysvascular Foot: A System of Diagnosis and Treatment." *Foot and Ankle, 2* (1981): 64–122.

1. Friedmann, L.W. ISPO Advanced Course: B/K and through knee amputations and prosthetics, Køge, Denmark, May 10–13, 1982.
2. MacMillan, A.H. Personal communication, 1978.
3. Ibid.
4. Herman, E. Personal communication, 1983.
5. Ibid.

During normal gait dynamics, all motions and forces oppose each other (see Gait-Forces, p. 2). This principle also applies during prosthetic gait.

Each motion, produced by muscular contraction, is controlled by (Gardiner, 1981):

- agonists, which produce movement by contraction
- antagonists, which relax or lengthen to control the movement without hindering it
- synergists, which refine the action of the agonists
- fixators, which fix or stabilize the origin of the synergists or agonists

Weakness in any of these groups produces a muscular imbalance that adversely affects the ability of all muscle groups to perform a coordinated movement, thus affecting both movement and stability (Gardiner, 1981).

For the amputee, the control of stump motions depends upon:

- lever length
- muscle contractibility
- proprioception
- joint position
- location and nature of the attachment of the muscles severed during the amputation
- control of the direction, intensity, and speed of the movement

Effective control of stump motions will aid in

- initiating the muscular forces required to produce gait
- providing stability for support during weight bearing
- augmenting momentum, thereby assisting velocity

To provide clarity, each stump motion will be analyzed individually. However, the clinician must remember that each movement or motion occurs as a result of coordinated muscle work performed simultaneously by several muscle groups (Gardiner, 1981). The intensity of muscle work demanded from each group depends upon the joint range position during the different phases of gait.

The hip extensor and flexor muscles control anteroposterior stability during the gait cycle (Radcliffe, 1981).

The control of stump hip extension is of primary functional importance to the transfemoral amputee. Hip extension aids in holding the body upright and provides the greatest muscular force shortly after heel strike (Inman et al., 1981).

STUMP MOTIONS: THEIR RELATIONSHIP TO GAIT FUNCTIONS AND RESULTANT TREATMENT CONSIDERATIONS

Anterior-Posterior Stump Forces

Stump Hip Extension (Transfemoral Amputation)

The stump extension or "push-back" motion also stabilizes the prosthetic knee joint during the stance phase. It also provides the main muscular force for the forward thrust of the body during the early part of the stance phase and controls the prosthetic stance stability. This movement is necessary for stump lever action and joint position control in ascending and descending stairs and inclines, climbing ladders, or in any other activities that require weight-bearing stability.

Reduced Functional Output. If the stump hip extensor muscles are weak, the gluteus maximus muscle is unable to stabilize the stump in extension, and consequently, the prosthetic knee joint becomes unstable during weight bearing. The transfemoral amputee may be hesitant to weight bear over the prosthesis for fear of the knee buckling. In order to overcome this unsteadiness, a manually locked or "safety knee" is required (see Knees, p. 206). The transfemoral amputee can then compensate by increasing the lumbar lordosis while leaning the trunk diagonally backward toward the prosthetic side (Hoppenfeld, 1976). This position biomechanically stabilizes the hip joint. This postural compensation begins at heel contact and continues past midstance. The hip extensor muscles are utilized in combination with the hip abductor muscles up to midstance only. Then, trunk leaning (biomechanical assistance) occurs to maintain a moderately stable, but shortened, prosthetic stance.

Kneeling is impossible because of pelvic instability in this position. When attempting to kneel, the center of gravity falls in front of the hip joints, and the trunk flexes forward because the weak hip extensor muscles are unable to assist in holding the trunk upright. The elongated hip extensor muscles are at a bio-mechanical disadvantage and are unable to counteract the pull of gravity.

Treatment Considerations. Stump hip extension practice is of prime importance in preparation for gait training. This stump motion is often the most difficult movement for the amputee to perform.

Exercising may be started in a prone position with a pillow under the pelvis. This exercise position (not to be used for rest periods) provides the gluteus maximus muscles with a slightly stretched starting position and permits the amputee to achieve a greater joint range of motion before the muscle end range contraction is achieved (Gardiner, 1981; Mensch, 1982). The pillow, if placed correctly under the pelvis, will also counteract excessive lumbar lordosis and will neutralize any compensatory movement.

Stump Hip Flexion (Transfemoral Amputation)

Stump hip flexion initiates the bending of the prosthetic knee joint following heel off on the prosthetic side. It then accelerates the prosthesis, providing swing phase power.

The hip flexor muscles also assist the trunk when moving from sitting to standing (Colthurst et al., 1973) by bringing the center of gravity in front of the hips. They not only initiate hip flexion but also stabilize the stump, together with the antagonists, in any required joint range position. This joint range control is necessary during all phases of gait.

Reduced Functional Output.   If hip flexor muscle weakness and/or a loss in hip extension range is present, the amputee adapts by utilizing a variety of compensatory movements. The most common deviations are trunk forward flexion and hip hiking. These movements replace and/or augment the hip flexor function, permitting the amputee to initiate step positions.

Trunk forward flexion is intensified when using crutches, a walker, or canes and is especially noticeable in the three point crutch gait. The amputee increases the support base, brings the center of gravity in front of both hip joints, and increases body weight support through the arms during ambulation (Mensch, 1979). This posture reduces weight bearing through the prosthesis and also demands less than full hip range of motion because the hip extension range is not fully utilized on the prosthetic side. The sound leg cannot overstep the prosthesis (unequal ground gain). However, increasing the support base stabilizes balance and gives the amputee a feeling of security. Amputees who have a marked hip flexion contracture often demonstrate increased lumbar lordosis when attempting to correct this stooped posture.

If the hip flexors are weak, the amputee can mobilize the prosthesis through hip hiking, a function of the quadratus lumborum muscle. The prosthetic swing phase is thus not initiated by the active hip flexion unlocking the prosthetic knee. Instead, the prosthesis accelerates forward in a pendular fashion. This is a gravity-assisted motion and results in a stiff prosthetic swing phase with little prosthetic knee flexion. The stance period on the remaining leg is prolonged. The gait pattern is asymmetrical and extremely tiring for the amputee.

Treatment Considerations.   It is not necessary to *overemphasize* stump hip flexion during an exercise program because the amputee automatically uses the stump, in the flexed position, as a balancing lever when transferring from bed to chair, during ambulation without the prosthesis, and during sitting periods with the trunk in a forward flexed position (Mensch, 1979, 1983). However, it is important to include some flexion exercises and to stress proprioceptive awareness of this stump motion.

The amputee should also be encouraged to maintain an upright posture during exercise sessions and gait practice. By doing so, the amputee can learn to shift the center of gravity back over the legs, resulting in better postural control and a more natural gait pattern.

Comparison of Hip Extension and Flexion Functions.   The main hip extensor muscle, the gluteus maximus, together with the hamstring muscles, provide the major muscular force needed to accomplish the body's forward thrust within the gait sequence. These muscles depend on weight bearing and ground reaction forces to function effectively.

Functional stump extension is more difficult, particularly in the presence of a hip flexion contracture, and, consequently, is harder for the amputee to learn.

The active function of the hip flexor muscles causes effective leg shortening (by joint flexion) in order to achieve ground clearance during swing phase. During the forward acceleration of the limb (swing phase), the hip flexors are assisted by momentum, and, consequently, the hip flexor muscles function with relative ease in comparison with the hip extensor muscles during the forward motion of the gait cycle.

Medial-Lateral Stability

The hip abductor and adductor muscle groups control the medial-lateral pelvic stability during prosthetic gait (Radcliffe, 1981).

Stump Hip Abduction (Transfemoral Amputation)

The hip abductor muscles hold the pelvis level during walking and when standing on one leg (Kapandji, 1970; Colthurst et al., 1973). Following transfemoral amputation, this pelvic stability is difficult to maintain because the hip abductor muscles, although remaining intact postsurgically, do not have the weight-bearing feedback of the natural leg. When contracting, they lead the femur laterally and can only provide pelvic stability if a firm lateral stump support (socket wall) is available to contract or lean against (New York University, 1975; Radcliffe, 1977, 1981).

Reduced Functional Output.   Weak hip abductor muscles on the prosthetic side cause a positive Trendelenburg sign as the pelvis drops to the sound side. Even a minimal degree of weakness can cause a marked postural deficit owing to the biomechanical disadvantage at which the hip abductor muscles must function. To compensate for the lack of pelvic stability caused by this weakness, the amputee eliminates the lateral pelvic shift and substitutes a moderate amount of lateral trunk bending toward the prosthetic side. This motion shifts the center of gravity laterally, directly over the prosthetic socket. This reduces the amount of muscle work required by the hip abductors to maintain pelvic stability on prosthetic stance and keeps the prosthetic foot within the normal walking base.

Abductor weakness of both hips in bilateral transfemoral amputees causes excessive lateral trunk bending toward each side, as well as a wide-based gait. The combination of these two compensatory movements produces a marked "waddling" gait pattern similar to that of a duck or clown. This form of ambulation is most tiring and energy consuming because of the increased amount of muscle work required to shift the center of gravity from one support side to the other.

Treatment Consideration.   Hip abductor muscles have to be strengthened, particularly in short stumps, to ensure pelvic stability on stance and to reduce energy-consuming gait deviations. Stump motion control can be initiated by giving manual resistance in the desired direction of the movement during exercise sessions. Functional stump abduction combined with hip extension control the position and, partially, the speed of the prosthetic gait pattern.

Stump Hip Adduction (Transfemoral Amputation)

The adductor muscle group counteracts abduction and external rotation and, as an antagonist, aids in pelvic stabilization on stance together with the hip abductor muscles (Kapandji, 1970; Colthurst et al., 1973). However, the complete function of the adductor muscle group within the gait cycle is not yet fully understood (Radcliffe, 1981).

Reduced Functional Output. Adductor weakness is seldom observed clinically (Colthurst et al., 1973; Gardiner, 1981) and does not appear to severely affect the amputee's gait. But if marked weakness is present, the amputee places the prosthesis in a toe-out position, walking with the prosthesis externally rotated in relation to the line of progression. Pelvic stability is not noticeably affected. (Radcliffe, 1977)

Adductor and internal rotator muscles will gradually weaken in bilateral transfemoral amputees owing to inactivity and prolonged sitting. To maintain a stable sitting balance, both stumps are abducted and externally rotated, which results in a broader sitting base but, at the same time, this position overstretches the adductor and internal rotator muscle groups.

Treatment Consideration. The adductor muscles draw the prosthesis toward body midline and, together with the abductor muscles, control the width of the walking base. The adductor muscles can be exercised in the supine or prone position. In this position, the pelvis must be level in relation to the axis of the spine to avoid hip hiking or a pelvic drop, since both of these compensatory pelvic motions inhibit the actual adduction motion.

Comparison of Abduction and Adduction Functions. Functional hip abduction is a more difficult movement for the amputee to accomplish. The stump hip abductor muscles influence the distance of the pelvic lateral shift while holding the pelvis level over the support leg. The abductors function at their peak during the stance phase (Inman et al., 1981). The actual anatomical length of the muscle group is rather short when one considers its required function. The adductor muscles, although assisting in pelvic stabilization, function mainly during the beginning and the end of the swing phase and, therefore, assist in stump hip flexion (Inman et al., 1981).

The stump hip rotators act in a synergetic fashion to refine the actions of the agonists.

Hip Rotators

The hip internal rotators function during the swing phase simultaneously with the hip flexor muscles, whereas the hip external rotators are active from midstance to heel off in combination with the hip extensor muscles (see Gait, p. 8). The rotators also perform a synergetic function coordinating the primary stump movers. These primary stump motions are hip abduction and extension. The external rotators provide a smooth transition from hip abduction to extension. Similarly, the internal rotators provide this same synergetic function between hip flexion and adduction. The hip rotator muscles assist in pelvic stabilization. Both rotational muscle groups control the amount of prosthetic rotation and have a bearing on balance control when standing and walking. This can be experienced

Stump Hip Internal and External Rotation (Transfemoral Amputation)

by standing on one leg while forcefully rotating the trunk over the stance leg. One will feel the effort required by the rotators (together with the foot invertors and evertors) to assist in maintaining the center of gravity over the stance leg. The foot placement in relation to the line of progression during the stance phase also is partially determined by the hip rotators together with the abductor and adductor muscles. The degree of hip rotation depends on the step length: the longer the stride, the greater the amount of hip rotation required (Inman et al., 1981).

The clinician must remember that certain hip joint range positions can cause a change in the direction of muscle fibers, thus altering the function of these muscle groups. For example, internal rotation past 40° causes the obturator externus (external rotator) and the pectineus (adductor, flexor, external rotator) to cease functioning as external rotators and to become internal rotators. The tensor facia lata (abductor and internal rotator) and the gluteus medius and minimus (abductors and internal rotators) then assume the role of the external rotators (Kapandji, 1970).

Reduced Functional Output. Decreased, or lack of, strength in the hip external or internal rotators causes the gait to appear stiff and shortens the step length. This problem (seldom seen in isolation) usually occurs in combination with weak hip flexor and extensor muscles. Compensation for reduced leg rotation may be made by increased trunk rotation.

Treatment Considerations. Since hip external and internal rotation contribute to balance control and, consequently, to gait stability, these motions must be practiced in preparation for gait training. In the transfemoral amputee, active rotational control of the prosthesis comes from the hip joint only. The amount of rotation possible depends upon the stump length and the suspension utilized. A suction socket wearer has free hip range control. A Silesian suspension will restrict prosthetic rotational movement to some extent, whereas a rigid pelvic belt will not allow active hip rotation to be transmitted through the prosthesis.

Comparison of Hip Internal and External Rotation Functions. Comparing the rotational movements, the hip external rotator muscles are more powerful and are aided in their function by some of the abductors (Kapandji, 1970). They perform in combination with the hip abductors and extensor muscles from mid-stance to toe-off and assist in providing a transitional muscular force in response to ground resistance, thus acting with predominant muscle forces and contributing to body velocity.

In contrast, the hip internal rotators are less numerous and less powerful and function in combination with the hip flexors and adductors. Their functions have the benefit of momentum assistance during the swing phase. Therefore, there is less demand on these muscles to produce force.

Stump Knee Functions

The transtibial stump extensor and flexor muscle groups provide force for both forward motion of the prosthesis and stance stability.

The knee extension movement is initiated by the quadriceps muscle group and controlled by its antagonists, the hamstring muscles. The coordinated interaction of these two muscle groups extends the knee joint to allow the prosthesis to reach heel contact. The quadriceps muscle group stabilizes the knee joint on weight bearing and is particularly active during stair walking, sitting down, and standing from sitting.

Reduced Functional Output. Nonamputees can usually feel their quadriceps muscles after quickly walking several flights of stairs. Tiring of the muscle groups becomes apparent when the muscle belly aches and a "hand push" over the muscle bulk is needed to assist stepping onto the next plateau (Hoppenfeld, 1976).

The transtibial amputee who has weak knee extensor muscles walks with a foot flat, bent knee gait, taking short steps that may result in either diminished or absent heel contact. When the stance phase is reached, knee stability is poor since the knee tends to flex because the quadriceps muscle is unable to overcome the ground reaction force acting on knee flexion and because of the action of the knee flexor muscles (Kapandji, 1970). The amputee compensates for this weakness by trunk forward flexion. This shifts the center of gravity in front of the knee joint, thus biomechanically assisting in knee joint stabilization.

Treatment Considerations. The quadriceps muscles have two major functions in gait: at the end of the swing phase, they extend the knee to allow the prosthesis to reach heel contact, whereas on weight bearing they also stabilize the knee joint. Following midstance, the quadriceps muscles are not active (Inman et al., 1981).

Early quadriceps muscle reeducation is of prime concern. Quadriceps contractions can be practiced immediately postsurgically when the stump is casted, followed by active knee extension exercises within knee range of movement as soon as the cast is removed.

The knee flexor muscles act primarily as a counterforce to the quadriceps muscle group in controlling the knee joint during gait. They are active in the first half of the stance phase, assisting in knee stabilization on weight bearing. They also decelerate the forward motion of the prosthesis at the end of swing phase. In non-weight-bearing situations, they allow for slight knee internal and external rotation when the knee joint is flexed.

Reduced Functional Output. Amputees with weak hamstring muscles may use more hip flexor power than necessary to produce knee flexion. This causes an uneven heel rise following prosthetic toe-off. During gait, uneven step length and/or hip hiking occur to compensate for decreased knee flexion. Weakness and/or a knee flexion contracture, particularly in a short transtibial stump, make ambulation difficult because of poor stump lever control. These amputees walk with a stiff knee gait (similar to patients who have a long leg cast). They eliminate active knee flexion intentionally by compensating with other gait devia-

Stump Knee Extension (Transtibial Amputation)

Stump Knee Flexion (Transtibial Amputation)

tions such as abduction and circumduction. This stiff knee gait pattern is energy consuming because the prosthesis is activated by hip flexion only (Saunders et al., 1953). The stiff knee posture over the prosthetic side places the stump directly over the socket on weight bearing. This gives the amputee a feeling of security. When the knee is kept stiff during the prosthetic swing phase, vaulting on the sound side occurs to allow prosthetic ground clearance.

Treatment Considerations.   The clinician must constantly be aware of the biarticular function of the hamstring muscles as hip extensors as well as knee flexors. Action in the knee strongly depends on the position of the hip (Kapandji, 1970). The presence of weak hip flexors will decrease the function of the hamstrings as knee flexors because their efficiency as knee flexors is enhanced when stretched by hip flexion.

Comparison of Knee Extension and Flexion Functions.   Both stump knee extension and flexion have major functions during the gait cycle.

The quadriceps muscle has to exert a strong muscular force to extend the knee and hold it within its required joint position. This can be illustrated by asking a healthy person to stand for a prolonged time with both knees in a bent position. Muscle tiring occurs relatively quickly.

The hamstring muscles have to absorb the impact of the prosthetic heel strike and contribute to holding the slightly flexed knee position during midstance.

The functions of knee extension and flexion are therefore divided into producing velocity and providing weight-bearing stability.

Summary   In preparation for ambulation, stump movements are assessed in terms of strength and range of motion. Individual stump exercises are practiced in an effort to ensure stump lever control during locomotion. The use of biofeedback, weights, and "hands-on" techniques, when correctly applied, will facilitate improvement of all stump movements. Manual contact is an integral part of treatment since it provides tactile input, enhancing stump proprioception and permitting the therapist to feel the correct direction, the amount of control, and the intensity of each stump movement (Gardiner, 1981).

The importance of stump extension and flexion (at any amputation level) must be emphasized because without functional control of these movements, gait velocity is compromised.

Stump extension exercises must always be emphasized because the extensor muscles provide strong muscle forces that contribute to postural control and body forward thrust.

The stump extensor muscles:

- assist in holding the body upright
- stabilize the prosthetic knee and thereby contribute to a safe prosthetic stance phase (in transfemoral amputations)
- stabilize the natural knee (in transtibial amputations)

- are antagonist to the knee flexor muscles
- counteract the development of flexion contractures

Flexion exercises are necessary but are of lesser importance. Flexion basically shortens the leg to allow it to swing forward and requires less muscular force because the motion is assisted by momentum during the swing phase. During the stance phase, flexion also has an impact-absorbing effect on locomotion.

The stump flexor muscles:

- Are antagonists for the extensor muscles.
- Are stabilizers for the extensor muscles.
- Are automatically used by the amputee as a balancing lever (in a hip flexion and/or knee flexion position) when walking on crutches without the prosthesis, when standing up and sitting down, and when transferring from bed to chair.
- Are used to provide positions of comfort during rest periods (e.g., sitting or curling up in bed). However, over prolonged periods these positions tend to overstretch the hip extensor muscles.

When considering the extensive automatic use of the flexors, one can see that, following amputation surgery, extensor muscle power has a tendency to weaken and, therefore, needs special attention during exercise training.

Although stressing stump extension and flexion motions, the clinicians must always be aware of the effects that other stump muscle groups, especially weak ones, have on gait. These groups also need to be exercised to achieve an energy efficient, safe gait pattern.

Colthurst, A.J.B., and Falconer, K.A. "Lower Extremity." *Manual Muscle Testing.*   References
    Toronto: University of Toronto, 1973, 1–23.
Gardiner, M.D. "An Introduction to Movement. The Stretch Stimulus and the Stretch
    Reflex. The Hip Adductors." *The principles of exercise therapy.* London: Bell and
    Hyman, 1981, 21–25, 82–83, 202–203.
Hoppenfeld, S. "Examination of Gait." *Physical Examination of the Spine and
    Extremities.* New York: Appleton-Century-Crofts, 1976, 133–141.
Inman, V.T., Ralston, H.J., and Todd, F. "Kinematics." *Human Walking.* Baltimore:
    Williams & Wilkins, 1981, 22–61.
Kapandji, I.A. "The Hips. The Knee." *The Physiology of the Joints,* 2nd ed. Edinburgh,
    Scot.: E. & S. Livingstone, 1970, vol. 2, 9–66, 72–134.
Mensch, G. "Prosthetic Gait Observation: Comparison of Bipedal and Quadrupedal
    Locomotion." Physiotherapy Canada, *31,* no. 5 (1979): 269–272.
Mensch, G. "Prosthetic Gait Training—Clinical Observations and Correction of Postural
    Gait Deviations." *Proceedings, the IXth International Congress of World Confedera-
    tion for Physical Thearpy,* Part 1. London: World Confederation for Physical Therapy,
    1982, 14–119.
Mensch, G. "Physiotherapy Following through-knee Amputations." *Prosthetics and
    Orthotics International, 7,* no. 2 (1983): 79–87.
New York University. "Socket Characteristics." *Lower-limb Prosthetics.* New York: New
    York University Post-Graduate Medical School, 1975, 199–207.
Radcliffe, C.W. "Above-knee Prosthetics." *Prosthetics and Orthotics International, 1*
    (1977): 146–160.

Radcliffe, C.W., and Eberhart, H.S. ''Applications to Lower Limb Prosthetics.'' In Inman, V.T., Ralston, H.J., and Todd, F., (eds) *Human Walking*. Baltimore: Williams & Wilkins, 1981, 129–134.

Saunders, J.B.D.M., Inman, V.T., and Eberhart, H.D. ''The Major Determinants in Normal and Pathological Gait.'' *Journal of Bone and Joint Surgery, 35A,* no. 3 (1953): 534–558.

3

Prosthetics and Prosthetic Gait

A lower extremity prosthesis consists of prosthetic components that include a foot, a joint or joints, a socket, and a suspension system. Special additional devices (e.g., torque absorber) can also be incorporated as the amputee's needs are identified.

A PHYSICAL THERAPY OVERVIEW OF PROSTHETICS

All components are essential to ensure functional performance by providing:

- weight-bearing stability (see Prosthetic Alignment, p. 232)
- optimum dynamic alignment (see Prosthetic Alignment, p. 234)
- sitting, standing, and walking comfort

In addition to these functional considerations, the cosmetic appearance of the prosthesis is equally important (Friedmann, 1978).

Each prosthesis is prescribed by a physician in consultation with the prosthetist and other team members. The prescription and selection of appropriate components is based on the amputee's specific requirements and must take into consideration (Foort, 1982):

- the level of amputation
- the reason for amputation
- the health status of the amputee
- the characteristics of the stump
- the amount of functional activity expected
- the weight of the prosthesis
- the age and sex of the amputee
- the comfort and appearance of the prosthesis (see Prosthetic Prescription and Checkout, p. 283)

Each prosthesis is custom made by the prosthetist. Therefore, prostheses are not interchangeable. The socket is fabricated according to the specific stump characteristics (see Amputation Levels, p. 31), whereas the dynamic alignment (see Prosthetic Alignment, p. 234) is adjusted to the individual gait pattern of each amputee. Prefabricated or mass-produced definitive prostheses are not available.

Prostheses have been used throughout history. The refinement of approaches to prosthetic fabrication has produced a variety of prostheses. Fabrication materials previously included wood, metal, and leather. More recently, plastics and foam have been introduced. Over the past 40 years, prosthetic designs have undergone considerable change (Radcliffe, 1977) as prosthetic fabrication has evolved from a creative art to also include the field of science. Researchers investigating:

- the biomechanics of human gait
- the principles of prosthetic alignment
- the suitability of materials
- the function of different prosthetic components

have greatly improved the prostheses of the 1980's.

The introduction of the endoskeletal, modular fabrication system has been a major development from the existing exoskeletal system.

An exoskeletal system supports the body weight by a hard, external, shell-like system fabricated from a plastic laminate. The construction and fixation of the components is permanent, making alignment alterations and repairs an involved task. Exoskeletal prostheses are functional and still popular because they are built to withstand the excessive "wear and tear" associated with heavy use. In addition, they can be utilized for amputees who require lighter weight, durable prostheses because their shell construction permits variations in the weight structure to accommodate the needs of these amputees.

The endoskeletal system, now frequently prescribed, transmits the body weight over an internal pipe system comparable with natural bone support. With this modular system, concealed by a cosmetic foam cover, each individual component can be easily exchanged. Alignment adjustments, replacements, and repairs are all readily accomplished. The endoskeletal system is basically lighter and is constant in weight compared with the exoskeletal prosthesis. This system is useful for moderate prosthetic users as well as for geriatric amputees. However, it can now also be prescribed for the rugged user because earlier component breakage problems have been solved by fabricating components of stronger materials. Replacement of the cosmetic foam cover is necessary from time to time.

Prosthetic Components

Researchers and manufacturers of prosthetic components and systems are constantly investigating new concepts and developing prototypes (see Recent Developments in Prosthetics, p. 337). Therefore, it is impossible to present every product available.

To introduce therapists to prosthetics and assist them in broadening their clinical skills, commonly prescribed prosthetic components have been selected for presentation and are dealt with according to their function and clinical indications.

This knowledge will permit the therapist to have an input into prosthetic prescription.

Sophisticated engineering designs and manufacturing details of prosthetic components (e.g., the working mechanism of the hydraulic knee unit) will not be considered.

Feet

Different models permit versatility in the selection of the most suitable design for the amputee's gait. Feet are available in many variations to accommodate the different sizes, heel height, and right–left selection necessary. Cosmetic feet with imitation toes are more readily accepted by some amputees for use with open-toed shoes or sandals.

Solid Ankle Cushion Heel (SACH) Foot.   The SACH foot is comparatively light in weight and has no mechanically moving parts. It is made of high density rubber and has an internal stabilizing keel that extends into the forefoot. The foot simulates the foreward rolling motion of the natural foot by passively responding to weight-bearing forces. On heel contact, the heel section, referred to as the heel bumper, compresses, partially absorbing ground impact and thus permitting plantarflexion. During midstance the foot provides stable weight-bearing support. Toe-off is possible because the end of the keel section in the forefoot acts as a passive toe break. Inversion and eversion are minimal and only simulated by compression. These functions permit some flexibility for walking over rough ground and give the foot a natural appearance. The amount of heel

(See Fig. 3–1)

Figure 3–1   SACH foot: cross section.

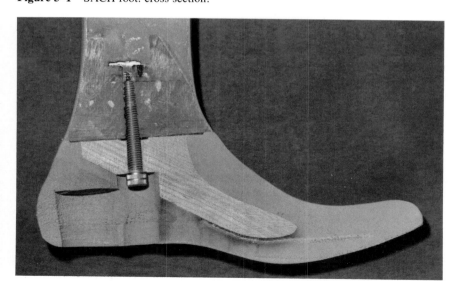

compression is determined by the density of the heel rubber (firm, soft) as well as by the amputee's weight and walking style.

SACH feet are indicated for all amputation levels and are most commonly prescribed (Fishman et al., 1975). They are particularly useful for geriatric amputees when the weight of the prosthesis must be considered. They are cosmetically acceptable and can be utilized for both exoskeletal and endoskeletal systems.

(See Fig. 3–2)

Stationary Attachment Flexible Endoskeleton (SAFE) Foot. The uniquely designed SAFE foot is an ''offshoot'' of the SACH foot. However, it is entirely different in its construction.

Embedded in foam, the foot features a solid union between the shank and foot by bolt attachment. A flexible keel simulates, in shape, the arch of the foot. It also includes a toe section and plantar ''ligaments'' (bands) that adapt to uneven ground while controlling the range of the flexible keel. The foot has no mechanical joints.

Heel contact and foot flat occur by heel bumper compression. Foot stability at midstance is possible because the ''ligaments'' are under stretch. Heel-off causes further ''ligament'' tension, activating the toe lever and, by doing so, duplicates the toe-off function. All of these features permit foot movement in all planes, absorb axial rotation, and allow the foot to adapt to standing sideways on an incline.

The SAFE foot will probably become more popular because of its adaptability and stability. It can be utilized for the exoskeletal and the endoskeletal prosthesis.

(See Fig. 3–3)

Single Axis Foot. The single axis foot has a horizontal axis that permits dorsi and plantarflexion movements. The foot motion is initiated by weight

Figure 3–2   SAFE foot: cross section.

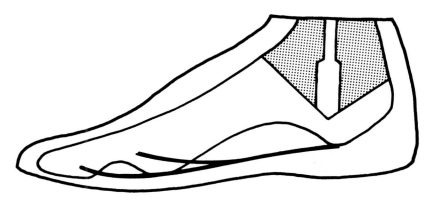

bearing, starting at heel contact. A bumper, placed posterior to the ankle axis, controls the amount of movement between shank and foot. A toe break is incorporated, either by building a mechanical segment into the forefoot or by constructing the distal foot portion from a softer material than the midfoot section. This particular foot, more rigid than the others, does not permit inversion and eversion and, therefore, increases foot stability.

A single axis foot is heavier than a SACH foot and not prescribed when the weight of the prosthesis is a factor. However, it is utilized where increased foot stability is required (e.g., when a bilateral transfemoral amputee with knee instability requires medial-lateral foot stability).

The single axis foot has traditionally been selected for transfemoral amputees with short stumps and hip disarticulations to provide stance stability. However, this trend is changing in favor of the SACH foot. A single axis foot can be utilized for both the exoskeletal and endoskeletal systems.

Multiaxis foot.   The multiaxis foot provides a multiaxis connection between the foot and shank sections through a bumper ring, permitting dorsiflexion and plantar flexion (which can be independently adjusted) as well as inversion and eversion, thus absorbing some axial rotation (Murray et al., 1982). The stationary keel section is surrounded by soft rubber that also provides moderate flexibility in the midsection. The foot can adapt to rough terrain and, therefore, is useful for amputees whose occupations demand walking on uneven ground (e.g., farmers, construction workers). It is available for both the exoskeletal and endoskeletal prosthetic systems.

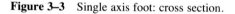

Figure 3–3   Single axis foot: cross section.

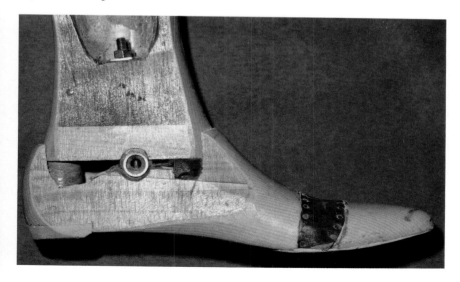

Knees

Prosthetic knee joints function like hinges and are activated by stump movements. They must flex easily and also provide stability under load. Several different knee joint designs are available. Some of these increase stance stability, whereas others enhance the gait pattern by assisting the swing phase (Radcliffe, 1977). Appropriate knee unit selection is difficult because, often, the ones involving more sophisticated engineering designs that improve function also add weight to the prosthesis.

Single-axis free-swinging knee.   The single-axis free-swinging knee is the most simple approach to duplicating knee function. It is a free-swinging hinge design that allows the shank to move freely in a pendular fashion toward knee extension. The movement of the shank is halted on extension by contact with a stop and will remain in extension provided:

- the prosthesis is in ground contact
- the stump simultaneously extends

The operation of this knee mechanism depends entirely on the position of the knee joint in relation to the hip and foot and on the amputee's ability to control the knee. It is simple, lightweight, and can be equipped with a knee extension aid and/or a manual locking device. These two adaptations enhance stance stability and are helpful for those elderly amputees who have stump hip extension weakness. The single axis knee can be incorporated into the exoskeletal as well as the endoskeletal system.

Knee Mechanisms Aiding in Stance Stability

The most crucial moment during gait occurs at the beginning of the stance phase. Knee instability is experienced by many, particularly the elderly transfemoral amputee. Knee joints that provide stance stability contribute to a safer, more confident gait.

Polycentric Knee.   The horizontal axis of rotation in the natural knee joint does not remain in the same position during flexion and extension. This change in position of the center of rotation occurs because the curves of the femoral condyles are not circular. If recorded, the position change produces an irregular curve and differs slightly between stance (when the shank is under load) and swing (when the shank is suspended) (Frankel, 1971; Blacharski, 1975; Page, 1979; Winter, 1981). One can simply say that in extension this axis is located more posteriorly and proximally, thus contributing to knee stability on weight bearing, whereas in flexion the center of rotation of the knee axis slides more anteriorly and distally, thus contributing to shortening the shank during swing.

(See Fig. 3–4)

Polycentric knees attempt to duplicate the function of the anatomical knee to provide increased knee stability. Different engineering systems are based on rolling designs and skidding actions as well as two- and four-bar linkage units (Radcliffe, 1977).

Figure 3–4   Position of the center of the knee axis during motion.

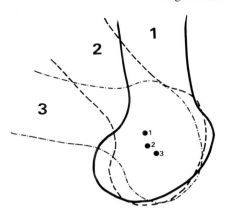

Four-bar Linkage Knee Mechanism.   The polycentric four-bar linkage knee unit appears to be the more commonly selected one. The polygon position of the bars not only projects the instant center of rotation proximally and posteriorly to give stance stability (Fernie, 1981) but also assists in shortening the prosthetic shank during swing by moving the center of rotation anteriorly and distally (Radcliffe, 1977). This is an additional safety factor since it assists in ground clearance.   *(See Fig. 3–5)*

The four-bar linkage unit is particularly useful for knee disarticulations since the stump length necessitates placing the prosthetic knee below the axis of the natural knee. The projection of the center of the knee rotation by the four-bar linkage unit provides a more natural gait since it nearly equalizes the levels of knee rotation and provides increased sitting comfort.

The knee mechanism is also specifically functional for short transfemoral stumps because it projects the horizontal knee axis closer to the stump, thereby assisting in stump leverage. It also helps the amputee to move more easily by giving the impression that the prosthesis is lighter.

Polycentric knees are available for both endoskeletal and exoskeletal prostheses.

Safety Knees.   Some transfemoral amputees have difficulty in controlling the prosthetic stance phase from heel contact to midstance and, consequently, may develop a fear of prosthetic knee buckling. To avoid knee instability, the safety knee is designed like a brake drum. Precisely fitting thigh and shank friction surfaces will lock or brake on weight bearing, even if full knee extension has not been accomplished. However, at the same time, the shank is able to swing freely during the prosthetic swing phase. The term ''safety knee'' can be misleading as these mechanisms provide only a safe weight-bearing range within the first 25° of knee flexion. This degree of weight-bearing ability in flexion is often referred to as

Figure 3–5   Four-bar linkage knee mechanism. The projected center of knee rotation is superimposed.

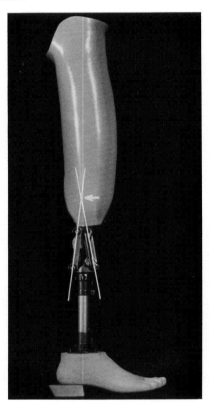

the "safe zone." Amputees must be made aware of and understand the limitations of these knee mechanisms.

Safety knees are indicated for the elderly, particularly if they have short transfemoral stumps with a hip flexion contracture or if hip extensor muscle weakness is present. Exoskeletal safety knees are heavier than endoskeletal safety knee units.

Knee Mechanisms
Assisting Swing Phase

In the normal knee, knee control varies inversely to the cadence speed (e.g., as walking speed increases, the forward motion of the shin is slowed down prior to its end range to prevent excessive, uncontrolled knee extension before heel contact). Swing phase control devices incorporate both constant and variable friction mechanisms in an attempt to duplicate the normal swing phase function.

Constant Friction Unit.   Constant friction units are preset to function satisfactorily at a certain walking speed. Therefore, they require a consistent gait velocity. If the amputee attempts to increase walking speed, the friction does not alter, and the shank of the prosthesis lags behind.

Variable Friction Units.   Variable friction units include hydraulic (fluid-filled) and pneumatic (air-filled) knee mechanisms and most closely simulate the normal gait by:

- regulating prosthetic heel rise
- controlling the amount and speed of prosthetic knee flexion
- providing a smooth prosthetic swing motion
- preventing terminal impact (see Gait Deviations, p. 304)
- adapting to the amputee's walking speed

and thus imitate, most closely, the functions of the quadriceps and hamstring muscles.

Both of these swing phase control units are angular velocity control devices that function like a shock absorber in a car, dampening the speed of the angular movement and providing resistance to any sudden and/or excessive motion.

Both hydraulic and pneumatic knee units have proven to be clinically reliable. However, adjustments of these devices can be very intricate. Physical therapists are strongly advised to consult with the prosthetist for alterations in the setting of these devices.

Hydraulic and pneumatic swing phase control units are indicated for amputees whose physical abilities and needs exceed those of a constant friction swing control unit. Therefore, they are most suitable for active prosthetic users.

The mechanisms are available for exoskeletal and endoskeletal prosthetic fabrication systems.

Knee mechanisms providing swing and stance phase control are sophisticated, expensive devices that are not yet routinely prescribed, although they are gaining popularity. Their use relies upon the availability of prosthetic services and, therefore, they are at present geographically dependent to some extent.

Knee Mechanisms Providing Swing and Stance Phase Control

MAUCH S'N'S*™ *(Stance and Swing) Knee Unit.   The MAUCH S'N'S™ knee unit is a dual function unit that provides stance stability in combination with hydraulic swing phase control. The stance feature provides the ability to bear weight over a flexed knee (of value when walking down an incline). A lever setting allows the amputee to either adjust the flexion setting or lock the knee to full extension. (This provides stability during long standing activities.)

The hydraulic swing phase control adapts to the amputee's walking speed and can also (if needed) be manually adjusted by the amputee.

TEH LIN*™ *Modular Knee Unit.   The TEH LIN™ modular knee unit is a design that combines a four-bar linkage system for stance stability with a self-adjusting pneumatic swing phase control system. The unit is modular, moderately lightweight, and designed for the active transfemoral prosthetic user. It is produced for use with the endoskeletal prosthesis.

General Information About Sockets and their Suspensions

Sockets are stump receptacles and provide an interface between the stump and the prosthesis. They are constructed to the anatomical contours of the individual stump size and shape and are adapted to the specific stump characteristics (see Amputation Levels, p. 32).

All sockets must fit securely:

- to provide functional lever control
- to provide stability for muscular control
- to avoid stump piston action
- to provide total contact (also in non-end-bearing stumps)
- to prevent distal edema and/or skin irritation (Levy, 1983)
- to permit stump tissues to receive uniform sensory feedback

during all phases of gait. Sockets must also be comfortable so that the stump can efficiently accommodate the forces resulting from gait dynamics in a pain-free manner.

Socket design principles are based on the assumption that a hard socket wall provides firm support for stump lever control and that stump tissue accommodation depends on tissue tolerance to external pressures. Pressure-tolerant tissues are compressed to ensure a snug fit between the stump and socket, whereas pressure-sensitive tissues are accommodated in the socket shape to give comfort by providing a relief in the socket wall (Radcliffe, 1977; Fernie, 1981; Foort, 1982; Murray et al., 1982).

In this way, pressure-sensitive and pressure tolerant tissues are correctly positioned within the socket. Muscle tissues can contract and relax against the socket walls without losing contact so that control between the stump and the prosthesis can be maintained. A snug fit facilitates prosthetic suspension because the muscles "grip" the socket wall while contracting. This redistribution of external pressure during casting causes socket diameters to look somewhat different than the actual stump shape. However, a functional environment is achieved for the stump.

Socket suspension systems differ in their designs and functions and are closely related to the type of socket they are suspending. Suspension is vitally important since it holds the prosthesis on the stump and, by doing so, helps to control the longitudinal rotation of the prosthesis. The suspension must always be nonrestrictive and comfortable.

Other Components

Additional prosthetic component parts, also designed to meet specific needs, will either enhance the function or the appearance of the prosthesis.

Torque Absorber. During normal gait, longitudinal rotation occurs in the lower extremities. This rotation or torsion is absorbed by the joints. Amputation disrupts this natural torque absorption mechanism because of the removal of the distal joint. Therefore, torsion takes place between the socket interface and the stump, causing a potential site for problems of skin shearing or breakdown.

A torque absorber minimizes this shearing action (felt more so in the long amputation stumps), improves weight-bearing comfort, and allows the active amputee to perform turning and shifting motions with more ease (e.g. snow shovelling, golf, etc.). It is not routinely prescribed for the geriatric amputee.

Torque absorbers are adjustable (they have a range of $\pm 20°$), are available for endoskeletal systems, and can be utilized for most amputation levels.

Knee Rotator. Cross-legged sitting is made possible for transfemoral amputees by adding a modular knee rotation unit to the prosthesis during fabrication. The rotating disc unit is positioned proximal to the knee mechanism and remains locked during walking. The range of available rotation is up to 360°. When rotation is needed, the disc bearings are released by push button, and the shank/foot section is then rotated. The degree of rotation is manually controlled by the amputee and takes place between the knee unit and the socket, thus eliminating stump skin shearing. When shank rotation is no longer required, the device is manually returned to the zero position, where the push button mechanism engages, locking the unit.

(See Fig. 3–6)

Figure 3–6   Knee rotator released.

This rotation component is convenient for amputees for:

- changing shoes
- crossing the legs
- sitting on the floor
- getting the prosthetic shank "out of the way" during driving

or any other activities that would normally require extensive hip internal or external rotation.

Cosmetic Covers. To improve the appearance of the prosthesis, different cosmetic covers are marketed. These covers are made of foam or elastic vinyl.

(See Fig. 3–7)   ***Foam Covers.*** An endoskeletal prosthesis is finished by concealing the pipe support system with foam. This foam is shaped to the anatomical contours of the thigh and/or shank and then protected by a durable cosmetic elastic stocking.

Figure 3–7   Cosmetic foam cover.

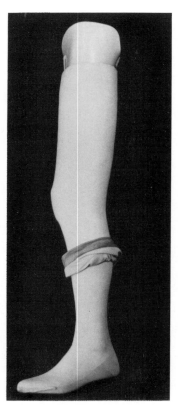

Source: Photograph courtesy of Otto Bock Orthopedic Industry of Canada Ltd.

The foam compresses when sitting and is cosmetically pleasing. However, prosthetic knee movement may be hindered if the foam is too dense.

The cosmetic stocking is held in place by a proximally incorporated elastic band that adheres to the socket. This stocking can be easily removed for washing and can be reapplied by the amputee.

Prosthetic Skin.   Prosthetic skin is a cosmetic cover for endoskeletal as   *(See Fig. 3–8)* well as exoskeletal prostheses. It is made from thin copolyvinyl elastic. The elastic skin adapts to the contours of the prosthesis and allows for unhindered movements of the prosthetic components. The prosthetic skin has to be gently cared for, protected from sharp objects, and washed with mild soap. It is applied by the prosthetist and mostly stays in place until replacement is indicated.

Stump Socks.   Stump socks are manufactured in different sizes, thickness (ply), and materials. They are worn with the prosthesis to provide stump comfort by reducing skin friction and absorbing perspiration. Stump measurements (length, proximal and distal girth) determine the stump sock size. Most three- and five-ply socks are made from wool and permit the amputee to control the snugness of the socket fit by increasing or decreasing the number of ply (e.g., two three-ply socks provide a thickness of six ply). When 10 to 12 ply are needed, socket adjustments should be made.

A stump sheath-sock combination (Daw Industries, Inc.) features a soft aerated sheath worn over the stump for comfort that is then covered by a woollen sock. Sheath and sock adhere to each other to function as one.

Figure 3–8   Prosthetic skin.

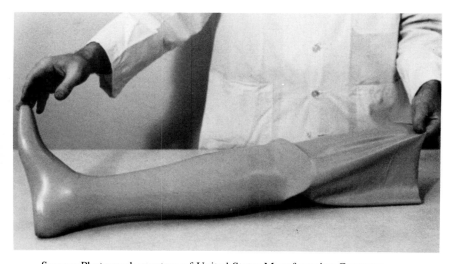

Source: Photograph courtesy of United States Manufacturing Company.

Clinical Comment. A stump sock is not required by amputees who have been fitted with a suction socket since skin–socket contact is needed to maintain suspension. However, a tube-like suction socket sheath (Daw Industries, Inc.) can be used to protect the skin around the proximal socket rim should skin irritation in this area be a problem.

Modular Assembly Systems

(See Fig. 3–9)

Researchers have developed various designs of endoskeletal, modular assembly systems (e.g., Otto Bock Orthopedic Industry Inc., United States Manufacturing Company, TEH LIN). Each system is functional and cosmetic and allows easy exchange of interdependent component parts only within its own system. Since prosthetic component parts are not standardized, an interchange of parts between these systems is not yet routinely possible (Foort, 1981).

Summary

Prosthetic components vary in function, weight, and appearance. The physical therapist, by observing the amputee during gait training sessions with a temporary prosthesis, can provide needed information for the prescription of the definitive prosthesis.

Prostheses

Each amputation level has specific prosthetic needs. The higher the level, the more complex the prosthetic fabrication becomes.

Figure 3–9   A modular assembly system.

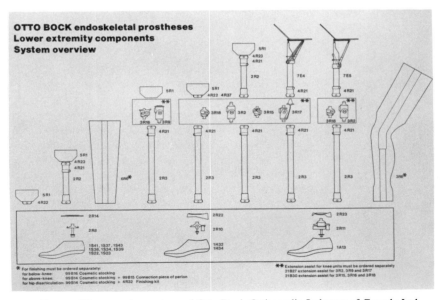

Source: Photograph courtesy of Otto Bock Orthopedic Industry of Canada Ltd.

A partial foot amputation does not require a laminated socket construction but, in order to function effectively, the residual foot needs support, total contact, and comfort. This is provided by a shoe or boot that may require reinforcement of the sole. The shoe or boot is fitted with a permanent soft or firm filler in the toe section or with a removable insert. Sometimes, depending on the length of the residual foot, the insert is connected to an arch support (Murray et al., 1982). These adjustments will:

- compensate for the lost forefoot lever function
- provide proximal total contact for stability
- prevent the remaining foot portion from sliding forward
- aid in balance and proprioception
- assist in the push-off phase

Comfortable insert contouring against the proximal portion of the remaining foot portion is most important, particularly since the toe break action occurs between the remaining foot portion and the insert.

To improve stability in the shortened foot, the forefoot insert can be attached to an ankle-foot orthosis similar in shape to a shoehorn brace (Staros et al., 1981). The flexible polyethylene design allows for mobility while providing anteroposterior, as well as medial-lateral, foot stability and moderate toe break resistance. This prosthetic–orthotic device can be transferred to other shoes if the toe box is large enough and the heel height is the same.

Prosthetic Replacements for Forefoot Amputations

(See Fig. 3–10)

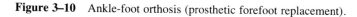

Figure 3–10 Ankle-foot orthosis (prosthetic forefoot replacement).

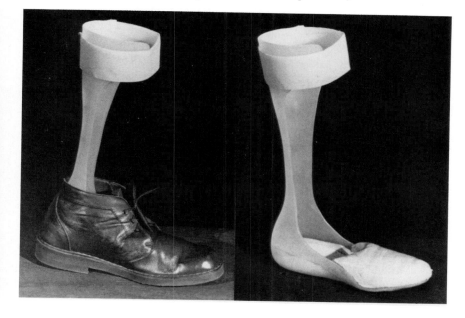

In very short forefoot stumps, fitting shoe inserts may present a problem since the heel portion must be encased by the ankle joint in order to obtain functional weight-bearing stability. The prosthetic replacement consists of a laced leather casing with a rigid forefoot section, constructed with an articulated toe break. This device has to be worn in a boot rather than a shoe.

In all replacement techniques, the shoe functions as the socket and the suspension. Correct shoe selection is, therefore, a prerequisite for successful fitting.

Ankle Disarticulation (Syme's) Prosthesis

The socket for a Syme's amputation is long when compared with the loss in leg length. The proximal brim extends to below the knee level to ensure effective stump lever control. When viewed from above, the inner socket outline is triangular proximally, narrowing distally to an almost oval shape before widening to provide room for the malleoli at the stump end. The anterior section has a prominent groove to provide relief for the tibial crest. This groove stabilizes the stump against the longitudinal rotational forces and thus reduces stump end torque action (Radcliffe, 1970). A snug fit is ensured over the entire stump length by soft tissue compression. The fabrication of the socket can be somewhat difficult because it must provide total contact to both the entire lower leg and the bulbous stump end.

An intimate socket fit is essential:

- to provide controlled end weight bearing over the distal heel pad
- to prevent heel pad shifting
- to permit the calf muscles to contract against the socket wall
- to ensure stump comfort

(See Fig. 3–11)

A socket wall opening or window must be provided so that the bulbous stump end can pass through the narrower distal section. The windowed opening can be placed either medially or posteriorly and is closed, with the cut-out section being held in place by straps and a velcro closure when the prosthesis is worn. Although necessary, this opening adversely affects the socket wall stability.

With regard to the position of the window, the medial opening provides better socket stability because the continuity of the posterior wall is maintained. The calf muscles thus have an uninterrupted posterior wall against which to contract. This, in turn, counteracts the anterior and posterior forces acting on the stump during gait. Conversely, because of its position, a posterior window causes posterior wall instability. However, in rare situations a posterior wall opening is utilized to accommodate fluctuations in stump size that some elderly amputees with vascular impairment experience during the course of the day (Foort, 1982).

The stump heel pad, unable to contract against the forces acting upon it, functions as a cushion by absorbing weight-bearing stresses during gait (see Ankle Disarticulations, p. 34). If the stump heel pad shifts, the diameter of the socket, which accommodates the heel pad, must be checked. If stump end weight bearing is still uncomfortable, the socket must be modified proximally. This is accomplished by extending the socket brim to a PTS design. This will distribute

Figure 3–11 Ankle disarticulation (Syme's) prosthesis.

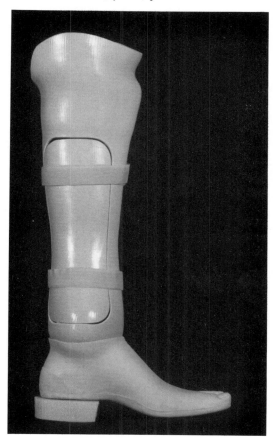

weight-bearing forces to the patellar tendon bar and the tibial flares, thus easing distal stump end discomfort (see Transtibial Prostheses, p. 218).

Suspension. The socket walls are contoured proximal to the malleoli. This narrows the distal shank section, thus maintaining the socket in correct alignment with the stump and minimizing piston action (see Stump Piston Action, p. 245). If the malleoli have been trimmed surgically (see Ankle Disarticulations, p. 34) and do not provide enough area to contour the socket so that the prosthesis is held in place, proximal socket modifications (PTS) are indicated to suspend the prosthesis. Calf muscle activity within a snug fitting shank section also aids in suspension control.

If the above modifications are successfully implemented, no further suspension should be necessary for this prosthesis.

Segmented Socket. An entirely different socket design for the ankle disarticulation prosthesis has been developed (The Hugh MacMillan Medical Centre, Toronto) to improve shank stability as well as cosmetic appearance. This prosthesis consists of two sockets. An inner, full length pliable socket is segmented by means of four to eight lengthwise slits placed through the narrow shank section. During donning, the inner socket expands temporarily to permit entry of the bulbous stump end. When the stump is positioned, the slits close and the inner socket provides an intimate stump socket interface for stump lever control. The rigid outer, nonwindowed socket receptacle ensures weight-bearing support and stability.[1] The total contact fit of the inner socket, as well as the combined inner socket and the outer receptacle that are snugly linked proximally and distally, provide suspension control.

The design has also been successfully utilized for other bulbous stumps. However the stump, functioning in the double socket prosthesis, will have a tendency to get hot, and donning and doffing require manual dexterity and strength.

Foot Component. A modified SACH foot is positioned distally directly under both socket types so that the weight-bearing line at midstance falls on the midfoot section (see Alignment, p. 232).

Cosmesis. The appearance of an ankle disarticulation prosthesis is not too attractive because the ankle section is always broader when compared with the remaining leg.

Transtibial Prostheses

Advances in below knee socket design ensure efficient socket fit regardless of below knee stump length. In these prostheses, foot and socket are joined by either endoskeletal or exoskeletal construction systems.

Patellar Tendon-
Bearing Prosthesis
(See Fig. 3–12)

The PTB transtibial socket provides total contact but is not an end-bearing socket (Foort, 1982). When viewed from the top it is roughly triangular in shape. The brims of the medially and laterally flaring socket sidewalls are approximately 2 in. higher than the level of the brim of the connecting posterior wall. The apex of the triangle, positioned anteriorly, provides relief for the tibial crest. Other areas of relief include the tibial tubercle, the fibular head, and the patella (Fernie, 1981; Foort, 1982; Murray et al., 1982).

The inner anterior wall in its upper third section also accommodates the patellar tendon bar. This inward protruding socket landmark is situated at a right angle to the tibial groove. With the socket set in slight flexion (see Prosthetic Alignment, p. 235), the patellar tendon bar:

- Permits the amputee to kneel against it on prosthetic weight bearing, thus reducing stump end bearing and transferring some weight-bearing control to the patellar tendon.

Figure 3–12 Transtibial prosthesis (PTB).

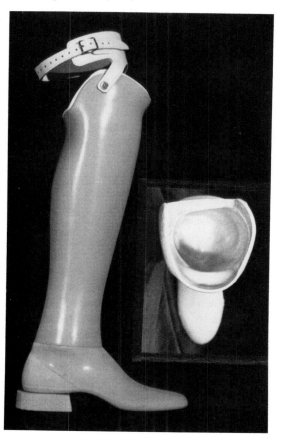

- Allows for improved proprioceptive feedback since the tissue surrounding the patellar tendon is designed by nature to accommodate weight bearing in the kneeling position.
- Aids marginally in socket suspension together with the contraction of the stump muscles against the socket walls. This occurs during the swing phase when the quadriceps muscles contract and the patellar tendon is able to "grip" the patellar tendon bar.

Medial and lateral wall flares extend to the level of the femoral condyles and provide medial-lateral joint stability, which is of particular benefit to the amputee with a short stump.

The posterior connecting wall is flared outwardly to permit knee flexion and provide comfort in the sitting position. The wall is shaped to allow relief for the hamstrings and gastrocnemius muscle tendons. The center of the proximal section of the posterior wall provides gentle compression of the soft tissues immediately below the popliteal fossa. This counterpressure facilitates patellar tendon weight bearing against the patellar tendon bar.

The total contact of the socket provides uniform proprioceptive feedback to all stump tissues and ensures moderate weight-bearing distribution over the total stump surface. The patellar tendon and the medial tibial flare function as specific weight-bearing areas to relieve distal stump end pressure (Foort, 1982).

Suspensions.   The patellar tendon-bearing socket can be suspended in several ways. Each suspension system has unique benefits that must be considered before the final prescription is made.

(See Fig. 3–13)

Figure-Eight Strap.   This strap arrangement is anchored to the lateral flare, crosses in front of the knee, leads posteriorly, returns to the front, again crosses in front of the knee, and is either buckled or fastened by a velcro closure on the opposite side. This strap is easily secured but needs frequent replacement since the webbing deteriorates with use.

Supracondylar Cuff Suspension Strap.   This suspension is made up of a forked leather strap anchored to the proximal medial and lateral socket walls and is joined to a leather strap that encircles the limb above the knee. The strap fastens with either a buckle or a D ring and a velcro closure. An elastic insert may be

Figure 3–13   Transtibial prosthetic suspension systems. Left to right: figure-eight strap, supracondylar cuff suspension, fork strap attachment, side bars and thigh corset.

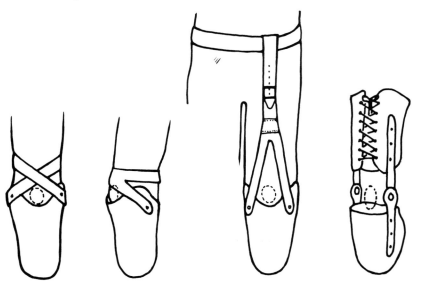

incorporated at the apex of the fork to improve the fit over the proximal patellar border.

These two types of suspension are functional, efficient, and commonly used. Adaptability in the placement and the type of closure used is most beneficial for amputees with decreased hand function.

However, some amputees find the closures bulky, and often females comment on the increased wear on stockings. Another drawback of these systems becomes evident in the particularly fleshy stump. The strap may not be able to provide sufficient suspension over the condyles and the patella, and the excessive soft tissue around the knee may cause the strap to slip down.

Suspension Modification. The supracondylar strap may be supplemented by an additional suspension assist provided by a fork strap attachment from the anterior socket wall to a waist belt. This additional support aids in socket suspension and also functions as a knee extension aid.

Rubber Sleeve Suspension. A silicone rubber sleeve placed partially over the socket and covering the knee and lower third of the thigh will also suspend a PTB prosthesis. This buckle-free suspension interferes least with clothing. Stump piston action is minimal because: *(See Fig. 3–14)*

- The texture of the rubber sleeve causes it to cling to the skin and the plastic laminate of the socket.
- The extent of skin covered by the sleeve provides a larger contact area over which to suspend the prosthesis compared with strap suspensions.

This system functions well for the particularly fleshy stump, provided the correct sleeve size is selected. The amputee must be taught to avoid the rolling down of the proximal sleeve rim that will create a constricting rubber band effect, adversely affecting the stump circulation. The sleeve is also difficult to put on, needs regular replacement and restricts ventilation, which may cause skin irritation. During sitting, knee flexion may be restricted by the sleeve, causing the amputee to respond by holding the knee extended.

Side Bars and Thigh Corset. Metal side bars and a thigh corset were more commonly used with the earlier plug fit sockets. This system actually combines the features of weight-bearing distribution and suspension. The side bars provide firm medial lateral knee joint stability. The snugly laced thigh corset functions as suspension and at the same time accommodates some weight bearing (Foort, 1982).

This suspension approach may be indicated: *(See Fig. 3–13)*

- when the transtibial stump is very short
- when an ''old timer'' prefers to remain with the plug fit socket
- when heavy physical work or participation in sports requires increased knee stability
- when the amputee is unable to bear weight completely through the socket because of stump sensitivity.

Figure 3–14   Rubber sleeve suspension.

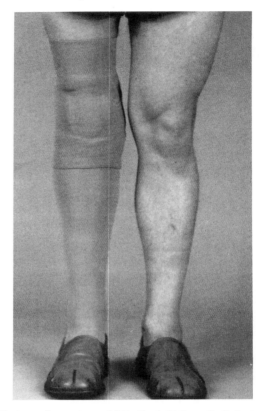

Source: Photograph courtesy of Otto Bock Orthopedic Industry of Canada Ltd.

Disadvantages include discomfort during prolonged sitting periods since thigh tissues bulge posteriorly when the knee is in flexion, even when side bars with polycentric hinges are utilized. Piston action (or relative motion between stump and socket) may be caused by a discrepancy in the position of the mechanical hinges in relation to the anatomical knee axis.

The side bars and thigh corset add weight to the prosthesis, and some amputees find it difficult to fasten the corset firmly enough to provide effective suspension. Since the development of the PTB socket, their use is seldom indicated.

Transtibial Suction Suspension.   This suspension method, developed in Sweden, requires the definitive prosthesis to be constructed in two parts. This inner malleable socket adheres to the stump contours and is held in place by suction with a valve placed distally. The inner socket is placed into an outer shell that functions as an exoskeletal frame, providing the connection between shank and foot and accommodating weight bearing. This method, while practiced in Sweden, is not yet commonly used on this continent.

The PTS socket (developed from the PTB socket) functions similarly to the PTB socket but differs somewhat because the medial and lateral socket brims are extended proximally. These modifications allow the socket walls to contour above the condyles and above the patella.

Patellar Tendon Supra-condylar Prosthesis

(See Fig. 3–15)

Suspension.   The socket is self-suspending. Suspension occurs by the compression of the soft tissues above the femoral condyles and the proximal patellar border.

Wedge Suspension.   If the self-suspension system is not entirely satisfactory (depending on the stump characteristics), a contoured wedge can be slipped

Figure 3–15   Transtibial prosthesis (PTS).

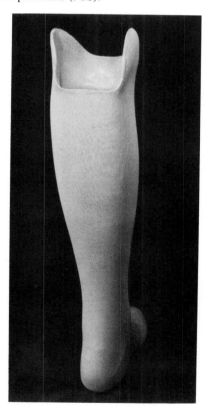

Source: Photograph courtesy of Otto Bock Orthopedic Industry of Canada Ltd.

Figure 3–16   Wedge suspension. Left: contoured wedge; right: removable wedge
section.

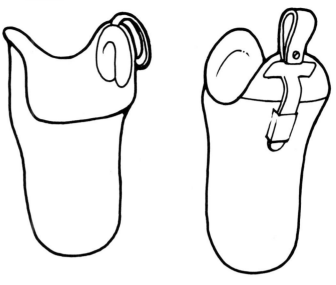

(See Fig. 3–16)

inside the socket just below the medial brim to increase the soft tissue compression
above the medial condyle.[2]

A different version of the removable wedge section can be constructed by
making the wedge a part of the proximal medial wall section. Instead of slipping
the wedge into place inside the socket, the amputee must position the entire wedge
section into a slot in the actual medial wall itself.

Transtibial Socket Liners

According to principles of socket design, fitting, and stump biomechanics,
the hard socket provides the best environment for stump function (Foort, 1982).

However, some amputees (primarily geriatric transtibial amputees with
tender stumps) find the hard socket difficult to tolerate. The amputees may have to
be fitted with either a socket liner or insert to provide comfort by cushioning
sensitive stump tissues.

Liners, produced from materials such as pelite, horsehide or silicone gel,
are shaped from the positive cast mold. When inserted into the socket, they
provide, along with the socket, total stump contact. These inserts occasionally
wear out and require replacement.

There has been discussion that a perfect socket fit should not require any type
of liner (Foort, 1982). However, clinically it has been reported that transtibial
amputees who have been fitted with an insert appreciate the socket lining. A
survey revealed that 54% of the PTB sockets fabricated for the amputees included
in the investigation, had an insert (Fishman et al., 1975).

The total contact fully end-bearing socket fits snugly over the entire stump shape. The proximal rim extends to the upper third of the thigh, and the distal portion broadens to accommodate the femoral condyles. Socket relief, if indicated, is provided for the patella. The socket narrows above the condyles and extends in an almost oval shape to the proximal rim. Socket modification for soft tissues is not required.

A window is situated at the medial lower third of the socket to permit donning and doffing. The window position is maintained by either buckled straps or a velcro closure. The window opening does not interefere with anteroposterior forces during gait.

Firm medial-lateral support is required to prevent shifting of the stump within the socket (Foort, 1982). The shifting contact would concentrate on the weight-bearing surface, causing skin friction over the bony areas. The socket length maximizes stump lever control for anteroposterior gait forces and also helps to minimize the longitudinal rotational forces between the stump and the socket interface.

Knee Disarticulation
Prosthesis

(See Fig. 3–17)

Figure 3–17   Knee disarticulation prosthesis.

Conversely, a short socket would reduce stump lever function and stability. Stump pressure proximally–anteriorly at heel contact and proximally–posteriorly at heel-off would result.

Suspension is provided by shaping the socket over the proximal aspect of the condyles. This is sufficient and comfortable; additional proximal suspension assistance is seldom required.

A knee disarticulation prosthesis functions best when a four-bar linkage knee mechanism (see Prosthetic Components, p. 207) is utilized. This unit projects the instant center of rotation of the knee upward, thus providing walking comfort by equalizing the level of the knee axis on both sides.

Socket Variations.   If stump end bearing causes discomfort, a modified quadrilateral socket shape is constructed to utilize additional weight-bearing capabilities over the ischial seat. A Silesian bandage may be used to augment the suspension over the condyles (see Transfemoral Prosthesis, p. 226).

Previously, knee disarticulation stumps were fitted with contoured, anteriorly laced, total contact leather sockets. Knee function was obtained with metal hinged joints, the uprights being attached to the leather socket and the exoskeletal shank. The clinician may still see some of these sockets.

The segmented socket technique has also been applied to knee disarticulation stumps (see Ankle Disarticulation Prostheses, p. 218).

If the amputee is active, a torque absorber may be considered during prosthetic prescription.

Foot Component.   A prosthetic foot, selected according to the individual needs and attached to the endoskeletal system, completes the prosthesis.

Cosmesis.   Although the appearance of the prosthesis during gait has improved with the development of the polycentric four-bar linkage knee mechanism, the cosmesis is still not fully comparable with prostheses for other amputation levels. The unbalanced thigh-shank ratio is apparent when sitting: the thigh protrudes, and the shorter shin section often does not allow foot-ground contact.

Transfemoral
Prosthesis

The transfemoral quadrilateral socket consists of four walls, and most of these sockets provide total stump contact. However, some amputees are fitted with an open ended design. Each wall performs a specific function that corresponds to gait dynamics. Both the anterior and posterior socket walls are designed to accommodate the flexion and extension stump forces during gait, whereas the medial and lateral socket walls contribute to prosthetic stance stability. The anterior and lateral socket brims are approximately 2 inches higher than the posterior and medial socket brims.

*(See Figs. 3–18
and 3–19)*

Posterior Wall.   The posterior socket brim provides an ischial shelf so that most of the body weight can be transmitted through the ischium to the prosthesis on weight bearing. The posterior wall is slanted forward when compared with a

Figure 3–18 Transfemoral prosthesis with Silesian bandage.

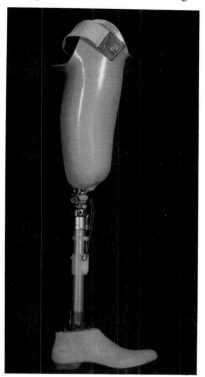

Figure 3–19 Quadrilateral socket: top view.

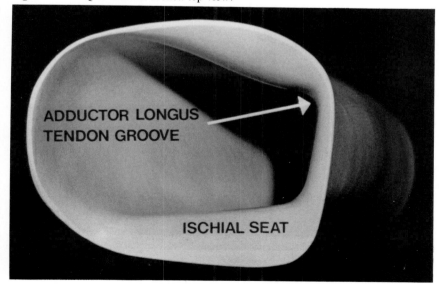

perpendicular line. This preflexion position slightly stretches the stump hip extensor muscles, creating more range for these muscles to control the prosthetic knee during stance.

Anterior Wall.   The higher brim of the anterior socket wall is necessary to provide the counter pressure that ensures that the ischial tuberosity does not slide off the ischial shelf (Radcliffe, 1977). The anterior wall fulfills this function by compressing the soft tissues of the femoral triangle.

Medial Wall.   The socket brim on the medial wall is low to prevent discomfort at the pubic ramus during stance. The anteroposterior width of the medial wall is crucial since it determines the socket diameter and, therefore, influences the accuracy of the fit of all four walls.

Lateral Wall.   The lateral wall is the key factor in providing medial-lateral pelvic stability during gait. It flares slightly, contouring over the greater trochanter. On stance, the entire wall must provide total contact support to the femur. This is important because the abductor muscles can only stabilize the pelvis if the femur is prevented from abducting (Radcliffe 1977, 1981). Three of the junctions of the walls are gently curved, wheras the anterior-medial corner provides a groove to accommodate the adductor longus tendon (Radcliffe 1977, 1981).

Suspensions.   Several factors determine the type of suspension indicated:

- the reason for amputation
- the stump length
- the projected activity level
- the age of the amputee

Suction.   Suction suspension is a self-suspending system and requires a precise socket fit. After donning the prosthesis and expelling all air, a valve is put into place. Negative pressure and socket skin contact will hold the prosthesis on the stump.

(See Fig. 3–20)

This type of suspension eliminates a belt system. However, some suction socket users prefer to have an additional simple strap suspension to help control hip rotation and to act as a back-up system in case the suction method should fail. According to a New York study (Fishman et al., 1975), 61% of the subjects were fitted with transfemoral suction sockets and, of these, approximately 50% were also equipped with additional suspension.

The suction socket is indicated for young athletic amputees who have medium to long transfemoral stumps and also for a few elderly amputees. This suspension method is not prescribed initially because complete stump maturation must be achieved before the amputee is able to effectively use suction suspension.

Figure 3–20   Suction socket.

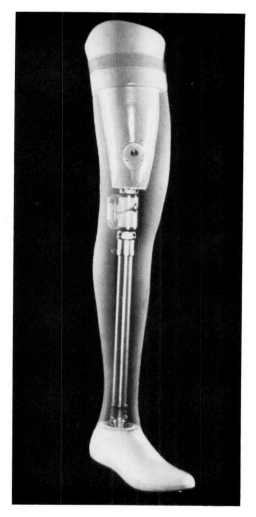

Source: Photograph courtesy of Otto Bock Orthopedic Industry of Canada Ltd.

A suction suspension is not prescribed for elderly amputees who have a history of heart problems and/or vascular insufficiency since most of these amputees are not able to stand on one leg in a stooped position long enough to "pump" the stump into the socket while donning the prosthesis. They find it difficult to tolerate the suction effect on the distal stump end. In addition, the stump volume fluctuations that occur if vascular insufficiency is a problem make these amputees unsuitable for suction suspension.

Semisuction.   Semisuction is achieved by using the suction valve system, but the amputee wears a stump sock that is useful in avoiding donning problems since this method eliminates pumping the stump into the socket. The semisuction method requires the addition of the Silesian bandage to keep the prosthesis in place.

Silesian Bandage.   The commonly used suspension for transfemoral sockets, either in addition to the suction or independently, is the Silesian bandage. The nonelastic webbing is anchored on the lateral socket wall over the greater trochanter. It leads posteriorly, slightly below the opposite pelvic crest in a ''hip-hugger'' fashion, and buckles through a D ring that is held by an anteriorly fastened fork strap. The Silesian bandage minimizes socket rotation and does not restrict hip mobility during sitting and walking.

Pelvic Belt.   The pelvic belt suspension system is somewhat more restricting. It consists of a metal joint (a pivoting anchor) and a steel section with anterior and posterior metal extensions at the pelvic level. These metal extensions accommodate the strap that buckles like a belt. The pelvic belt is indicated for very short stumps when the Silesian bandage does not provide adequate lateral stability. The pelvic belt system provides security in suspending the prosthesis but restricts hip mobility, particularly hip rotation, thus contributing to a more rigid gait. Sitting is not quite as comfortable as with other suspension systems.

Shoulder Harness.   A shoulder harness functions like suspenders, using shoulder straps to secure the prosthesis. It can be utilized in very short stumps that have a tendency to slip out of the socket when sitting, as a modification to other existing suspension systems, or on rare occasions to adapt to specific needs (e.g., colostomy). It was previously popular to suspend plug fit sockets. However, with the introduction of the quadrilateral socket design, the shoulder harness has become almost obsolete.

Foot Component.   The selection of the foot component attached to either an endo- or exoskeletal system depends on the activity level of the amputee.

Hip Disarticulation
Prosthesis
(See Fig. 3–21)

The total contact, snugly fitting, bucket-shaped socket contours around and under the innominate bone on the amputated side and extends broadly over the innominate bone on the sound side. The proximal socket rim is shaped to, and extends over, both pelvic crests. This molding over the pelvic bones on both sides provides the suspension and is necessary to hold the prosthesis vertical during the swing phase (McLaurin, 1970). The distal socket rim on the sound side is positioned so that the remaining hip joint can move freely. All rims must be contoured to provide comfort during walking and sitting.

The plastic-laminated socket contributes to pelvic stability and must be sturdy distally in order to transmit body weight and provide a solid base for the attachment of the prosthetic hip joint. The density of the socket material decreases over the sound side, making this socket area pliable for easier donning of the prosthesis.

Figure 3–21　Hip disarticulation prosthesis.

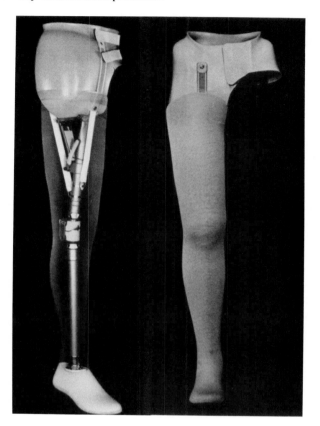

Source: Photograph courtesy of Otto Bock Orthopedic Industry of Canada Ltd.

Donning and doffing require a socket opening that is usually positioned anteriorly. Closure is obtained with straps and buckles tightened by clamps.

The front opening maintains the integrity of the lateral walls and ensures a firm buttock-sitting position over the prosthesis, thus preventing medial sliding on weight bearing. It also offers medial-lateral pelvic support. A side opening is only occasionally constructed to facilitate donning. However, medial-lateral socket support is somewhat compromised.

The prescribed hip, knee, and foot components are assembled under the socket according to alignment principles (see Alignment, p. 241). A torque absorber may be included to add functional comfort for an active prosthetic user.

The endoskeletal prosthesis is cosmetically completed with a long leg foam cover shaped to the contours of the remaining leg.

Hemipelvectomy
Prosthesis

A hemipelvectomy prosthesis, seldom seen clinically, is fabricated in a similar fashion to the hip disarticulation prosthesis. Major bucket modifications are necessary and intricate seating adaptations are required. Auxiliary suspension is also needed because half of the pelvis is missing. Functional use of this type of prosthesis is rarely, if ever, achieved. Since the fitting requirements are so specialized, the therapist treating a person with this amputation level must have close liaison with the prosthetist.

Summary

If biomechanics and the mechanical functions of each prosthesis are understood, gait training becomes a logical sequence of events. It is the responsibility of the physical therapist to maintain clinical competence by keeping up-to-date with developments in the rapidly advancing field of prosthetics (see Recent Development in Prosthetics, p. 337).

Prosthetic Alignment

Alignment means the assembly or placement of parts into a line or in a specific relationship to each other. Several prosthetic alignment systems exist and are clinically accepted and used. The basics of one of these systems, commonly utilized, are discussed.

Prosthetic alignment is established in two phases and is accomplished by positioning the socket and the prescribed component parts, in relation to the stump, so that the prosthesis can function most effectively for the individual amputee's gait pattern (Fernie, 1981; Foort, 1982).

Initially, the prosthetist establishes the static alignment or, as it is sometimes called, the bench alignment of the prosthesis in the workshop. This static alignment relates to stable or constant conditions. Optimal dynamic alignment, accommodating forces not in equilibrium, is next obtained when the amputee is wearing the prosthesis by adjusting or offsetting the various component parts from their original position in order to meet the differing biomechanical needs of the amputee. These changes must be made without compromising the stability of the prosthesis.

Alignment must take into consideration the

- level of amputation
- stump strength, joint range of motion, and coordination
- socket position
- foot position in relation to the socket
- resultant prosthetic load line forces
- preexisting postural problems and habits of the amputee
- functional ability expected
- comfort of the prosthesis

Load Line.   A combination of forward momentum, weight bearing, resultant ground reaction forces, and stump muscle action determines the positioning of the prosthetic load line (Radcliffe, 1977). The load line can be visualized as a path from the center of gravity of the body to the center of pressure of the foot in contact with the ground. The position of the load line depends on the position of the prosthesis in relation to the motion and moves (owing to the forward momentum) during the stance phase, from the heel to the toes, causing either a flexion or extension moment. A moment is the result of a force producing motion at an axis or pivot point (Fernie, 1981). This moment influences the degree of extension and flexion movements.

This initial alignment provides prosthetic stance stability and is established by using a vertical reference or indicator line that is closely related to the line of gravity (see Gait, p. 4).

Static Alignment (Bench Alignment)

Transtibial Prosthesis. In the transtibial prosthesis, when viewed from the side, the indicator line for the anteroposterior forces is measured from the middle of the medial-tibial plateau (MTP) to slightly forward of the prosthetic ankle joint (Mital, 1971; Fernie, 1981; Foort, 1982). This ensures balanced foot leverage during the entire stance phase.

(See Fig. 3–22)

The reference line to achieve medial-lateral stability, viewed posteriorly, bisects the posterior tibial rim and the center of the prosthetic heel. This ensures stable and equal foot contact during midstance.

Transfemoral Prosthesis. Static alignment for the transfemoral prosthesis is based on one of two commonly used reference lines. One line is established by using a plumb line dropped from the trochanter. This lateral reference line, the trochanter-knee-ankle (TKA) line determines the position of the foot in relation to the socket and provides the center point of the base support. It also helps the prosthetist to identify the position of the prosthetic knee. The TKA line passes from the trochanter to just forward of the ankle joint. The knee axis is located slightly posterior to the proximal and distal reference points.

(See Fig. 3–23)

Figure 3–22 Static alignment: reference line for transtibial prosthesis.

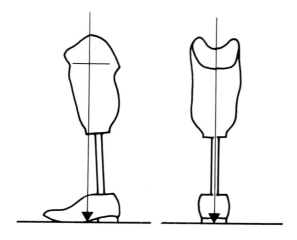

Figure 3–23   Static alignment: reference line for transfemoral prosthesis.

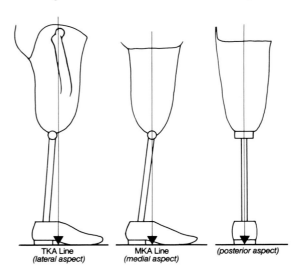

The other, the MKA (center of medial socket brim, knee, ankle) line is a medial reference line for the same plane. The knee axis is located on a line between the proximal and distal reference points. This is because the prosthetic knee axis, although positioned parallel to the ground, is moderately externally rotated in relation to the line of progression (Radcliffe, 1977) and is thus positioned more forward medially than laterally. Both perpendicular reference lines ensure prosthetic knee stability on midstance.

The reference line for medial–lateral stability originates from 2.5 cm lateral to the ischium. This line then passes through the center of the knee axis and the center of the prosthetic heel. The position of this line provides stump comfort and equal, stable foot contact during midstance.

Dynamic Alignment

In addition to stance stability, a prosthesis must also permit ease of functional mobility. Dynamic alignment is adjusted during early gait-training practice by changing the static alignment settings without sacrificing stability, in order to meet the amputee's needs during walking. Effective dynamic alignment is accomplished by finding the best relationship between the stump and all the prosthetic components (socket, knee, and foot) so that the amputee can activate the prosthesis smoothly, efficiently, and comfortably. Correct dynamic alignment provides the basis for a safe, energy-efficient prosthetic gait pattern.

Socket Preflexion

During the initial static alignment phase, the socket is positioned in slight flexion in relation to the lateral reference line. The amount of flexion can then be adjusted during the dynamic alignment. Factors affecting the extent of socket flexion include

- joint range of movement
- stump length
- step length
- socket weight-bearing distribution
- foot position
- gait pattern
- comfort

Transtibial Socket Preflexion. A preflexed transtibial socket (on the average 3–5°) permits the natural knee to function within a more normal joint range on midstance. If the socket is not slightly flexed, the knee would be forced into hyperextension on midstance. This would result in an unnatural, arrhythmic, uncomfortable gait pattern and would have detrimental effects on the anatomical structures of the knee over a period of time. Socket preflexion also increases the effectiveness of the weight-bearing potential of the patellar tendon in PTB and PTS sockets. When combined with posterior counter pressure, the stump can lean onto the patellar tendon.

The preflexed socket tilt also influences the positioning of the prosthetic foot. The foot must be slightly dorsiflexed for weight-bearing stability on midstance and to permit easier ground clearance during the swing phase. The amount of dorsiflexion is directly related to the amount of socket flexion. *(See Fig. 3–24)*

Transfemoral Socket Preflexion. A preflexed transfemoral socket (on the average 5–7°) assists in stance stability by placing the hip extensor muscles on a slight stretch, thus permitting them to function more efficiently in a "push back" motion just following heel strike. At this time, the tendency is for the prosthetic

---

Figure 3–24 Socket preflexion influencing foot position.

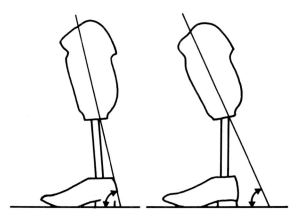

knee to flex because the load line passes behind the knee. Stump hip extension must be controlled to counteract this flexion movement. Socket preflexion is then individually adjusted to permit normal step length and also to accommodate stump muscle weakness or lack of range of movements. This allows the amputee to achieve and hold prosthetic knee extension while the stump is in a slight hip flexion position. Socket preflexion also helps to maintain the position of the ischial tuberosity on the ischial seat during hip extension movements.

Clinical Comment.   The longer the stump lever, the more difficult socket preflexion becomes, especially when accommodating for joint contractures. In the transtibial prosthesis, a long flexed stump lever would place the foot too far posteriorly, and in the transfemoral prosthesis it would place the prosthetic knee joint too far anteriorly.

The amount of possible socket preflexion is determined by stump length and function, the position of the foot, socket comfort, and the resultant smooth gait pattern. Exact socket flexion alignment will ensure optimal anteroposterior equalization of the forces acting on the stump during ambulation.

Foot Position

A correctly aligned prosthetic foot has optimum ground contact on midstance, with the weight carried over the midfoot section. The degree of toe-out in relation to the line of progression is adjusted to correspond with the remaining foot.

Alignment Settings

Any alignment change has an effect on the stump and on the gait pattern because the distribution of the forces acting on the stump is altered. The clinician must not only be aware of the implications of each alignment adjustment, but also be able to suggest or implement the corrective measures necessary to equalize the forces acting on the stump during gait.

Transtibial Alignment Settings and Their Effects on Gait

The position between the socket and the prosthetic foot can be altered with a coupling device. This alignment tool, temporarily positioned under the socket, can slide or tilt the socket in the anteroposterior and medial-lateral planes and tilt in flexion-extension as well as in abduction and adduction. Specific alignment errors cause specific gait deviations, and may result in clinical signs such as discomfort or pressure areas. To clearly show resultant stump pressure areas, schematic malalignment drawings have been exaggerated.

Socket–Foot Correlation: Lateral Aspect.

(See Fig. 3–25)

- The socket is placed anteriorly in relation to the foot, or the foot is set too far back.
- The load line passes anterior to the center of the base of support, causing a knee flexion moment.
- The shortened forefoot lever contributes to forced knee flexion and accelerates the stance phase from heel strike to midstance.
- The stump experiences proximal-posterior and distal-anterior pressures.

Figure 3–25   Socket placed anteriorly in relation to the foot.

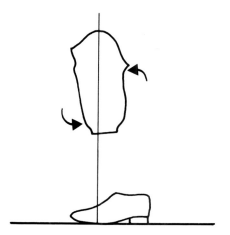

- The socket is placed posteriorly in relation to the foot, or the foot is set too far forward.
- The load line passes posterior to the center of the base of support, causing a knee extension moment (hyperextension).
- The forefoot lever is longer, causing a delay from midstance to toe-off that makes knee flexion more difficult.
- The stump experiences proximal-anterior and distal-posterior pressures.

(See Fig. 3–26)

Figure 3–26   Socket placed posteriorly in relation to the foot.

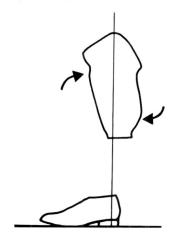

Figure 3–27   Socket placed laterally in relation to the foot.

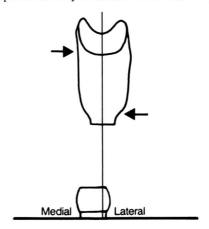

Socket–Foot Correlation: Posterior Aspect.

(See Fig. 3–27)

- The socket is placed laterally in relation to the foot, or the foot is placed too for medially (inset).
- The load line passes lateral to the center of the base of support, forcing the knee into varus.
- The stump experiences proximal-medial and distal-lateral pressures.
- The gait base is narrowed.
- The gait adaptations include lateral instability, which forces the amputee to use hip abduction to compensate balance and alleviate stump pressure.

Figure 3–28   Socket placed medially in relation to the foot.

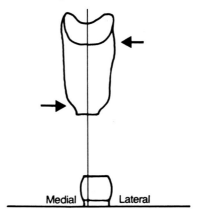

- The socket is placed medially, or the foot is placed, too far laterally (outset).   *(See Fig. 3–28)*
- The load line passes medial to the center of the base of support, forcing the knee into valgus.
- The stump experiences proximal-lateral and distal-medial pressures.
- The gait base increases.
- The gait adaptations include drawing the stump toward midline to avoid stump discomfort.

This may also result in lateral trunk bending toward the amputated side.

Foot-tilting Positions in Relation to the Socket: Lateral Aspect.

- Too much foot dorsiflexion.   *(See Fig. 3–29)*
- The load line passes anterior to the center of the base of support, forcing the knee into flexion.
- The gait is accelerated from midstance to toe-off. The prosthesis appears short owing to the increased knee flexion thrust that also results in excessive hip flexion.
- The stump experiences proximal-posterior and distal-anterior pressures.

- Too much plantar flexion of the foot.   *(See Fig. 3–30)*
- The load line passes posterior to the center of the base of support forcing the knee into extension.
- The gait is slowed from midstance to toe-off. The prosthesis appears too long owing to the extension thrust.
- The stump experiences proximal-anterior and distal-posterior pressure.
- The amputee abducts and externally rotates to avoid stump discomfort.

Figure 3–29   Too much dorsiflexion.

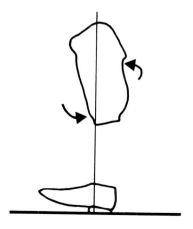

Figure 3–30   Too much plantar flexion.

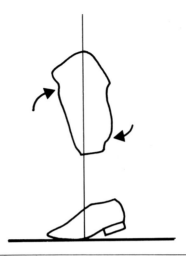

Foot-tilting Positions in Relation to the Socket: Posterior Aspect.

(See Fig. 3–31)

Foot Inversion

- Foot inversion reduces the foot weight-bearing surface and requires the amputee to walk on the outside of the foot.
- The load line passes lateral to the center of the base of support, causing a varus moment.
- The stump experiences proximal-medial and distal-lateral pressures.

Figure 3–31   Foot inversion.

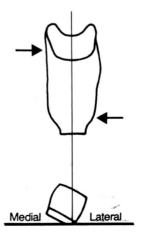

Figure 3–32 Foot eversion.

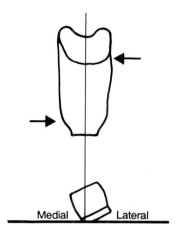

Medial   Lateral

Foot Eversion   *(See Fig. 3–32)*

- Foot eversion reduces the foot weight-bearing surface and requires the amputee to walk on the inside of the foot.
- The load line passes medial to the center of the base of support, causing a valgus moment.
- The stump experiences proximal-lateral and distal-medial pressures.

As in transtibial amputations, the fit and the position of the prosthetic socket in relation to the foot are equally critical for smooth prosthetic performance in transfemoral amputations. The additional factor to be considered during alignment is the location of the prosthetic knee joint.

Transfemoral
Alignment Settings and
Their Effects on Gait

The placement of the prosthetic knee, in relation to the proximal and distal reference points, is crucial since its position controls the degree of prosthetic stance stability. The more posterior the knee axis is set to the reference line, the more the prosthetic knee stability increases. However, this stance safety factor, often considered for the elderly amputee, makes it physically more difficult for the amputee to initiate prosthetic knee flexion in preparation for the swing phase. This occurs because the load line force remains in front of the prosthetic knee, thus causing an extension moment (Radcliffe 1977, Fernie 1981).

(See Fig. 3–33)

If the knee axis is placed anterior to the reference line, initiating the swing phase is much easier because the load line passes behind the prosthetic joint, thus creating a flexion moment. However, to achieve prosthetic midstance stability, the amputee requires stronger hip extensor muscle control to provide the counterforce necessary to prevent the artificial knee from buckling when under load.

The lateral reference line for the static alignment of this prosthesis passes through the trochanter, bisects the base of the socket, and passes in front of the

Hip Disarticulation
Alignment Settings and
Their Effects on Gait

Figure 3–33   The effect of knee positioning on prosthetic stability.

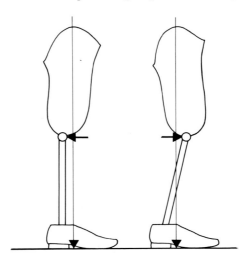

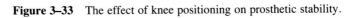

Figure 3–34   Static alignment: reference line for hip disarticulation prosthesis.

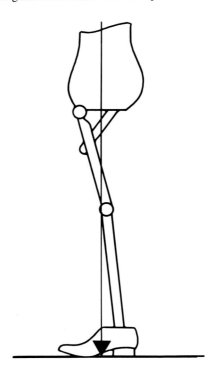

knee and ankle joint. The axis of the hip joint is positioned parallel to the ground and in front of the natural joint at the anterior border of the socket base. This permits stance stability since the weight-bearing line passes between the prosthetic hip and knee joint. *(See Fig. 3–34)*

When viewing the prosthesis from the front, the clinician can see that the hip joint position, in relation to the body midline, determines the width of the walking base.

Optimum dynamic alignment is achieved by finding a position that provides the balance between the prosthetic hip and knee joint over the foot.

The prosthesis is activated by lumbar movement. A pelvic tilt, together with forward momentum, slants the socket forward and up. This places the load line behind the knee. The knee flexion moment then initiates the prosthetic swing phase.

Alignment errors in positioning the hip and knee joints, or the foot component, will affect either the stability or the mobility of the prosthesis and thus decrease the functional efficiency during gait.

Incorrect prosthetic leg length is a vertical alignment error that affects the horizontal alignment of the pelvis, thus introducing gait deviations.

Incorrect Prosthetic Leg Length (Trans-femoral and Transtibial Levels)

Prosthesis Too Long. Throughout the gait cycle, the pelvis (in transfemoral amputations) moves with the prosthesis, and during stance it actually sits on the socket brim. If the prosthesis is too long, the pelvis is forced by the prosthesis to rise higher than normal to achieve midstance. This pushes the body upward and causes a postural imbalance.

A similar, excessive, upward motion occurs in transtibial amputees whose prostheses are too long. However, it is not as noticeable because it is partially accommodated by the natural knee joint.

Biomechanically, it is difficult for amputees to achieve midstance because:

- The body has to rise unnaturally against gravity to reach its vertical undulation peak (see Undulating Pathways, p. 5).
- The load line increases the knee flexion moment at an altered angle.

These factors contribute to a slowing of the phase from heel contact to midstance (like going uphill) when compared with the velocity of the entire cycle.

In transfemoral amputees only, excessive prosthetic leg length also increases ischial tuberosity pressure. This pressure will be felt at its strongest from midstance to heel-off, with the prosthetic knee in extension. Following midstance, the amputee experiences a prosthetic acceleration caused by the dropping of the center of gravity (like going downhill) that some amputees express as a prosthetic "push."

The transtibial amputee requires an increased amount of quadriceps work (similar to prolonged standing on a flexed knee) to balance over the too long prosthesis. The acceleration in the second part of the stance phase is partially initiated by pelvic drop-off (see Gait Deviations, p. 282) and by passive forced prosthetic toe-off.

During prosthetic swing, toe tripping can occur with both transfemoral and transtibial amputees, particularly if the gait velocity is slow.

The amputee adjusts posturally by holding the prosthesis further away from the body midline. In both amputation levels, this results in either an abducted or circumducted gait pattern often associated with lateral trunk bending toward the sound side or by vaulting (see Gait Deviations, p. 324).

Prosthesis Too Short.   Many amputees, both transfemoral and transtibial, request that their prosthesis be aligned slightly shorter (up to 1 cm) compared with the sound leg. This is sometimes acceptable since it helps when walking over rough terrain and permits uncomplicated ground clearance during the prosthetic swing phase.

However, a marked insufficient prosthetic leg length (more than 1 cm shorter), although giving the initial impression that the prosthetic gait is easily accomplished, introduces undesirable postural deviations.

Prosthetic midstance is achieved with less physical effort, and less joint range is required because the rising of the center of gravity on the amputated side does not occur. This results in an increased pelvic drop over the prosthesis at midstance. Thus, to maintain balance, both transfemoral and transtibial amputees laterally bend the trunk toward the affected side, which, in turn, reduces the function of the abductor muscles.

Extra unilateral trunk muscle power is required on the sound side to hold the trunk upright, and the sound leg has to work harder to raise the body's center of gravity during gait.

This gait pattern causes exaggerated unilateral spinal motion and may result in secondary low back pain. If this situation becomes chronic, trunk muscle atrophy can occur on the same side as the amputation.

Clinical Comments.   An apparent increase in prosthetic leg length can be caused by stump edema, preventing the stump from fully entering the socket. Conversely, an apparent prosthetic shortening can be the result of additional stump shrinkage, causing excessive penetration into the prosthetic socket. This is often expressed as perineal discomfort in transfemoral amputees or as stump end sensitivity in transtibial amputees.

In the nonamputee, leg length discrepancy can be experienced by walking with a thick-soled shoe on one foot and no shoe on the other. Increased muscle work will be felt in the leg wearing the shoe as it accommodates for the leg length discrepancy.

Donning in Relation to Alignment

Donning the prosthesis correctly has a major bearing on the prosthetic alignment. The stump–socket interface requires an intimate fit (see General Information about Sockets and their Suspensions, p. 210) and the socket suspension must be secure to maintain the socket position. Any malalignment between socket and stump will result in gait deviations. Therefore, the stump position has to be checked before each gait practice session begins (see Donning and Doffing of the Prosthesis, p. 247).

Two types of piston action can be observed, both of which will affect prosthetic gait.

Stump Piston Action

Poor Suspension or Socket Diameter Too Large. The stump pistons up and down in the socket because either the suspension system is inadequate or the socket diameter is too large, causing the intimate socket fit to be lost. Precise lever control is lacking, and skin friction can result.

Excessive Soft Stump Tissues. Excessive soft stump tissues are difficult to control because, although the stump contact may be firm, the excess soft tissue is mobile. During stance, the body weight compresses these tissues and shifts them in an upward direction. During swing, the weight of the prosthesis will pull these tissues down. This causes "tissue pumping," which increases stress, particularly on the distal stump on weight bearing, and may result in stump discomfort.

The intimate correlation of the stump function, socket fit, suspension, and component alignment is based on the effect of the forces acting on the stump. The skill of the clinician lies in the ability to understand the relationship of these factors, the alignment principles, and the actions of the force vectors, thus enabling diagnosis of gait deviations that are related to the prosthetic fit and the alignment of the prosthesis.

Close liaison with the prosthetist ensures alignment proficiency to meet the static and dynamic alignment requirements of each individual amputee.

Summary

Blacharski, P.A., Somerset, J.H., and Murray, D.G. "A three-dimensional Study of the Kinetics of the Human Knee." *Journal of Biomechanics, 8* (1975): 375–384.

Fishman, S., Berger, N., and Watkins, D. "A Survey of Prosthetics—1973–74." *Orthotics and Prosthetics, 29,* no. 3 (1975): 15–20.

Foort, J. "Comments on Orthopaedic Research in Amputation Surgery, Prosthetics and Orthotics by N.C. McCollough." *Prosthetics and Orthotics International, 5,* no. 2 (1981), 97–102.

Foort, J. "Prosthetic Fitting and Components—Lower Extremity Amputees." In S.N. Banerjee, ed. *Rehabilitation Management of Amputees.* Baltimore, Md.: Williams & Wilkins, 1982, 42–98.

Fernie, G.R. "Biomechanics of Fitting. Prosthetic Mechanism." In J.P. Kostuik and R. Gillespie, eds. *Amputation Surgery and Rehabilitation: The Toronto Experience.* New York: Churchill Livingstone, 1981, 259–265, 269–271.

Frankel, V.G., Burstein, A.H., and Brooks, D.B. "Biomechanics of Internal Derangement of the Knee." *Journal of Bone and Joint Surgery, 53-A,* no. 5 (1971): 945–962.

Friedman, L.W. "Training-Adult." *The Psychological Rehabilitation of the Amputee.* Springfield, Ill.: Chas. C. Thomas, 1978, 44–66.

Levy, S.W. "Stump Edema Syndrome." *Skin Problems of the Amputee.* St. Louis, Mo.: Warren H. Green, 1983, 143–153.

References

McLaurin, C.A. ''The Canadian Hip Disarticulation Prosthesis.'' In G. Murdoch, ed. *Prosthetic and Orthotic Practice*. London: Edward Arnold, 1970, 285–302.

Mital, M.A., and Pierce, D.S. ''Below-knee Prosthesis.'' *Amputees and Their Prostheses*. Boston: Little, Brown, 1971, 147–154.

Murray, D., and Fisher, F.R. ''Amputation Levels.'' *Handbook of Amputations and Prostheses*. Ottawa: University of Ottawa, 1982, 45–77.

Page, R.A. ''The Instantaneous Axis of Knee Rotation. In *Report: Department of Health and Social Security. Biomechanical Research and Development Unit (BRADU)*. Roehamptom: 1979, 61–68.

Radcliffe, C.W. ''The Biomechanics of the Syme Prosthesis.'' *Selected Articles from Artificial Limbs*. Huntington, N.Y.: Robert E. Krieger, 1970, 273–282.

Radcliffe, C.W. ''Above-Knee Prosthesis.'' *Prosthetics and Orthotics International*, 1 (1977): 146–160.

Radcliffe, C.W. ''Applications to Lower Limb Prosthetics.'' In V.T. Inman, H.J. Ralston, F. Todd, (eds.) *Human Walking*. Baltimore, Md.: Williams & Wilkins, 1981, 129–148.

Staros, A., and Goralnik, B. ''Partial Foot Prosthesis. *Atlas of Limb Prosthetics*. (American Academy of Orthopedic Surgeons.) St. Louis, Mo.: C.V. Mosby, 1981, 293–295.

Winter, D.A. ''Use of Kinetic Analysis in the Diagnostics of Pathological Gait. *Physiotherapy Canada*, 33, no. 4 (1981): 208–214.

Notes

1. Sova, M. The segmented socket. Presentation, CAPO Convention, Vancouver, B.C.: April 3–6, 1984.
2. Kuhn, R. Discussion, ISPO World Congress, Montreux, Switzerland, October 1974.

GAIT TRAINING

The progression to gait-training activities will provide a realistic picture of the amputee's ambulation potential and will also give an indication of the prosthetic components most appropriate for the final prosthetic prescription.

Gait training is the most important aspect of amputation rehabilitation and involves more than just teaching the amputee to walk. The gait-training program must also include teaching the amputee to:

- don and doff the prosthesis
- stand up and sit down
- practice balance and step positions
- learn advanced activities (e.g., navigating stairs, ramps, obstacles and rough ground, crossing at intersections, falling [not always practiced] and getting up from the floor)

During all these activities, the therapist concentrates on analyzing and correcting gait deviations (see Gait Deviations, p. 282).

Gait-training Unit

To practice these skills, the amputee is initially fitted with a gait-training unit. This unit is a temporary prosthesis and consists of a plastic socket (at times prefabricated) and an endoskeletal component system (see Modular Assembly Systems, p. 241). The device replaces the rigid dressing as well as other postoperative dressings and is prescribed as soon as the stump tissues can tolerate partial weight bearing.

The gait-training unit fulfills several important functions. These consist of:

- promoting stump shrinkage and shaping (see Stump Shrinkage and Shaping Techniques: Gait-training Unit, p. 139)
- conditioning the stump so that it can tolerate the forces acting upon it during gait
- exercising stump lever functions
- stimulating proprioception, coordination, and balance
- decreasing stump contractures
- permitting early gait practice
- providing a method by which the amputee can increase gait endurance
- acting as a preliminary evaluation tool before the definitive prosthesis is prescribed

Gait-training units are utilized for all amputation levels. They must be precisely aligned and suspended and, if indicated, have a functional knee unit to ensure:

- correct proprioceptive feedback
- accurate biomechanical functioning
- stump comfort

Alignment adjustments are ongoing during the gait-training period until the optimum dynamic alignment has been achieved prior to the construction or completion of the definitive prosthesis.

Donning and Doffing the Prosthesis

A prosthetic socket can be compared with a shoe in that it must fit well and be comfortable. All sockets are constructed to accommodate the anatomical contours of the stump (see General Information About Sockets and Their Suspensions, p. 210) and must be donned accordingly. If the stump is incorrectly positioned, the prosthesis will be malaligned. Socket malalignment will always cause gait deviations (see Donning in Relation to Alignment, p. 244) and can also result in stump pain and/or injury. Therefore, correct stump placement in the socket is vital. Gait training begins by learning to don the prosthesis correctly.

Donning the Transtibial Prosthesis

There are several specific steps to follow in the donning of the transtibial prosthesis that will ensure stump comfort and correct stump lever control.

1. The amputee, sitting in the chair, removes the bandage or shrinker sock.
2. The stump is checked for any abrasions or reddened areas before the stump sock is put on. The stump sock(s) must always be wrinkle free. If the amputee wears a soft inner liner, it is then placed over the sock.
3. The extension of the wheelchair sitting board is lowered or pushed in (see Wheelchair Sitting Boards; p. 72).
4. The prosthesis is placed in front of the amputee with the heel in floor contact, placing the prosthesis at a slight angle towards the stump.

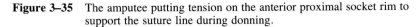

Figure 3–35   The amputee putting tension on the anterior proximal socket rim to support the suture line during donning.

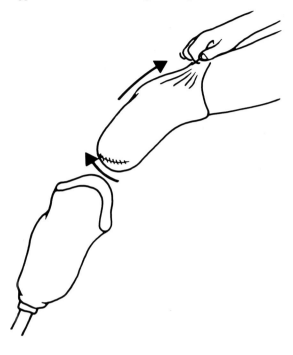

(See Fig. 3–35)

5. The amputee puts tension on the anterior proximal sock rim, to provide suture line support during donning.
6. The knee is held in approximately 40–45° of flexion. The stump enters the socket, sliding downward and pressing against the posterior wall. This backward motion will compress the soft tissues of the posterior aspect of the stump, thus preventing abrasion of the tibial crest on the patellar tendon bar during donning.
7. The suspension is secured when the amputee feels that the stump has penetrated sufficiently and is positioned correctly in the socket.

A brief period of weight bearing following initial donning will allow the therapist to check that the stump–socket interface is correctly aligned before gait training begins. This is done by checking:

- the position of the patella in relation to the anterior socket rim
- the position of the posterior socket rim
- the prosthetic leg length (see Incorrect Prosthetic Leg Length, p. 243).

Donning the transfemoral prosthesis is perhaps more difficult because the amputee must concentrate on controlling the prosthetic knee joint while correctly aligning the socket on the stump before securing the suspension. The donning procedure depends upon the socket construction. A conventional quadrilateral socket requires a stump sock, whereas a suction socket has stump–skin contact.

The Conventional Socket. When donning a conventional quadrilateral socket, the amputee sits forward in the chair. The bandage is removed, and the stump skin examined.

1. The stump sock is donned and must be wrinkle free.
2. The prosthetic knee is placed in 90° of flexion, with the foot flat on the floor. This shortens the lever produced by the prosthesis, thereby allowing the amputee to control the prosthetic socket more easily during donning. It also prevents socket rotation.
3. The stump is then placed into the socket. The adductor longus tendon groove is used as a landmark for correct socket placement. (If the patient wears a soft inner liner it is donned before inserting the stump into the rigid outer socket [Baumgartner, 1979].)
4. The amputee then stands on the remaining leg, manually holding the socket in place, and draws the prosthesis under the hip. Once prosthetic knee extension control has been achieved, the amputee can bear weight on the prosthesis.
5. The suspension is then secured. It is important to remind the amputee to maintain weight bearing on the prosthesis while fastening the suspension. The firm ground contact holds the prosthesis in position and thus prevents internal rotation of the prosthesis on the stump.

The Suction Socket. The suction socket does not slide on quite as easily. It is donned with the aid of either a length of stockinette (exceeding stump length) pulled over the stump, or a 10-cm-width bandage that is wrapped in circular turns around the stump. The amputee then stands up and inserts the distal end of the stockinette or bandage into the socket, threading it through the valve opening. With the trunk in forward flexion and the prosthesis held in knee extension, the stump is then "pumped" into the socket while the stockinette or bandage is pulled downward with each downward pumping motion.

(See Fig. 3–36)

Initially, this may be difficult because an equal pull is necessary to place all stump tissues evenly within the socket. When donning is complete, the stockinette or bandage has passed through the valve opening, and the stump skin is in direct and total contact with the inner socket walls. The valve is then inserted, preventing air entry and keeping the socket in place.

Weight bearing is necessary in order to judge both the correct stump–socket interface and the alignment prior to gait activities. This is done by checking to ensure that the:

Figure 3–36   Wrapping the stump to don a suction socket.

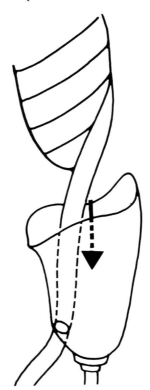

- Adductor longus groove accommodates the tendon.
- Adductor area tissues are placed against the medial socket wall.
- Ischial tuberosity is sitting on the ischial shelf. The latter is tested by asking the amputee to lean forward. The therapist places a finger on the ischial shelf and asks the amputee to straighten up. One can then feel if contact is present.
- Leg length is correct.

Clinical Comments.   In donning the conventional transfemoral socket, "bunching" of the stump sock may occur, especially at the medial socket brim, preventing the stump from fully entering the socket. This can also result in pinching. If this occurs, the sock should be stretched over the outer socket brim prior to donning. This may help prevent the stump sock from slipping inside the socket.

Some transfemoral amputees have, or will develop, sufficient strength and balance to don the prosthesis while standing. However, initially they should be taught to start the procedure sitting to ensure that they learn to precisely align the socket on the stump.

If a socket becomes loose, extra stump socks should be used to maintain a firm contact between socket and stump. Conversely, one can reduce the number of stump socks if the socket is too tight.

If the distal stump is somewhat bulbous (in transtibial as well as in transfemoral stump levels), the amputee may require a ''pull'' sock, to assist in the donning of the prosthesis. The ''pull'' sock, usually made of an open-ended stockinette, is worn over the stump sock.

An opening, placed on the medial-distal aspect of the socket (similar to a valve opening in a suction socket), allows the amputee to pull the stump into the socket with the extra sock while holding on to the stump sock with the other hand.

Donning the prosthesis must be practiced repeatedly. It is particularly difficult for the elderly transfemoral amputee to learn to don the prosthesis. If correct donning is not mastered, the amputee, after discharge from the rehabilitation center, loses motivation and will not use any acquired walking skills.

The basic procedure for doffing the prosthesis is similar for both transtibial and transfemoral amputees.

The amputee:

Doffing the Prosthesis

1. Returns to the sitting position.
2. Unfastens the suspension.
3. Removes the stump from the socket. The transtibial amputee should exert a backward pressure while lifting the stump out of the socket, again to prevent abrading the tibial crest on the patellar tendon bar.
4. Removes the stump sock.
5. Examines the stump skin for any abrasions or incorrect pressure points.
6. Reapplies the stump bandage or shrinker sock.

Doffing the prosthesis rarely presents a problem since it requires minimal balance skills. However, the immediate reapplication of the stump bandage or shrinker sock must be reinforced.

Standing up and sitting down with the prosthesis are achieved primarily through the work of the remaining leg and with the aid of crutches. Regardless of the amputation level, the prosthesis is positioned forward. This permits unrestricted knee motion on the amputated side and, thus, does not hinder movements of the remaining leg during the change in position.

Standing Up and Sitting Down

The amputee is instructed to:

Standing Up
(See Fig. 3–37)

1. sit forward in the chair
2. bend the remaining leg slightly more than 90°, with the foot placed firmly on the ground
3. position the prosthetic foot ahead of the remaining foot

Figure 3–37   Getting off a chair.

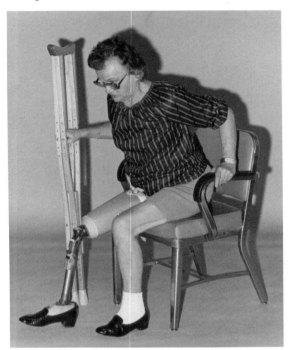

4. place the crutches on the prosthetic side, holding both handles with one hand
5. hold onto the chair armrest with the other hand
6. lean the trunk forward slightly
7. push simultaneously on the armrest, crutch handles, and the remaining leg to bring the body into standing position with the weight supported over the remaining leg
8. bring crutches into position
9. draw the prosthesis under the trunk so that both feet are in a parallel position
10. adjust to and maintain balance before beginning to walk

When rising from an exercise mat or a bed, the same procedure is followed with the exception that armrests are not available to assist in standing. The ambulation aid (crutches, walker, canes) is placed nearby, and elbows are extended with the hands pushing the hips off the mat or bed. Additional hip and knee extensor strength as well as arm strength is required since the position of the mat or bed is often lower than the wheelchair seat. Again, as an important safety factor, balance must be maintained before taking any steps.

The hesitant walker, tired after gait practice and wanting to sit down quickly, often forgets the most basic safety procedures. The amputee is therefore instructed to:

1. Back up slowly until the remaining leg is in contact with the chair. This tactile feedback will ensure that the chair is close enough for sitting.
2. Place the prosthesis one step forward. This allows for easier hip and knee flexion when sitting.
3. Position the crutches next to the prosthesis, gripping both crutch handles with one hand.
4. Reach with the other hand for the chair armrest while bending the remaining leg and using the crutches for support.
5. Grip the armrest firmly for support and slowly lower the hips into sitting.
6. Place the crutches within easy reach.
7. Reposition the prosthesis in a comfortable sitting position.

Transtibial amputees prefer sitting with the prosthesis placed slightly forward since the knee feels unrestricted and the suspension may exert less tension.

Transfemoral amputees, depending on the chair height, will place their prosthesis so that anterior socket rim pressure is avoided during sitting. These amputees, as well as knee disarticulation amputees, are also advised to have the foot supported on the floor, the wheelchair foot rest, or, if indicated, a foot stool. This prevents anterior-distal stump pressure that could occur if the prosthesis is "hanging" unsupported.

Consistent repetition and practice of the correct procedure for sitting and standing before gait activities begin will maximize the amputee's ability to automatically perform these activities in a safe manner.

Balance and step position exercises are important prerequisites for prosthetic gait. Initially, the amputee must consciously:

- practice feeling, moving, and positioning the prosthesis
- experience motion limitation imposed by the prosthesis
- learn how to recover balance (see Balance Control, p. 17)

This is necessary to:

- allow weight transfer from one leg to the other
- encourage a coordinated rhythmic gait pattern
- negotiate difficult and unfamiliar terrain (e.g., rough ground, icy surfaces)
- recover from a sudden unforeseen imbalance (e.g., being jostled in a crowd)

Initially, balance exercises are practiced between parallel bars. The bars provide stability and security as the amputee uses arm support to prevent any sudden uncontrolled stump weight bearing. A mirror at the end of the parallel bars provides visual feedback, useful for postural corrections.

The position of the therapist will change in relation to the amputee depending upon the direction of the stimulus needed to assist or resist in the correction of postural deviations.

As the amputee gains confidence in basic balance skills, progression to more advanced balance activities will further enhance locomotor independence.

Basic Balance Exercises

Some examples of basic balancing exercises have been selected to assist therapists in teaching balance control. During these exercises, manual contact is used extensively, both to facilitate movement through controlled resistance as well as to passively correct posture.

The starting position for these exercises requires the amputee to stand between the parallel bars with:

- hands on the bars
- feet even, approximately 10–15 cm apart
- weight equally distributed over both legs
- trunk posture upright

Mastering balance exercises improves the amputee's prosthetic skills and provides confidence for gait and more complicated tasks.

(See Fig. 3–38)

Exercise: Anteroposterior Weight Shifting with Hips and Knee Extended

Purpose: to enable the amputee to feel how much anterior and posterior shifting is possible without losing balance

---

Figure 3–38 Anterior–posterior weight shifting with hips and knees extended: postural deviations and corrective treatment.

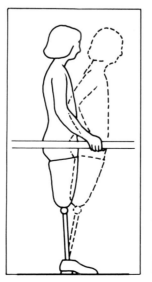
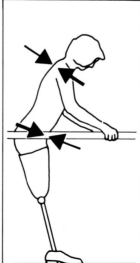
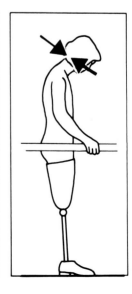

Comment: movement during this exercise is minimal and is primarily controlled by the foot and ankle of the remaining leg.

Deviations: compensatory actions include:

- weight bearing through the remaining leg and arms only
- head and trunk held in forward flexion
- hip flexion during both forward and backward motions

Corrective Treatment: the amputee returns to the starting position.

- Diagonally directed manual resistance over the occipital area will encourage head and trunk extension.
- Posteriorly directed resistance to the anterior aspect of the pelvic crest with the forward motion, and anteriorly directed resistance to the shoulders with the backward motion, will help to encourage a more upright posture, counteracting trunk flexion.

Exercise: Lateral Weight Shifting *(See Fig. 3–39)*

Purpose: to allow the amputee to feel and correct the lateral pelvic shift as weight is transferred from one leg to the other while maintaining an upright trunk posture.

Comment: this movement encourages the amputee to use the hip abductor muscles to maintain pelvic stability on stance.

Figure 3–39   The pelvis shifting laterally over the support leg: postural deviation and corrective treatment.

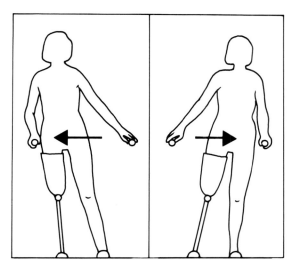
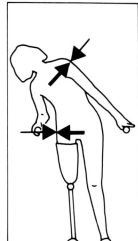

Deviations: compensatory actions include:

- lateral trunk bending toward the prosthetic side on prosthetic weight bearing
- hip flexion with lateral trunk bending toward the prosthetic side
- positive Trendelenburg sign on the weight-bearing side

Corrective Treatment: The amputee returns to the starting position.

- The therapist to increase the amputee's awareness of the correct pelvic motion uses manual resistance against the lateral pelvis on the amputated side to give direction so that the amputee can correct the pelvic movement. Simultaneous resistance to the opposite shoulder will help to correct lateral trunk bending.

(See Figs. 3–40a, b) **Exercise:** Circular Pelvic Rotations (Clockwise and Counterclockwise) over Both Legs with Shoulders Remaining Over the Stance Position

Purpose: to teach the amputee to control the combination of anterior, posterior, and lateral pelvic movements necessary for a smooth gait pattern.

Deviations: compensatory actions include:

- uneven pelvic rotation, with a wider arc over the remaining leg
- trunk flexion and lateral trunk bending over the prosthesis

Corrective Treatment: the amputee returns to the starting position.

- The therapist passively corrects the lateral trunk bending.
- Manual resistance is given to the pelvis against the direction of the movement. This facilitation incorporates the anterior, posterior, and lateral movements. The changing of hand positions must be smooth so that the amputee receives the correct input to ensure the continuity of the movement.

(See Fig. 3–41) **Exercise:** Raising Both Arms above the Head

Purpose: to help the amputee learn to distribute weight equally over both feet, without arm support, with an upright trunk posture.

Comment: shoulder pathology or weakness may limit the amputee's ability to raise the arms above shoulder level.

Deviations: compensatory actions include:

- arms held at 90° to the trunk rather than raised above the head
- increased lumbar lordosis
- trunk and hip flexion
- unequal weight bearing (decreased on the prosthetic side)

Figure 3–40(a)   Pelvic rotations (clockwise and counterclockwise).

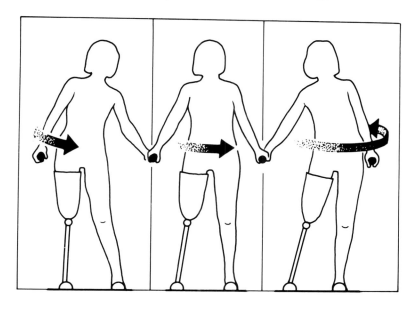

Figure 3–40(b)   Postural deviations and corrective treatment.

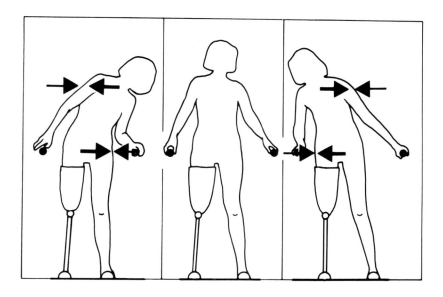

Figure 3–41   Raising both arms above the head: postural deviations and corrective treatment.

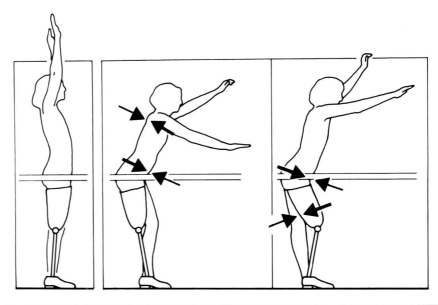

Corrective Treatment: the amputee returns to the starting position.

- The amputee alternately holds the bar with one hand while raising the other arm to experience the entire shoulder range possible.
- The amputee is then encouraged to attempt to raise both arms simultaneously.
- Downward-directed manual resistance over the occipital area will encourage trunk extension during single arm raising.
- Manual resistance to the anterior pelvis will counteract hip flexion during single arm raising.
- The use of an overhead ambulation aid (see Posture Control Device, p. 266) will also encourage an upright trunk posture.

(See Figs. 3–42a, b)   ***Exercise:*** Trunk Rotation with Simultaneous Alternating Arm Swing (Forward and Backward to Shoulder Level)

Purpose: to teach the amputee to maintain balance while incorporating trunk rotation into movement.

Comment: trunk rotation can be increased by instructing the amputee to turn the head toward the hand in the back swing position.

Deviations: compensatory actions include:

Figure 3–42(a)   Trunk rotation with simultaneous alternating arm swing (forward and backward to shoulder level).

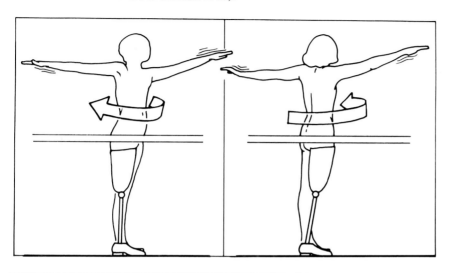

Figure 3–42(b)   Postural deviations and corrective treatment.

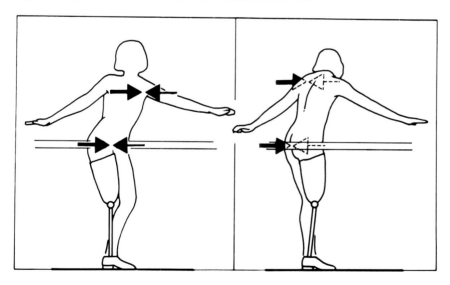

- Decreased weight bearing when rotating toward the prosthetic side. The amputee has difficulty turning the head toward the backward arm swing.
- Hip and trunk flexion on the prosthetic side with backward arm swing.

Corrective Treatment: The amputee returns to the starting position.

- Practice unilateral arm swing while the other arm holds onto the parallel bar.
- When rotating to the right, manual resistance to the anterior aspect of the left shoulder and the posterior aspect of the right hip will help guide the spinal rotation movement. Hand positions are changed to the right shoulder and left hip for rotation to the left.

(See Fig. 3–43)

Exercise: Alternate Knee Flexion and Extension

Purpose: to teach knee control to both transtibial and transfemoral amputees.

Comment: the prosthetic heel will rise with knee flexion because the foot is bolted to the shank, eliminating ankle movement.

Deviations: compensatory actions include:

- unequal weight bearing (decreased on the prosthetic side)
- lateral trunk bending over the sound side when the prosthetic knee bends
- abrupt prosthetic knee flexion and extension (in knee disarticulation and transfemoral amputations)
- prosthetic knee buckling

Corrective Treatment: the amputee returns to the starting position.

- Manual resistance to stump hip extension and flexion (transfemoral) and knee extension and flexion (transtibial) encourages knee control and

---

Figure 3–43   Alternate knee flexion and extension: postural deviations and corrective treatment.

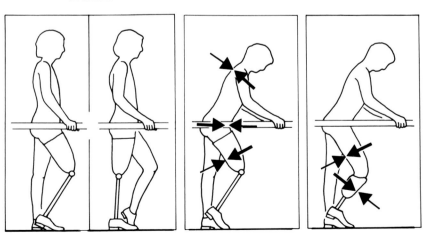

provides feedback to the stump through the socket. The prosthesis must maintain ground contact for the amputee to experience the correct movement.

- Lateral trunk bending is corrected, and correct lateral pelvic movement is reviewed.

Once the amputee can maintain or recover balance in these basic positions, without exaggerated postural compensation, progression can be made to practicing step position. Balance skills are further improved according to the amputee's ability by selectively introducing more difficult balance exercises, such as:

- Standing on the remaining leg and crossing the prosthesis first anteriorly and then posteriorly. Reverse the procedure by standing on the prosthesis, with the remaining leg crossing in both directions.
- Standing on the remaining leg, lifting the prosthesis using hip flexion, then standing on the prosthesis, lifting the remaining leg off the ground. Prolonged standing on the prosthesis often proves to be difficult.
- Catching a ball from different angles.

The prosthetic swing and stance phase are practiced separately to ensure that the amputee can correctly integrate the individual gait components into the total gait pattern (Koerner, 1980). Some physical therapists elect to begin practicing step positions by first teaching the prosthetic swing phase. They initially rely on the stability of the remaining leg. Other physical therapists believe that the prosthetic stance phase should be taught first. They consider this to be a safer method. Clinically it may be advisable to be guided by the degree of competence demonstrated by the amputee during balance exercises.

Progression to Practicing Step Positions

Prosthetic Swing Phase. The sequence of movements necessary to accomplish prosthetic swing will teach the amputee:

- to initiate prosthetic swing
- to practice the pelvic forward thrust on the prosthetic side
- to transfer weight from one double support period to the next
- to place the foot correctly at prosthetic heel strike
- to maintain an upright posture throughout the prosthetic swing phase

Starting Position. The amputee assumes a step position between the parallel bars (hands secured), with the remaining leg placed anteriorly and the prosthesis placed posteriorly, approximately a hip's breadth apart. The exercise begins with the body weight being shifted over the prosthesis.

(See Fig. 3–44)

Exercise Sequence. To propel the body forward, the amputee practices a combination of movements. These consist of:

- forceful prosthetic heel and toe off using stump hip extension
- transferring the weight forward to the remaining leg
- hip extension of the remaining leg

Figure 3–44 Prosthetic swing phase.

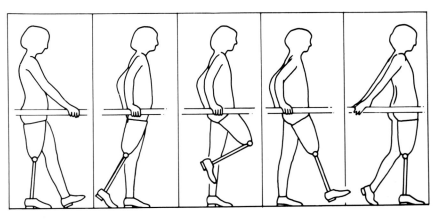

These synchronized movements result in a forward pelvic thrust on the prosthetic side. This then allows stump hip flexion to accelerate the prosthesis into the swing phase. During prosthetic midswing, the weight is held by the remaining leg until the prosthesis reaches heel contact and foot flat in the forward position. Prosthetic weight bearing with the pelvis over the prosthesis, combined with stump hip extension, completes the exercise sequence.

The prosthesis is pulled back into the starting position to repeat the movement sequence until the pattern becomes smoothly coordinated.

Common deviations:

- absent or incomplete forward pelvic thrust
- long prosthetic step
- hesitant step
- lack of prosthetic heel contact as the foot progresses immediately into foot flat
- prosthesis held as an appendage rather than purposefully activated
- knee flexion of the remaining leg on stance

The lack of pelvic forward thrust encourages trunk forward flexion and gives the appearance of the prosthesis being "left behind." Reasons leading to the lack of pelvic forward thrust include:

- weak hip extensor muscles
- the presence of a hip flexion contracture
- reduced spinal rotation
- elimination of active initiation of prosthetic knee flexion
- inaccurate timing of weight transfer
- prosthetic knee axis set too far back

Corrective Treatment.   The amputee returns to the starting position.

- Resistance to the anterior pelvis on the prosthetic side will facilitate the forward pelvic thrust movement. Simultaneous resistance to the occipital area during pelvic forward thrust practice will encourage a more upright trunk posture (see Basic Balance Exercises, p. 254)
- The amputee is instructed to assume a short step position with the sound heel being placed slightly ahead of the prosthetic foot.
- Rhythmic weight shifting is practiced in the step position without initiating prosthetic swing.
- Strong stump hip extension (transfemoral amputees) and hip and knee extension (transtibial amputees) are emphasized on heel contact to stabilize the knee before progression to foot flat. If this is not achieved, the amputee will attempt to bear weight on a partially flexed and, therefore, unstable, knee. This will result in:
    the knee buckling on weight beraing
    the knee ''snapping'' into extension during foot flat

Although the amputee is bearing weight alternately on both legs, the primary focus during this exercise is on the initiation and control of the prosthetic swing phase.

Prosthetic Stance Phase.   The sequence of motions necessary to control the prosthetic stance phase will teach the amputee:

- to achieve prosthetic stance stability
- to initiate the pelvic forward thrust on the sound side
- to transfer weight from one double support period to the next
- to feel the body forward motion over the prosthesis
- to maintain an upright posture throughout the prosthetic stance phase

Starting Position.   The amputee assumes a step position between the parallel bars (hands secured), with the prosthesis placed anteriorly and the remaining leg placed posteriorly, approximately a hip's breadth apart.   *(See Fig. 3–45)*

Exercise Sequence.   To propel the body forward, the amputee practices a combination of movements. These consist of:

- forceful heel- and toe-off using hip extension and plantar flexion
- the transfer of weight forward onto the prosthesis
- stump hip extension to control prosthetic knee stability

These synchronized movements result in a pelvic forward thrust on the sound side. This then allows hip flexion to accelerate the remaining leg into swing. During midswing the weight is over the prosthesis, with the stump maintaining forceful hip extension to keep the prosthetic knee stable until the remaining leg reaches heel contact and foot flat. At this moment, the weight transfers to the

Figure 3–45   Prosthetic stance phase.

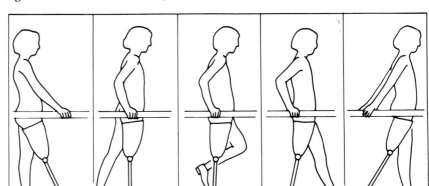

remaining leg, with the hip extended and the pelvis positioned directly over the support leg. Prosthetic knee flexion then occurs.

Using hip extension, the remaining leg returns to the starting position, and the motion sequence is practiced until the amputee can comfortably control prosthetic weight bearing throughout the stance phase.

Common deviations:

- decreased or absent pelvic forward thrust on the sound side
- a short step forward, with the remaining leg causing shortening of the prosthetic stance phase
- lateral trunk bending over the prosthesis when the remaining leg leaves the ground
- trunk forward flexion used to bring the body weight in front of the prosthetic knee

Corrective Treatment.   The amputee returns to the starting position.

- Stabilization of the prosthetic knee on stance must be practiced and is assisted by the therapist, who braces the prosthesis with one leg and, therefore, provides prosthetic foot and knee countersupport. The therapist then holds one hand over the gluteal muscles and the other over the anterior chest wall, thus providing further proprioceptive input. This will also ensure an upright trunk posture and permit the amputee to bear weight on the prosthesis with more confidence.
- Manual resistance to the anterior and posterior aspects of the knee (transtibial amputee) during stance will enhance the amputee's awareness of the muscle work necessary to control knee stability on stance.

(See Fig. 3–46)

Figure 3–46   Practicing knee stabilization with the transtibial amputee.

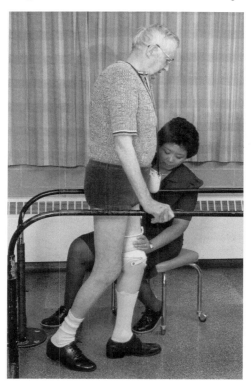

When both the prosthetic swing and stance phase and the skill of stepping backwards as well as sideways are properly controlled by the amputee, progression to walking takes place. Walking begins in the parallel bars and advances to crutches. With further skill, confidence and endurance, the amputee progresses to cane(s) or may walk without additional aids. However, if the amputee demonstrates gait deviations during treatment progression, a return to the previous level is advised (e.g., crutches reverting to parallel bars) to further practice the correct gait pattern. This will give the amputee an additional opportunity to acquire a safe and energy efficient gait.

The utilization of sensory feedback techniques during gait training will enhance the amputee's awareness of:

Sensory Feedback Techniques

- the amount of weight bearing applied
- the muscular effort required to perform the movement
- the direction and control of movements
- the dynamic body posture

Conventional Sensory Feedback Techniques

Three conventional and effective techniques are tactile, verbal, and visual stimulation. Sensory input can be further enhanced by the use of biofeedback equipment.

Tactile Stimulation. Precise hand positioning in relation to the movement and the amount of resistance or assistance given will greatly influence the direction, intensity and speed of the movement performed (see Progression to Practicing Step Positions, p. 261).

Manual contact is an excellent clinical teaching technique. The amputee is guided by hand, and the therapist, through contact, can judge the quality of the movements performed.

Verbal Stimulation. Instructions or commands, augmented by touch, are helpful to prompt postural corrections during gait training. Instructions must be clear and concise. In addition, the timing of the words is important since instructions must coincide precisely with the gait phase being corrected. The amputee must understand exactly the gait sequence and the postural faults and know how to correct them (Netz et al., 1981). Problems or confusion may occur if instructions are not clear and immediate.

Visual Stimulation. A full-length mirror placed at the end of the parallel bars helps to show amputees any postural faults while standing. However, when progression is made to walking, amputees may have difficulty concentrating on both the walking pattern and simultaneously improving their posture in the mirror image (Netz et al., 1981).

In the absence of specialized sensory feedback equipment, tactile, verbal and visual stimulation techniques, combined with an in-depth knowledge of gait deviations and their corrections, provide basic and reliable means for competent and individualized gait training.

Biofeedback Equipment

Special equipment or devices monitoring or assisting the amputee's performance can augment, stimulate and/or record gait-training activities. These include the use of a:

- posture control device
- videotape recorder
- EMG biofeedback unit
- limb load monitor (LLM)
- system for controlling ambulation pressure (SCAP III™)
- pedynograph

Posture Control Device. When using crutches or a walker, some amputees have a tendency to walk with a stooped gait. The overhead ambulation aid counteracts trunk forward flexion. The ceiling-suspended posture control device runs on a track, is height adjustable, and has a pivoting mechanism and a

Figure 3–47   Posture control device.

handle bar. By reaching overhead with both arms, the amputee places the center of   *(See Fig. 3–47)*
gravity over the hips and straightens up, thus counteracting trunk flexion. Using an
overhead arm swing when walking (which is made possible by the pivoting
mechanism) also encourages natural spinal rotation, which is often markedly
restricted when using gait aids (Mensch, 1983). The overhead device can also be
beneficial in the early phases of gait training to facilitate correct hip joint positioning during step practice. The posture correction can be felt by the amputee and
hopefully will be incorporated in the gait pattern as ambulation activities progress.

Videotape Recorder.   The replay of videotape recordings showing gait
practice sessions from different angles permits both the amputee and the therapist
to critically evaluate the gait performance following treatment sessions. The
amputee can then concentrate fully on recognizing gait appearance, step timing,
gait faults and postural deviations. If videotapes are kept as records, they can be
used for an objective comparison to analyze progression or regression in the gait
pattern over an extended period of time. Videotaping may also be beneficial in
encouraging amputees to improve their quality of walking (Netz et al., 1981).

Being able to sit back and objectively look at the ''finer points'' that will make the gait more natural may motivate some amputees to try harder.

EMG Biofeedback Unit.   The EMG biofeedback unit measures myoelectrical signals. These signals are picked up by sensors that produce audio signals proportional in volume and/or frequency to the amount of muscle work expended. The system is used to teach and facilitate relaxation, stimulation and reeducation of muscles, either during stump exercising (e.g., the sensors can be applied to the quadriceps muscle group if knee instability is apparent in a transtibial amputee) or in conjunction with gait training (EMG Handbook, 1979).

Electrode placement must be specific so that the pertinent muscle groups produce the signal. However, the procedure of placing EMG sensors inside a transfemoral socket to stimulate stump hip extension is not recommended, since they often cause localized skin pressure and skin irritation.

Limb Load Monitor.   This sensory feedback device will provide ''proportional, precise information about the weight-bearing force applied through the lower limb'' (Wannstedt et al., 1978). During the immediate postoperative phase, the LLM is used to *limit* the amputee's weight bearing (see Immediate Postoperative Treatment—Weight-Bearing Control, p. 93). During the active rehabilitation and the prosthetic gait-training phase, the LLM is used to *increase* weight bearing to equalize the weight distribution over both legs during ambulation.

A force sensor, shaped like an insole, is inserted into the shoe under the prosthesis and is connected by a cable to the portable control box. There are two modes of feedback that can be utilized. In one, the pitch of the auditory signal is calibrated to decrease with increased weight bearing. The signal stops when full loading has been achieved. In the other, the signal is absent until the desired amount of weight bearing has been attained, with the intensity of the signal increasing if too much weight is applied (Gapsis et al., 1982). The amputee must learn to correlate the sound to the weight-bearing intensity. The LLM is a useful adjunct to gait training since it partially compensates for the lost sensory perception of the foot as a result of the amputation.

Knee Control Device.   The knee control device is a quality and quantity feedback trainer that assists hip disarticulation, transfemoral, and knee disarticulation amputees in learning prosthetic knee control. It has a knee switch, a heel switch, and a control box. A sound signal received openly or through an earpiece indicates that the prosthetic knee is flexed (during swing). The absence of the sound means that the prosthetic knee is in extension, and thus weight bearing is safe (Fernie et al., 1978; Gilbert et al., 1982). The control box is also equipped with a light and an error counter. When the sound signal is turned off, a small light will alert the therapist when an error has been made (e.g., weight-bearing attempt in knee flexion). The errors are counted with the error counter to provide an objective measure of the amputee's progress (Fernie et al., 1978).

The addition of a foot switch step counter can also be useful because the error count, in comparison with the step count, supplies a quantitative measure of improved gait performance (Fernie et al., 1978).

System for Controlling Ambulation Pressure. The SCAP III™ system uses two sensors (mechanical load transducers), one under the heel and the other under the sole of the prosthetic foot (shoe insert). An audible signal is produced when the threshold of the preset amount of weight bearing has been reached (by pressure transfer to a bellow system). The sensors are synchronized in order to elicit a summated signal as the foot position changes from heel contact to toe off (King et al., 1972). Settings are continuously adjustable from 15 to 60 lb.

Pedynograph. The pedynograph, not commonly used, monitors and documents weight bearing, walking speed, and smoothness of the prosthetic gait. A force transducer attached to the pylon and placed between the foot and socket emits signals that are transmitted via a cable to a mobile oscilloscope. A camera placed over the oscilloscope takes a photograph of the recordings that can be used as a permanent record (Symington et al., 1979).

Pedynograms can be obtained during gait-training sessions. The tracings document weight-bearing intensity in kilograms throughout the gait cycle. For instance, discrepancies such as the reduction of prosthetic weight bearing at midstance, when actually full weight bearing should be applied, are plainly shown. The recordings help the therapist to adjust treatments accordingly.

Summary

Increased awareness of the need to supplement visual observations during gait training (Krebs et al., 1985), to better control the amount of weight bearing (King et al., 1972), to obtain qualitative and quantitative measures (Saleh et al., 1985), and to provide a meaningful biomechanical analysis has led to the development of gait-training equipment and biofeedback devices. The information provided by some of this equipment will probably provide the basis of future research statistics. However, physical therapists who do not have access to these devices should not feel that they cannot provide adequate gait training for their amputee patients using the more conventional training methods. Physical therapy assessment, treatment planning, clinical expertise, and the use of verbal, manual, and visual stimulation cannot be replaced by any equipment, however sophisticated.

Progression to Independent Ambulation

Once the amputee can ambulate safely under supervision with the training unit and any necessary walking aids, progress is made to independent walking outside of the physical therapy department.

Amputees often become very dependent on the presence of their treating therapist in whom they have confidence. To gain self-confidence and independence and to increase their walking tolerance, recent amputees must be encouraged to walk and to use their training unit during activities of daily living on the ward.

Although supervision and assistance is available, the amputee is not under as close scrutiny as during normal gait-training sessions.

In a rehabilitation setting, patients are usually transported to their therapies via wheelchair, since this often saves time. As the amputee progresses, however, consideration must be given to weaning from the wheelchair, especially if a wheelchair is not needed at home. This process of weaning must be paced according to the amputee's tolerance and can be facilitated by chairs situated ''along the way'' to permit rest periods.

Independence is also encouraged by weekend home visits prior to discharge. In the familiar home environment, the amputee is encouraged to adapt ambulation activities to specific meaningful tasks (e.g., walking to the bathroom or standing and stooping to remove food from the oven).

By encouraging independent ambulation, the therapist may alleviate some of the amputee's anxiety, upon discharge, related to the psychological support provided during the treatment in a rehabilitation center (Kindon et al., 1982).

Increasing Prosthetic-wearing Tolerance

During initial gait-training activities, the amputee may come to view the training unit as a treatment tool that is used *only* during physical therapy sessions for walking. These perceptions are reinforced by the therapist, who initially may limit the use of the training unit to treatment sessions only because of concerns about the amutee's ability:

- to correctly don the training unit independently
- to safely transfer
- to control step positions and balance
- to recognize stump problems during and after ambulation

However, the therapist must also consider that gradually increasing the prosthetic-wearing tolerance will facilitate:

- acclimatization of the stump to the socket
- integration of the training unit into the amputee's body image (Friedmann, 1978)

Once the amputee can safely transfer and correctly don the training unit, it is taken to the ward where it is worn for gradually increasing periods of time. The rationale for this routine is that the amputee, by discharge, will be able to wear the training unit for the entire day. The amputee is also requested to record the actual wearing time on a flow chart provided. The therapist, noticing any decrease in wearing time and/or lack of progress, will thereby be alerted to possible problems and be able to provide guidance.

Often, amputees are discharged from a rehabilitation ward and continue physical therapy treatments on an out-patient basis while still using the training unit or temporary prosthesis. At this time, when adapting to a regular life-style, the amputee should use the training prosthesis throughout the day. If however, the amputee is only donning the device at home for short walking periods, then the therapist must investigate the possible reason or reasons for the reduced prosthetic activities so that corrective measures can be implemented immediately.

Learning to master advanced gait activities will increase the amputee's ambulation skills, encourage independence, and provide increased self-confidence. Practice sessions for these increasingly difficult tasks include:

Advanced Activities

- navigating stairs, curbs, ramps
- attempting to turn around
- picking up objects
- clearing obstacles
- coping with unusual ground conditions
- falling and getting up

Regardless of whether the amputee uses crutches or walks without any external support, the remaining leg performs the major work required for these bilateral activities. The prosthesis provides stability or is positioned in such a way that it will not interfere with the functional task being performed by the remaining leg.

Several stair-walking techniques can be taught. One step at a time is a commonly used pattern. Overstepping, as in regular stair walking, may be accomplished by the amputee with a longer amputation stump (e.g., ankle disarticulations), but it is seldom practiced by amputees who have higher level amputations or by the elderly amputee.

Stairs, Curbs, and Ramps

Stairs: Stepping Up.   The body weight is placed over the extended prosthesis. The remaining leg steps up with the trunk easing gently forward. This transfers the body weight over the remaining foot so that the remaining leg can complete the upward step. The prosthesis follows and is placed on the same step beside the remaining leg. The procedure is repeated.

(See Fig. 3–48)

Stairs: Stepping Down.   The body weight is held by the remaining leg. The prosthesis, held in extension, steps down first while the remaining leg, with the knee flexing, follows to be placed beside the prosthesis. The procedure is repeated.

Using Crutches.   The same method is practiced with the crutches supporting the prosthesis.

Using Crutches and a Handrail.   Again the same method is utilized. Both crutches are held on one side while the amputee holds the handrail with the other hand. Crutch support and the grip on the rail assist the prosthesis.

When using gait aids, it is important to teach the amputee the art of *stepping down* (a controlled movement) and not allow the amputee to hop down (an uncontrolled and extremely unsafe manner in which to navigate steps).

Figure 3–48   Stair walking, one step at a time.

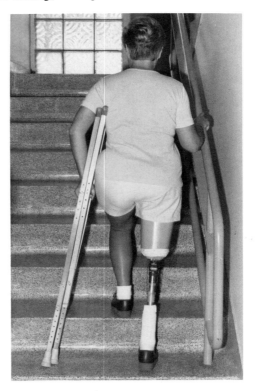

(See Fig. 3–49)

"Jack Knifing" Techniques.   Using the jack knife technique, the transfemoral amputee can descend stairs by overstepping. The prosthetic foot is placed so that the forefoot extends past the step. In this way, stance stability can be maintained, and descending can be initiated by hip flexion. Hip flexion, combined with weight bearing and the ground reaction force passing behind the knee, will flex the prosthesis, allowing the remaining leg to step down. This technique is abrupt and requires excellent timing and coordination by the amputee.

Clinical Comment.   Stair-walking techniques may have to be adapted to the actual dimensions of the steps. Descending on narrow steps requires the amputee to place the prosthesis at an angle to the line of progression. This provides sufficient foot ground contact on a narrow step to give prosthetic stance stability.

Curbs.   The procedures for stepping up and down curbs are identical to climbing stairs. The remaining leg initiates the stepping up while the prosthesis precedes in stepping down.

Figure 3–49   Starting position for jack knifing.

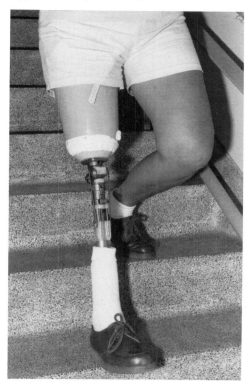

Ramps.   The same principles as in stair walking also apply to walking on steep slopes, except that the amputee approaches the slope at an angle to the line of progression. The remaining leg leads with a sideways step in the upward direction while the extended prosthesis, held parallel to the remaining leg, follows. The procedure is reversed when descending the slope with the prosthesis leading.

If the amputee attempts to ascend by facing the slope, the prosthetic foot would be forced into dorsiflexion by the incline, thus hindering both prosthetic knee extension and the overstepping by the remaining leg. Conversely, going downhill, the slope would have a plantar flexion effect on the prosthetic foot, thus causing forced prosthetic knee flexion.

Pivoting on the prosthesis should be avoided since a pivot motion causes skin friction at the stump–socket interface. The amputee is advised to use several small alternating steps to complete the turn, with the remaining leg on the outside of the circle.

Turning Around

(See Fig. 3–50)

Figure 3–50 Stepping around instead of pivoting.

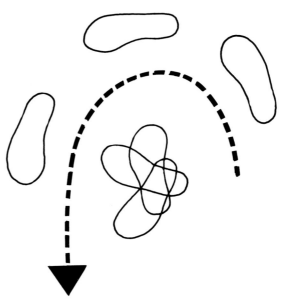

Picking Objects Off the Ground

Objects can be picked off the ground either by trunk flexion only or by the combined flexion of the trunk, the hips, and the remaining knee. The amputee is instructed to:

1. Assume a step position, the remaining leg forward, close to the item to be picked off the floor.
2. Place the body weight over the remaining leg, then flex the hips and the remaining knee.
3. Reach for the item.
4. Rise by extending the remaining leg and the trunk.

With the prosthesis in the rear position, unhindered movements by the remaining leg are possible.

Clearing Obstacles

The most reasonable approach to clearing objects is by walking around them. If this is not possible, the amputee must assess if stepping over the barrier is feasible. The therapist can set up an obstacle course by using sandbags, a board, and a marked restricted area (imaginary hole) that must be negotiated.

1. The amputee approaches the obstacle.
2. The weight is shifted to the remaining leg.
3. Forceful hip flexion on the amputated side, and sometimes leaning the trunk backwards, "throws" the prosthesis over the obstacle.
4. The prosthetic knee is then forcefully extended on ground contact past the obstacle.

5. Weight transfer, continued prosthetic knee extension, and trunk forward flexion permit overstepping with the remaining leg.

Clinical Comments. It is important for the amputee to learn to judge the distance away from the obstacle to allow for prosthetic clearance without tripping. A common error during practice is to pause and hold the prosthesis over the obstacle. This causes the prosthetic shank to flex in suspension (gravity), and the momentum to reach heel contact is then lost. Abduction and/or circumduction may be necessary to assist in clearing obstacles.

Unusual Ground Conditions

Ground surface conditions, partially weather dependent, can be firm, soft (mud), wet, dusty, rough, slippery (ice), etc. Adjustments to unusual ground conditions may be required for safety.

The most common way to walk on unusual ground conditions is to wear shoes that have nonslip soles or to put on protective rubber boots and use small controlled steps with or without gait aids.

Ice. A flip-up winter grip can be clipped to a cane or crutches. The spike, when positioned downward, provides a firm hold when walking on ice and snow. *(See Fig. 3–51)*

Figure 3–51 Flip-up winter grip in up and down position.

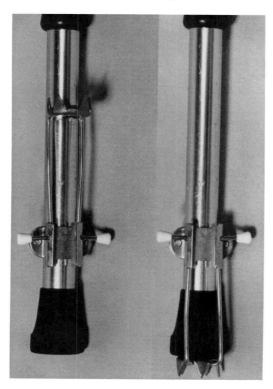

A pushbutton device allows the spike to be positioned out of the way when their function is not required.

Metal grip bars buckled under shoes are effective to prevent slipping on ice but are cumbersome. The rigid bar restricts the foot-rolling motion, and the device has to be put on and taken off as needed because the cleats on the bar are sharp and can easily scratch other surfaces (floors).

A simple, but unconventional, method of pulling a woollen work sock over the shoe fitted to the prosthesis will provide some protection from slipping on ice and snow if other methods are not readily available.

Gravel.   Small steps and/or one step at a time, rather than overstepping are recommended to ensure a sound footing on gravel or sandy ground.

Falling and Getting Up

Most falls occur because the prosthetic knee buckles, a foot slips or trips, or the amputee loses balance for other reasons. Learning to fall can be practiced by young and active amputees. The not so active, elderly amputees should only be told how to respond to falling, thus preventing any possible injury resulting from a practice fall.

Falls.   Since all falls occur unexpectedly, it is difficult for amputees to decide quickly which procedure to use for a forward, a sideway, or a backward fall. Therefore, basic falling principles must be simple. and must always be remembered (Mensch, 1983).

1. Let go of crutches and canes: they hinder body self-protection.
2. Immediately flex the body. Body flexion cushions the impact, whereas extension intensifies the impact.
3. Use hands if possible to lessen the impact.

Practice sessions for falling require a soft, thick mat. The amputee, standing on the mat, must first concentrate to think out the falling procedure, then relax before the practice fall is attempted. Forward falling is practiced with both hands absorbing the impact. Backward and sideway falls (use caution) require instant trunk and neck flexion to avoid the head striking the ground.

Getting Up from Supine.

(Figure 3–52 a to g)

A The prosthesis is in extension.
B The remaining leg is flexed.
C The amputee rolls over the remaining leg using momentum to achieve the kneeling position.
D Both arms and hands push the trunk backward over the remaining foot to obtain foot–floor contact.
E Both hands and the remaining leg then exert pressure to help raise the body to stand up.

F Hand pressure over the thigh assists in knee extension preparation for standing.

G The prosthesis is brought forward to achieve a stable stance.

Figure 3–52(a) Getting off the floor from supine.

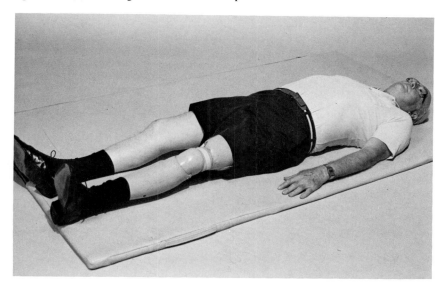

Figure 3–52(b) The remaining leg is flexed.

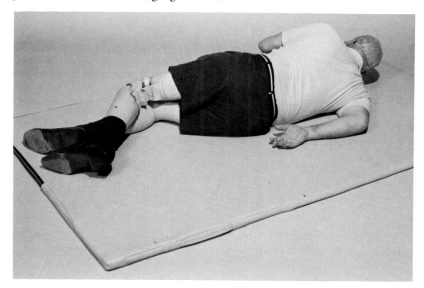

Figure 3–52(c)   The amputee rolls around the remaining leg using momentum.

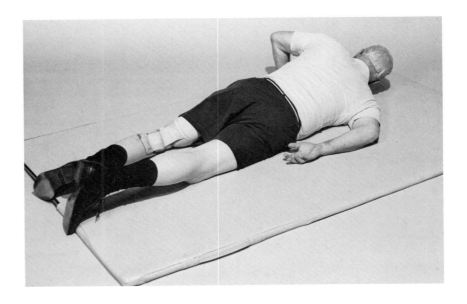

Figure 3–52(d)   Both arms and hands push the trunk backward over the remaining foot to obtain foot–floor contact.

Figure 3–52(e) Both hands and the remaining leg then exert pressure to help raise the body.

Figure 3–52(f) Hand pressure over the thigh assists in knee extension preparation for standing.

Figure 3–52(g)   The prosthesis is brought forward to achieve a stable stance.

Getting Up from Floor Sitting.

1. The prosthesis is extended.
2. The remaining leg is flexed, with the foot having ground contact close to the trunk.
3. The extended arms are positioned slightly backward to brace the trunk.
4. The amputee turns toward the natural leg and uses momentum to reach the kneeling position.
5. The trunk weight is transferred backward to bring the center of gravity over the quadriceps so the foot can attain the foot–floor contact.
6. Both hands and the remaining leg then exert pressure to help the body stand up.
7. The prosthesis is brought forward to achieve a stable stance.

Getting up is difficult to learn and requires repeated practice. Amputees who are able to get up are less afraid of falling.

Clinical Comments. Sometimes the amputee will hold on to nearby furniture to get up, or will place one hand over the quadriceps muscle to assist by pushing while straightening the knee and hip of the remaining leg.

Learning to master these activities depends upon the amputee's:

Summary

- health status and age
- level of amputation
- coordination and balance
- motivation

Therapists must offer continuous supervision and guidance throughout the entire advanced activity training phase until the amputee performs all activities naturally and with ease.

Prosthetic proficiency rewards the amputee with physical independence. The level of skill achieved varies greatly among amputees, and a return to a completely satisfactory life-style is possible for many. Some elect to lead a quiet life, whereas others like to travel, enjoy dancing, or participate in sporting activities (see Sports, p. 343).

References

Baumgartner, R.F. "Knee Disarticulation versus above-knee Amputation." *Prosthetics and Orthotics International, 3* (1979): 15–19.

Cyborg Corporation. "Applying the J33 to Muscle Re-education." *EMG J33 handbook.* Boston, Ma.: 1979, 12–15.

Fernie, G., Holden, J., and Soto, M. "Biofeedback Training of Knee Control in the above-knee Amputee." *American Journal of Physical Medicine, 57*, no. 4 (1978): 161–166.

Friedmann, L.W. "Patient Reactions to Amputation. Training-Adult." *The Psychological Rehabilitation of the Amputee.* Springfield, Ill.: Chas. C. Thomas, 1978, 44–66.

Gapsis, J.J., Grabois, M., Borrell, R.M., Menken, S.A., and Kelly, M. "Limb Load Monitor: Evaluation of a Sensory Feedback Device for Controlled Weight Bearing." *Archives of Physical Medicine and Rehabilitation, 63* (January 1982): 38–41.

Gilbert, J.A., Maxwell, G.M., George, R.T., and McElhaney, J.H. "Technical Note—Auditory Feedback of Knee Angle for Amputees." *Prosthetics and Orthotics International, 6* (1982): 103–104.

Kindon, D., and Pearce, T. "Psychological Assessment and Management of the Amputee." In S.N. Banerjee, ed. *Rehabilitation Management of Amputees.* Baltimore, Md.: Williams & Wilkins, 1982, 350–371.

King, P.S., Gerhardt, J.J., Pfeiffer, E.A., Usselman, L.B., and Fowlks, E.W. "System for Controlling Ambulation Pressure (SCAP III) in Patients with Disabilities of the Lower Extremity." *American Journal of Physical Medicine, 51*, no. 1 (1972): 9–15.

Koerner, I.B. *Normal Human Locomotion and the Gait of the Amputee.* Alberta: University of Alberta, 1980.

Krebs, D.E., Edelstein, J.E., and Fishman, S. "Reliability of Observational Kinematic Gait Analysis. *Physical Therapy*, July 65, no. 7 (1985): 1027–1033.

Mensch, G. "Posture Control Device." *Physiotherapy Canada, 35*, no. 3 (May/June 1983): 152–153.

Mensch, G. "Physiotherapy Following through-knee Amputation." *Prosthetics and Orthotics International, 7* (1983): 79–87.

Netz, P., Wersen, K., and Wetterberg, M. "Videotape Recording—A Complimentary Aid for the Walking Training of Lower Limb Amputees." *Prosthetics and Orthotics International, 5*, (1981): 147–150.

Saleh, M., and Murdoch, G. "In Defence of Gait Analysis, Observation and Measurement in Gait Assessment. *Journal of Bone and Joint Surgery, 67B,* no. 2 (1985): 237–241.

Symington, D.C., Lowe, P.J., and Olney, S.J. "The Pedynograph: A Clinical Tool for Force Measurement and Gait Analysis in Lower Extremity Amputees. *Archives of Physical Medicine and Rehabilitation,* 60 (February 1979): 56–61.

Wannstedt, G.T., and Herman, R.M. "Use of Augmented Sensory Feedback to Achieve Symmetrical Standing. *Physical Therapy, 58,* no. 5 (May 1978): 553–559.

Recommended Reading

New York University. "Gait and Activities Training." *Lower-limb prosthetics.* New York: Prosthetics and Orthotics, New York University Post-Graduate Medical School, 1977, 255–274.

Vultee, F.E. "Physical Treatment and Training of Amputees." *Atlas of Limb Prosthetics,* St. Louis, Mo.: C.V. Mosby, 1981, vol. II 313–337.

GAIT DEVIATIONS

Prosthetic gait is complex, and the reasons leading to gait deviations are many and diverse. The underlying cause(s) of the different gait deviations must be identified to correct and/or improve the amputee's gait pattern.

Prosthetic gait examination requires that the therapist:

- evaluate specific gait characteristics by separating the dominant gait deviation from the associated postural adaptations that may be observed as a result of the dominant gait deviation
- identify any intrinsic components that affect the gait pattern in terms of medical problems as well as static and/or dynamic locomotor problems
- recognize that extrinsic components such as prosthetic reasons and/or environmental factors may also contribute to gait faults.

Evaluating prosthetic gait is often difficult because, regardless of the underlying cause(s), *all* gait deviations are demonstrated posturally. Precise analysis and separation of the causative factors requires repeated investigation and critical subjective and objective observation. For example, intrinsic or extrinsic factors may cause stump pain that will result in a gait deviation. The manifestation of a gait deviation depends on the origin, the severity, and the anatomical location of the pain, as well as to when the pain is experienced during the gait cycle.

A comprehensive chart system describing commonly observed gait deviations and their possible causative factors will assist clinicians in problem identification so that the appropriate corrective measures can be initiated.

Transtibial gait deviations (see Table 3–1, p. 284) are less evident because the function of the natural knee joint has been preserved, making prosthetic gait more natural. In comparison, transfemoral gait deviations (see Table 3–2, p. 292) are usually more pronounced because the amputee must accommodate for the loss of the knee joint.

The prosthetic gait pattern, like "normal" gait, is not consistent because additional variables, such as the individual's physical or mental state, atmospheric conditions (temperature, humidity), and other environmental factors (ground conditions), influence gait performance. Amputees also tend to demonstrate different walking patterns when being observed in a clinical setting compared with when they are left to walk on their own.

Precise observation and analysis of prosthetic gait, viewed from the front, side, and back, will determine the best treatment intervention. However, the clinician must realistically accept that gait deviations, particularly at the higher amputation levels, cannot be entirely eliminated. Inherent postural characteristics and difficulty in adapting to the biomechanical changes produced by the amputation often prevent the amputee from achieving the "perfect" prosthetic gait.

The definitive prosthesis is generally prescribed 2–5 months following amputation surgery (there are exceptions to this estimated time frame) when optimum stump maturation has occurred and when the amputee has demonstrated sufficient functional ability with a training unit or a temporary prosthesis. The amputee team physician, with input from the prosthetist, the physical therapist, and the amputee (e.g., request for interchangeable feet to allow for variation in shoe heel heights), prescribes the prosthesis. The prescription explicitly specifies:

PROSTHETIC PRESCRIPTION AND CHECKOUT

- socket features
- type of lining (if indicated)
- suspension system(s)
- foot component
- type(s) of joint(s) (if indicated)
- special device(s) (if indicated)
- stump sock requirements
- endo- or exoskeletal system

The period of time required to fabricate a prosthesis depends on local conditions and the availability of prosthetic components (rarely used parts may not be in stock). If the amputee is discharged prior to final fitting, a short period of readmission may be advisable, particularly if the amputee lives any distance from the rehabilitation center, to construct and complete the prosthesis as specified and to ensure optimum function and comfort.

The active rehabilitation phase ends with a final and detailed examination of the definitive prosthesis.

Prosthetic Checkout

During the prosthetic checkout, the team compares the actual prosthesis with the written prescription. The following points are evaluated:

- socket fit (contours, diameter, contact)
- suspension efficiency (socket self-suspension, belt and strap positions, suction system)
- static alignment (anteroposterior and medial–lateral)
- dynamic alignment
- leg length
- comfort
- cosmetic appearance

(Text continues on p. 326)

TABLE 3–1   Description of Transtibial Gait Deviations: Their Effects and Causative Components

Dominant Gait Deviation and its Characteristics	Compensatory Postural Adaptations Associated with the Dominant Gait Fault
Excessive Knee Flexion from Heel Contact to Midstance 	trunk forward flexion lateral trunk bending toward the prosthetic side center of gravity drops lack of heel contact weight bearing over prosthetic forefoot resulting in heelrise reduced arm swing prosthesis appears to be too short

Figure 3–53   Excessive knee flexion from prosthetic heel contact to midstance.

| *Sudden Early Knee Flexion at End of Midstance*  | prolonged prosthetic heel off
sudden forward step with sound leg
prolonged stance phase on sound side
arrhythmic gait pattern |

Figure 3–54   Premature knee flexion at the end of midstance.

Intrinsic Components		Extrinsic Components	
Medical Considerations and Static Locomotor Problems	**Dynamic Locomotor Problems**	**Prosthetic Reasons**	**Environmental Factors**
knee flexion contracture hip flexion contracture decreased quadriceps muscle strength weak hip extensor muscles anterior-distal stump pain	poor balance lack of confidence decreased proprioception bilateral knee flexion lowers center of gravity and increases stance stability temporarily (tiring)	foot set in dorsiflexion socket aligned in too much flexion socket set too far forward in relation to foot stiff heel (SACH foot) stiff plantarflexion bumper (conventional foot) posterior displacement of suspension strap prosthesis too long	slippery ground surface conditions premature progression of gait aids (e.g. crutches to canes) walking downhill
poor proprioception flexion contracture knee instability weak hip extensor muscles anterior-distal stump pain	hesitant gait habit not corrected during early gait training	excessive dorsiflexion of prosthetic foot keel of SACH foot too short socket placed anterior in relation to foot socket too loose	slippery ground conditions walking downhill

TABLE 3–1 continued

Dominant Gait Deviation and its Characteristics	Compensatory Postural Adaptations Associated with the Dominant Gait Fault
Excessive Knee Flexion Prior to Toe–Off knee flexion increases too quickly as the center of gravity passes over the foot	pelvic drop and shoulder drop on prosthetic side quick forward step with sound leg to recover balance trunk forward flexion as a reaction to excessive knee flexion spinal rotation towards prosthetic side prolonged stance on sound side arrhythmic gait pattern

Figure 3–55   Excessive knee flexion prior to prosthetic toe-off.

Insufficient or Absent Knee Flexion From Heel Contact to Mid-stance (difficult to demonstrate with correct socket alignment)	prolonged foot flat as center of gravity has to rise hip abduction on prosthetic side vaulting on sound side reduced spinal rotation

Figure 3–56   Insufficient or absent knee flexion from heel strike to midstance.

Intrinsic Components		Extrinsic Components	
Medical Considerations and Static Locomotor Problems	**Dynamic Locomotor Problems**	**Prosthetic Reasons**	**Environmental Factors**
hip and/or knee flexion contracture knee instability anterior-distal stump pain poor proprioception weak hip extensor muscles short stump	fatigue inability to control knee motions elimination of pelvic forward thrust amputee feels weight of the prosthesis sudden and/or unexpected increase in weight bearing	excessive dorsi-flexion of prosthetic foot too much socket flexion anterior socket placement in relation to foot prosthetic foot too small prosthetic foot too soft (SACH)	walking downhill wearing higher heeled shoes without prosthetic alignment change slippery ground conditions
anterior-distal stump pain decreased quadriceps strength excessive soft tissue in popliteal area	habit decreased proprioception fear of knee buckling small steps	too much plantarflexion of prosthetic foot too soft plantarflexion bumper (conventional foot) too soft heel cushion in SACH foot posterior socket placement in relation to foot prosthesis too short	walking uphill wearing lower heeled shoes without prosthetic alignment change

TABLE 3–1 continued

Dominant Gait Deviation and its Characteristics	Compensatory Postural Adaptations Associated with the Dominant Gait Fault
Delayed Knee Flexion at End of Stance Phase (difficult to demonstrate with correct socket alignment)	trunk forward leaning delayed toe off on prosthetic side decreased swing phase on sound side unequal ground gain, sound leg leading vaulting on sound side

Figure 3–57   Delayed knee flexion in the latter part of stance.

Excessive Lateral Thrust medial wall presses against the stump, lateral wall gapes during midstance	excessive lateral pelvic shift to center the weight over the socket pelvic drop on sound side

Figure 3–58   Excessive lateral thrust.

Intrinsic Components		Extrinsic Components	
Medical Considerations and Static Locomotor Problems	**Dynamic Locomotor Problems**	**Prosthetic Reasons**	**Environmental Factors**
weak hip flexor muscles posterior-distal stump pain	lack of pelvic forward thrust prolonged weight bearing with knee held in extension causes knee extension moment actively extended knee causes prosthetic foot to rise	excessive posterior socket placement in relation to the foot foot too large excessive foot plantarflexion socket aligned with posterior tilt prosthetic foot too hard (SACH)	walking up an incline walking up stairs
medial collateral ligament weakness preexisting joint pathology (bandy knee) distal-medial stump pain weak hip abductors (positive Trendelenburg sign)	preexisting gait pattern wider walking base as sound leg abducts to compensate for adduction	excessive medial placement of the prosthetic foot socket set too far lateral in relation to foot socket too large	walking on rough ground

TABLE 3–1 continued

Dominant Gait Deviation and its Characteristics	Compensatory Postural Adaptations Associated with the Dominant Gait Fault
Medial and Lateral Whips occur from toe off to mid swing whips are recognized by the direction the prosthetic heel turns in relation to the center line of the shank medial whips occur more frequently than lateral whips	trunk turning toward prosthetic side at heel off hip external rotation at toe off resulting in medial whip hip internal rotation at toe off resulting in lateral whip prosthetic forefoot pivoting prolonged mid stance on sound side

Figure 3–59   Medial whip.

Insufficient Weight Bearing during prosthetic mid stance	prosthesis abducted cane braced, slightly abducted, against sound hip shoulder elevated on sound side during weight transfer to cane bilateral shoulder elevation to increase weight bearing through both arms if walker is used shortened stance on prosthetic side prolonged stance on sound side

Figure 3–60   Insufficient weight bearing.

Intrinsic Components		Extrinsic Components	
Medical Considerations and Static Locomotor Problems	**Dynamic Locomotor Problems**	**Prosthetic Reasons**	**Environmental Factors**
weak hip rotators knee instability	slightly prolonged swing phase because prosthesis does not swing straight through active hip external or internal rotation decreased pelvic forward thrust action strong external rotators assist weak hip extensor muscles	suspension loose malalignment of hinges (thigh corset) toe break improperly aligned (conventional foot) stiff SACH foot causing pivot posterior-medial brim pressure at knee flexion	rough ground walking uphill
stump hypersensitivity short stump decreased quadriceps strength knee instability	fear of the knee buckling anticipation of stump pain early training problem	socket too large socket too small distal socket contact missing	initial reliance on gait aids

TABLE 3–2   **Description of Transfemoral Gait Deviations: Their Effects and Causative Components**

Dominant Gait Deviation and its Characteristics	Compensatory Postural Adaptations Associated with the Dominant Gait Fault
Abducted Gait lateral placement of the prosthesis away from the body midline during swing and stance phase the sound foot is placed at a normal distance from the line of progression while the prosthesis is placed an excessive distance from the line of progression the increase in the width of the walking base is caused by the prosthetic placement only	moderate lateral trunk bending toward the prosthetic side, but can also be observed toward the sound side unequal and/or reduced arm swing decreased spinal rotation insufficient prosthetic knee flexion prosthesis moderately internally rotated prolonged stance on sound leg uneven timing moderate hip hiking vaulting

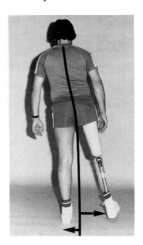

Figure 3–61   Abducted gait.

Intrinsic Components		Extrinsic Components	
Medical Considerations and Static Locomotor Problems	**Dynamic Locomotor Problems**	**Prosthetic Reasons**	**Environmental Factors**
adductor roll abduction contracture hip flexion contracture weak hip flexors pain on distal lateral stump surface generalized skin sensitivity weak hip adductors weak hip extensors weak hip abductors on the sound side cause a pelvic drop on the prosthetic side resulting in apparent lengthening of prosthesis incomplete insertion of stump into prosthetic socket	poor balance inability to extend stump through full range of motion fear of knee buckling inability to perform pelvic thrust	prosthesis too long improperly shaped lateral wall medial socket wall too high prosthesis aligned with wide base inadequate suspension excessive knee friction medial lateral dimension of socket brim too narrow	rough ground inclines carrying a heavy object on the sound side progression from crutches to one cane strenuous ambulation on uneven ground

TABLE 3–2 continued

Dominant Gait Deviation and its Characteristics	Compensatory Postural Adaptations Associated with the Dominant Gait Fault
Circumducted Gait amputee swings the prosthesis in an arc away from the body midline during swing phase foot placement on stance returns to an accepted distance from the line of progression walking base is normal on double support with both feet placed at an accepted distance from the line of progression	arm swing on the prosthetic side is reduced arm swing on the sound side is increased and the arm is held in slight abduction using the contralateral arm as momentum during circumducted prosthetic swing phase shoulder elevation on the sound side apparent reduced or absent prosthetic knee flexion moderate hip hiking on prosthetic side provides ground clearance occasional vaulting which prolongs the midstance phase on the sound side permitting time for the prosthesis to be accelerated forward internal rotation of prosthesis on heel contact head forward flexion

Figure 3–62 Circumducted gait.

Intrinsic Components		Extrinsic Components	
Medical Considerations and Static Locomotor Problems	**Dynamic Locomotor Problems**	**Prosthetic Reasons**	**Environmental Factors**
short stump causing inadequate lever control	inability to initiate prosthetic knee flexion	prosthesis too long	avoiding obstacles
pistoning due to flabby stump tissues	the circumducted swing eliminates the correct prosthetic swing phase sequence, easing the forward motion of the prosthesis	too much prosthetic knee friction	pivoting on sound leg using prosthesis to initiate motion and to improve standing balance
weak hip flexors		too much knee alignment stability	
painful anterior distal stump		excessive plantar flexion of prosthetic foot	
abduction contracture			
weak hip abductors on the sound side causing a drop on the prosthetic side resulting in an apparent lengthening of the prosthesis	less energy consumption by the stump	pistoning due to oversized socket diameter	
	more energy consumption by the sound leg because of prolonged stance phase	socket is too small	
		loose suspension	
		excessively strong extension assist of prosthetic knee	
	potential to become a permanent habit		
	lack of confidence in control of prosthetic knee		

TABLE 3–2 continued

Dominant Gait Deviation and its Characteristics	Compensatory Postural Adaptations Associated with the Dominant Gait Fault
Lateral Trunk Bending the trunk flexes laterally from body midline toward the prosthetic side to center the trunk weight directly over the socket during stance phase during prosthetic swing phase the trunk returns to midline walking base is normal with feet positioned at an equal distance from the line of progression	contralateral arm is held in abduction in combination with shoulder elevation to counter balance trunk weight over the prosthetic socket occurs predominantly toward the prosthetic side but can also be observed toward the opposite side arm swing on prosthetic side reduced unequal timing lateral pelvic drop trunk forward flexion head forward flexion

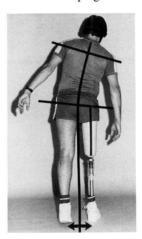

Figure 3–63   Lateral trunk bending.

Intrinsic Components		Extrinsic Components	
Medical Considerations and Static Locomotor Problems	**Dynamic Locomotor Problems**	**Prosthetic Reasons**	**Environmental Factors**
short stump causing inadequate lever control	shifting center of gravity with upper trunk because of inability to laterally shift the pelvis over the prosthetic side	prosthesis is too short	carrying heavy object on sound side (counter balances weight)
stump painful distally and laterally	poor balance potential to become a permanent habit because the trunk is used as a long lever to shift the center of gravity over the stance leg. This is easier for some amputees who find lateral pelvic shift difficult	high medial wall lateral distal socket counter pressure on tender area inadequate lateral wall contact socket too loose inadequate lateral tilt of socket medial-lateral diameter of the socket is too wide	incorrect use of cane (incorrect side) incorrect height of cane walking parallel to a slope to counteract gravity pull on the trunk thus aiding balance
weak hip abductors on the prosthetic side			
reduction of trunk muscle tone on the prosthetic side	lateral trunk bending occurs toward the sound side during running due to increased prosthetic step length		
adductor roll	poor reciprocation		

TABLE 3–2 continued

Dominant Gait Deviation and its Characteristics	**Compensatory Postural Adaptations Associated with the Dominant Gait Fault**
Rotation of Forefoot on Heel Strike the foot externally rotates on prosthetic heel contact prior to foot flat walking base normal	excessive prosthetic heel compression causes the prosthesis to rotate active hip external rotation on the prosthetic side resulting in a forefoot toe out position which causes the trunk to proceed at an angle to the line of progression arms held in slight abduction particularly on the sound side to control balance during rotation of the forefoot prosthesis, at times, may be slightly abducted as well as externally rotated medial whip can be a resultant deviation terminal swing impact

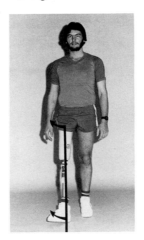

Figure 3–64   Rotation of forefoot on heel strike.

Intrinsic Components		Extrinsic Components	
Medical Considerations and Static Locomotor Problems	**Dynamic Locomotor Problems**	**Prosthetic Reasons**	**Environmental Factors**
excessively soft stump tissue permits passive rotational mobility weak hip internal rotators external rotation contracture (rarely seen in isolation)	pivoting caused by active hip external rotation excessive heel strike decreased prosthetic weight bearing if walking aid is used prolonged time on prosthetic heel habit using excessive active hip external rotation on heel strike	heel cushion too rigid (SACH foot) stiff plantar flexion bumper (conventional foot) inadequate suspension too much toe out built into prosthesis loose socket fit prosthetic foot set too far posteriorly excessive tissue mobility in suction socket wearers	slippery ground incorrect shoe height on prosthetic side (lower heel than aligned for) rigid shoe

TABLE 3–2 continued

Dominant Gait Deviation and its Characteristics	Compensatory Postural Adaptations Associated with the Dominant Gait Fault
Medial and Lateral Whips altered heel trajectory in space following toe off of prosthetic foot, either medial or lateral to the center line of the shank whips can be caused by rotational forces at the hip, knee or foot level the prosthetic foot returns to mid position at mid swing medial whips are more common than lateral whips	prolonged midstance on sound leg trunk rotation decreased as spinal motion follows hip rotation decreased arm swing arm on sound side slightly abducted to aid balance walking at an angle to the line of progression favouring either hip internal or external rotation head forward flexion knee flexion always present otherwise whip would not occur

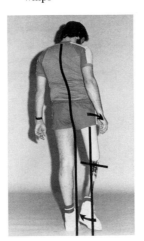

Figure 3–65   Medial whip.

Intrinsic Components		Extrinsic Components	
Medical Considerations and Static Locomotor Problems	**Dynamic Locomotor Problems**	**Prosthetic Reasons**	**Environmental Factors**
excessive amount of soft tissue on stump contracture combinations at hip which may involve internal or external rotation ranges weak hip rotators	faulty habit by using excessive active hip internal or external rotation incorrect fastening of suspension belt pulling the socket into internal rotation excessive hip flexion on toe off combined with rotation contractures causing lack of control of the prosthesis	incorrect alignment of prosthetic knee axis (normal alignment 5-10° external rotation in relation to hip axis) internal rotation of the knee axis causes a lateral whip external rotation of knee axis causes medial whip knee axis not set horizontally to the ground toe break not set at right angle to the line of progression	rough ground

TABLE 3–2 continued

Dominant Gait Deviation and its Characteristics	Compensatory Postural Adaptations Associated with the Dominant Gait Fault

Uneven Heel Rise
caused by excessive
    prosthetic knee flexion
    following toe off
 	
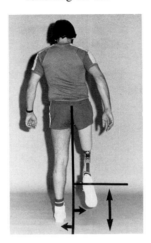
Figure 3–66   Uneven heel rise.
	excessive heel rise lengthens
	    prosthetic swing phase and
	    therefore midstance on the
	    sound leg is prolonged
	swing phase is prolonged
	    because heel rises higher
	    than normal and then has to
	    return to follow the normal
	    swing phase pattern
	both arms are slightly
	    abducted during the
	    midstance phase on the
	    sound side to assist balance
	moderate trunk bending
	    toward the sound side
	excessive heel rise is
	    occasionally accompanied
	    by a medial or lateral whip
	head forward flexion
	at prosthetic toe off, weak hip
	    extensors are unable to
	    perform total hip extension
	    therefore stump flexion is
	    initiated too forcefully and
	    too soon in the gait cycle

Intrinsic Components		Extrinsic Components	
Medical Considerations and Static Locomotor Problems	**Dynamic Locomotor Problems**	**Prosthetic Reasons**	**Environmental Factors**
decreased hip extension range weak hip extensors	using excessive force for prosthetic knee flexion patient feels the weight of the prosthesis dropping away from ischial weight bearing too early during the gait cycle poor control of the prosthesis	insufficient prosthetic knee joint friction extension aid too loose knee axis higher than sound side	stepping over obstacles wearing heavier shoes than worn at the time of prosthetic fitting

TABLE 3–2 continued

Dominant Gait Deviation and its Characteristics	Compensatory Postural Adaptations Associated with the Dominant Gait Fault
Terminal Swing Impact caused by excessive socket acceleration during prosthetic swing to achieve strong prosthetic knee extension prior to heel contact knee extension "impact" audible prior to heel strike	trunk is hyperextended to increase the intensity of the impact of forced prosthetic knee extension arms abducted to assist balancing on stance with the sound leg therefore arm swing is reduced on prosthetic knee extension heel is too far from the ground requiring prolonged midstance on the sound leg during prosthetic impact decreased trunk rotation prosthetic heel is forced to the ground to maintain knee extension following heel contact excessive hip extension is required to maintain prosthetic knee extension head forward flexion

Figure 3–67   Terminal swing impact.

Foot Slap following heel contact the forefoot forcefully hits the ground	unequal step rhythm slight trunk forward flexion on heel contact followed by exaggerated trunk extension on midstance prolonged stance on sound leg

Figure 3–68   Foot slap.

Intrinsic Components		Extrinsic Components	
Medical Considerations and Static Locomotor Problems	**Dynamic Locomotor Problems**	**Prosthetic Reasons**	**Environmental Factors**
short stump causing poor lever control weak hip flexors the weight of the prosthesis forces the patient to accelerate the prosthesis more forcefully than necessary	lack of confidence in the function of the prosthetic knee causes the amputee to use more power than necessary to force the knee into extension decreased proprioception causes the patient to use the auditory and sensory feedback to ensure prosthetic knee stability signals when the prosthetic knee is stable for weight bearing (auditory-vibration feedback for the visually impaired amputee)	insufficient knee friction too much tension on the extension aid	wearing of heavier shoe than worn at time of prosthetic fitting
	ensuring prosthetic knee extension by driving the prosthesis with excessive force onto heel contact decreased confidence in prosthetic knee mechanism	soft heel cushion worn posterior bumper loose ankle joint in single axis foot prosthetic foot placed too far anteriorly	

TABLE 3–2 continued

Dominant Gait Deviation and its Characteristics	Compensatory Postural Adaptations Associated with the Dominant Gait Fault
Unequal Step Rhythms Recorded in Foot Positions Relative to the Line of Progression These are: b Unequal Ground Gain (often referred to as uneven step length) c Uneven Timing d Walking at an Angle to the Line of Progression (crab gait) these deviations are closely related and pertain to foot positions, time and distance thus producing a halting non-rhythmical gait pattern both steps are of equal length but their pattern is offset causing unequal timing as well as poor step positions during gait predominantly, the prosthesis is leading, the sound leg, providing the stabilizing support, follows	short prosthetic step hesitant gait reduction of spinal rotation pausing on sound leg during stance unequal arm swing hip hiking eliminating initiation of prosthetic knee flexion patient does not utilize prosthetic knee flexion to initiate swing momentum of pendular motion advances prosthesis, resulting in a long step because of elimination of knee flexion not extending hip from midstance on avoiding toe-off long prosthetic step due to excessive hip flexion lack of stability on prosthetic stance causes the amputee to quickly accelerate the sound leg to provide additional support

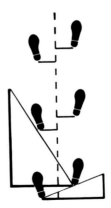

Figure 3–69(b)   Unequal step rhythms recorded in foot positions relative to the line of progression: unequal ground gain.

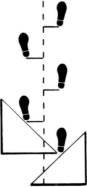

Figure 3–69(a)   Unequal step rhythms recorded in foot positions relative to the line of progression: equal step pattern.

Intrinsic Components		Extrinsic Components	
Medical Considerations and Static Locomotor Problems	**Dynamic Locomotor Problems**	**Prosthetic Reasons**	**Environmental Factors**
generalized stump pain marked lumbar lordosis decrease in hip extension range weak hip extensors weak hip abductors	short prosthetic stance caused by lack of confidence in prosthetic knee poor proprioception in judging prosthetic foot placement feeling of insecurity amputee tries to hoist the weight of the prosthesis rather than activate it	insufficient knee friction insufficient initial socket flexion socket aligned too far forward	using a walker encourages uneven step patterns as it presents a barrier to forward progression

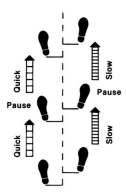

Figure 3–69(c) Unequal step rhythms recorded in foot positions relative to the line of progression: uneven timing.

Figure 3–69(d) Unequal step rhythms recorded in foot positions relative to the line of progression: walking at an angle to the line of progression (crab gait).

TABLE 3–2 continued

Dominant Gait Deviation and its Characteristics	Compensatory Postural Adaptations Associated with the Dominant Gait Fault
Unequal Arm Swing reciprocal arm swing is eliminated the arm on the prosthetic side is held closer to the prosthesis and the ipsilateral arm provides the movement	trunk rotation reduced hand contact on socket accompanies both hip flexion and extension arm on sound side held in slight abduction arm swing on sound side shows moderate range prolonged double support unequal step rhythms

Figure 3–70   Unequal arm swing.

Intrinsic Components		Extrinsic Components	
Medical Considerations and Static Locomotor Problems	**Dynamic Locomotor Problems**	**Prosthetic Reasons**	**Environmental Factors**
stump pain short stump weak hip extensors	hesitant gait pattern limiting stump motion short steps amputee unaccustomed to weight of prosthesis amputee hesitant to initiate prosthetic knee flexion poor balance	inadequate socket suspension pistoning loose socket	progression of walking aids (e.g. from crutches to canes) increasing prosthetic weight bearing

TABLE 3–2 continued

Dominant Gait Deviation and its Characteristics	Compensatory Postural Adaptations Associated with the Dominant Gait Fault
Trunk Forward Flexion trunk leans forward bringing the center of gravity in front of the hip and knee joints trunk remains in forward flexion position during swing and stance phase of both legs	reduced step length hip extension missing for pelvic thrust moderate hip hiking on prosthetic swing pausing on sound leg prosthetic knee flexion reduced or absent restricted trunk rotation uneven timing occasional shoulder elevation on sound side with use of cane hesitant gait pattern reciprocal arm swing missing head forward flexion

Figure 3–71   Trunk forward flexion.

Intrinsic Components		Extrinsic Components	
Medical Considerations and Static Locomotor Problems	**Dynamic Locomotor Problems**	**Prosthetic Reasons**	**Environmental Factors**
hip flexion contracture	poor balance	knee instability	walking aid too
weak hip flexors	motion utilized to	too much flexion	short
lack of proprioception	assist prosthetic	built into socket	walking aid
painful stump	knee stabilization	socket too wide	held too far
weak hip extensors	during stance	poor suspension	away from
painful ischial seating	inability to initiate	tight suspension	body
arthritic spinal changes	prosthetic knee	belt	walking on
	flexion	tight socket	uneven
	head forward flexion	diameter causing	ground
	used to assist	anterior distal	habit from
	proprioception for	stump pain	walking with
	prosthetic foot	insufficient socket	walking
	placement	flexion	frame
	hesitant gait due to		
	insecurity		
	amputee		
	unaccustomed to		
	the weight of the		
	prosthesis, stops		
	prosthetic step		
	prior to stance		
	completion		

TABLE 3–2 continued

Dominant Gait Deviation and its Characteristics	Compensatory Postural Adaptations Associated with the Dominant Gait Fault
Lumbar Lordosis with Excessive Hip Flexion - With Walking Aid trunk flexion is dominant at prosthetic heel contact lumbar lordosing occurs at prosthetic midstance with cane support to assist trunk into upright position when using a walker less trunk movement is noticeable	inability to accomplish pelvic forward thrust difficulty extending prosthetic knee no spinal rotation prolonged double support the cane is carried too far forward to accommodate trunk weight arm swing on prosthetic side missing hesitant gait uneven timing unequal step rhythm prosthetic leg appears too short

Figure 3–72   Lumbar lordosis with excessive hip flexion: with walking aid.

Intrinsic Components		Extrinsic Components	
Medical Considerations and Static Locomotor Problems	**Dynamic Locomotor Problems**	**Prosthetic Reasons**	**Environmental Factors**
tight iliopsoas muscle	poor balance	prosthesis too heavy	incorrect use of gait aids
hip flexion contracture	use of cane provides a wider standing base	reduced knee friction	
weak hip extensors			
short stump	short steps	posterior socket wall contact incomplete	
weak abdominals	uneven step timing		
distal stump sensitivity	decreased spinal rotation	insufficient socket pre-flexion	
protruding abdomen	head forward flexion		
weak hip flexors			
pain at ischial seat level on weight bearing			

TABLE 3–2 continued

Dominant Gait Deviation and its Characteristics	Compensatory Postural Adaptations Associated with the Dominant Gait Fault
Lumbar Lordosis with Excessive Hip Flexion - Without Walking Aid an excessive lumbar lordosis maintains the trunk upright counteracting a marked hip flexion position (see-saw trunk motion) trunk forward flexion occurs from prosthetic heel contact to mid stance lumbar lordosis occurs from midstance to toe-off/heel-off	moderate lateral trunk bending towards prosthetic side at times a wider walking base is evident forceful heel contact lumbar lordosis replaces pelvic forward thrust increased alternating arm swing arms held in slight abduction to initiate momentum for prosthetic acceleration increased spinal rotation

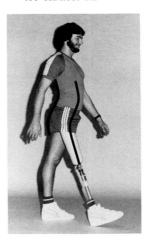

Figure 3–73   Lumbar lordosis with excessive hip flexion: without walking aid.

Intrinsic Components		Extrinsic Components	
Medical Considerations and Static Locomotor Problems	**Dynamic Locomotor Problems**	**Prosthetic Reasons**	**Environmental Factors**
tight iliopsoas muscle hip flexion contracture weak hip extensors short stump weak abdominals sensitive stump end obese abdomen weak hip flexors	potential to become a permanent habit use of trunk to mobilize prosthesis rather than active stump motions patient is unaccustomed to the weight of the prosthesis	loss of lateral wall contact inadequate suspension reduced knee friction posterior socket wall contact incomplete insufficient socket pre-flexion	more evident with increased walking speed

TABLE 3–2 continued

Dominant Gait Deviation and its Characteristics	Compensatory Postural Adaptations Associated with the Dominant Gait Fault
Prosthetic Knee Instability caused by delayed stump extension motion on heel contact	VARIATION a during stance on the sound side the trunk leans backward to give momentum to the end of prosthetic swing
VARIATION a trunk leans back to help in accelerating prosthetic swing. This forced motion is followed by a pause at the end of the prosthetic swing phase	center of gravity is behind the hip joint at midstance on sound leg increased prosthetic swing
the pause causes the prosthetic knee to flex (gravitational forces)	VARIATION b prolonged double support both arms held in abduction to aid balance for prolonged stance on swing leg uneven arm swing
gait phase progresses to foot flat (heel contact missing)	
the center of gravity remains behind the knee joint causing knee instability	
VARIATION b similar technique however less forceful hip flexion is utilized and heel contact is present	
center of gravity still remains behind the prosthetic knee	
in both variations the amputee is unable to counteract the knee flexion moment occurring at the prosthetic knee. This results in a rapid, alternating movement at the knee until the center of gravity falls in front of the knee joint and full weight bearing occurs on the prosthesis	
stabilization occurs at midstance	

Figure 3–74(a)   Prosthetic knee instability: pausing at midsv

Intrinsic Components		Extrinsic Components	
Medical Considerations and Static Locomotor Problems	**Dynamic Locomotor Problems**	**Prosthetic Reasons**	**Environmental Factors**
decreased proprioception weak hip extensors hip flexion contracture short stump painful distal stump decreased stump skin sensation	heel contact unsafe for weight bearing affecting balance as amputee has to learn stump lever control emphasizing hip extension	plantar flexion resistance too great causing knee to buckle at heel strike excessive dorsiflexion in prosthetic foot causing quick accelerating motion of the prosthesis onto foot flat (uncontrolled) excessive socket preflexion socket set too far posteriorly knee axis set too far anteriorly prosthetic knee center located anterior to TKA line	walking down an incline using a walker encourages elimination of pelvic forward thrust because the arms transfer body weight to the walker thus the center of gravity falls too far forward uneven ground

Figure 3–74(b)   Prosthetic knee instability: heel contact with a delay in stump hip extension.

TABLE 3–2 continued

Dominant Gait Deviation and its Characteristics	Compensatory Postural Adaptations Associated with the Dominant Gait Fault
Vaulting rising on toes on the sound side so that the extended prosthesis can swing through with momentum and shoulder elevation to provide prosthetic ground clearance prosthetic knee flexion is eliminated	reduced hip flexion on prosthetic side lack of active initiation of prosthetic knee flexion due to missing ground contact unequal arm swing shoulder elevation on prosthetic side arms slightly abducted to aid balance during prolonged stance on sound side prosthesis sometimes held in internal rotation no pelvic forward thrust sometimes combined with hiking on the prosthetic side quadratus lumborum is used to hoist the trunk initiating incorrect gait motion reduced spinal rotation

Figure 3–75   Vaulting.

Intrinsic Components		Extrinsic Components	
Medical Considerations and Static Locomotor Problems	Dynamic Locomotor Problems	Prosthetic Reasons	Environmental Factors
short stump	fear of stubbing toe	prosthesis too long	clearing obstacles
painful hip	fear of uncontrolled knee buckling	foot in excessive plantar flexion	increasing walking speed (in young amputees)
painful stump	extra height at midstance permits toe clearance	inadequate suspension resulting in excessive pistoning	
weak hip flexors	lack of confidence in prosthesis	excessive knee friction	
	habit practiced by younger amputees to avoid activating prosthetic components	too much knee stability built into prosthetic alignment	
		extension aid too tight	

TABLE 3–2 continued

Dominant Gait Deviation and its Characteristics	Compensatory Postural Adaptations Associated with the Dominant Gait Fault
Hip Hiking	elimination of prosthetic knee flexion
quadratus lumborum muscle action to shorten prosthesis during swing	reduced spinal rotation
	ipsilateral rotation of the trunk and prosthesis toward the prosthetic side
elimination of prosthetic knee flexion	marked hip flexion
amputee hikes the hip to eliminate weight bearing which is necessary to initiate knee flexion	reduction of alternating arm swing
	uneven timing
hip held in active flexion before heel contact	pelvic forward thrust missing
prosthesis can be accelerated by pendular motion	hip flexion increased by trunk forward flexion

Figure 3–76   Hip hiking.

Intrinsic Components		Extrinsic Components	
Medical Considerations and Static Locomotor Problems	**Dynamic Locomotor Problems**	**Prosthetic Reasons**	**Environmental Factors**
painful stump hip flexion contracture weak hip flexors short stump	decreased proprioception inability to produce pelvic forward thrust patient has not adapted to weight of the prosthesis habit amputee hoists the weight of the prosthesis rather than activate it	prosthesis too long excessive friction in prosthetic knee excessive knee stability built into alignment inadequate suspension prosthesis too heavy	trying to go up stairs with prosthesis leading

TABLE 3–2 continued

Dominant Gait Deviation and its Characteristics	Compensatory Postural Adaptations Associated with the Dominant Gait Fault
Inability to Initiate Prosthetic Knee Flexion prosthesis held in knee extension with center of gravity in front of the knee and weight bearing on the ischial seat prosthetic knee remains in extension during heel– off to toe–off the amputee pauses at toe- off arms are held backwards as the amputee attempts to initiate prosthetic knee flexion the amputee purposely hip hikes to allow for the pendular forward action of the extended prosthesis	hesitant gait pattern with a delay at prosthetic toe-off reduced trunk rotation prosthetic abduction or circumduction vaulting on sound leg used during prosthetic swing to clear the ground either hip hiking or shoulder elevation utilized to initiate prosthetic swing hand on prosthetic side holds onto the prosthesis

Figure 3–77   Inability to initiate prosthetic knee flexion.

Intrinsic Components		Extrinsic Components	
Medical Considerations and Static Locomotor Problems	**Dynamic Locomotor Problems**	**Prosthetic Reasons**	**Environmental Factors**
weak hip flexors anterior distal stump pain restricted hip range of motion (O.A.) decreased skin sensation excessive stump soft tissue short stump	inability to use pelvic and hip motions to produce pelvic forward thrust decreased proprioception	too much knee stability prosthetic knee axis lower than anatomical knee axis stiff prosthetic foot prosthesis too short socket too large toe break too far anterior prosthetic foot too large	walking uphill using a walker center of gravity too far forward to initiate controlled prosthetic swing

TABLE 3–2 continued

Dominant Gait Deviation and its Characteristics	Compensatory Postural Adaptations Associated with the Dominant Gait Fault
Drop Off at End of Stance Phase dropping of the pelvis on the prosthetic side just following midstance to toe–off results in dropping of the trunk on the prosthetic side the center of gravity drops on the prosthetic side strong contraction of hip abductors on the sound side prevents the amputee from losing balance and falling sideways	decreased arm swing decreased trunk rotation hip internal rotation on prosthetic side uncontrolled prosthetic knee flexion acceleration of gait phase from midstance to toe–off unequal timing unequal step pattern

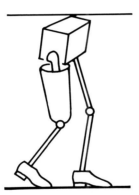

Figure 3–78   Drop-off at end of stance phase.

Intrinsic Components		Extrinsic Components	
Medical Considerations and Static Locomotor Problems	**Dynamic Locomotor Problems**	**Prosthetic Reasons**	**Environmental Factors**
weak hip flexors weak abdominals weak quadratus lumborum weak abductors on sound side	a hesitant gait reduces the amount of acceleration force in pelvic forward thrust which brings the center of gravity toward the supporting side loss of momentum and the biomechanical forces produced by dorsiflexion of the prosthetic foot cause the pelvic drop	excessive dorsiflexion of prosthetic foot keel of SACH foot too short toe break too far posterior (conventional foot) prosthetic alignment too stable socket too far anterior over the foot resulting in a push forward by the posterior socket wall thus causing the knee to collapse and the pelvis to follow prosthetic socket downwards socket diameter too large incorrect positioning of suspension belt prosthetic foot too small (rare) prosthetic knee in hyperextension	walking downhill

When the prosthesis is donned correctly, all features are reviewed in standing, sitting, and during walking. The gait pattern is observed, excessive piston action (see Stump Piston Action, p. 245) is investigated, and any gait deviations are noted. Then the prosthesis is doffed, and the stump is examined immediately for any skin discoloration, weight-bearing distribution markings, and excessive perspiration. The prosthesis itself is inspected for workmanship. A checklist specific to the prosthetic characteristics of each amputation level will help to ensure that all aspects are investigated and that all findings are recorded.

Following necessary adjustments, a recheck must be done to confirm that the prosthesis has been completed according to specifications.

A postdischarge clinic recall system will permit the team to monitor the amputee's performance and prosthetic-wearing tolerance, to examine the stump and the remaining leg, to check the condition of the prosthesis, and to provide advice and support where needed. Suggested time intervals are 1 month, 3 months, 6 months, and 1 year postdischarge. Following the first year, traumatic amputees can be seen annually; however, dysvascular amputees should be followed every 6 months.

Since a high percentage of amputees are elderly and have to cope with other medical problems in addition to walking with a prosthesis (see Amputation Incidence, Causes, Associated Diseases, and Conditions, p. 22), it is most important to follow through with a reassessment to maintain the level of independence achieved during rehabilitation. It must also be stressed to the amputee that the Amputation Clinic team is always available. A procedure should be in place whereby amputees can request appointments prior to their scheduled recall visit, should help be needed.

Recommended Reading

New York University. "Check-out of below-knee Prosthesis. Check-out of above-knee Prosthesis. Check-out of Hip Disarticulation and Hemipelvic Prosthesis." *Lower-limb Prosthetics*. New York: Prosthetics and Orthotics, New York University Post-graduate Medical School, 1977, 283–331.

BILATERAL AMPUTATIONS

Losing both legs is devastating. Adjustment to this disability, physically, socially, and emotionally, requires not only balance, strength, coordination, and determination but also the acceptance of major life-style changes.

Bilateral amputees need the same treatment considerations as unilateral amputees. However, all problems are intensified, and the rehabilitation period is prolonged. It is therefore particularly important to adhere to all basic rehabilitation principles. The ability to walk with two prostheses depends largely on the health status, the amputation levels, and whether the amputee was a prosthetic user prior to losing the second leg (Kostuik, 1981). The extent of functional problems varies greatly for different amputation levels as well as from one amputee to another. However, every effort should be made to rehabilitate bilateral amputees to their maximum *functional* capacity. The treatment aim for many high level bilateral amputees will be wheelchair independence.

Balance problems (see Balance Control, p. 17) and increased energy requirements (see Energy Expenditure, p. 18) make learning to walk with two prostheses difficult. It is harder for bilateral amputees to maintain balance because of:

- unequal stump length
- uneven body distribution (top heavy)
- severe loss of proprioception

These factors result in a slow reaction to any shift in body balance.

The higher the levels of amputation, the more difficult it becomes to maintain balance and the greater the amount of energy required for locomotion (English, 1981). Many amputees with severe cardiovascular disease are unable to generate this amount of energy, and, therefore, their ambulation potential is poor.

To prepare the bilateral amputee for independent bed mobility, safe transfer procedures, and gait training, physical therapy treatments must focus specifically on:

- contracture prevention
- upper extremity strength
- trunk flexion and extension
- stump functions
- sitting balance and transfers
- donning two prostheses

Contracture Prevention. Fixed flexion contractures present severe mobility problems for bilateral amputees (see Positioning, p. 70). They complicate prosthetic fitting, making it even harder for the amputee to balance, and result in poor posture control, thus hindering prosthetic locomotion in several ways (Holliday, 1981). Prevention of contractures is therefore one of the major immediate postoperative objectives (Murdoch, 1977).

Upper Extremities. The ability to bear weight efficiently through both arms is a prerequisite for maintaining *any* type of mobility for bilateral amputees. Arm strength is required to sit up, to move in bed, to transfer, to use crutches, and to propel a wheelchair. Specific exercises are indicated for elbow extension and wrist and hand function and must be maintained.

Trunk Flexion and Extension. Prolonged sitting keeps the abdominal muscles inactive and overstretches the hip extensor muscles, resulting in muscle weakness. This decreases the amputee's ability to control sitting and, subsequently, standing balance. The effort of trying to sit up becomes increasingly more difficult.

Strong abdominal muscles, together with strong back extensor muscles, control trunk movements and help to maintain an upright posture during sitting, standing, and walking. Abdominal exercises should include trunk flexion and rotation to maintain thoracic and lumbar mobility. Back extension exercises must be practiced in prone, alternately raising the trunk from shoulder level to stimulate the latissimus dorsi muscles, and raising both stumps to contract the gluteal muscle groups. The amputee should eventually be able to perform trunk flexion and extension against resistance, since these muscles are needed not only for gait activities, but also for wheelchair propulsion.

Stump Functions. (See Stump Motions: Their Relationship to Gait Functions and Resultant Treatment Considerations, p. 191). Stump mobility, stump muscle strength, and the ability to stabilize a joint at any point within its range (Vultee, 1981) are essential for accomplishing prosthetic gait. Assessment of stump muscle strength will indicate to the therapist which muscle groups require intensive training prior to prosthetic fitting.

Sitting Balance and Transfers. Bilateral amputees spend a great deal of time sitting. By doing so they flex, abduct, and externally rotate both stumps. This broadens the sitting base (see Balance Control, p. 17), which helps to support sitting balance. However, this position also encourages contracture development. Active and resisted adduction, internal rotation, and hip extension exercises must therefore be a part of the bilateral amputee's exercise program to counteract the inactivity of these muscle groups during prolonged sitting.

Practicing transfers is equally important to encourage the amputee's independence. The transfer technique taught must be adapted to the individual's needs; e.g., a bilateral amputee with one ankle disarticulation (prosthesis donned in bed) and one transfemoral amputation (prosthesis donned when sitting) can practice a standing transfer (see Transfer, p. 79), whereas a bilateral amputee who has two short transfemoral stumps may need a trapeze and a transfer board or sufficient arm strength to get from bed to chair (see Bilateral Transfemoral Amputations, p. 331). Transfer techniques are practiced regardless of whether the amputee will be a prosthetic user or not.

Donning Two Prostheses. Learning to don both prostheses is a difficult task. It can be accomplished in several ways.

Bilateral transtibial amputees manage best when sitting in a chair because floor contact, following stump entry, helps in positioning the socket correctly (see Donning of the Transtibial Prosthesis, p. 247).

Bilateral transfemoral amputees are best advised to start practicing donning their prostheses while still in bed. This prevents unexpected knee buckling and gives the amputee ample time to secure the suspension system. When suspension belt fastening can be controlled, the amputee can advance to donning both prostheses while sitting in a chair between parallel bars. Initially, help is provided, but eventually each amputee must learn to master the donning procedure independently to ensure continuation of gait. Often bilateral amputees lose the skill of walking after discharge because the procedure of donning both prostheses correctly is too cumbersome and team supervision is not available to reinforce the procedure. Tedious training is indicated to perfect the amputee's proficiency in donning both prostheses.

Gait training considerations for bilateral amputees depend on the stump level combination. Bilateral transtibial amputees have a better chance of learning to walk safely than amputees with higher amputation levels since the knee joints provide voluntary controlled stability during weight bearing. Gait training commences when the recent stump has healed, with the longer and/or stronger stump becoming the dominant leg. The recent stump must be healed so that equal weight-bearing distribution over both prostheses can be achieved during balancing exercises (see Basic Balancing Exercises, p. 254). The practice of standing and ambulating in parallel bars prior to healing of the recent stump with only the primary prosthesis is unsound. If this is done, the amputee must center the prosthesis directly under the trunk and maintain balance in a biomechanically incorrect position. The prosthetic socket is not aligned for balancing in this fashion, and the stump experiences indescribable weight-bearing stresses from incorrectly applied forces (Mensch et al., 1982).

Gait Training for Bilateral Amputees

Most bilateral amputees are fitted with their prostheses slightly shorter than the natural leg length. This lowers the center of gravity and aids in stance stability. Balance is further controlled by adopting a wider walking base. Gait velocity and step length decreases with higher amputation levels in unilateral amputees (Sulzle et al., 1978). This is even more markedly observed in bilateral amputees.

With both knee joints preserved, the prognosis for learning to walk is good. Gait is accomplished with a slightly wider walking base. Standing initially with two prostheses at first gives the amputee a feeling of being on stilts, which requires conscious balance control. Just as for unilateral amputees, balance exercises must be practiced before steps are taken. If bilateral amputations occur simultaneously, treatment progression is usually slower than when the amputee first loses one leg and, at a later time, the other. The gait, although slower, is stable and functional. The use of a cane is recommended to aid stability when walking is recommended. Bilateral transtibial amputees are expected to be ADL independent (hygiene, dressing, transfers, donning the prostheses, using stairs, getting in and out of a car).

Bilateral Transtibial Amputations

Rising from a Chair.

1. Secure wheelchair brakes.
2. Sit forward on the seat.
3. Bend knees to 90° and place prosthetic feet parallel and flat on the ground (if the knees are bent more than 90°, the prosthetic heels will rise).
4. Lean trunk over prostheses. This is necessary to bring the center of gravity forward.
5. Push on both arm rests while straightening both knees.

6. Come to the standing position.
7. Balance before walking.

Stair Walking.   A handrail and/or gait aids are used for safety.

1. The amputee stands close to the step.
2. The dominant leg steps up first.
3. The trunk leans forward to place the dominant leg in a position to bring the body up while the subdominant leg provides some force (push) to accomplish the step.
4. The subdominant leg is positioned on the same step, and the pattern is repeated.

For going downstairs, the procedure is reversed. The subdominant leg steps down first while the dominant leg, controlling knee flexion, holds the body weight until the downward step is completed. Young, healthy amputees are able to use the alternate step pattern on stairs.

Transtibial/
Transfemoral
Amputations

This stump level combination introduces even more inequality in stump length and with it unequal body weight distribution (laterally unbalanced) and unequal proprioceptive sensation. Learning to walk becomes more difficult. The amputee has to rely primarily on the transtibial amputation side. Young, healthy amputees can cope; however, older amputees who have cardiovascular problems may not continue to walk regularly. Balance training must be intense. The width of the walking base increases. The gait is stable under controlled conditions. Canes should always be used. Most amputees with only one knee joint will use a wheelchair in addition to walking with their prostheses (Hunter et al., 1978). ADL independence will be achieved by most, while difficult tasks such as stair walking are accomplished by only a few of these amputees.

Rising from a Chair.

1. Secure wheelchair brakes.
2. Sit diagonally forward on the chair seat with the transtibial side turned toward the chair.
3. Position a walker in front of both legs.
4. Bend natural knee to 90°, with the prosthetic foot placed flat on the ground.
5. Position transfemoral prosthesis forward, with the prosthetic knee in extension.
6. Lean trunk over transtibial stump to bring center of gravity forward.
7. Push both arms on the wheelchair arm rests while straightening the natural knee.
8. Pull the transfemoral prosthesis under the trunk into a stable stance position by locking the prosthetic knee when rising.
9. Place both hands on the walker.

10. Balance on both prostheses before stepping ahead with the dominant leg.

Stair Walking.

1. The amputee stands close to the step.
2. The prosthetic knee is consciously locked.
3. The amputee reaches ahead with one hand and holds onto the rail while the other hand has crutch or cane support.
4. The transtibial prosthesis steps up.
5. The trunk leans well over the forward leg, and stepping up is accomplished by knee extension and arm support (pushing on the crutch or cane and pulling on the rail).
6. The transfemoral prosthesis follows and is placed on the same step. The sequence is repeated.

Going downstairs, the transfemoral prosthesis steps down, first with the prosthetic knee consciously locked before full weight is transferred, while the remaining knee joint has to control the descent.

For physically fit amputees, gait is possible. However, for most, the physical limitations posed by these amputation levels are enormous. Most bilateral transfemoral amputees will rely on a wheelchair as well as on their prostheses to get about. Geriatric amputees with two short stumps will not walk. Wheelchair mobility is then the treatment aim.

If any potential for ambulation is identified, gait training may begin with stubby prostheses (Mital et al., 1971; Wainapel et al., 1985). Stubby prostheses are sockets with rocker bottoms used for standing and modified walking. Without knee joints and the center of gravity considerably lowered, stubby prostheses provide stability and reduce the hazard of falling. Mobility, however, is restricted to level walking. Sitting on an average height chair presents problems since the amputee has to rely on arm strength to reach the sitting level. The cosmesis is not good, but occasionally bilateral transfemoral amputees elect to remain with stubby prostheses since the energy cost to use them is less than walking with conventional transfemoral prostheses.

If prosthetic fitting is considered, the prescription should include one free-swinging knee and one safety knee (the latter on the shorter stump side). Two safety knees may complicate a fall since the prosthetic knees would remain stable at a time when joint flexion is needed (see Falling, p. 276). One must consider the alignment of the knee axes. If the axes are set too far posterior to the weight-bearing lines, activation of the prosthetic knees becomes more difficult. The selection of the firmness of the heel cushion in the prosthetic feet also has an effect on knee function.

The gait pattern demonstrates a wide stance base that aids in balance. During locomotion, marked lateral trunk flexion occurs to place the center of gravity over the stance leg. Trunk flexion and lumbar lordosis are evident, both when using gait

Bilateral Transfemoral Amputations

(See Fig. 3–79)

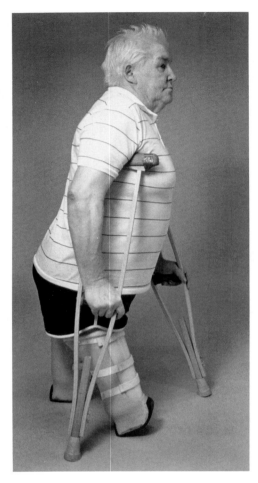

Figure 3–79 Walking with stubby prostheses.

aids and also when walking free. Steps are slow and deliberate, with forced knee flexion and extension.

Transfer from Bed to Chair, Prostheses Donned. Transfer from bed to chair with prostheses donned must occur in two phases because of the inability of the bilateral transfemoral amputee to rotate sufficiently to transfer directly to the chair.

Phase One. The amputee sits at the edge of the bed with both feet flat on the ground. The hospital bed is positioned higher than the wheelchair seat. Prosthetic knee extension necessary for the transfer is biomechanically easier to accomplish from the higher level because joint angulation at hips and prosthetic knees is less compared with sitting at a standard chair height (Burdett et al., 1985). A walker in front allows the amputee to lean forward and exert pressure on the frame while extending first one and then the other prosthesis to achieve the standing position. Small steps, not pivoting (see Turning Around, p. 273), will bring the amputee in front of the wheelchair seat.

Phase Two.   With one leg forward and the other in contact with the chair, the amputee leans over the walker while reaching for the arm rests. The knee in contact with the chair flexes (by hip flexion) while the arms control the sitting speed. The knee unit of the forward-positioned prosthesis will flex when sitting.

Transfer from Bed to Chair Using a Trapeze.   (See Transfers with an Overhead Assistive Device, p. 82).

1. The seat of the wheelchair is placed directly against the side of the bed at a level so that the amputee can use the trapeze or T bar to transfer.
2. The brakes are secured.
3. The amputee uses the ''push–pull'' method to maneuver with the back against the chair seat (see Figure 2–15).
4. Arm push-ups and a transfer board placed to bridge the bed and chair help the amputee to get onto the chair seat.

Rising from a Chair.

1. The wheelchair is placed to face the parallel bars, with brakes secured.
2. The amputee sits forward on the seat, placing both prosthetic feet flat on the ground.
3. The amputee then leans forward with one hand holding onto the bar while the other hand is placed in the push position on the wheelchair arm rest.
4. While using the push–pull method to elevate the trunk, both artificial knees are locked as quickly as possible.
5. Stance must be secure before walking.

Stair Walking.   It is easier for the bilateral transfemoral amputee to use forearm crutches during stair walking since trunk mobility is not restricted.   *(See Fig. 3–80)*

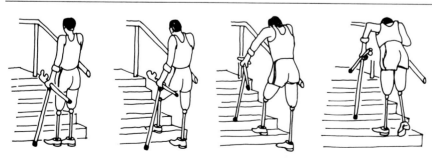

Figure 3–80   Bilateral transfemoral amputee ascending stairs.

1. The amputee stands in front of the stairs.
2. While one hand reaches up the rail, the other uses crutch support (with the second crutch carried along).
3. The amputee flexes one hip until the prosthetic foot reaches the step above.
4. The support crutch is then placed one step further up.
5. The trunk leans forward.
6. By pulling on the rail and pushing on the crutch, the trunk is elevated and stump hip extension must lock the prosthetic knee.
7. The second prosthesis follows, and step one is completed. The sequence is repeated.

When stepping down, both feet must overlap the step. The crutch advances, and the other hand reaches ahead on the rail. Full weight is exerted through both arms. One prosthesis remains in extension, and the other uses hip hiking and a pendulum motion to step down. This allows the other leg to flex and follow. Arm strength must be maintained until the second prosthesis is stable.

Summary

The energy cost of walking is high. Under the guidance of an occupational therapist, the amputee must learn to conserve energy by planning activities ahead. The occupational therapist will also carefully consider the amputee's wheelchair needs. The main concern for wheelchair safety is stability. This requires using a wheelchair that has the axis of the rear wheel set further back than in a standard wheelchair to counterbalance the weight loss of both legs.

As in unilateral amputations, short stumps (transtibial and transfemoral) have less lever control, less muscle power, and less weight-bearing surface compared with the long stump. Therefore, short stumps have to work harder. This limits endurance. These and other limitations will influence the bilateral amputee's life-style.

Coping requires adaptation, knowing how much can be done, learning to practice energy-saving measures, and remaining physically active.

References

Burdett, G., Habasevich, R., Pisciotta, J., and Simon, R. "Biomechanical Comparison of Rising from Two Types of Chairs." *Physical Therapy, 65*, no. 8 (1985): 1177–1183.

English, E. "The Energy Cost of Walking for the Lower Extremity Amputee. In J.P. Kostuik and R. Gillespie, eds. *Amputation Surgery and Rehabilitation: The Toronto Experience*, New York: Churchill Livingstone, 1981, 311–314.

Holliday, J.P. "Prevention of Contractures. In J.P. Kostuik and R. Gillespie, eds. *Amputation Surgery and Rehabilitation: The Toronto Experience*, New York: Churchill Livingstone, 1981, 224–226.

Hunter, G.A., and Holliday, P. "Review of Function in Bilateral Lower Limb Amputees." *The Canadian Journal of Surgery, 21*, no. 2 (1978): 176–178.

Kostuik, J.P. "Indications, Levels and Limiting Factors in Amputation Surgery of the Lower Extremity. In J.P. Kostuik and R. Gillespie, eds. *Amputation Surgery and Rehabilitation: The Toronto Experience*. New York: Churchill Livingstone, 1981, 17–25.

Mensch, G., and Ellis, P. "Bilateral Amputees." In S.N. Banerjee, ed. *Rehabilitation Management of Amputees*, Baltimore, Md.: Williams & Wilkins, 1982, 231–233.

Mital, M.A., and Pierce, D.S. "Stubbies." *Amputees and Their Prostheses*, Boston, Ma.: Little, Brown, 1971, 117–119.

Murdoch, G. "Amputation Surgery in the Lower Extremity." *Prosthetics and Orthotics International, 1* (1977): 183–192.

Sulzle, G., Pagliarulo, M., Rodgers, M., and Jordan, C. "Energetics of Amputee Gait." *Orthopedic Clinics of North America, 9*, no. 2 (1978): 358–362.

Vultee, F.E. "Detailed Physical Treatment." *Atlas of Limb Prosthetics*. St. Louis, Mo.: C.V. Mosby, 1981, vol. II, 323.

Wainapel, S.F., March, H., and Steve, L. "Stubby Prostheses: An Alternative to Conventional Prosthetic Devices." *Archives of Physical Medicine and Rehabilitation*, 66 (1985): 264–266.

4

Other Points of Interest

Computer Aided Design (CAD), Computer Aided Manufacturing (CAM), and shape-sensing techniques used in industry can now be applied to prosthetics. They will eventually permit major advances in socket fit technology. The rapid pace of these research projects may result in dramatic changes in the design and construction of prostheses in the near future. Although several centers are involved in CAD/CAM projects, only the work of three of these centers are mentioned here.

The Medical Engineering Resources Unit (MERU) of the University of British Columbia developed an interactive prototype Computer Aided Socket Design (CASD) system (Saunders, et al., 1985), which replaces the procedure of hand crafting the modified stump model needed for socket fabrication. The CASD system will eventually simplify socket construction by eliminating the guesswork of cast modifications and by controlling the quality of shape.

CAD

Manually obtained stump measurements are used to modify a computer stored ''primitive'' socket shape. The outlines of the modified socket shape are then visible on a graphic screen, and the prosthetist, using a manual override mode (Saunders et al., 1985), can further refine the socket design. All data are stored for future reference.

Presently the CASD system is programmed to design transtibial socket shapes only. The system is, however, capable of modifying any shape.

Foort demonstrated this technique at the 1983 ISPO (International Society for Prosthetics and Orthotics) World Congress in London, England. He took stump measurements of amputees attending the Congress, telephoned the measurements to Vancouver, and had the sockets delivered by air to London.

The Bioengineering Centre at the University College London (UCL), England is researching computer-controlled carving techniques of stump shapes

CAM

337

(Lawrence et al., 1985) and methods of socket production by using the Rapidform thermoplastic manufacturing process (Davies et al., 1985).

The UCL carver is a specially developed, computer-numerically controlled (CNC) milling machine. The unit produces a shape replication (model) from data provided by CASD or other sources, thus providing the CAD/CAM link between designing and manufacturing (Lawrence et al., 1985).

The UCL research team also adapted the vacuum-forming process to automated polypropylene socket production by developing the Rapidform microprocessor-controlled vacuum-forming machine. The UCL shape replication, or a model constructed by conventional methods, can be used with the Rapidform process.

Both transtibial and transfemoral sockets have been fitted satisfactorily in this manner.

The total CAD/CAM automated-fitting procedure requires approximately 75–90 min. Measuring takes 5–10 min; CASD, 5–10 min; carving, 20 min; Rapidforming, 20 min; and assembly, 15 min (Saunders et al., 1985). Experimental transtibial CAD/CAM fittings conducted jointly in Canada and Britain confirm that, once the method is perfected, it is possible to produce a prosthesis using a computer-based socket model (Foort et al., 1985).

Comment.   There is a potential for fitting amputees who live in remote areas. By sending measurements to a center where CAD/CAM facilities are available, these amputees could benefit, long distance, from a service that may not be available to them locally.

Shape Sensing

Shape sensing is a process that has existed in theory for many years but has only recently become a reality through the use of computer recordings, measurements, and equations.

Shape sensing applied to prosthetics, a research project under way at West Park Research, University of Toronto, utilizes laser beams to duplicate shapes and body segments (Fernie et al., 1984, 1985). The data of multidimensional stump shape measurements is stored directly in the computer. The technique is accurate and eliminates the manual measuring process.

The system, which can be linked to other CAD/CAM projects, will eventually have several advantages, such as standardized measuring techniques and faster socket fabrication, and will provide valid data to study stump shape changes that occur over the years.

The shape-sensing system is already used to evaluate the shape of stump plaster models, before and after modification, by using printouts of superimposed computer drawings of the same model (Fernie et al., 1984). This demonstrates the amount of variation that occurs during the modification process and is of particular help to student prosthetists.

Summary

The developments of these projects, laser beam shape sensing (Toronto), shape modifications (Vancouver), and carving production methods (London), have been accomplished through a collaborative effort between these research centers. With the expansion of computer technology into prosthetics, the education of prosthetists will now require a knowledge of physics, mathematics, mechanics, biomechanics, and characteristics of materials (Klasson, 1985).

As a point of interest, it is noted that prosthetists in Sweden are now classified as orthopedic engineers.

The Flexible Socket System

Another development of immediate benefit to transfemoral amputees is the fitting of the flexible socket system. This totally new concept in socket design challenges existing hard socket-fitting principles. The first design application of this approach to socket fitting was initiated by Iceland's Össur Kristinsson, a prosthetist. He, together with the Een-Holmgren Company of Sweden, perfected the original model (Kristinsson, 1983) and successfully fitted over 300 transfemoral amputees. Further development of the Scandinavian flexible socket (SFS) fitting technique is being carried out in the United States (Pritham et al., 1985). New York University named their project the Icelandic, Swedish, New York (ISNY) socket. Germany offers the IPOS (Integrated Prosthetic and Orthotic Systems) Flex-socket.

The concept of a flexible socket design differs biomechanically from the hard socket principles (see General Information about Sockets and Their Suspensions, p. 210). The traditional hard socket, a single structure, serves two functions: weight bearing and stump accommodation. The flexible socket, however, consists of two components. The first is the socket itself. It is quadrilateral in shape and vacuum formed from a thin-walled, transparent polyethylene and provides total contact. The second component is the carbon fiber support frame, which gives the prosthesis stability, transmits weight-bearing forces, and acts as a socket receptacle. Both components, when assembled, function as one.[1]

(See Fig. 4–1)

The main advantages of the flexible socket are its pliability, which provides stump comfort during all phases of gait and when sitting, and the ability of the socket to change shape during stump movements without altering socket volume.[2] Other advantages include increased sensation and proprioception (the stump can feel through the socket, e.g., sitting on a firm or soft surface), faster heat dissemination, and stump visibility owing to the thinner socket material.

The Flexible Socket

(See Fig. 4–2)

Medial-lateral stability during weight bearing appears to be controlled by placing the stump fluid mass under pressure, thus filling the socket completely while the socket walls hold tight, providing stability.[3]

The carbon fiber frame covers 25% of the stump area and leaves 75% of the stump area free. It has a cup-like base in which the socket must sit to prevent socket abduction, a medial strut (or upright) to accommodate weight-bearing stresses, and two proximal arms that grip the socket anteriorly and posteriorly.

The Support Frame

The socket–frame combination can be assembled with any available knee unit. The suspension system requires some modifications because of the dual nature of the design. Alignment principles remain unchanged.

Figure 4–1   ISNY suction socket assembled.

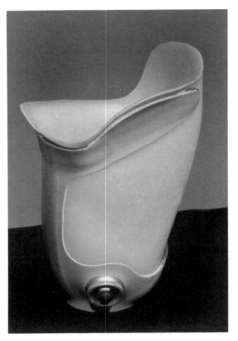

Figure 4–2   Demonstration of socket flexibility.

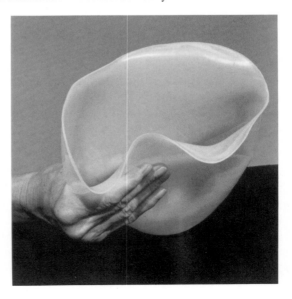

The initial success in fitting transfemoral amputees with flexible sockets has encouraged New York University to experiment in fitting transtibial amputees with a flexible socket system. The socket construction itself is problem free. At the time of writing, the support-frame design needed further refinement.

Clinical Comments. The acceptance of the flexible socket system by amputees is remarkable and can be attributed to the increased stump comfort. Therefore, it is anticipated that more of these fittings will soon be seen in clinics. Research is still indicated to answer several questions, such as how much load can this socket system take, and when does load interfere with function.

Physical therapy treatments are the same. Therapists, however, will observe that most amputees fitted with the flexible socket system are pleased with comfort and function and will demonstrate less pronounced gait deviations.

This new approach to transfemoral socket fitting, recently introduced by the University of California, Los Angeles (UCLA), deviates entirely in shape, contour and concept from existing transfemoral socket fitting principles (Sabolich, 1985). When compared to the conventional quadrilateral socket, CAT-CAM's major differences include a change in the socket's medial-lateral (M/L) and anterior-posterior (A/P) diameters, the accommodation of the ischial tuberosity *within* the socket and as a result, an altered socket brim. The socket shape (transverse view) is oval in the anterior-posterior direction. One can simply say that the stump tissues which used to be compressed front to back, are now compressed from side to side.

A markedly reduced M/L diameter brings the lateral wall surface closer to the femur and, thus, more precisely controls the position of the femoral adduction angle. The brim of the lateral wall contours firmly into the soft tissues above the greater trochanter. Biomechanically, this femoral adduction control enhances the work of the medial-lateral muscle forces during prosthetic stance.

The expanded A/P diameter of the CAT-CAM design provides extra space for extensor and flexor muscle action. In this way, these muscles, no longer compressed, can function more naturally. The extra A/P space also accommodates the ischial tuberosity and, partially the gluteus muscles within the socket. This containment of bone and muscle combined with the narrower M/L diameter and the resulting femoral adduction control is biomechanically significant as it causes a "locking" or fixation of the ischial tuberosity at prosthetic midstance. It is also said to contribute to the spreading of weight bearing over a large anatomical area. Furthermore, this containment seems to allow the amputee to achieve a better controlled prosthetic heel strike because the socket and the tuberosity remain in contact.

This "locking" of the ischial tuberosity in the CAT-CAM design does not occur in quadrilateral sockets. In a quadrilateral socket, the larger M/L diameter permits a wider femoral abduction range and thus can allow the ischial tuberosity, which is sitting outside the socket on a shelf, to shift when gluteus medius muscle activity causes the femur to abduct against the socket wall. This affects the efficiency of the hip abductor muscles, causing the amputee to compensate with either an abducted gait or lateral trunk bending over the prosthesis.

Sabolich (1985), who greatly contributed to the development of the CAT-CAM socket design, reports that even amputees with short transfemoral stumps find CAT-CAM sockets more comfortable, functional and less tiring than the quadrilateral socket design.

Sabolich (1985) recommends that all amputees, including previous quadrilateral socket users, undergo intensive physical therapy to specifically strengthen weakened abductor muscles, so that they can utilize CAT-CAM sockets effectively.

Summary

The preceding section highlights some of the recent developments in prosthetics to make clinicians aware of the focus of future trends.

References

Davies, R.M., Lawrence, R.B., Routledge, P.E., and Knox, W. "The Rapidform Process for Automated Thermoplastic Socket Production." *Prosthetics and Orthotics International,* 9 (1985): 27–30.

Fernie, G.R., Halsall, A.P., and Ruder, K. "Shape Sensing as an Educational Aid for Student Prosthetists." *Prosthetics and Orthotics International,* 8 (1984): 87–90.

Fernie, G.R., Griggs, G., Bartlett, S., and Lumau, K. "Shape Sensing for Computer Aided Below-knee Prosthetic Socket Design." *Prosthetics and Orthotics International,* 9 (1985): 12–16.

Foort, J., Spiers, R., and Bannon, M. "Experimental Fittings of Sockets for Below-knee Amputees Using Computer Aided Design and Manufacturing Techniques. *Prosthetics and Orthotics International,* 9 (1985): 46–47.

Klasson, B. "Computer Aided Design, Computer Aided Manufacture and Other Computer Aids in Prosthetics and Orthotics." *Prosthetics and Orthotics International,* 9 (1985): 3–11.

Lawrence, R.B., Knox, W., and Crawford, H.V. "Prosthetic Shape Replication Using a Computer Controlled Carving Technique." *Prosthetics and Orthotics International,* 9 (1985): 23–26.

Pritham, C.H., Fillauer, C., and Fillauer, K. "Experience with the Scandinavian Flexible Socket." *Orthotics and Prosthetics,* 39, no. 2 (1985): 17–32.

Sabolich, J. "Contoured Adducted Trochanteric-Controlled Alignment Method (CAT-CAM): Introduction and Basic Principles." *Clinical Prosthetics and Orthotics,* 9 (1985): (4) 15–26.

Saunders, C.G., Foort, J., Bannon, M., Lean, D., and Panych, L. "Computer Aided Design of Prosthetic Sockets for Below-knee Amputees." *Prosthetics and Orthotics Internatioinal,* 9 (1985): 17–22.

Notes

1. Fishman, S. Discussion at ISPO's Executive Board Meeting, Copenhagen, January 1984.
2. Ibid.
3. Berger, N. ISPO Seminar, Vancouver, April 1984.

Recommended Reading

Mensch, G. "ISPO Seminar Features New Flexible Socket for Amputees. *Physiotherapy Canada,* 36, no. 4 (1984): 208–209.

For healthy and physically fit amputees, rehabilitation will not be complete until they can enjoy, and even compete in, sports activities. Depending on the type of sport, they will participate with or without their prosthesis. Prosthetic adaptations may be required, and occasionally an additional prosthesis will be designed and fabricated to meet the specific functional needs of a particular sport (Kegel et al., 1980). Transtibial amputees can usually participate in most sports, whereas certain sports activities become somewhat more challenging for transfemoral amputees.

Sports activities that lower extremity amputees may select include swimming, bowling, curling, snow skiing, water skiing, golf, wind surfing, sailing, skating, ice hockey, bicycling, and, more recently, running.

Some sports-adapted prosthetic devices are highlighted here so that clinicians may visualize the relationship between the prosthesis and the requirements of the sport.

Prosthetic modifications for a hockey player with a transtibial amputation may include a thigh corset that will protect the stump from a checking impact and improve knee stability by minimizing rotational forces on the natural knee. Golfers (any amputation level) need a torque absorber in order to achieve a more natural club swing. Curling requires increased foot dorsiflexion when delivering curling stones. This position can be prosthetically provided for transtibial amputees by incorporating an Otto Bock safety knee (reversed) between the distal end of the shank and the prosthetic foot. The safety knee then allows the ankle to dorsiflex so that the natural knee can drop to the ice. The posteriorly placed tubing helps the prosthesis return to its upright position (Chadderton, 1983).

Most transtibial snow skiers use their prosthesis without adaptations, whereas transfemoral snow skiers elect to ski without their prosthesis. This is necessary because a prosthetic knee that flexes enough for skiing cannot hold the

SPORTS

(See Fig. 4–3)

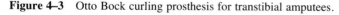

Figure 4–3   Otto Bock curling prosthesis for transtibial amputees.

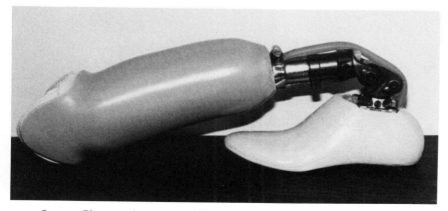

Source: Photograph courtesy of The War Amputations of Canada.

Figure 4–4   Skiing without a prosthesis using outriggers.

Source: Photograph courtesy of William Darby.

Figure 4–5   Karl Hilzinger during the filming of the ski movie "Downhill, Any Way You Can."

Source: Reprinted from *CHAMP Magazine,* Vol. 1, 1983, The War Amputations of Canada.

body weight. Aluminum elbow crutches are converted into outrigger ski poles (Davis, 1981) to provide balance in a lateral direction. *(See Fig. 4–4)*

Skiing for bilateral transfemoral amputees is possible, although unusual. Karl Hilzinger, a business man and physical education consultant for the Child Amputee Program (CHAMP) of the War Amputations of Canada (and also a former professional football player), designed his own stubby prostheses for skiing. He teaches downhill skiing to amputees in the winter (Chadderton, 1983) and enjoys playing golf in the summer. *(See Fig. 4–5)*

Water skiing is performed without the prosthesis, whereas wind surfing requires the use of a prosthesis (see Utility Prosthesis, p. 350) for balance, calculated weight transfers, and body position change while operating the sail board. *(See Fig. 4–6)*

(See Fig. 4–7)

One of our transfemoral amputees designed and constructed a sailor's peg leg for boating. The components include a socket, a tapered wooden hollow shank that is filled with 12 oz of his favorite liquid, and a large safety crutch tip. The prosthesis has no moving parts but has a little tap medially in the lower shank section. Hence, the proverbial "hollow leg."

Recently, several young amputees have become newsworthy because of their athletic endeavors in fields that have more traditionally been monopolized by "two-legged" individuals. Some of these amputees include Terry Fox, Jeff Keith, and Steven Fonyo. They are representative of a vital group of athletes who enjoy

Figure 4–6 Water skiing.

Source: Photograph courtesy of William Darby.

Figure 4–7   Windsurfing with utility prosthesis.

Source: Photograph courtesy of William Darby.

the challenge of participating actively in sports such as long distance running (see The Terry Fox Running Prosthesis, p. 346).

Most athletes are usually very knowledgeable about the training required to participate in their chosen sport. They also have a basic idea of what their prosthetic requirements might entail. The task for the Amputation Clinic team is to evaluate whether these concepts can be transposed into prosthetic components that are already available or that may be realistically designed and fabricated.

These developments have made Amputation Clinic teams more cognizant of specific needs that must be fulfilled for these amputees within the scope of rehabilitation. The results are the development and design of specific components for sports activities as well as recreational prostheses.

The Terry Fox Running Prosthesis

The styles of walking and running differ. During walking, both feet have simultaneous ground contact when the gait cycle alternates from stance to swing. However, during running there is an instant when both legs are simultaneously off the ground (Wells et al 1971, Hughes et al 1979, Brody, 1980; Inman et al., 1981).

During running:

- step length, joint angulation, and body velocity increase
- heel contact occurs with increased intensity and at a less acute angle
- active knee and foot control are necessary to achieve stable midstance over a flexed knee

Transfemoral amputees who have been fitted with a standard prosthesis cannot use the normal running pattern because they are unable to overcome the intensity of the ground reaction force following heel contact. They are also unable to keep the prosthetic knee stable in slight flexion during the stance phase. To compensate for these deficiencies, they must add an extra hop with the sound leg. This allows extra time for the prosthesis to swing through and reach heel contact at

Running with a Conventional Transfemoral Prosthesis

(See Fig. 4–8)

Figure 4–8   Transfemoral amputee running pattern.

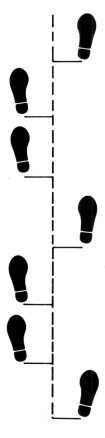

a more vertical angle. Thus, the amputee can draw the prosthesis into extension and maintain this position on midstance. On observation, this hop–skip running style is abrupt, energy consuming, and accomplished at the expense of a reduced running speed.

The Terry Fox Idea

To improve this unnatural running style, Terry Fox, a Canadian long distance runner, experimentally incorporated a telescoping mechanism into the shank section of his conventional transfemoral prosthesis. His untimely death left this project incomplete. However, his idea was adopted by the prosthetic team at the Chedoke–McMaster Hospitals, Hamilton, Ontario. They developed a prototype of the Terry Fox running prosthesis that has as its main feature, a heavy duty

Figure 4–9   Spring mechanism in the Terry Fox Running Prosthesis.

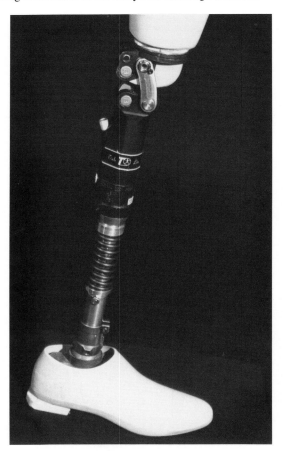

Source: From ''The Terry Fox Running Prosthesis'' by G. Mensch and P. Ellis, 1982, *Physiotherapy Canada, 36,* p. 346. Copyright 1982 by Canadian Physiotherapy Association. Reprinted by permission.

precompressed spring incorporated into the shank section. Other components   *(See Fig. 4–9)*
include a quadrilateral suction socket, a polycentric knee with swing and stance
phase control, and a multiaxis foot.

   The Spring Mechanism.   The amount of spring precompression has to be
individually set and depends on several factors; e.g., body weight and velocity. It
is adjusted so that the spring remains inactive during walking but will activate
when running.
   The spring has several functions. The ability of the spring to compress
provides stump comfort by cushioning the ground impact and also slightly shortens the prosthesis. This decreases the knee flexion movement and helps the
amputee achieve prosthetic knee extension without the effort of raising the center
of gravity of the body (see The Undulating Pathways, p. 5). The potential energy resulting from spring compression when weight bearing is converted into
kinetic energy as weight bearing is decreased during the latter phase of stance. In

Figure 4–10   Running with the Terry Fox Running Prosthesis.

   Source: From ''The Terry Fox Running Prosthesis'' by G. Mensch and P. Ellis,
1982, *Physiotherapy Canada, 36,* p. 346. Copyright 1982 by Canadian Physiotherapy
Association. Reprinted by permission.

(See Fig. 4–10)

theory, the released energy will intensify prosthetic toe-off, assisting the forward projection of the prosthesis into swing phase (Mensch et al., 1984).

With the spring mechanism, the amputee can hop on the prosthesis and stride jump, two functions (not possible on a conventional prosthesis) that are most useful in such sports as basketball or volleyball.

Summary

After further clinical testing, this prototype prosthesis may soon become more widely available to transfemoral amputees who wish to participate in sports that require running.

The SEATTLE Foot

Another exciting development for the athletic amputee is the SEATTLE foot, which (among 12 other winners) received the Presidential Award for Design Excellence. It is presently undergoing a nationwide field evaluation in the United States prior to its commercial release (Burgess, 1985).

The design consists of a cantilevered thermoplastic keel spring cosmetically covered with foam. During weight bearing, the keel section gradually stores energy that is released at the end of the stance phase. This bounce-off effect simulates forefoot muscle activity and should make walking, and also running, more effective and less tiring. One of the field testers was the American long distance runner Jeff Keith who used four SEATTLE feet during his 8-month run across the United States.

The Utility Prosthesis

Most amputees who enjoy swimming do so without a prosthesis. When attempting to swim for the first time after the amputation, many amputees experience a buoyancy imbalance. This feeling of trunk tipping is usually easily overcome when the amputee adjusts to moving in water.

(See Fig. 4–11)

A utility prosthesis is of waterproof endoskeletal construction. The socket is in direct stump contact, the double-walled shank section has drill holes so that water can enter the shank to add weight that will counteract the floating tendency of the prosthesis in water. The foot has a nonslip sole (Chadderton, 1983).

An amputee who has a utility prosthesis will usually use it to walk to the water, either on the beach or at the pool side, and then doff it. However, some transtibial amputees elect to swim with their utility prosthesis since it allows them to step up and down ladders, get on a diving board, and use fins.

Other ''wet'' uses include taking showers, wind surfing, and boating.

Summary

The coexistence of expertise in amputation rehabilitation and sports medicine is rarely found in one physical therapist. The therapist specializing in amputation rehabilitation will provide the best advice by acting in close liaison with experts (e.g., sports physical therapists, trainers) in specific fields to gain insight into the individualized requirements for the sport in which the amputee chooses to participate. Once the appropriate prosthesis or prosthetic adaptations have been dispensed and relevant restrictions (if any) to the specific training program have been identified, the amputee should be referred to a community

Figure 4–11 Utility prosthesis.

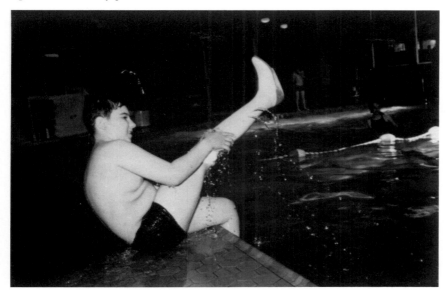

Source: Reprinted from *CHAMP Magazine,* Vol. 1, 1983, The War Amputations of Canada.

resource where physical facilities and monitoring are available to carry out independent training.

References

Brody, D.M. "Running Injuries—Biomechanical Factors." *Clinical Symposia,* 32, no. 4 (1980): 3–5.

Burgess, E.M. "Letter to the Editor." *Prosthetics and Orthotics International,* 9 (1985): 55–56.

Chadderton, B. "DOWNHILL, Any Way You Can." *Champ,* 1 (1983): 14–17.

Chadderton, H.C. "Otto Bock Curling Limb." *The Fragment,* 141 (1983): 40.

Chadderton, H.C. "Swimming Legs." *Champ,* 1 (1983): 8–11.

Davis, W.M. "Skiing." *Aids to Make You Able.* New York: Beaufort Books, 1981, 129.

Hughes, J., and Jacobs, N. "Normal Human Locomotion." *Prosthetics and Orthotics International,* 3 (1979): 4–12.

Inman, V.T., Ralston, H.J., and Todd, F. "The Process of Walking." *Human Walking.* Baltimore, Md.: Williams & Wilkins, 1981, 2–3.

Kegel, B., Webster, J.C., and Burgess, E.M. "Recreational Activities of Lower Extremity Amputees: A Survey." *Archives of Physical Medicine and Rehabilitation.* 61 (1980): 258–264.

Mensch, G., and Ellis, P. "The Terry Fox Running Prosthesis." *Physiotherapy Canada,* 36, no. 6 (1984): 245–246.

Wells, K.F. "Running." *Kinesiology, the Scientific Basis of Human Motion,* 5th ed. Philadelphia, Pa.: Saunders, 1971, 423–425.

Conclusion

The treatment of lower extremity amputees is a stimulating and challenging field of practice for physical therapists in that it can involve both direct patient care and research.

This text presents the practitioner with a variety of guidelines for clinical approaches to current practice. It will give physical therapists a better understanding and appreciation of future developments, and, it is hoped, will encourage our colleagues to evaluate and validate, with well-designed controlled clinical trials, the efficacy and effectiveness of these established approaches.

Index

A

Abdominal contraction exercise, 77
Abdominal muscle, 75
Abrasion, 180–181
Acceleration, 4, 15
    electromyographic muscle action, 15
Adductor roll, 176–177
    bandaging, 132–134
Adhesion
    friction to mobilize, 156–158
    hypertrophic scar, 157–158
    joint range problems, 177–178
    surgical scar, 157
Afferent input, 17
Aging, 27
Air splint, 62–63
    disadvantages, 63
    techniques, 62–63
Alignment, 232–245
    donning, 244–245
    dynamic, 234
    settings, 236
        hip disarticulation, 241–243
        transfemoral, 241
        transtibial, 236–241
    static, 233–234
    temporary gait device, 86
Ambulation
    early activities, 84–94
    progression to, 269–270
Amputation. See also Specific type
    bilateral, 326–334

balance problems, 327
contracture, 327
donning two prostheses, 328–329
gait training, 329
increased energy requirements, 327
rising from chair, 329–331
sitting balance, 328
stairs, 330, 331
stump function, 328
transfemoral, 331–334
transfer, 328
transtibial, 329–330
transtibial/transfemoral, 330–331
trunk flexion and extension, 327–328
upper extremity, 327
    causes, 21–22
    incidence, 21
Amputee role model, preoperative visit, 50
Ankle disarticulation, 34–37
    gait, 36–37
    prosthesis, 216–218
        cosmesis, 218
        foot component, 218
        segmented socket, 218
        suspension, 217
    rigid dressing, 87–88
    stump bandaging, 127–128
    stump characteristics, 34–36
    treatment considerations, 35–36
Arm raising exercise, 256–258
Arm swing, unequal, 308–309
Arteriosclerosis, 23

Assessment
  chart, 99–106
    medical history, 98–107
    physical examination, 107–111
    social history, 107
  diabetic gangrene, 98–107
  gross motor functions, 110–111
  malignancy, 98
  remaining leg, 107
  stump, 108–110
  team conference, 111
  trauma, 98
  trunk, 110
  upper extremity, 107–111
  vascular deficiencies, 98–107
Atelectasis, 53
Atherosclerosis, 23
Avocation, 101

B
Balance, 1
  control, 17–18
  exercises, 254–265
  learning, 18
  trunk, 49
Bandage
  adductor roll, 132–134
  advantages, 121
  alternatives to, 186
  ankle disarticulation, 127–128
  bulbous soft tissue, 134
  clinical opinion against, 135
  contraindications, 124
  disadvantages, 121
  dog ear, 134–135
  elastic, 61
    postoperative vs. preprosthetic, 61
    standard, 121–122
  forefoot amputation, 126–127
  hip disarticulation, 131–132
  hygiene, 125
  knee disarticulation, 129–130
  lightweight, 121
  objectives, 120
  patient education, 124–125
  removal, 123
  selection, 121
  stump, 120–135
  Syme's amputation, 127–128
  techniques, 124–125
  tension, 122
  transfemoral amputation, 130–131
  transtibial amputation, 128–129

Base unit, 86
Bath, contrast, 186
Bed, positioning in, 70–72
  prone lying, 70–72
  stump positioning, 70
Betadine, 171
Biofeedback equipment, 266–269
Blister, 181–182
Blood pressure, 26
Body, 2
  extension exercise, 76
Bone
  end sensitivity, 184
  pain, 66
  protrusion, 173
  spur, 184
  tumor, primary malignant, 27–28
Buerger's disease, 24
  cigarette smoking, 26

C
Calcification, 23
Cast
  change indications, 57–58
  position, 56
  pressure pain, 68
  rotation, 56–57
  serial, 161
  slippage, 56–57
  suspension, 56–57
  windowed, 168–170
Chest, postoperative care, 52–53
Cicatrin, 172
Cigarette smoking, 26
Circulation, lower extremity, 103
Claudication
  intermittent, 188–189
  pain, 118–119
Communication, 101
Complications, nurse liaison, 170
Compress, wet, 172–173
Compression markings, 122
Compression pumping, intermittent, 137–138
  advantages, 137
  disadvantages, 137–138
Computer Aided Design, 337–338
Computer Aided Manufacturing, 337
Computer Aided Socket Design, 337
Contact dermatitis, 182
Contoured Adducted Trochanteric-Controlled
  Adjustment Method (CAT-CAM), 341–342
Contracture, 140–161. See also Specific type
  active exercises, 158

ambulation, 158–159
  bilateral amputation, 327
  characteristics, 141
  classification system, 141
  manual stretch techniques, 149–152
  measurement, 147
  pain, 147–149
  range of motion, 178–179
  treatment goals, 141
Controlled environment treatment, 63–65
  disadvantages, 64
  techniques, 63–64
Coordination, 49
Cosmetic cover, 212–213
Curb, 272
Cyst
  epidermal, 183–184
  sebaceous, 183–184

D

Debrisan, 172
Deceleration, 4, 15–16
  electromyographic muscle action, 15–16
Deformity, congenital, 28
Desensitizing techniques, 149, 185–186
Diabetes mellitus, 22, 24–25
  atherosclerosis, 25
  infection, 25–26
  long term effects, 25
  symptoms, 25
  test results, 25
  ulceration, 25
Dietician, 45
Distance, 5
Dog ear
  bandaging, 134–135
  stump shape, 175–176
Donning, alignment, 244–245
Double support, 4, 10
Dressing, 54–65
  air splint, 62–63
    disadvantages, 63
    techniques, 63
  controlled environment treatment, 63–65
    disadvantages, 64
    techniques, 63–64
  rigid
    ambulation characteristics, 86–92
    ankle disarticulation, 87–88
    benefits, 55
    cast change indications, 57–58
    cast position, 56

cast rotation, 56–57
    cast slippage, 56–57
    cast suspension, 56–57
    disadvantages, 55
    fundamental concepts, 55–58
    gait training attachment unit, 55–56
    hip disarticulation, 92
    history, 54–55
    knee disarticulation, 90–91
    vs. semirigid, 59–60
    Syme's amputation, 87–88
    technique, 55
    transfemoral amputation, 90–91
    transtibial amputation, 88–90
  semirigid, 58–60
    indications, 58
    vs. rigid, 59–60
    technique, 58–59
    transtibial amputation application, 58–59
  soft, 60–62
    disadvantages, 61
    techniques, 60–61
  Unna paste. See Unna paste dressing
    wound, 172–173

E

Edema, 108, 118
  stump, 119–120, 175
Efferent output, 17
Elase, 172
Elderly patient, 39, 40, 42
  exercises, 49–50
  preoperative care, 46–47
EMG biofeedback, 159
  unit, 268
Emotional aspects, 46, 113
  amputee role model, 50
Endoskeletal system, 202
Energy requirements, 1, 18–20
  prostheses vs. wheelchair, 19–20
Equinus deformity, 33–34
  gait, 33–34
  treatment considerations, 33
Equipment, preoperative presentation, 50
Exercise, 49–50, 74–79
  abdominal contraction, 77
  active, contracture, 158
  arm raising, 256–258
  balance, 254–265
  elderly patient, 49–50
  gluteal muscle contraction, 76
  hip abduction, 76–77

hip adduction, 76–77
isometric, 75–77
    progression into motion, 78–79
knee flexion and extension, 260–261
pelvic rotation, circular, 256
quadriceps contraction, 75–76
remaining leg, 78
step positions, 261–265
total body extension, 76
trunk rotation with arm swing, 258–260
weight shifting
    anteroposterior, 254–255
    lateral, 255–256
Exoskeletal system, 202
Extended care facility, 101

F
Fall, 276–281
getting up, 276–281
    from floor sitting, 280–281
    from supine, 276–279
Family, 101
Foam cover, 212–213
Foot
    amputation, longitudinal partial, 34
    deformity, 33
        gait, 33–34
        treatment considerations, 33
    eversion, 241
    multiaxis, 205
    position, 236
    prosthetic components, 203–205
    single axis, 204–205
    slap, 304–305
    Solid Ankle Cushion Heel (SACH), 203–204
    Stationary Attachment Flexible Endoskeleton
        (SAFE), 204
Foot flat, 4, 11, 12
    electromyographic muscle action, 11
    forces, 11
Force
    body motion, 2
    gravitational, 2
    ground reaction, 2
    muscle, 2
    weight-bearing, 2
Forefoot amputation, 32–34
    gait, 33–34
    prosthesis, 215–216
    stump bandaging, 126–127
    stump characteristics, 32–33
    treatment considerations, 33

G
Gait, 1–20
abducted, 292–293
ankle disarticulation, 34–37
bipedal, 3–4
    vs. quadrupedal, 3
circumducted, 294–295
cycle, 4–9
deviation, 282–283
equinus deformity, 33–34
factors affecting, 1–3
foot deformity, 33–34
forefoot amputation, 33–34
hemipelvectomy, 42
hip disarticulation, 42
knee disarticulation, 40
stump motion, 191–199
toe amputation, 32
training, 246–281
transfemoral amputation, 41–42
transtibial amputation, 38
Gait-training attachment unit, 55–56
Gait-training unit, 139, 246–247
    ambulation without, 94
    transfer, 81–82
Gangrene, 23, 173
    diabetic, 98–107
Gauze, dry sterile, 172
Gluteal muscle contraction exercise, 76
Gravel, 276
Gravity, 2
    line of, 3, 4
Gritti-Stokes amputation, 76
Ground reaction force, 2

H
Hallux. See Toe
Healing, delayed, 108, 163
Heat, 149
Heel, 118
Heel contact, 4, 10–11
    electromyographic muscle action, 11
    forces, 10
Heel off, 4, 13–14
    electromyographic muscle action, 14
    forces, 13–14
Heel rise, uneven, 302–303
Heel strike, 284–287, 298–299
Hemipelvectomy, 42
    gait, 42
    prosthesis, 232
    stump characteristics, 42

treatment, 42
young patients, 42
Hip
    abduction, 194
        compared to adduction, 195
        exercise, 76–77
        reduced functional output, 194
        treatment, 194
    adduction, 194–195
        compared to abduction, 195
        exercise, 76–77
        reduced functional output, 195
        treatment, 195
    disarticulation, 42
        alignment setting, 241–243
        gait, 42
        prosthesis, 230–231
        rigid dressing, 92
        stump bandaging, 131–132
        stump characteristics, 42
        treatment, 42
        young patient, 42
    extension, 191–192
        compared to flexion, 193–194
        reduced functional output, 192
        treatment, 192
    extensor muscle, 75
    flexion, 192–193
        compared to extension, 193–194
        excessive, 312–315
        reduced functional output, 193
        treatment, 193
    flexor muscle, 75
    hiking, 320–321
    rotator, 195–196
        internal vs. external, 196
        reduced functional output, 196
        treatment, 196
    stretching, 152–154
History
    medical, 98–107
    social, 107
Hobby, 101
Hold-relax technique, 151–152
Home, 101
Hydrogen peroxide, 172
Hygeol, 170–171
Hygiene, 114–119
    bandaging, 125
    claudication pain, 118–119
    edema, 118
    heel, 118
    malleoli, 118
    remaining leg, 115

shoes, 117–118
socks, 115, 118
stump, 114–115
Hypertension, 26

I
Ice, 149, 275–276
    pack, 187
Infection, 21–22
    diabetes, 25–26
    severe, 173
    ultraviolet irradiation, 165
    vascular disease, 25–26
    whirlpool bath, 167
Infrared irradiation, 187
Insulin, 24
Irradiation. See Specific types

J
Joint contracture, 142, 145–146
    flexion and extension synergy, 146
    osteoarthritis, 145
    rheumatoid arthritis, 145
    trauma, 146
Joint pathology, 179

K
Knee
    constant friction unit, 208–209
    control device, 268–269
    disarticulation, 39–40
        elderly patient, 40
        gait, 40
        prosthesis, 225–226
        rigid dressing, 90–91
        stump bandaging, 129–130
        stump characteristics, 39
        treatment, 39–40
    extension, 197
        compared to flexion, 198
        reduced functional output, 197
        treatment, 197
    flexion, 197–198
        absent, 286–287
        compared to extension, 198
        delayed, 288–289
        excessive, 284–285, 286–287
        inability to initiate, 222–323
        insufficient, 286–287
        premature, 284–285

reduced functional output, 197
    treatment, 198
flexion and extension exercise, 260–261
four-bar linkage mechanism, 207
function, 196–198
polycentric, 206
prosthetic components, 206
prosthetic instability, 316–317
rotator, 211–212
safety, 207–208
single-axis free-swinging, 206
stance stability mechanism, 206–208
stretching, 154–155
swing phase mechanism, 208–209
swing and stance phase control mechanism, 209–210
variable friction unit, 209

L

Lateral thrust, excessive, 288–289
Lateral whip, 290–291, 300–301
Leg length, prosthetic, 243–244
Level
    ankle disarticulation, 34–37
        gait, 36–37
        stump characteristics, 34–36
        treatment considerations, 35–36
    forefoot, 32–34
        gait, 33–34
        stump characteristics, 32–33
        treatment considerations, 33
    hemipelvectomy
        gait, 42
        stump characteristics, 42
        treatment considerations, 42
        young, 42
    hip disarticulation, 42
        gait, 42
        stump characteristics, 42
        treatment considerations, 42
        young, 42
    knee disarticulation, 39–40
        elderly, 40
        gait, 40
        stump characteristics, 39
        treatment considerations, 39–40
    longitudinal partial foot, 34
    toe, 32
        gait, 32
        treatment considerations, 32
    transfemoral, 40–42
        elderly, 42

    gait, 41–42
        stump characteristics, 40
        treatment considerations, 40–41
        young, 41
    transtibial, 38–39
        elderly, 39
        gait, 38
        stump characteristics, 37
        treatment considerations, 38
        young, 38, 39
Life-style factors, 26–27
Limb discrepancy, 21–22, 28
Limb load monitor, 268
Line of progression, 1, 306–307
Load line, 232–233
Lordosis, lumbar, 312–315
Lower extremity, 102–104
    circulation, 103
    joint range of motion, 104
    motor function, 104
    pain, 103
    sensation, 103

M

Malignancy, assessment, 98
Manual stretch technique, 149–152
MAUCH S'N'S knee unit, 209
Medial whip, 290–291, 300–301
Medical status, 100
Medication, 53–54
    topical, 170–172
Midstance, 12, 13, 284–285, 286–287
    electromyographic muscle action, 13
    forces, 13
Midswing, 4, 15, 16, 316–317
    electromyographic muscle action, 15
Modular assembly system, 214
Motion
    opposing, 1
    progression into, 78–79
Motivation, 101
Motor function
    gross, 106
        assessment, 110–111
    lower extremity, 104
    trunk, 105
    upper extremity, 105
Muscle contracture, 141–145
    preexisting tightness
        orthopedic, 143–144
        neurological, 144
    soft tissue retraction

orthopedic, 144
   neurological, 144–145
Muscle cramping, 67
Muscle force, 2

N

Necrosis, 173
Nerve
   pain, 67
   stimulation, transcutaneous electrical, 149
Neuroma, 184
Nurse, 45
Nutrition, 26–27, 112

O

Obstacle, 274–275
Occupational therapist, 45
Opposing motion, 1
Op-site® dressing, 173
Osteomyelitis, 25–26
Osteosarcoma, 27–28
Overhead assist device, 82–83
Overhead bar, 82–83

P

Pain
   bone, 66
   cast pressure, 68
   claudication, 118–119
   clinical evaluation, 65–70
   contracture, 147–149
   extrinsic origin, 68–69
   intrinsic origin, 65–68
   lower extremity, 103
   nerve, 67
   phantom limb, 69
   socket fit, 68–69
   stump, 53, 68–69, 110
   vascular, 66–67
   wound, 67–68
Pathway, undulating, 5–8
   coronal plane, 7
   sagittal and coronal combined, 7
   sagittal plane, 6–7
   transverse plane, 8
Patient education, 46, 47–48, 112–114
   goals, 112
   group sessions, 112–113
   stump bandaging, 124–125
Pedynograph, 269

Pelvic rotation exercise, 256
Pelvis, 8–10
Perspiration, increased, 48
Phantom limb pain, 69
Phantom limb sensation, 47–48, 69, 75, 103
Physical assessment, preoperative, 48–49
Physical therapist, 45
Physician, 45
Pneumatic walking aid, 138–139
   advantages, 138
   disadvantages, 139
Pneumonia, 53
Positioning, 70–74
   bed, 70–72
   wheelchair sitting board, 72–73
Postoperative care
   immediate, 52–65
      chest care, 52–53
      stump dressing, 54–63
   medical status, 53–54
Posture control device, 266–267
Preoperative care, 46–50
   equipment presentation, 50
Pressure area, 180–181
Proprioception, 17
Prosthesis, 214–232
   ankle disarticulation, 216–218
   checkout, 283
   components, 202–214
   doffing, 251
   fitting preparation, 97
   forefoot amputation, 215–216
   hemipelvectomy, 232
   hip disarticulation, 230–231
   increased tolerance, 270–271
   knee disarticulation, 225–226
   leg length, 86
   patellar tendon-bearing, 218–223
      figure-eight strap, 220
      rubber sleeve suspension, 221
      side bar, 221–222
      supracondylar cuff suspension, 220–221
      suspension, 220–223
      suspension modification, 221
      thigh corset, 221–222
      transtibial suction suspension, 222–223
   patellar tendon supracondylar, 223–224
      suspension, 223
      wedge suspension, 223–224
   prescription, 283
   Syme's amputation, 216–218
   temporary alignment, 85–86
   Terry Fox running, 346–347, 348–350

spring mechanism, 349–350
too long, 243–244
too short, 244
transfemoral amputation, 226–230
donning, 249
static alignment, 233–234
transtibial amputation, 218–225
donning, 247–248
static alignment, 233
utility, 350
Prosthetic skin, 213
Prosthetic stance, 263–265
common deviations, 264
corrective treatment, 264–265
exercise sequence, 263–264
starting position, 263
Prosthetic swing, 261–263
common deviations, 262
corrective treatment, 263
exercise sequence, 261–262
starting position, 261
Prosthetist, 45
liaison with, 185
Proviodine, 171
Psychological aspects, 46, 113
amputee role model, 50
Psychologist, 45
Pyrexia, 53

Q

Quadriceps contraction exercise, 75–76

R

Ramp, 273
Range of motion, 49
contracture, 178–179
decreased, 109
joint pathology, 179
lower extremity, 104
problems, 177–180
spasticity, 179
trunk, 105
upper extremity, 105
Record keeping, 111
Rehabilitation
assessment, 97–111
chart, 99–106
defined, 45
Rehabilitation team, 45–46
assessment conference, 111

Remaining leg
assessment, 107
claudication, 188–189
exercises, 78
hygiene, 115
Respiratory function, 48–49
Rotation, forefoot, 298–299
Rotator, knee, 211–212
Rub
moist salt, 185–186
sand, 185–186
Running, 4, 346–350
Terry Fox running prosthesis, 346–347, 348–350
transfemoral prosthesis, 347–348

S

SACH foot, 203–204
SAFE foot, 204
Savlon, 171
Scar
adhesions, friction to mobilize, 156–158
contractures, 146, 156–158
hypertrophic, 146–147
adhesions, 157–158
joint range problems, 177–180
surgical, 146
adhesions, 157
SEATTLE foot, 350
Sensation
lower extremity, 103
phantom limb, 47–48, 69, 75, 103
Sensory feedback technique, 265–269
Sensory impairment, 109
Sensory stimulation technique, 159–160
Shape sensing, 338
Shoe, 117–118
prosthetic, 50
Shoulder girdle, 9
Shrinker sock, 135–137
advantages, 137
disadvantages, 137
fitting, 135–136
selecting, 135
suspension, 136–137
Sinus, ultraviolet irradiation, 165–166
Sitting down, 253
Skin
condition, 49
contracture, 142, 146–147
hypertrophic scarring, 146–147
surgical scar, 146
graft, 176

prosthetic, 213
    sensation, 49
Sleep pattern, 53
Snow skiing, 343–345
Social worker, 45
Socket, 210
    conventional, 249
    diameter too large, 245
    foot-tilting position, 238–240
    inadequate fit, 68–69
    position, 85–86
    preflexion, 234–236
    segmented, ankle disarticulation, 218
    suction, 249–250
    system
        flexible, 339
        support frame, 339
    transtibial liner, 224
Socket-foot correlation, 236–238
Socks, 115, 118
    stump, 213–214
Soft tissue, bulbous
    bandaging, 134
    stump shape problems, 175
Solid Ankle Cushion Heel foot (SACH), 203–204
Spasticity, 179
Spine
    C curved, 3
    S curved, 3
Splinting
    indications, 161
    serial casting, 161
    treatment, 161
Sports, 343
Stability, medial-lateral, 194–195
Stairs, 271–272
    crutches, 271
    crutches and handrail, 271–272
    jack knifing techniques, 272
    stepping down, 271–272
    stepping up, 271
Stance, 288–289
Stance phase, 10–14
    drop-off, 324–325
Standing up, 251–252
Stationary Attachment Flexible Endoskeleton (SAFE)
    foot, 204
Step position exercise, 261–265
Step rhythm, unequal, 306–307
Strength, 49
    decreased, 109
Stretching
    active assisted, 149

hip, 152–154
    prone, 154
    side lying, 152–154
knee, 154–156
    prone, 156
    sitting, 154
    supine, 154
passive, 149
positions, 152–156
Stride length, 5
Stump
    amputation-associated disease symptoms, 185–190
    assessment, 108–110
    bandaging, 120–135
    bilateral amputation, 328
    bleeding, 53
    bulbous soft tissue, 175
    characteristics, 31
        ankle disarticulation, 34–36
        forefoot amputation, 32–33
        hemipelvectomy, 42
        hip disarticulation, 42
        knee disarticulation, 39
        transfemoral amputation, 40
        transtibial amputation, 37
    claudication, 188–189
    cold, 188
    complications, 162–190
    control, 191
    dressing. See Dressing
    edema, 119–120, 175
    excessive soft tissue, 245
    forces
        anterior-posterior, 191-194
        hip rotators, 195–196
        knee functions, 196–198
        medial-lateral stability, 194–195
        transtibial amputation, 197–198
    hygiene, 114–115
    hypersensitive, 185–187
        alternatives to bandaging, 186
        desensitizing techniques, 185–186
        thermal modalities, 186–187
    immobilization, 163–170
    insensitive, 189
    motion, 191–199
    pain, 53, 69, 110, 187–188
    piston action, 245
    positioning, 70
    redundant tissue, 175
    shape
        adductor roll, 176–177
        problems, 175–177

shaping techniques, 119–140
skin graft, 176
shrinkage, 119–140
skin fold, 175–176
socks, 213–214
transtibial amputation, 341
Stump-socket interface, 180–184
  abrasion, 180–181
  bone end sensitivity, 184
  bone spur, 184
  contact dermatitis, 182
  epidermal cyst, 183–184
  neuroma, 184
  pressure area, 180–181
  sebaceous cyst, 183–184
  venous restriction, 182
  verrucose hyperplasia, 182–183
Support phase, 10
  double, 4, 10
Surgery, 99
Suspension, 86, 210
  ankle disarticulation, 217
  patellar tendon-bearing, 220–223
  patellar tendon supracondylar, 223
  poor, 245
  Syme's amputation, 217
  system, 85–86
  transfemoral amputation, 228–230
Swimming, 350
Swing impact, terminal, 304–305
Swing phase, 4
Syme's amputation
  prosthesis, 216–218
    cosmesis, 218
    foot component, 218
    segmented socket, 218
    suspension, 217
  rigid dressing, 87–88
  stump bandaging, 127–128
System for Controlling Ambulation Pressure
  (SCAP III), 269

T
Tactile stimulation, 160, 266
TEH LIN modular knee unit, 209–210
Telfa film, 172
Terry Fox running prosthesis, 346–347, 348–350
Tobacco use, 26
Toe amputation, 32
  gait, 32
  treatment considerations, 32
Toe-off, 4, 14, 286–287

electromyographic muscle action, 14
  forces, 14
Torque absorber, 210–211
Trapeze, 333
Transcutaneous electrical nerve stimulation (TENS),
  149, 187–188
Transfemoral amputation, 40–42
  bilateral, 331–334
    bed to chair transfer, 332–333
    rising from chair, 333
    stair walking, 333–334
    trapeze, 333
  elderly, 42
  gait, 41–42
    deviation, 292–325
  prosthesis, 218–225, 226–230
    anterior wall, 228
    foot component, 230
    lateral wall, 228
    medial wall, 228
    posterior wall, 226–228
    suspensions, 228–230
  quadrilateral socket, 226–228
  rigid dressing, 90–91
  socket preflexion, 235–236
  stump
    bandaging, 130–131
    characteristics, 40
    forces, 191–196
  treatment, 40–41
  young patients, 41
Transfer, 50, 79–84
  bed to chair, 79–81
  bilateral amputation, 328
  gait-training unit, 81–82
  overhead assist device, 82–83
Transtibial amputation, 38–39
  bilateral, 329–330
  elderly, 39
  gait, 38
    deviation, 284–291
  rigid dressing, 88–90
  semirigid dressing, 58–60
  socket preflexion, 235
  stump bandaging, 128–129
  stump characteristics, 37
  stump forces, 197–198
  treatment considerations, 38
  Unna paste dressing, 58–59
  young, 38, 39
Transtibial/transfemoral amputation, bilateral, 330–331
Trauma, 21–22
  amputation due to, 27

assessment, 98
  joint contracture, 146
Treatment, early, goals, 54
Trunk, assessment, 110
  balance, 49
  extensor muscle, 75
  forward flexion, 310–311
  joint range of motion, 105
  motor function, 105
  rotation exercise, 258–260
Tumor, malignant, 21–22
Turning around, 273

U
Ulcer, ultraviolet irradiation, 165
Ulceration, 23, 24
Ultrasound, 149, 184
Ultraviolet irradiation, 163–167
  clean wound, 163–165
  infections, 165
  sinus, 165–166
  ulcer, 165
Undulating pathway, 5–8
Unna paste dressing, 58–60
  indications, 58
  vs. rigid, 59–60
  technique, 58–59
  transtibial amputation application, 58–59
Upper extremity
  assessment, 107–111
  motor function, 105
  range of motion, 105

V
Vascular deficiency, assessment, 98–107
Vascular disease, 21–22, 22–24
  infection, 25–26
Vascular pain, 66–67
Vasospastic disorders, 24
Vaulting, 318–319
Verbal stimulation, 266

Verrucose hyperplasia, 182–183
Vibrator, 186
Videotape recorder, 267–268
Visual stimulation, 266
Vocation, 101
Vocational counselor, 45

W
Walker, 50
Walking aid, 312–315
  pneumatic. See Pneumatic walking aid
Water skiing, 345
Weight bearing, 31–32
  control, 93
  force, 2
  initial practice, 84
  insufficient, 290–291
  postoperative training, 84
  problems, 180–184
  progression, 93–94
  tolerance, 84–85
Weight shifting exercise
  anteroposterior, 254–255
  lateral, 255–256
Weight transference, 93
Wheelchair sitting board, 72–73
Whirlpool bath, 163, 167, 187
Wind surfing, 345
Wound
  dressing, 172–173
  pain, 67–68
    deep, 68
    infection, 68
    superficial, 67–68
  taping, 163, 167–168
    suture line, 168
    wound support, 168
  ultraviolet irradiation, 163–165

Y
Young patient, 38, 39, 41, 42

About the Authors

GERTRUDE MENSCH, M.C.P.A. received her physical therapy education in Leipzig, Germany and completed her Canadian Physiotherapy Association membership examinations at the University of Toronto in 1956. She began to develop her expertise in amputation rehabilitation by attending several postgraduate courses in Prosthetics and Orthotics at New York University's Postgraduate Medical School in the 1960s. She continued to further upgrade her expertise by attending advanced courses in amputation management offered by the International Society for Prosthetics and Orthotics in Copenhagen and London.

In collaboration with Dr. A.H. MacMillan, F.R.C.S.(C.) she helped establish the Amputation Rehabilitation Services for the Hamilton Civic Hospitals.

Mrs. Mensch teaches at both the University and College levels in Medicine and in Physical Therapy and Occupational Therapy and has conducted amputation rehabilitation seminars and instructional courses in North America and Europe. She has presented several papers at international congresses in Amsterdam, Montreux, Montreal, New York, Tel Aviv, Bologna, Stockholm, Copenhagen, and London, has published articles in different professional journals, and has written a chapter, together with Mrs. Ellis, in Rehabilitation Management of Amputees.

In 1980, Mrs. Mensch was elected to serve for a triannum on the International Executive Board of the International Society for Prosthetics and Orthotics. She was reelected in 1983 to serve for a second term. In 1983 she received the distinct honor of ISPO Fellowship.

PATRICIA M. ELLIS, DIP. P. & O.T., M.C.P.A., O.T.(C) graduated from the University of Toronto in 1970. During her early years in clinical practice, her main focus was in the field of orthopedics.

The existence of the Regional Amputee Assessment Clinic at the Henderson General Hospital and her involvement with the rehabilitation of lower extremity amputees prompted her attendance at the Post Graduate Prosthetics Course at New York University, New York in 1977.

Since 1977 she has been actively involved in the teaching of the amputations component in the Mohawk–McMaster Programs in Physiotherapy and Occupational Therapy, Hamilton, Ontario. She has also presented several clinical papers at multidisciplinary conferences and has had articles published in professional journals.

She is presently participating with a research team in a project that will compare the energy requirements of running with a conventional transfemoral prosthesis and the recently designed Terry Fox Running Prosthesis.